Praise for the First Edition of The Arkansas Handbook

"Brimming with interesting tidbits about Arkansas ... The real attraction of the *Handbook* is having comprehensive information about Arkansas contained in one volume ... The *Handbook* features much more than lists of facts and numbers. It is enlivened by folk remedies, the odd names of some Arkansas towns, mini-profiles of famous Arkansans, popular sayings, traditional quilt patterns, old-fashioned recipes, travel tips and sports statistics ... A natural gift for anyone interested in Arkansas."
– *The Arkansas Gazette*

"A little bit of everything ... Even a life-long Arkansan can get an education."
– *The Arkansas Democrat*

"This everything-you-always-wanted-to-know-about-Arkansas-but-didn't-know-where-to-look book is highly recommended. It's a natural for anyone's library on the natural state."
– *Cabot Star Herald*

"Just about every imaginable subject ... Highly informative and easy to read."
– Ernie Deane, *Baxter Bulletin*

"Hundreds of fascinating facts and anecdotes ... "
– *El Dorado News-Times*

The Arkansas Handbook by Diann Sutherlin was first published in 1983 and went through three printings. Now the "everything-you-always-wanted-to-know-about-Arkansas-but-didn't-know-where-to-look book" is back in an all-new, completely revised second edition that includes even more facts, more fun and more trivia on the natural state

D0814170

For Ron Robinson —
with best wishes.

Diann Sutherlin
8-24-96

THE ARKANSAS HANDBOOK

DIANN SUTHERLIN

FLY-BY-NIGHT PRESS

Little Rock, Arkansas

Fly-By-Night Press
200 North Bowman Road
Suite 482
Little Rock, AR 72211

Copyright © 1996 by Diann Sutherlin

Printed and manufactured in the United States of America. All rights reserved.
No part of this book may be reproduced in any form or by any electronic or
mechanical means including information storage and retrieval systems without
permission in writing from the publisher, except by a reviewer who may quote
brief passages in a review.

ISBN 0-932531-03-2

Library of Congress Catalog Card Number 95-90761

Second Edition, First Printing

Production by Moonlights

Cover design by Pat LaGrone

Recognizing the importance of preserving what is written, this book is printed
on acid-free paper.

*For my husband Craig Smith whose formidable talent
is surpassed only by his infinite patience*

*And for our children Quentin, Lindsey and Blair –
sorry about all the burned grilled cheese sandwiches*

WHAT'S INSIDE

PREFACE TO THE SECOND EDITION

INTRODUCTION

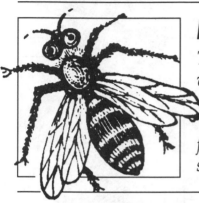

ARKANSAS AT A GLANCE ... 5

The Cliff's Notes guide to the state – where we're located, how we got our name, what the weather's like, what we're famous for, plus everything from our favorite vehicle to the official state bug.

THE ARKANSAS IMAGE ... 15

The historical perspective – what others have said about us, and why. Plus Arkansas in the movies, state songs, the famous "Arkansaw Traveler," and, oh yes, Whitewater.

FAMOUS ARKANSANS ..39

From Bronco Billy Anderson to Sam Walton – the good, the bad, the ugly, the rich, the poor, and the indicted.

Contents

TOP ATTRACTIONS ... 333

Everything to see and do – from playing the ponies at Oaklawn to floating the Buffalo River. From exploring Blanchard Springs Caverns to playing the dulcimer at the Ozark Folk Center.

STATE PARKS 355

Information on everything from the Crater of Diamonds to the Arkansas Oil and Brine Museum, with a guide to the state tourist information centers.

ARKANSAS HISTORY 377

What happened when – featuring a dateline of important events, Arkansas firsts and a section on our Indian heritage.

ARKANSAS GOVERNMENT 405

Map of congressional districts, constitutional officers, governors past and present, voter info, county seats and Arkansas women in Congress.

ARKANSAS BUSINESS .. 415

Fortune 500 companies, top ten manufacturing employers, Arkansas' big bucks earners, agriculture stats, plus our top ten funky business names.

PREFACE TO THE SECOND EDITION

Every effort has been made to ensure that *The Arkansas Handbook* is accurate and up-to-date. However, due to the very nature of the book, certain information is subject to change. Businesses are bought and sold. Facilities alter their hours of operation and fees. When making plans to visit attractions, points of interest, fairs or festivals, it's always recommended that you contact your destination in advance to verify information.

INTRODUCTION

When the first *Arkansas Handbook* appeared in 1983, most people in the United States – much less the world – knew very little about Arkansas. And what they *thought* they knew made them a tad nervous.

But nine years later, when Bill Clinton ran for president, our small state suddenly found itself under a large microscope. Reporters arrived by the planeload, giddy with anticipation of what weirdness they might uncover. With their preconceived bumpkin caricatures firmly in mind, they swarmed the state, sucking up sound bites and pull-quotes from the locals. Smugly, they reported back to civilization that Arkansas was indeed a peculiar place where the natives eat funny stuff like fried dill pickles and say funny things like, "I'm *fixin'* to." *The Wall Street Journal* got on its high horse and labeled the entire state "a congenitally violent place."

Annoying as this travesty has become, it's certainly nothing new for Arkansas. Fact is, we've had public relations problems from the git-go. Case in point: "Whenever I told people in the East and North that I was going to Arkansas, they yelled at me as if I planned to enter a robber's den. The whole state was said to swarm with outlaws and murderers ..." This from German writer Frederick Gerstaecker in 1868. Yep, those stereotypes hang on tighter than a seed tick.

In reality, Arkansas is brimming with ambiguities, contradictions and eccentricities. It is precisely these qualities that make Arkansas so maddening and at the same time so appealing. Arkansas was never the aristocratic Old South of mint juleps, magnolias, and "you-alls" wafting on the breeze. It was more the hardscrabble frontier where malcontents and desperadoes took refuge. The pioneers who later came to settle the territory were independent, courageous folk. And hard work and risk-taking are still respected here, as evidenced by the number of success-ful entrepreneurs our little state has spawned. This is truly a land of opportunity.

Arkansas is like a big high school. With only two million people, there's an intimacy, a shared history, a sense of community that extends to the entire state. It's not six degrees of separation here – it's more like two or three. Everybody knows everybody or knows someone who knows them. I have come to appreciate the off-beat character that is Arkansas, and I delight in it. I love the roadside stand that boasts an unlikely inventory of "chairs, birdseed and collards." I love floating down the Buffalo River, my canoe flanked by rock bass clearly visible in the pristine water. I love the blaze of sugar maples in northwest Arkansas in the fall, and the white lace of dogwood that trims the Hot Springs Highway in the spring. And I can't help but grin when I pass Glenda's Hair-Go-Round on a lonesome south Arkansas backroad with a sign out front that says "Walk-ins welcome." If that's not optimism, I don't know what is.

The Arkansas Handbook is an effort to document the facts and figures of our state, to provide a valuable reference for natives and visitors alike on places to go and things to do. But the book is also an attempt to capture the spirit and flavor of Arkansas – our history, our customs, our language, even our junk food. It is a compilation of the good, the bad and the weird – everything that makes this state unique.

No, Arkansas isn't perfect. Yes, we have our problems. But for better or worse, I'm proud to call it home. And in the immortal words of *True Grit's* Mattie Ross, "People who don't like Arkansas can go to the devil!"

That pretty well covers it.

Diann Sutherlin
Little Rock
May 1, 1996

ARKANSAS AT A GLANCE

Facts at your fingertips!

For those who may be unfamiliar with our fair state, here's the Cliff's Notes. However, if you prefer all the juicy details of Arkansiana, hang on – the best is yet to come.

FAST FACTS

Population	2,350,725
Capital	Little Rock
Counties	75
Time Zone	Central
Area Code	501
Postal Abbreviation	AR
Size Rank	27th
Statehood	Admitted June 15, 1836, 25th state
Per Capita Income	$15,994 (1993), 49th
Area	53,187 square miles (includes 600,000 acres of water)
Extreme Length	240 miles
Extreme Width	275 miles
Mountains	Ozarks to the north, Ouachitas (WASH-uh-tahz) in the west-central
National Forests	Three forests cover 2.4 million acres: Ouachita, Ozark, St. Francis
State Parks	48
Avg. Annual Temp.	61.4 degrees F
Highest Elevation	Mount Magazine; 2,753 feet above sea level
Main Rivers	Mississippi, Red, Arkansas, White, St. Francis, Ouachita

Legal Drinking Age	21. Some counties are dry, however; Sunday sales by local law
Curfews	Many cities have them for kids under 18
Favorite Vehicle	Chevy Pickup
Major Crops	Rice, soybeans, cotton
Major Businesses	Wal-Mart, Dillard's, TCBY, Tyson's, Alltel, J.B. Hunt
Minerals	Petroleum, natural gas, bromine
State Tree	Pine
State Flower	Apple Blossom
State Bird	Mockingbird
State Gem	Diamond
State Insect	Honey Bee
State Fruit/Vegetable	Tomato
State Mineral	Quartz Crystal
State Rock	Bauxite
State Instrument	Fiddle
State Dance	Square Dance
State Mammal	White-tail Deer
State Beverage	Milk
State Nickname	The Natural State
State Anthem	"Arkansas"
State Motto	Regnat Populus (The People Rule)

GLAD YOU ASKED: Answers for frequently asked questions

WHERE IS ARKANSAS ANYHOW?

Contrary to what George Bush said in 1992, Arkansas is not a small state between Texas and Oklahoma. In point of fact, Arkansas is a small southern state bounded on the west by Texas and Oklahoma; on the north by Missouri; on the east by the Mississippi River, which separates Arkansas from Mississippi and Tennessee; on the south by Louisiana.

HOW DID ARKANSAS GET ITS NAME?

Arkansas means "downstream people" and comes from the name of an extinct Indian tribe called Quapaw or Oo-gaq-pa. (The Quapaw were one of the native tribes living in Arkansas when the white men arrived. They had apparently moved downstream to make their homes.) From that jumping off point, the derivation of our name seems to be a classic example of the parlor game "Gossip" where one person tells another person who tells another, etc. until when the last person in the line hears the message it bears no resemblance to the original one. The Algonquin Indians pronounced the name of the tribe Oo-ka-na-sa. The French Jesuit Marquette's version was Arkansoa; La Salle wrote Arkensa; De Tonti liked Arkancas; and at long last, La Harpe penned the now-familiar Arkansas. When the state was admitted to the Union in 1836, it was spelled Arkansas. The Legislature of 1881 appointed a committee to ascertain the rightful pronunciation of the last syllable, and the result was a resolution declaring the pronunciation to be "ARK-an-saw."

WHAT'S IT LIKE THERE?

The state is small and for the most part, the natives are friendly, decent and (dare we summon up visions of Mayberry) downright neighborly. That is not to say we don't enjoy Yankee-baiting when the opportunity arises. Everybody knows everybody – or knows somebody who knows them. Almost 68% of us were born here. The state is still largely rural and agricultural with 46.5% of us living outside urban areas. By and large, Arkansas remains a naturally pretty, unspoiled state. The upper part is hilly, the lower and eastern parts are flat. Arkansas has more rivers, streams and lakes than you can shake a stick at. And speaking of sticks, the state is flush with trees. In fact, 65% of the state is forestland. The countryside is dotted with soybean fields, chicken houses and major home gardens where turnip greens, watermelons, squash and tomatoes thrive. Ironically, although Arkansas is a relatively poor state, there are also an amazing number of people in the state with really big bucks.

HOW'S THE WEATHER?

The weather here is a lot like our people and our politics. Unpredictable. Generally speaking the state is blessed with a favorable climate year-round. The winters are short, but it does get cold. It snows more in the northwest part, particularly in January and February. In the south, winter may bring ice storms that wreak havoc with the pine trees and power lines, but there's rarely enough snow to amount to anything. Summers are pretty hot and sticky statewide, and temperatures sometimes pass the 100 degree mark, particularly in the valleys. Rainfall is normally abundant and well distributed throughout the year. However, the state is no stranger to crop-scorching droughts or flash floods. Disastrous floods are rare these days, since the construction of levees and dams. But while Arkansas was spared the flood of 1993, the great flood of 1927 inundated one fifth of the state. Autumn is the driest time of the year. Spring is tornado season (though tornadoes can occur anytime). Arkansas ranks number three in tornado fatalities. Arkansas also experienced the greatest earthquake in North America, the New Madrid Quake of 1811-1812.

SO WHAT DO PEOPLE DO FOR A LIVING IN ARKANSAS?

Well, it's not all moonshine and varmint hides, as you might have been led to believe. Since Arkansas is primarily agricultural, a lot of people farm, growing almost every crop that can be grown in the temperate zone except for citrus fruit. Arkansas is the number one producer of rice and broilers in the country and number three in catfish production. Tourism is also a major industry. The entrepreneurial spirit is alive and well. Businesses like Dillard's, Aromatique, TCBY and Wal-Mart started here, and it's probably safe to say that most Americans know more about Sam Walton than they do about Woodrow Wilson.

A FEW THINGS ARKANSAS IS FAMOUS FOR

★ **The Clintons**
Bill, the 42nd President of the United States, and Hillary Rodham Clinton, First Lady.

★ **Wal-Mart**
Headquartered in Bentonville.

★ **Watermelons**
A place called Hope, Bill's birthplace, claims to be the watermelon capital of the known universe. In 1985 Ivan Bright made the Guinness Book of World Records with his 260-pound melon. His record still stands.

★ **Potpourri**
Patti Upton's mega bucks fragrance business Aromatique, built from pine cones and petals, is head-quartered in Heber Springs.

★ **Basketball**
Nolan Richardson's Razorbacks won the NCAA championship in 1994.

★ **Quartz Crystals**
Montgomery County is the quartz capital of the world and literally glitters. Rock shops and mining opportunities abound.

★ **Dillard's Department Stores** Founded by Arkansan William Dillard, this national retail giant is headquartered in Little Rock.

★ **Frozen Yogurt**
Founded by Frank Hickingbotham, the TCBY corporate offices are located in the tallest building in the state, the 40-story TCBY Tower in downtown Little Rock.

★ **Mountain Valley Water**
This famous mineral water is bottled here and shipped all over the U.S. and several foreign countries. Corporate headquarters, Hot Springs.

★ **Bricks** Malvern, Arkansas, produces more brick than any place else in the world.

★ **Retirement**
Next to Florida, Ark-ansas has the highest percentage of residents over the age of 60.

★ **Trout**
The current world-record brown trout was caught by Rip Collins, May 9, 1992, on the Little Red River. The whopper weighed in at 40 pounds, 4 ounces.

★ **Diamonds**
Yep. Arkansas has the only diamond mine in North America. And it's open to the public for prospecting.

★ **Stephens Investments** One of the largest investment firms outside of Wall Street. Founded by brothers Jack and Witt and headquartered in downtown Little Rock.

★ **Pickles**
Atkins packs a passel of 'em, including pickled peppers.

★ **Rice**
Arkansas is the number one producer of rice in the U.S. The largest rice mill in the world can be found at Stuttgart.

★ **Chickens**
Does the name Tyson ring a bell? Arkansas is the nation's leading producer of commercial broilers. Springdale is chicken central.

★ **Tomatoes**
We don't produce the *most*. We rank 15th. But we do produce some of the best tomatoes in the country. If you've never eaten a Bradley County Pink, you've never tasted a real tomato.

★ **Tornadoes**
We're number three in tornado fatalities.

★ **Ducks and Rice**
A tasty combo. Stuttgart is known as the duck and rice capital of the world.

★ **Catfish**
We're the number three producers of these farm-raised whiskered delicacies.

PULLING RANK

Here's how our state stacks up with other states:

#1 in broilers, bricks, bromine, rice and quartz crystals
#1 in deaths from strokes
#1 in spinach canning
#1 in incidence of blastomycosis,
   a fungal infection
#1 high school basketball tournament
#2 in elderly population
#3 in SPAM consumption
#3 in catfish production
#3 in tornado fatalities
#4 in percentage of smokers
#4 in obesity
#5 in cotton production
#5 worst roads
#10 on the 1994 Most Boring List from Boring Institute
#15 in harvested acreage
#15 in tomatoes
#27 in size
#32 in apple production
#49 in per capita state and local taxes
#49 in per capita income

DETAILS. . . DETAILS. . .

"We need an official fish!"

Stay with us, folks. Arkansas has an officially designated symbol for just about everything you can think of. Put a bunch of politicians in a room for more than fifteen minutes and one of 'em is bound to propose a new official symbol. Case in point: Senator Mike Todd of Paragould sponsored Senate Bill 490 on behalf of his daughter Leah and a contingent of other fifth-graders to designate the catfish, "the most easily recognizable fish of all Arkansas fish," as the official state fish. The 80th General Assembly of 1995 didn't take the bait and the bill sank, like the maligned bottom feeder it touted. No official fish. At least not yet.

• STATE FLOWER

The pink and white apple blossom was adopted as the Arkansas state flower by the 33rd General Assembly of 1901. The apple blossom was chosen because at that time Arkansas was known as the apple state and sometimes called "The Land of the Big Red Apple." At one time Benton County was the chief apple-producing county in the United States. Today Arkansas ranks 32nd in apple production.

• STATE BIRD

The mockingbird was adopted as the state bird by the 47th General Assembly of 1929. An excellent mimic, the mockingbird can perfectly imitate the song of other birds.

• STATE TREE

The pine was adopted as the state tree by the 52nd General Assembly of 1939. It is the shortleaf or yellow pine, and may grow to be 100 feet tall. The pine is a major resource of the state's paper industry.

• STATE GEM

The diamond was adopted as the state gem by the 66th General Assembly of 1967. Arkansas is the only diamond-producing state in the Union.

• STATE MINERAL

The quartz crystal was adopted in 1967. Arkansas is the number one producer of quartz crystals in the U.S. and, most likely, the world.

• STATE ROCK

Bauxite was adopted in 1967. At one time, Arkansas produced 97% of the nation's bauxite, an essential ore in the making of aluminum.

• STATE INSECT

Yes, we even have a state insect. The honeybee was adopted by the General Assembly of 1973. The rhetoric in support of the honey bee compared the bee to Arkansans as diligent, productive and willing workers. It was also noted that without the honey bees' pollination of crops, agriculture in the state would be in quite a fix.

• STATE FRUIT/ VEGETABLE

The South Arkansas Vine Ripe Pink tomato was adopted
as the state fruit and vegetable by the General Assembly
of 1987. The tomato is botanically a fruit and is used as
a vegetable.

• STATE MUSICAL INSTRUMENT

The fiddle was adopted as the state instrument
by the General Assembly of 1985. Otherwise
known as the violin, the instrument has been
commonly associated with Arkansas music and culture.

• STATE BEVERAGE

UDDERLY
DELICIOUS

Milk was adopted as the
state beverage by the
General Assembly of 1985.
Dairy farming was once an
important part of Arkansas
agriculture with 536,000 head of
milk cows in 1945. By 1993 the number
of milk cows in the state had dwindled to
only 64,000 head.

• STATE AMERICAN FOLK DANCE

The square dance was adopted in 1991. (According to the
legislative act which made the square dance official, our
state's national and international reputation would be
enhanced by adopting a state dance. Go figure.)

• STATE MAMMAL

The white-tail deer was adopted in 1993. The
state's most important game species, white-tail
range in all 75 counties.

• STATE FLAG

In 1912, the Pine Bluff Chapter of the Daughters of the American
Revolution voted to present the newly christened battleship *Arkansas*
with three flags: a U.S. flag, a Navy flag and an Arkansas flag. They
wrote the secretary of state for a state flag and discovered that their
plan had a slight hitch – Arkansas didn't have a state flag. The DAR
sponsored a contest and from 65 entries, the flag designed by DAR
member Miss Willie K. Hocker of Pine Bluff was chosen. The red, white
and blue Arkansas state flag was officially adopted by the General

Assembly of 1913. The 25 stars around the border of the diamond indicate Arkansas as the 25th state admitted to the Union. The three large blue stars below the name have a double meaning: signifying Spain, France and the United States to which Arkansas successively belonged; and signifying Arkansas as the third state formed out of the Louisiana Purchase. The large star above "Arkansas" commemorates the Confederacy, and the diamond sign signifies Arkansas as the only diamond-producing state in the Union.

• SALUTE TO THE FLAG

" I salute the Arkansas Flag with its diamond and stars. We pledge our loyalty to thee."

• THE ARKANSAS CREED

I believe in Arkansas as a land of opportunity and promise.

I believe in the rich heritage of Arkansas, and I honor the men and women who created this heritage.

I believe in the youth of Arkansas who will build our future.

I am proud of my State. I will uphold its constitution, obey its laws, and work for the good of all its citizens.

• OFFICIAL NICKNAME: THE NATURAL CHOICE

Arkansas has been called many things, some even printable. We have been known as "The Bear State," "The Wonder State," "The Hot Water State," and even "The Toothpick State"– a reference to the bowie knife or "Arkansas toothpick." During the 1930s we were even referred to as "The Guinea Pig State" because of the state's willingness to participate in agricultural experiments. In 1953 "The Land of Opportunity" was adopted as our official nickname by the 59th General Assembly. Around 1971, the state tourism industry was looking for a catchy slogan to promote the state. The task fell to advertising agency Cranford Johnson Robinson. The brilliant result was "Arkansas is a Natural" and the slogan caught on like wildfire. The now-famous moniker was conceived by then-agency copywriter Jackye Shipley Finch and designed by art director Jim Johnson. Some years later, a variation of the slogan was also put into service – "Arkansas: The Natural State." After years of seeing the phrase adorn everything from car tags to T-shirts, the 80th General Assembly in 1995 decided it was only natural to make it legal and passed legislation making Arkansas' new official nickname "The Natural State."

• STATE SEAL

The eagle in the lower half of the circle of the seal holds in his beak a scroll inscribed with the state motto, "Regnat Populus," Latin for "the people rule." He clutches a bunch of arrows in one claw and an olive branch in the other. The breast of the eagle is covered with a shield bearing images of a steamboat, a beehive, a plow and a sheaf of wheat, symbols of Arkansas' agricultural wealth. The steamboats which traveled rivers were a major factor in the state's early development. Above the eagle is the Goddess of Liberty, holding a wreath in one hand and a liberty pole with cap in the other. The goddess, wreath and pole are surrounded by a circle of stars and rays. The figure to the left of the eagle is the Angel of Mercy, supporting the shield against the breast of the eagle with her left hand. The Sword of Justice is to the right of the shield. The seal was adopted in its basic form in 1864, and in its present form in 1907.

• STATE SONGS

In 1917, the Arkansas Legislature adopted "Arkansas" by Eva Ware Barnett as our state song. It remained our state song until 1947 when a tiff developed between the state and Mrs. Barnett who held the copyright. The Legislature of 1947 changed the official song to "The Arkansas Traveler" and appointed a committee to draft suitable words and music to be adapted from the old fiddle tune. As generally happens when committees undertake to create, the results were less than desired and the song was not popular among the school children forced to sing it, according to the Secretary of State's Historical Report of 1968. So in 1963, the Legislature persuaded Mrs. Barnett to relinquish her copyright to the state and the state re-established "Arkansas" as the official state song. In 1987. Following Arkansas' sesquicentennial (150th) birthday in 1986, the General Assembly adopted a few more official songs to commemorate the occasion. They decided to make Mrs. Barnett's song the official state anthem and "The Arkansas Traveler" became our official state historical song. Two new songs, "Arkansas" (You Run Deep In Me) by Wayland Holyfield and "Oh, Arkansas" by Terry Rose and Gary Klaff, were designated as official state songs. (The lyrics to the two more recent songs can be found in the section *Arkansas Image*.)

OFFICIAL STATE ANTHEM

"Arkansas"

Words and music by Eva Ware Barnett. First adopted in 1917 as the state song. Adopted in 1987 by the General Assembly as the official state anthem.

I am thinking tonight of the Southland,
Of the home of my childhood days,
Where I roamed through the woods and the meadows,
By the mill and the brook that plays;
Where the roses are in bloom,
And the sweet magnolia too,
Where the jasmine is white,
And the fields are violet blue,
There a welcome awaits all her children
Who have wandered afar from home.

Chorus
ARKANSAS, ARKANSAS, 'TIS A NAME DEAR,
'TIS THE PLACE I CALL "HOME, SWEET HOME;"
ARKANSAS, ARKANSAS , I SALUTE THEE,
FROM THY SHELTER NO MORE I'LL ROAM.

'Tis a land full of joy and of sunshine,
Rich in pearls and diamonds rare,
Full of hope, faith and love for the stranger
Who may pass 'neath her portals fair;
There the rice fields are full.
And the cotton, corn and hay,
There the fruits of the field
Bloom in winter months and May,
'Tis the land that I love, first of all, dear,
And to her let us all give a cheer.

Repeat CHORUS

OFFICIAL STATE HISTORICAL SONG

"The Arkansas Traveler"

Lyrics by the Arkansas State Song Selection Committee, 1947. Music by Colonel Sandford "Sandy" Faulkner, about 1850. Adopted in 1987 by the General Assembly as the official state historical song.

On a lonely road quite long ago
A trav'ler trod with fiddle and a bow;
While rambling thru the country rich and grand,
He quickly sensed the magic and the beauty of the land.

Chorus
FOR THE WONDER STATE WE'LL SING A SONG,
AND LIFT OUR VOICES LOUD AND LONG.
FOR THE WONDER STATE WE'LL SHOUT HURRAH!
AND PRAISE THE OPPORTUNITIES WE FIND IN ARKANSAS.

Many years have passed, the trav'lers gay
Repeat the tune along the highway;
And every voice that sings the glad refrain
Re-echoes from the mountains to the fields of growing grain.

Repeat CHORUS

THE ARKANSAS IMAGE

What we have here is failure to communicate

If outsiders have a problem defining Arkansas, so do Arkansans. Over the years we've called our home "The Bear State," "The Toothpick State," "The Wonder State," "The Land of Opportunity," and "The Natural State." Visitors have reported sightings of neighborly natives and inbred barbarians, shy hillbillies and sly billionaires. Why the confusion? Here's an attempt to shed some light on the development of the Arkansas image.

Interior of a Typical Arkansas Home?

From the 1904 pamphlet by Indiana native Marion Hughes, who spent three years in southwestern Arkansas. Mr. Hughes' unflattering portrait of the state was entitled: *Three Years in Arkansaw. A Complete History of the Funny, Unreasonable, Rich, Rare and Peculiar things that Happened, Transpired and Turned Up during My Three Years of Life Down in Old Arkansaw.*

FROM LUM & ABNER TO BILL & HILL

The following is a brief historical overview of Arkansas' persistent public relations problem.

■ THE TOOTHPICK STATE

Even after Arkansas became a state in 1836, a visit here was an opportunity to venture beyond the pale of civilization. The terms "bowie knife" and "Arkansas toothpick" were used interchangeably, and came to symbolize the lawless volatility of our frontier life. Duels, desperadoes, horse thieves – we had it all. The event that "cemented the state's association with the bloody blade," as historian William B. Worthen has pointed out, came in 1837, when the speaker of the house stabbed to death a fellow legislator during debate.

■ ARKANSAS TALL TALES

Next came the jokes and tall tales. The most famous was "The Big Bear of Arkansas" by Thomas Bangs Thorpe of Louisiana; it first appeared in 1841 and was translated into several languages. An avalanche of such stuff soon followed. From *Kit, the Arkansas Traveler*, a long-running comedy that wowed them up north, to "Change the Name of Arkansas?," a humorous ersatz speech, America couldn't get enough cornpone silliness about the state. Even one of our own, writer Charles Fenton "Fent" Mercer Noland of Batesville got in his two-cents worth.
During his 20-year career, Fent contributed some 225 tall tales about the Arkansas outdoors to the New York *Spirit of the Times*, a weekly newspaper for sportsmen.

■ THE ARKANSAW TRAVELER

In the 1850s, a humorous skit and fiddle tune called "The Arkansaw Traveler" became popular on the frontier [see below]. Generally credited to Arkansan Sandy Faulkner, it consisted of a dialogue of *non sequiturs* between a lost traveler and a backwoods homesteader. Later, painter Edward Payson Washburn produced a famous rendition of the piece, which was relentlessly copied for years and displayed over many a tavern bar. Together, they helped solidify our growing bumpkin image.

■ OPIE & THE SLOW TRAIN

There was no stopping it now. From 1882-87 Arkansas journalist Opie Read edited *The Arkansaw Traveler*, a weekly newspaper filled with more tall tales and funny stories; eventually he so annoyed his readers that he was forced to move the journal to Chicago. There, a few years later, humorist Thomas W. Jackson wrote and published *On a Slow Train Through Arkansaw* (1903), a wildly successful joke book that remained in print for almost a half century. This jewel was followed by other popular pamphlets in a similar vein, such as *Three Years in Arkansaw* by Marion Hughes. We had become the Polish joke of the day.

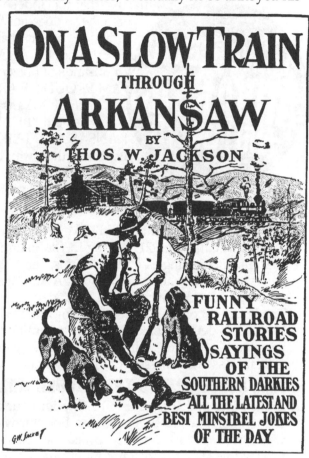

■ JEFF DAVIS

No, not *that* Jeff Davis. This guy wasn't the leader of the Confederacy, he was the governor of Arkansas. He was also a foaming-at-the-mouth demagogue whose gallus-popping speechifying mesmerized even the young Huey Long. Davis' race-baiting screeds drew unpleasant national attention to Arkansas in the early part of the 20th century, smearing the state's backwoods image with a nasty undertone of bigotry. (Some credit him, if that's the word, with coining the term "redneck.")

■ BOOSTERISM

In the 1920s a group of businessmen across the state formed the Arkansas Advancement Association to "preach the gospel of Arkansas." Its charter was to position the state "before the world in a garb so attractive that it is indeed a hard-hearted person who does not fall a victim to the attractions of this charming young miss." To this end, the AAA manufactured thousands of booster buttons, such as: "I AM PROUD OF ARKANSAS," meant to be worn by Arkansans on trips outside the state, and "I HAVE BEEN TO AR-KANSAS AND I LIKE IT" to be pinned to visitors on their way back home. Later, the group hired former governor Charles Brough to stump the country promoting his home state.

■ H. L. MENCKEN

The great American critic didn't like the South in general or Arkansas in particular. In 1921, writing in *The Smart Set*, he first attacked the "miasmatic jungles," "dead brains," and "brummagen mountebanks" of "a state almost fabulous." Arkansans took offense, denouncing Mencken as a Bolshevik, and, even worse, a damn Yankee. The President of the Arkansas Advancement Association demanded Mencken's deportation, mistakenly assuming he was an alien. Ten years later, Mencken, oblivious, lit into us again. This time the General Assembly passed a motion to pray for his soul.

■ LUM, ABNER, DIZZY & THE BAZOOKA MAN

In the 1930s and 40s, comedians Chester Lauck and Norris Goff (Lum and Abner, respectively) and Bob Burns (who popularized a wacky musical instrument he called the "bazooka") joked about their native state to radio and movie audiences in the millions. Lauck and Goff's cracker-barrel humor centered around the Jot 'em Down general store in mythical Pine Ridge, while Burns picked on Van Buren. In addition, sports fans were also following the exploits of colorful Dizzy Dean, an Arkie pitching ace who could really "far that tater."

■ THE CRISIS

In 1957 Gov. Orval Faubus defied a federal court order to integrate public schools. Soon the world was treated to daily coverage of snarling guard dogs and race-baiting white mobs. Arkansas was no longer funny. In time, the turmoil passed, but a vast amount of damage was done to the state's reputation. As writer Gene Lyons has observed, "Yankees who couldn't locate the Ozark Mountains on a map to save their lives knew all about the Little Rock Central High integration crisis of 1957 – and therefore all they needed to know about Arkansas."

■ WIN

After Faubus, Arkansas was lucky to have a progressive politician step up to the plate. Multi-millionaire Republican Winthrop Rockefeller did much to counteract the Faubus years. *Time* magazine even featured him on its cover in 1966 – "The Transformation of Arkansas." To win the job, Rockefeller handily defeated a segregationist diehard. Arkansas breathed a sigh of relief, hoping perhaps the bad old days were finally past.

■ CREATION SCIENCE

In 1981 the Arkansas General Assembly, in its wisdom, passed the so-called Creation Science Law, which mandated that biblical fundamentalism be included in classroom discussions of evolution. This notorious piece of legislation was soon thrown out by the courts as unconstitutional, but not before Arkansas found itself the butt of ridicule.

■ BILL CLINTON, PART I

In 1992, when Gov. Bill Clinton made his successful bid for the presidency, the world once again turned its attention to Arkansas, but this time liked what it saw, for the most part. No one could doubt the affection of "the man from Hope" for his native land, and press reports generally painted a pleasing picture of a land filled with natural wonders and friendly people.

■ BILL CLINTON, PART II

Then came the morning after. Hopeful the Clinton presidency would bury the hillbilly caricature forever, Arkansans had their faces stuck into it once again by Whitewater. Reporters by the planeload scurried over the state, filing stories depicting Arkansas as a moral wasteland ("A congenitally violent place," *The Wall Street Journal* called us – and they're from New York). Talk show hosts had a field day and the Bubba days were back with a vengeance.

The Arkansaw Traveler

This famous fiddle tune is the best-known piece of folklore associated with the state. It is generally credited to Colonel Sandford "Sandy" Faulkner, a prominent Little Rock plantation owner who claimed the story was inspired by an actual conversation with an Arkansas backwoodsman. The skit soon attained widespread popularity, aided by a play, *Kit, The Arkansas Traveler*, which delighted New York audiences in the 1880s.

Artist Edward Payson Washburn's representation of "The Arkansaw Traveler" is the state's most famous painting. Innumerable copies have been made over the years. (A painting that is purported to be the original was donated by Washburn's family and is on display at the Arkansas History Commission, though the authenticity is still debated.) Since 1941 governors have awarded "Arkansas Traveler" certificates to distinguished citizens and visitors.

Although some citizens resented "The Arkansaw Traveler," feeling it helped promote an unfortunate hillbilly image for the state, the piece has sustained a remarkable longevity. The dialogue has appeared in many different forms since its first publication in 1858. The version printed here is the one given in Fred Allsopp's *Folklore of Romantic Arkansas*.

Artist Edward Payson Washburn's representation of *The Arkansaw Traveler* is displayed at the Arkansas History Commission.

An Arkansaw Traveler, riding a fine white horse, lost his trail. After wandering around in rain and mud he came to a log cabin with its owner, a "squatter," seated on an old whisky barrel near the door of his cabin playing a fiddle. The following dialogue ensued, while the squatter continued to play over and over a few bars of a tune that never ended.

Traveler: Hello, stranger.

Squatter: Hello, yourself.

Traveler: Can I get to stay all night with you?

Squatter: You can git to go to hell.

Traveler: Have you any spirits here?

Squatter: Lots of 'em. Sal saw one last night by that ole holler gum, and it nearly skeered her to death.

Traveler: You mistake my meaning; have you got any liquor?

Squatter: Had some yesterday, but Ole Bose he got in and lapped all uv it out'n the pot.

Traveler: You don't understand me. I don't mean pot liquor. I'm wet and cold, and want some whisky. Have you got any?

Squatter: Oh, yes — I drank the last this morning.

Traveler: I'm hungry, haven't had a thing since morning. Can't you give me something to eat?

Squatter: Hain't a damned thing in the house. Not a mouthful of meat or a dust of meal here.

Traveler: Well, can't you give my horse something?

Squatter: Got nothin' to feed him on.

Traveler: How far is it to the next house?

Squatter: Stranger! I don't know, I've never been thar.

Traveler: Well, do you know who lives here?

Squatter: I do.

Traveler: As I'm so bold, then, what might your name be?

Squatter: It might be Dick, and it might be Tom; but it lacks a damned sight of it.

Traveler: Sir! will you tell me where this road goes to?

Squatter: It's never been any whar since I've lived here, it's always thar when I git up in the mornin'.

Traveler: Well, how far is it to where it forks?

Squatter: It don't fork at all, but it splits up like the devil.

Traveler: As I'm not likely to get to any other house tonight, can't you let me sleep in yours, and I'll tie my horse to a tree, and do without anything to eat or drink.

Squatter: My house leaks. Thar's only one dry spot in it, and me and Sal sleeps on it. And that thar tree is the ole woman's persimmon, you can't tie to it, 'case she don't want 'em shuk off. She 'lows to make beer out'n um.

Traveler: Why don't you finish covering your house, and stop the leaks?

Squatter: It's been raining all day.

Traveler: Well, why don't you do it in dry weather?

Squatter: It don't leak then.

Traveler: As there seems to be nothing alive about your place but children, how do you do here, anyhow?

Squatter: Putty well, I thank you, how do you do yourself?

Traveler: I mean what do you do for a living here?

Squatter: Keep tavern and sell whisky.

Traveler: Well, I told you I wanted some whisky.

Squatter: Stranger! I bought a bar'l mor'n a week ago. You see me and Sal went shares. After we got it here, we only had a bit tweenst us, and Sal, she didn't want to use hern fust, nor me mine. You see I had a spiggin' in one end, and she in tother. So she takes a drink out'n my end, and pays me the bit for it; and then I'd take un out'n hern, and give her the bit. Well, we's getting along fust-rate, till Dick, damned skulking skunk, he bourn a hole on the bottom to suck at and the next time I went to buy a drink, they wurnt none thar.

Traveler: I'm sorry your whisky's all gone; but, my friend, why don't you play the balance of that tune.

Squatter: It's got no balance to it.

Traveler: I mean you don't play the whole of it.

Squatter: Stranger, can you play the fiddle?

Traveler: Yes, a little sometimes.

Squatter: You don't look like a fiddlur, but ef you think you can play any more onto that thar tune, you kin just git down and try.

(The traveler gets down and plays the whole of it.)

Squatter: Stranger, take a half dozen cheers and sot down. Sal, stir yourself round like a six-horse team in a mud hole. Go round in the holler, whar I killed that buck this mornin' cut off some of the best pieces, and fotch it and cook it for me and this gentleman, directly. Raise up the board under the head of the bed and git the old black jug I hid from Dick, and give us some whisky; I know thar's some left yit. Till, drive Old Bose out'n the bread tray, then clime up in the loft, and git the rag that's got the sugar tied in it. Dick, carry the gentleman's hoss round under the shed, give him some fodder and corn, as much as he kin eat.

Till: Dad, thar ain't knive enouff for to sot the table.

Squatter: Whar's big butch, little butch, ole case, cob-handle, granny's knife, and the one I handled yesterday? That's nuff to sot any gentleman's table with, without you've lost um. Damn me, stranger, ef you can't stay as long as you please, and I'll give you plenty to eat and drink. Will you have coffee for supper?

Traveler: Yes, sir.

Squatter: I'll be hanged if you do tho', we don't have nothin' that way here, but Grub Hyson, and I reckon it's mighty good with sweetnin'. Play away, stranger, you kin sleep on the dry spot tonight.

Traveler: *(After about two hours' fiddling)* – My friend, can't you tell me about the road I'm to travel tomorrow?

Squatter: Tomorrow! Stranger, you won't get out'n these diggins for six weeks. But when it gits so you kin start, you see that big sloo over thar? Well, you have to git crost that, then you take the road up the bank, and in a mile you'll come to a two acre and a half corn-patch, the corn is mitely in the weeds, but you needn't mind that, just ride on. About a mile and a half, or two miles, from that you'll come to the damndest swamp you ever struck in all your travels; it's boggy enough to mire a saddle blanket. Thar's a fust-rate road about six feet under thar.

Traveler: How am I to get at it?

Squatter: You can't git at it nary time, till the weather stiffens down sum. Well, about a mile beyant, you come to a place whar thur's two roads. You kin take the right hand ef you want to, you'll follow it a mile or so, and you'll find it's run out; you'll then have to come back and try the left, when you git about two miles on that, you may know you are wrong, fur there ain't any road thar. You'll then think you are mighty lucky ef you kin find the way back to my house, where you can come and play that tune as long as you please.

DID YOU KNOW?

Gheap Thrills!!!

As an indication of the popularity of *The Arkansaw Traveler,* the 1908 Sears catalog featured an ad for Columbia Records' "Four Winners," which could be purchased for 18¢ a pop. The ad read *"The Arkansaw Traveler* **No. 511098** This is a talking and musical selection descriptive of an Arkansaw native sitting in front of his cabin door scraping his fiddle and replying to the questions of a traveler with a great variety of witty sallies... This record is full of jokes and laughter and humorous fiddling. Don't overlook this one in making up your list." The other three "winners" were: *Uncle Josh's Husking Bee Dance, Backyard Conversation Between Two Jealous Washerwomen,* and *The Night Alarm* ("A wonderful descriptive selection by the full Columbia orchestra representing an alarm of fire at night").

SAY WHAT?

A lot of people have said a lot of nice and not-so-nice things about Arkansas over the years. Here's a brief sampling:

■ "... the expedition is believed to have spent almost half of its time in a single state – one that for De Soto and his men became an ecological and geographical trap. That state was Arkansas."
– *Archaeology* magazine, 1993, concerning *Hernando de Soto's 1539 exploration of America*

■ "They [the native Americans of Arkansas] have cabins made with the bark of cedar; they have no other worship than the adoration of all sorts of animals. Their country is very beautiful, having abundance of peach, plum and apple trees, and vines flourish there; buffaloes, deer, stags, bears, turkeys, are very numerous."
– *Henry de Tonti, 1682*

■ "In 1816 we made up about thirty families and lived there two years in all the luxuries of life that a new country could afford, such as buffalo, bear, deer, and elk and fish and honey ... We had no doctors nor lawyers those happy days."
– *John Billingsley*

> **"the asylum of the most wicked persons without doubt, in all the Indies"**
>
> *Spanish provincial official, 1770*

■ "We here behold the assembled tributaries, flowing in a smooth, broad, deep, and majestic current between banks of the richest alluvion, covered with the most vigorous growth of vegetable life, and skirted at a short distance by mountains of the most imposing grandeur."
– *Henry R. Schoolcraft, 1819, at the confluence of the Buffalo and White rivers*

■ "This country is very new, and society very uncultivated. They are at this place particularly very fond of Balls and Loo [a card game] parties. ... They have one fiddler who can play one tune, they can dance but one figure, which is a kind of reel or cotillion, they commence at dark and hold on until day light, when each of the fair sex saddles her own pony, mounts and trudges home. The men generally hold on longer at the card table. At these card tables I have seen Grandfather, Grandmother, son and daughter, and grand-daughters all engaged in gambling as eager to make money as if playing with any one else. It is not uncommon to lose 150 or two hundred dollars in a night, or they may win. This appears to be their principal vice and it is a

great one . . ."
– James Miller, first governor of Arkansas Territory, 1820

■ "Travel in Arkansas during the first quarter of the nineteenth century involved hard, back-breaking work, whether it was hauling at a keelboat towrope (cordelle) or prying a wagon out of axle-deep mud. There were panthers in the woods, snags and sand bars in the rivers, and outlaws ready to turn their hands either to highway robbery or piracy as the chance offered. Anyone who spoke of a 'pleasure trip' would have been considered a humorist or a madman."
– Arkansas: A Guide to the State, 1941

■ "We are much disturbed in mind by what we are told is in the newspapers. It is said that the man who is sent to Congress by the White People of Arkansas has written to them and said that the President has ordered a Large part of Lovelys purchase [a buffer zone guaranteed to the Cherokees] to be surveyed and sold, and that it will, very soon, be settled by the Whites. This makes us very uneasy."
– Cherokee Nation Council, 1826

■ "Oh, Arkansas! How great would be thy name, if you could

puke up all the villains and send them back to their former homes."
– Antoine Barraque, a farmer who lost some hogs to thieves, c. 1834

■ "Between the 33rd and 37th degrees in north latitude lies a vast tract of country that has taken the name of Arkansas, from the principal river that waters it. It is bounded on one side by the confines of Mexico, on the other by the Mississippi. Numberless streams cross it in every direction; the climate is mild and the soil productive, and it is inhabited by only a few wandering hordes of savages."
– Alexis de Tocqueville, Democracy in America, 1835-40

■ "With the Indian territory to the west of them already filling up with tribe after tribe driven west of the Mississippi, Arkansas had become an outpost, where every really good man had in him something of the frontiersman and knew how to use his knife and gun."
– John Gould Fletcher, Arkansas, 1947

■ ". . . mainly a refuge for forgers, bankrupts, murderers, horse thieves, and gamblers."
– George Featherstonhaugh, English geologist, 1835

■ "Foreigners are constantly visiting every part of the United

> **"If I could rest anywhere it would be in Arkansaw where the men are of the real half-horse, half-alligator breed such as grows nowhere else on the face of the universal earth."**
>
> Davy Crockett, 1834

States and yet very few, if any have ever visited Arkansas. They all seem to be frightened away by the numerous stories of Arkansas murders . . . "
– *English traveler, 1839*

■ "'Where did all that happen?' asked a cynical-looking Hoosier.
'Happen! happened in Arkansaw: where else could it have happened, but in the creation State, the finishing-up country – a State where the *sile* runs down to the centre of the 'arth, and government gives you a title to every inch of it?   Then its airs – just breathe them, and they will make you snort like a horse. It's a State without a fault, it is.'"
– *Thomas Bangs Thorpe, "The Big Bear of Arkansas," 1841*

■ "You have made a great mistake as to our inhabitants, the people composing our community are the enterprising Citizens of Europe and America from the first Citys and Countys of Maine & every other state till you reach New Orleans & for urbanity we think we could compare with any country without a blush. The people are a Churchgoing people & they greatly pride in being orderly when at Church ... Many of our Citizens have been of the unfortunate & came here to get

homes and repair their conditions. This many of them will soon do as they are industrious."
– *John Meek, 1842*

■ "... the wilderness is their home; they scorn the city and multitude; neither have they house or lands; wherever night overtakes them they pitch their tents and herd their flocks; 'and when the railroad starts, they will start also, to go whither it cannot come,' so strong is their love for semi-civilized life, so great their aversion for improvement of whatever kind."
– *DeBow's Review, 1857*

■ "Traveler: 'Well, where does this road go to?'
Squatter: 'It don't go nowhere – just stays right here.'"
– *Sandy Faulkner, The Arkansaw Traveler, 1858*

■ "Arkansas is sometimes known as the Bear State, and many of its people at that time were singularly bearish and rude. The self-estimate of such men was sometimes colossal, and their vanities as sensitive as hair-triggers. . . . It is wonderful what trivial causes were sufficient to irritate them. A little preoccupation in one's own personal affairs, a monosyllabic word, a look of doubt, or a hesitating answer, made them flare up hotly."
– *Sir Henry Morton Stanley, 1860-61*

> "Of all I had seen in America it [Arkansas] was the one which pleased me most ... I shall never forget the happy days there, where many a pure heart beats under a coarse frock or leather hunting shirt."
> *Frederick Gerstaecker, German travel writer, 1843*

■ "But what a wretched reputation the poor land had in the United States! Whenever I told people in the East and North that I was going to Arkansas, they yelled at me as if I planned to enter a robber's den. The whole state was said to swarm with outlaws and murderers . . . "
– *Frederick Gerstaecker, 1868*

■ "Arkansas was a perfect *terra incognita*. The way to get there was unknown; and what it was, or was like, if you did get there was still more an unrevealed mystery."
– *Cephas Washburn, missionary, 1869*

■ "Arkansas! There I lived the best years of my youth ... There I felt free and independent for the first time. There in the wilderness I found a home more beautiful and magnificent than any I could have then imagined. For me, the word itself was magic."
– *Frederick Gerstaecker, 1872*

■ "Notorious ruffians, desperadoes and outlaws have been sufficiently abundant in this region to give the whole community a bad reputation, which has been rendered worse by report and exaggeration. The ill name of Arkansas has extended beyond the seas, until the English and French press has chosen this as the specious field for the practice of barbarities more than usually startling."
– *New York Tribune, 1873*

■ ". . . civilized people had no more desire to go there than to Central Africa."
– *Scribner's Monthly, c. 1873*

■ ". . . a bilious hog and corn-eating people."
– *The New York Times, 1874*

■ "Few countries offer greater inducements and combine more advantages for the home-seeker and capitalist than Arkansas."
– *North American Review, 1885*

■ "These Arkansas lunkheads couldn't come up to Shakespeare. What they wanted was low comedy – and maybe something rather worse than low comedy."
– *Mark Twain, The Adventures of Huckleberry Finn, 1885*

■ "Pity those benighted natives that are born and bred in the wild prairies, forests or swamps of Arkansas, far away from the influence of church, school, or civic intercourse."
– *Missionary, c. 1894*

■ "As soon as the train reaches the great pine belt of Arkansas, one becomes aware of the intoxication of the resinous air. It is heavy,

> "Arkansas is not a part of the world for which Jesus Christ died."
>
> *Lost traveler, emerging from a week in a swamp, c. 1839*

fragrant with the odor from the vast pine tracts and its subtle influence contains a prophecy of the spirit of the little city afar in the hills."
– *Stephen Crane, 1895*

■ "Society in Arkansas is [no longer] in a chaotic and unorganized state. The people do not spend their time in idleness, ruffianism and outlawry. It is a mistake that citizens of Arkansas carry pistols and bowie knives in their pockets in place of carpenters' rules and plug tobacco."
– *Railroad company brochure, 1896*

■ "I would like to flee like a wounded hart into Arkansas . . ."
– *Oscar Wilde, c. 1897*

■ "It was down in the state of Arkansas I rode on the slowest train I ever saw. It stopped at every house. When it came to a double house it stopped twice. They made so many stops I said, 'Conductor, what have we stopped for now?' He said, 'There are some cattle on the track.' We ran a little ways further and stopped again. I said, 'What is the matter now?' He said, 'We have caught up with those cattle again. . .' A lady said, 'Conductor, can't this train make any better time

than this?' He said, 'If you ain't satisfied with this train, you can get off and walk.' She said she would, only her folks didn't expect her til the train got there. A lady handed the conductor two tickets, one whole ticket and a half ticket. He said, 'Who is the half ticket for?' She said, 'My boy.' He said, 'He's not a boy; he's a man. Under twelve, half fare, over twelve full fare.' She said, 'He was under twelve when we started . . .'"
– *Thomas W. Jackson, On a Slow Train Through Arkansaw, 1903*

■ " . . . trackless, unexplored Arkansas, a state still almost fabulous. (Who, indeed, has ever been in it? I know New Yorkers who have been in Cochin China, Kafristan, Paraguay, Somaliland and West Virginia, but not one who has ever penetrated the miasmatic jungles of Arkansas.)"
– *H. L. Mencken, 1921*

■ " . . . the apex of moronia."
– *H. L. Mencken, 1931*

■ "There is a reign of terror in the cotton country of eastern Arkansas. The plantation system involves the most stark serfdom and exploitation that is left in the Western World."
– *Norman Thomas, 1935*

" . . . little that is true is really known of the state and no other people have been more misunderstood."
The New York Times, 1874

■ "... it is probably the most untouched and unawakened of all American states."
– *John Gunther, Inside USA, 1946*

■ "After forty years I don't remember their names or even the names of the places where we worked in eastern Arkansas, but I will always remember how we were treated in a kindly and Christian manner."
– *Edwin Pelz,*
WWII German prisoner of war

■ "Arkansas, part delta and part mountain, part magnolia and part moonshine, where a horse is a 'critter' and a heifer is a 'cow brute' ... "
– *Time magazine,1957*

■ "The most deliberately unprogressive people in the United States."
– *Vance Randolph, c. 1963*

■ "I also remember how the music used to sound down there in Arkansas when I was visiting my grandfather ... that blues, church, back-road funk kind of thing ... So when I started taking music lessons I might already had some idea of what I wanted my music to sound like."
– *Miles Davis, c. 1965*

■ "Arkansas is a curious state. ... What brings it all together, however, is football."
– *Dan Jenkins, Sports Illustrated, 1969*

■ "It doesn't sound like a state. It sounds like a small country."
– *Philip Roth, in conversation with Gene Lyons, 1981*

■ "There probably is no place in America where you can get a worse meal than Arkansas. They eat something there called 'chicken-fried steak.' I don't know what it is. I tried it once, swallowed one bite, and was in bed sick for two days. ... There's no question that Arkansas has few redeeming qualities."
– *Mike Royko, 1982*

■ "Better bring your checkbook ... this kind of place won't stay a secret long."
Promotional brochure on Whitewater Development, c. 1985

■ "Not as bad as you might imagine."
– *Calvin Trillin (his suggested state license plate motto), c. 1988*

■ "If anybody asked me to pick the happiest four or five years of my life, it would be my time in Arkansas."
– *Pat Summerall, c. 1990*

■ "... the lowest of the low."
– *George Bush, 1992*

■ "The state seems to be a congenitally violent place, and full of colorful characters with stories to tell, axes to grind and secrets of their own to protect."
– *The Wall Street Journal, 1994*

"Tell your mama, tell your pa, gonna send you back to Arkansas."

Ray Charles, 1959

■ "Then we have a few more drinks and listen to the Arkansans talk politics: kickbacks, rake-offs, payola and lined pockets; hush money, slush funds, booty and swag; bond-deal pork and tax-break plums; contract grift, construction graft, sweetheart legislation of every kind; plus jobbery, junkets and palm grease. If one-tenth of what I heard is true, everybody in the state of Arkansas is going to spend eternity in perdition. And if none of what I heard is true, they're all damned to hell anyway for being the biggest liars ever."
– P. J. O'Rourke, _Rolling Stone,_ 1994

■ "Bill Clinton's rise began in a corrupt, old-fashioned state where even murder is winked at ... What's new about drugs, sex, corruption, the red-neck mafia, money laundering or murder in Arkansas? What's new about dogs having fleas?"
– _The London Times,_ 1994

■ "Arkansas – sell it!"
– _Bob Dole, 1995 (the senator's number one recommendation on how to balance the federal budget, proclaimed during an appearance on "Late Night with David Letterman")_

■ "People who don't like Arkansas can go to the devil!"
– _Mattie Ross, heroine of Charles Portis' immortal_ True Grit

HOLLYWOOD GOES ARKANSAS

Since 1929 moviemakers have been shooting in Arkansas. Some of America's best directors (King Vidor, Elia Kazan, Martin Scorsese, Mike Nichols) and most popular stars (Gregory Peck, Burt Reynolds, Susan Sarandon) have all made films inside the state. Remember the Old Mill in the opening sequence of _Gone With The Wind_? Shot in North Little Rock. How about _A Face in the Crowd_, the 1955 classic starring Lee Remick and Andy Griffith? Filmed in Piggott. Okay, they haven't all been classics. There've been plenty of movies in the "White Lightning" genre, complete with potbellied sheriffs, rednecks and dim-witted large-haired, large-busted gals. Surprise. Surprise. But things are definitely changing for the better.

Filmmaking in Arkansas didn't really get going until the 1960s, then picked up considerably once the state established a film commission. There are a host of reasons why making a movie in Arkansas makes good sense, and low cost is only one of them. The state offers a rich diversity of locations: we've got your Delta, forests, lakes, antebellum South, rural hamlets, Depression-era towns, mountains, Confederate battlefields, as well as contemporary cities. We also have fully operational vintage railroads and an exact 3/4 replica of the U.S. Capitol. Not bad for a small state. Here's a list of movies filmed entirely or partially in our state, starting with the most recent.

Film	Year	Director	Location
Sling Blade	1995	Billy Bob Thornton	Benton
Tuskegee Airmen	1995	Robert Markowitz	Fort Smith
Separated by Murder	1994	Donald Wyre	West Memphis
Frank and Jesse	1993	Robert Boris	Van Buren/Prairie Grove/Eureka Springs
The Client	1993	Joel Schumacher	West Memphis/ Hughes
The Firm	1992	Sydney Pollack	West Memphis/Marion
The War Room	1992	D. A. Pennebaker	Little Rock
The Ernest Green Story	1992	Eric Laneuville	Little Rock
Nancy Ziggenmeyer Story: Taking Back My Life	1991	Harry Winer	West Memphis
One False Move	1990	Carl Franklin	Clarendon/Cotton Plant
Stone Cold	1990	Craig Baxley	Little Rock/Conway/ North Little Rock/Rison
Top Cop	1989	Mark Maness	Little Rock
Little Marines	1989	A.J. Hickson	Bryant
Too Scared to Laugh	1988	Demp Dempsey	Little Rock/North Little Rock
Great Balls of Fire	1988	Jim McBride	West Memphis
Heart of Dixie	1988	Martin Davidson	West Memphis
Rosalie Goes Shopping	1988	Percy Adlon	Stuttgart/Little Rock
Contemporary Gladiators	1988	Anthony Elmore	Jacksonville
Savage Fury	1988	Paul Clark	Conway
Stay Tuned for Murder	1987	Gary Jones	Little Rock
Biloxi Blues	1987	Mike Nichols	Ft. Smith/Van Buren
Pass the Ammo	1987	David Beaird	Eureka Springs
Three for the Road	1986	Bill Norton	Little Rock/Hot Springs
Final Field Trip	1986	John Braden	Little Rock

End of the Line	1986	Jay Russell	Benton/Little Rock/ North Little Rock/ England
Amerika	1986	Donald Wyre	Little Rock
Man Outside	1985	Mark Stouffer	Fayetteville
North and South	1985	Richard Heffron	Camden
North and South Part 2	1985	Kevin Connor	Camden
Under Siege	1985	Roger Young	Little Rock
Summer's End	1984	Beth Brickell	Camden
The Legend of Boggy Creek Part 2	1983	Charles Pierce	Texarkana
A Soldier's Story	1983	Norman Jewison	Ft. Smith/ Clarendon/ Little Rock
The Blue and the Gray	1981	Andrew McLaglen	Ft. Smith/Fayetteville
Crisis at Central High	1980	Lamont Johnson	Little Rock
Cody	1979	Bob Blackburn	Pine Bluff
Mark Twain: Beneath the Laughter	1979	Larry Yust	Little Rock
Okinnnagan's Day	1977	Dwayne Daily	Texarkana
High Pursuit	1979	John Braden	Harrison
September 30, 1955	1976	James Bridges	Conway
The Day It Came To Earth	1976	Harry Thomason	Little Rock
The Town That Dreaded Sundown	1976	Charles Pierce	Texarkana
Wishbone Cutter	1976	Earl B. Smith	Harrison
Fighting Mad	1975	Jonathan Demme	Springdale
Sweet Sweet Connie	1975	John Braden	Little Rock
The Great Lester Boggs	1974	Harry Thomason	Little Rock
Bootleggers	1973	Charles Pierce	Mountain Home

Title	Year	Director	Location
So Sad About Gloria	1973	Harry Thomason	Little Rock
Encounter With the Unknown	1972	Harry Thomason	Little Rock
The Legend of Boggy Creek	1972	Charles Pierce	Texarkana
White Lightning	1972	Joseph Sargent	Little Rock
Boxcar Bertha	1972	Martin Scorsese	Camden
Two-Lane Blacktop	1970	Monte Hellman	Conway
Welcome Home Soldier Boys	1971	Richard Compton	Central Arkansas
Smoke in the Wind	1971	Joseph Kane	West Arkansas
Bloody Mama	1969	Roger Corman	Camden
The Sporting Club	1969	Larry Peerce	Hot Springs
A Face in the Crowd	1955	Elia Kazan	Piggott
Gone With The Wind	1939	Victor Fleming	North Little Rock
Hallelujah!	1929	King Vidor	East Arkansas

SOURCE: Arkansas Motion Picture Development Office

SOMETHING TO SING ABOUT

In 1986 Arkansas celebrated her 150th birthday, and our attention was focused on enhancing her less-than-stellar image. As a consequence, a couple of new ditties appeared proclaiming the joys of our state. In 1987, the General Assembly designated these new tunes "official state songs," (because, as we've learned, legislators love all things official). To refresh your memory, our "official state anthem" is "Arkansas," by Eva Ware Barnett. Our "official state historical song" is "The Arkansas Traveler," music by Sandy Faulkner. (Words to these two traditional numbers are in *Arkansas at a Glance.*) Below are the lyrics to our most recent odes to Arkansas.

"Arkansas" *(You Run Deep in Me) by Wayland Holyfield*

> October morning in the Ozark Mountains,
> Hills ablazing like that sun in the sky.
> I fell in love there and the fire's still burning
> A flame that never will die.

> *CHORUS:*
> OH, I MAY WANDER, BUT WHEN I DO
> I WILL NEVER BE FAR FROM YOU.
> YOU'RE IN MY BLOOD AND I KNOW YOU'LL ALWAYS BE.
> ARKANSAS, YOU RUN DEEP IN ME.

> Moonlight dancing on a delta levee,
> To a band of frogs and whippoorwill
> I lost my heart there one July evening
> And it's still there, I can tell.

> Repeat *CHORUS*

> Magnolia blooming, Mama smiling,
> Mallards sailing on a December wind.
> God bless the memories I keep recalling
> Like an old familiar friend.

> Repeat *CHORUS*

> And there's a river rambling through the fields and valleys,
> Smooth and steady as she makes her way south,
> A lot like the people whose name she carries.
> She goes strong and she goes proud.

> Repeat *CHORUS*

"Oh, Arkansas" *by Terry Rose and Gary Klaff*

It's the spirit of the mountains and the spirit of the Delta,
It's the spirit of the Capitol dome.
It's the spirit of the river and the spirit of the lakes,
It's the spirit that's in each and every home.
It's the spirit of the people and the spirit of the land,
It's the spirit of tomorrow and today.

CHORUS:
OH ARKANSAS, OH ARKANSAS, ARKANSAS, U.S.A.
IT'S THE SPIRIT OF FRIENDSHIP, IT'S THE SPIRIT OF HOPE
IT'S THE RAZORBACKS EVERY GAME THEY PLAY.
OH, ARKANSAS, OH ARKANSAS, ARKANSAS, U.S.A.

It's the spirit of the forest, it's the spirit of the eagle
It's the spirit of the country that we love.
It's the spirit of pride that we all feel deep inside
It's the spirit that shines from above.
It's the spirit of our fathers, it's the spirit of our kids,
It's the spirit of the music that we play.

Oh Arkansas, Oh Arkansas, Oh Arkansas, U.S.A
Oh Arkansas, Oh Arkansas, Oh Arkansas, U.S.A.
Oh Arkansas, Oh Arkansas, Oh Arkansas, U.S.A.

"The Grand New State of Arkansas"

This little jingle was written around 1836 to let people know Arkansas was no longer a territory but a "grand new state." (A grand new state where women can carry their share of the workload, it would seem.)

I love the girl from Arkansaw
Who can saw more wood than her
maw can saw
And can saw much more than her paw can saw
In the grand new state of Arkansaw.

SOURCE: *Arkansas Yesterday and Today*, Knoop and Grant

THE LAND OF OPPORTUNITY

THE WHO, WHAT, WHEN & WHERE OF WHITEWATER

The origins of the Whitewater scandal can be traced back to August 2, 1978, when two married couples jointly purchased a 230-acre tract along the White River in Marion County in northern Arkansas for approximately $203,000. The new owners were James and Susan McDougal and their friends Bill and Hillary Clinton. At the time, Bill Clinton was the state attorney general; three months later he would be elected to his first term as governor.

Just over a year later, on September 30, 1979, the foursome transferred their land to the Whitewater Development Corporation, a new company they had formed to sell lots for vacation homes. They put in roads, built a model home, and produced sales literature ("One weekend here and you'll never want to live anywhere else") – but their marketing efforts proved unsuccessful.

James McDougal (who served briefly as Gov. Clinton's economic-development adviser) later acquired Madison Guaranty Savings and Loan Association, which collapsed in 1989 at a cost of $65 million to U. S. taxpayers. In 1990 McDougal was acquitted on charges of bank fraud.

During the 1992 presidential primary campaign, questions were first raised regarding the Clintons' involvement in the land deal and the possibility of financial irregularities and/or illegal or unethical conduct. Bill and Hillary Clinton maintained they were passive investors who had lost $68,900 on the venture. The press soon lost interest in the story.

Ultimately, the Clintons sold their half-interest in Whitewater in December 1992, when Bill Clinton was President-elect. The attorney who handled the sale was a fellow partner of Hillary Clinton in the Rose Law Firm, Vincent Foster. Foster became a White House counsel and later committed suicide on July 20, 1993. Hours after his death, a Whitewater file was removed from his office. When this incident was revealed, it helped fuel the scandal that people now refer to as Whitewater.

Amid the subsequent swirl of accusations and innuendo, difficult questions emerged: Was cash from Madison Guaranty improperly funneled into Clinton's 1984 gubernatorial campaign? Did the Clintons receive a sweetheart deal on Whitewater? Did Clinton-appointed state regulators go easy on the S&L? Was it ethical for Hillary Clinton to represent McDougal, her business partner, before a banking regulator appointed by her husband? Did the Clintons underpay federal income taxes?

The clamor for investigation grew strident. In early 1994 Attorney General Janet Reno appointed Wall Street lawyer Robert Fiske, a Republican, to serve as special counsel. A few months later, on August 5, a federal judicial panel replaced Fiske with Kenneth Starr, a former Republican judge. Committees in both the House and Senate scheduled hearings, which proved rancorous and highly partisan.

On August 17, 1995, Starr obtained indictments against Gov. Jim Guy Tucker and former Clinton partners James and Susan McDougal on 21 counts involving alleged financial improprieties unconnected with the Whitewater development. The following year, on May 28, all were found guilty. That same day, Tucker announced his intention to resign on July 15. However, moments before Lt. Gov. Mike Huckabee, a Republican, was scheduled to take the oath of office on that date, Tucker reneged on his pledge, precipitating demands for his impeachment. By the close of day, Tucker was persuaded finally to step aside.

Throughout the entire Whitewater controversy, the Clintons have steadfastly denied wrongdoing. "When this is over," said Hillary Clinton in 1994, "it's going to be the same story we've been telling for two years. We made a bad investment, we lost money, and that's all there is to it."

FAMOUS ARKANSANS
The Good, the Bad, the Ugly... the Indicted

What follows is a decidedly eclectic mix, as any grouping that includes Levon Helm, Helen Gurley Brown, Douglas MacArthur and Eldridge Cleaver would have to be. A word of caution: Not everyone here is a native of the state. We've embraced a very liberal interpretation of what constitutes an Arkansan. Some of the famous folks on our list were born here, but moved away as children (K. T. Oslin left after only two weeks); some were born and raised here, then moved away to become famous (Dick Powell); some were born elsewhere but moved here and became famous (Sam Walton); some were already famous – or notorious – by the time they got here (Gerald L. K. Smith); and a few were actually born here, raised here and became famous here (Bill Clinton). All, however, are guaranteed to be celebrated in one way or another.

JULIE ADAMS ACTRESS (b. Betty May Adams, 10/26/1926, Waterloo, IA) Raised in Little Rock, this beautiful, dark-haired actress broke into Hollywood in the early 1950s, appearing in big-budget productions like *Bright Victory* and *Bend of the River* before finding her niche in B-movies, including the cult classic, *The Creature from the Black Lagoon* (as the beauty carried off by the beast).

SUSAN ALAMO CULT LEADER (b. Edith Opal Horn, 1925?, Dyer, AR; d. 4/8/82, Tulsa, OK) The worldwide Tony and Susan Alamo Christian Foundation, described by *People* as "a dangerous and secretive religious group," was once centered in the town of Alma, in northwest Arkansas. The pair started off in the 1960s with a street ministry in Hollywood's Sunset Strip. In the 1970s they shifted operations to Arkansas. The Alamos were known for living lavishly while their zombie-like followers slaved for subsistence wages or no pay at all. When Susan Alamo died of cancer, her body was placed on permanent display on the grounds, but was mysteriously removed from its crypt in 1991 and remains missing to this day. The cult is now headquartered near Los Angeles. In 1994 Tony Alamo (aka Bernie Lazar Hoffman) was sentenced to prison for income tax fraud.

KATHERINE ALEXANDER

ACTRESS (b. 9/22/1901, Ft. Smith, AR; d. 1981) A veteran Broadway performer, Alexander also played supporting roles in many movies, including: *The Barretts of Wimpole Street, The Painted Veil* and *The Hunchback of Notre Dame.*

CATHERINE THARP ALTVATER

ARTIST (b. 1907, Little Rock, AR; d. 10/9/84, Jacksonville, FL) Nature watercolorist Altvater's work hangs in countless museums, including the Museum of Modern Art. She was the first woman to hold office in the American Watercolor Society. Although she lived most of her professional life in New York, Altvater spent 10 years of her retirement in Scott, Arkansas.

BRONCO BILLY ANDERSON *ACTOR*

(b. Max Aaronson, 3/21/1882, Little Rock, AR; d. 1/20/71, South Pasadena, CA) The first cowboy star of moving pictures, Anderson (aka Gilbert M. Anderson) played three separate roles in the first movie with a plot, the 13-minute *Great Train Robbery* (1903). As Bronco Billy, he starred in (and often wrote and directed) almost 400 films, later forming his own production company, Essanay (with Charlie Chaplin and Ben Turpin under contract). In 1958, Anderson, who grew up in Pine Bluff, was awarded a special honorary Oscar.

MAYA ANGELOU *POET, AUTHOR (b.*

Marguerite Annie Johnson, 4/4/1928, St. Louis, MO) Raised in Stamps, where she helped her grandmother run a small general store, the multi-talented Angelou became a professional dancer before finally trying her hand at writing. She is a National Book Award nominee for her autobiographical *I Know Why the Caged Bird Sings* (1970), a Pulitzer Prize nominee for her book of verse, *Just Give me a Cool Drink of Water 'Fore I Die* (1972), a Tony Award nominee for her performance in *Look Away* (1975), and an Emmy Award nominee for her portrayal of Kunta Kinte's grandmother in TV's *Roots* (1977). In 1993 she captivated the nation at the Clinton inauguration by reciting her commemorative poem, "On the Pulse of Morning." (The name "Maya" is her older brother's childhood nickname for her; "Angelou" is a variation of her first husband's surname, Angelos.)

KATHARINE ANTHONY *BIOGRAPHER*

(b. 11/27/1877, Roseville, AR; d. 11/20/1965, New York, NY) A biographer of famous women, Anthony's works include: *Catherine the Great* (1925), *Louisa May Alcott* (1938), *Dolly Madison: Her Life and Times* (1949), and *Susan B. Anthony* (1954).

DONNA AXUM *MISS AMERICA 1964*

(b. 1/3/1942, El Dorado, AR) As the first baby born in El Dorado in 1942, Donna Axum won a prize, the first of many. Her highest accolade arrived in September 1963, when she accepted the Miss America crown – Arkansas' first. Following her reign, she earned an MA in speech and drama from the U of A in 1968. Axum has been married three times – first briefly to a college classmate, next to a speaker of the Texas House of Representatives (they were divorced after his conviction on conspiring to accept a bribe) and

Donna Axum, with Miss America emcee Bert Parks

finally to an oil company exec. Today she is a freelance image consultant in Oklahoma. Axum is the author of *The Outer You, The Inner You*, a volume of beauty secrets and inspirational messages. ➤ *See also:* Elizabeth Ward Gracen.

DAISY BATES *CIVIL RIGHTS ACTIVIST* (b. Daisy Lee Gatson, 11/11/1914, Huttig, AR) As the Arkansas president of the NAACP, Bates led the fight to integrate Little Rock's Central High School, starting in September 1957, when she served as mentor to the Little Rock Nine. Throughout the

crisis, she and her husband, L. C., who together published the weekly *Arkansas State Press*, were subjected to vicious harassment, including a bombing at their home. In 1959 they were forced to fold the *State Press*. Daisy Bates resigned her NAACP post and, in 1960, she and her husband moved to New York. In 1962 her book, *The Long Shadow of Little Rock*, was published. Eventually the couple returned to the state. L. C. Bates died in 1980 at age 79. Daisy Bates revived the old *State Press* in 1984, eventually selling it. Over the years, she has been honored many times for her leadership in the American civil rights movement. Stevie Wonder performed at her gala 80th birthday bash in Little Rock. ➤ *See also:* Orval Faubus, Ernest Green, the Little Rock Nine.

MORGAN BEATTY *JOURNALIST* (b. 9/6/1902, Little Rock, AR; d. 7/4/75, Antigua Island) Best known as a radio commentator for NBC from 1941 until 1967, Beatty also anchored the

Daisy Bates, with husband L.C. and members of the "Little Rock Nine," Thanksgiving Day, 1957

DuMont Evening News and worked 14 years as an AP reporter.

EARL BELL *CHAMPION POLE VAULTER (b. 8/25/1955, Jonesboro, AR)* A former world-record pole vaulter (1976) and Olympic bronze medalist (1984), Bell started vaulting into a sawdust pit in his back yard when he was only five years old.

BLACK OAK ARKANSAS *ROCK GROUP* Originally called Knowbody Else, this dynamic Jonesboro-based band emerged as one of the top-grossing acts of the 1970s. Their eponymous 1971 debut album (featuring songs like "When Electricity Came to Arkansas" and "Hills of Arkansas") went gold, as did *High on the Hog* in 1976. The group's biggest hit was their 1974 cover of "Jim Dandy." At the peak of their fame, fans stole so many Black Oak city limit signs that the town council voted to stop putting them back up. Personnel problems and declining sales forced the band to break up in 1979. Original members: Tommy Aldridge, Pat Daugherty, Jimmy Henderson, Stan "Goober" Knight, Jim Dandy Mangrum, Ricky Reynolds. ➤ *See also:* Jim Dandy Mangrum.

JAMES BLACK *KNIFEMAKER (b. 1800?, PA or NJ; d. 1872, Hempstead County, AR)* Legendary Washington blacksmith Black is popularly credited with forging the first bowie knife, ostensibly for Jim Bowie, who later died at the Alamo. In his late 30s, the knifemaker lost his sight, became a ward of the county and finally went insane.

JOHN BLOOM *See* Joe Bob Briggs.

FRANK BONNER *ACTOR (b. Frank Woodrow Boers Jr., 2/28/1942, Little Rock, AR)* Best known for his portrayal of station manager Herb Tarlek (who always kept a Razorback coffee mug on his desk) on the long-running TV series "WKRP in Cincinnati," Bonner grew up in Malvern.

Frank Bonner

JAMES BRIDGES *FILM DIRECTOR, SCREENWRITER (b. 2/3/1936, Paris, AR; d. 6/6/93, Los Angeles, CA)* Bridges received an Oscar nomination for his screenplay for *The China Syndrome*, which he also directed. He grew up in Logan County and attended Arkansas State Teachers College, leaving in the 1950s for Los Angeles. In 1970 Bridges wrote and directed one of the critical hits of the decade, *The Paper Chase*. In 1977 he filmed his highly personal *September 30, 1955*, about events in the lives of a group of Arkansas students on the day James Dean died. Starring Richard Thomas, most of the movie was shot in Conway. Other films: *Urban Cowboy, Mike's Murder, Perfect,* and *Bright Lights, Big City*.

JOE BOB BRIGGS *WRITER, PER-FORMER (b. John Irving Bloom, 1958?, Dallas, TX)* A former president of the Parkview High School student council and sports reporter for the *Arkansas Democrat*, Bloom created his famous alter ego Joe Bob Briggs while at the *Dallas Times-Herald*. Briggs, a redneck drive-in movie reviewer, became wildly popular and branched out nationally with increasing success. In addition to writing a syndicated column, newsletter, and several Joe Bob books, Bloom has hosted a cable show, performed stand-up comedy and appeared in movies like *Great Balls of Fire* and *Casino*.

ELTON BRITT *SINGER (b. James Britt Baker, 7/7/1917, Marshall, AR; d. 6/23/72, McConnellsburg, PA)* One of country music's main attractions of the 1940s and 50s, Britt was born in Arkansas but reared primarily in Oklahoma. Half Cherokee and half Irish, Britt was discovered by talent scouts while literally plowing a field on the family farm at age 14. He was promptly signed to a contract, rushed to Los Angeles and within days was singing on the radio. Soon afterward he began recording for RCA, eventually producing over 56 albums. During WWII Britt emerged as one of America's most popular entertainers. His rendition of "There's a Star Spangled Banner Waving Somewhere," sold over four

million records. He also appeared in several movies.

FOOTSIE BRITT *MILITARY HERO (b. Maurice L. Britt, 6/29/1919, Carlisle, AR; d. 11/26/95, Little Rock, AR)* Raised in Lonoke, Britt led several lives – professional football player, certified war hero, and notable Arkansas politician. Nicknamed "Footsie" as a boy, Britt played end for the Detroit Lions. In WWII he was the first soldier to win the four top medals for gallantry, including the Congressional Medal of Honor. Wounded in four different battles, he lost his right arm and severely injured a foot. From 1967 - 71 Britt served as Republican lieutenant governor. (His cousin was actress Dorothy Lamour.)

LOU BROCK *HALL-OF-FAME OUT-FIELDER (b. Louis Clark Brock, 6/18/1939, El Dorado, AR)* Brock was raised in abject poverty in Collinston, LA, after his father abandoned the family. His phenomenal .542 college sophomore batting average attracted big league interest and in 1961 he joined the Chicago Cubs. Three years later, in one of baseball's most infamous trades, Brock went to St. Louis and immediately sparked the Cardinals' drive to the world championship. In 1974 the left-fielder swiped 118 stolen bases, setting a record. Brock entered the Hall of Fame in 1985. About his native state, Brock has said: "Arkansas is called the Land of Opportunity, and I got out at the first opportunity."

DEE BROWN *WRITER (b. 2/28/1908, Alberta, LA)* Brown's unsparing 1970 history of the government's war against the American Indians, *Bury My Heart at Wounded Knee*, brought him instant international acclaim. It has sold more than a million copies in the U.S. alone and been translated into over 20 languages. Although born in Louisiana, Brown moved to Arkansas at the age of five and was raised and educated here, eventually leaving in the 1930s. After retiring in 1972 from a full professorship at the University of Illinois, he returned here to live. Among this distinguished author's many other books are: *Hear That Lonesome Whistle Blow, Creek Mary's Blood, Killdeer Mountain*, and *The American Spa*, a history of Hot Springs.

HELEN GURLEY BROWN *EDITOR, WRITER* (b. 2/18/1922, Green Forest, AR) Longtime *Cosmopolitan* magazine editor Brown's carefree Arkansas childhood was shattered at age 10 when her father, a former state legislator who worked for the Game and Fish Commission, was crushed to death in an elevator accident at the state Capitol. Her destitute mother was forced to move the family to Los Angeles to live with relatives. Trained as a secretary, Brown held 17 jobs in 25 years before becoming

a successful advertising copywriter. In 1959 she married movie producer David Brown (whose later hits would include *The Sting, Jaws* and *A Few Good Men*). When he suggested she write a book, the result was the 1962 bestseller, *Sex and the Single Girl*. In 1965 the Hearst Corporation, in a last-ditch effort to revive the moribund *Cosmopolitan*, hired her as editor-in-chief and the Cosmo Girl was born. Under Brown's indefatigable leadership, the magazine's circulation began a spectacular climb. A tireless promoter, her tiny, painfully thin (105 pounds) presence has been a fixture of talk shows for three decades.

Jim Ed Brown

JIM ED BROWN *SINGER (b. James Edward Brown, 4/1/1934, Sparkman, AR)* Brown has had two wildly successful careers as a performer: first, as a member of a popular vocal group, The Browns, along with his sisters; then, as a solo entertainer. Brown was raised on a farm, the son of a sawmill owner. In 1953, as a forestry major at Arkansas A&M, he entered a Little Rock talent contest on a dare. He won first prize, then called up his sister Maxine from the audience and forced her to join him in a duet. A success, they were soon performing (along with sister

Bonnie) on "The Louisiana Hayride" and "Ozark Jamboree." Later they signed an RCA contract. Their 1959 smash "The Three Bells" sold 100,000 copies a week at its height. In 1967 the sisters retired to raise families. As a solo artist, Brown's hits include: "Regular on My Mind," "Pop-A-Top," and "Morning." ➤ *See also:* The Browns.

THE BROWNS *SINGING GROUP (Maxine: b. 4/27/1932, Sampti, LA; James Edward: b. 4/1/1934, Sparkman, AR; Bonnie: b. 7/31/1937; Sparkman, AR)* An extremely popular vocal trio from the 1950s and 60s, the Browns' hits included "The Three Bells," which sold over three million records in 1959, "Scarlet Ribbons," and "The Old Lamplighter." For a time, the group owned a supper club in Pine Bluff. The Browns disbanded in 1967.
➤ *See also:* Jim Ed Brown.

FRANK BROYLES *FOOTBALL COACH (b. John Frank Broyles, 12/26/1924, Decatur, GA)* Longtime czar of U of A athletics, Broyles built one of America's most successful college sports programs. At Georgia Tech he lettered in three sports. Following assistant coaching jobs at Baylor, Florida and Georgia Tech, he spent a year as Missouri head coach before coming to Arkansas in 1957, where nobody figured he'd remain long. By the time he retired after the 1976 season, his teams had won seven SWC championships and a national title (1964). His win-loss record is the best in Hog history: 144-58-5 (a .707 winning percentage). From 1974 he has also served as athletic director, switch-ing the Razorbacks from the SWC to the SEC in 1990, and making hires like Eddie Sutton, Lou Holtz, John McDonnell and Nolan Richardson. And for nine years he was ABC's top college color commentator. ➤ *See also:* Ken Hatfield, Nolan Richardson, Barry Switzer.

BEAR BRYANT *FOOTBALL COACH (b. Paul William Bryant, 9/11/1913, Moro Bottom, AR; d. 1/26/83, Tuscaloosa, AL)* The winningest major-college football coach of all time, Bryant was born on a small farm near Fordyce, one of 11 children reared in grinding poverty. He played tackle for the Fordyce Redbugs and earned his nickname after wrestling a bear at the Fordyce Theater in his teens. He played end at the University of Alabama, then stayed on after graduation as an assistant coach. He spent four years there, then two at Vanderbilt. In 1941 Bryant almost came to Arkansas as head coach. At the end of the season he was offered the job, but took a couple of days to think it over. On December 7 he planned to accept, but Pearl Harbor intervened, and Bryant joined the Navy instead. After the war he headed up programs at Maryland, Kentucky and Texas A&M before returning to his alma mater in 1958. In his 25 seasons at Alabama, he grew into a legend. Raspy-voiced and craggy-faced, always decked out in his trademark houndstooth-checked hat, Bryant coached the Tide to six national championships, seven perfect regular seasons and a record 24 straight bowls. Overall, his college coaching record was 323-85-17. Bryant's ties to his birthplace remained strong all his life. On the morning he died, in fact, he told his doctor that he was planning to go back to Arkansas and do some duck hunting.

BETTY BUMPERS *PEACE ACTIVIST (b. Betty Flanagan, 1/11/1925, Grand Prairie, AR)* Wife of long-time Arkansas senator Dale, Betty Bumpers is the founder of Peace Links, a national non-partisan organization through which women strive to end the nuclear threat. Spurred by a discussion with her teenage daughter on the possible after-effects of a nuclear war, Bumpers obtained a grant in 1982 from a foundation set up by Winthrop Rockefeller, the man her husband had defeated in the 1970 governor's race. Today, Peace Links has over 30,000 members nationwide. Betty Bumpers' hero: Eleanor Roosevelt.

BOB BURNS *ENTERTAINER (b. William Robert Burn, 8/2/1891, Greenwood, AR; d. 2/2/56, Encino, CA)* One of the top radio and movie comedians of the 1930s and 40s, Burns [he added the "s" to the family name after he entered show business] made a fortune serenading audiences with a musical contraption he called the bazooka and telling tall tales about mythical relatives back home in Van Buren, Arkansas, where he was raised. The son of a civil engineer, Burns was reared in a well-to-do family, but was forced to wear dresses until he was almost five. He taught himself to play the piano, mandolin, harmonica, trombone, violin, cornet and guitar. In 1910, he invented his own instrument, a noisemaker he dubbed the bazooka.

As a Marine in WWI he won the rifle championship of the American Expeditionary Forces and was decorated by Gen. Pershing. Back in the states, Burns knocked around in show business before landing a spot on the Rudy Vallee radio show. His dry humor caught on with the public. Later Bing Crosby brought him to Hollywood. Listening to Burns and his bazooka on the Kraft Music Hall became a Thursday night ritual. Among his movies: *The Singing Vagabond, The Big Broadcast of 1937, Waikiki Wedding,* and *The Arkansas Traveler.* During WWII, as the Army was testing a new rocket launcher, GIs tagged it the "bazooka" after Burns' celebrated instrument, and the name stuck. In the 1950s, Burns retired. Shrewd real

Bob Burns, with his "bazooka"

estate investments in the San Fernando Valley had made him one of the richest men in show business.

GLEN CAMPBELL *ENTERTAINER (b. Glen Travis Campbell, 4/22/1936, Billstown, AR)* Recording star, TV host, movie actor – Campbell has succeeded at it all. Born to share-cropper parents, Campbell was the seventh son of a seventh son. At 13 he performed with his Uncle Boo at the Forestry Festival and stole the show. Three years later, he dropped out of school and joined a band in Ari-zona. At 17 he married his pregnant 15-year-old girl-friend, then moved to LA where he developed a reputation as a top session man. After signing a record contract he hit it big in 1967, when "Gentle On My Mind" and "By the Time I Get to Phoenix" topped the charts, eventually earning him three Grammys. Other hits: "Wichita Lineman," "Galveston," "Rhinestone Cowboy," "Southern Nights." Next he con-quered TV with the very popular *Glen Campbell Goodtime Hour* ("Hi! I'm Glen Campbell!"), which ran four years on CBS. In 1969 he starred with John Wayne in one of

Glen Campbell

the year's top-grossing movies, *True Grit*, based on the best-selling novel by fellow Arkansan Charles Portis. By the 1970s, however, wild living had reduced the Goodtime Man to hard times. His second marriage collapsed in 1976 and he quickly remarried the ex-wife of singer Mac Davis, who left him four years later. In 1980 he began a stormy affair with country singer Tanya Tucker. Eventually, Campbell remarried a fourth time, rediscovered religion and gave up cocaine and alcohol. Today, an evangelical Christian, he still earns well over $1 million annually. In 1994 he published a tell-all autobiography, *Rhinestone Cowboy*.
➤ *See also:* Charles Portis.

HATTIE CARAWAY *FIRST WOMAN ELECTED TO THE SENATE (b. Hatty [sic] Ophelia Wyatt, 2/1/1878, Bakerville, TN; d. 12/21/50, Falls Church, VA)* Cara-way started off as a classic house-wife who raised three sons (one became a Brigadier General in WWII) and followed her husband Thaddeus to Congress. When he died in 1931 the surprised widow found herself appointed to his office. Nicknamed "The Little Lady in Black" because she always wore widow's weeds, she was expected to tend to her knitting and step aside the next November when

Hattie Caraway

some duly elected male would take back the job. Thus, everyone was astonished when she decided to run for the office herself. Nobody counted on a wild card in the election – Huey Long. The Louisiana senator had befriended Caraway after she endorsed his "Share the Wealth" proposal and engineered a guerrilla-style campaign that propelled the widow to an upset primary victory. Now officially the first woman to win a full term in the Senate, "Silent Hattie" rarely made a speech and never entered debate ("I haven't the heart to take a minute away from the men," she said. "The poor dears love it so"). But she worked hard at her job – she traveled to work by

streetcar and usually brought her own lunch – and in 1938 was re-elected for six more years. Her career was filled with firsts: first woman to preside over the Senate, first woman Senate committee chairman, first woman senior senator, first woman to conduct a Senate committee hearing. In 1944 she lost to J. William Fulbright. During the last session of the 78th Congress, the Senate rose in an unprecedented tribute.

JOHNNY CASH *ENTERTAINER*
(b. 2/26/1932, Cleveland County, AR)
Born in a three-room railroad shack to a sharecropper family, the future "Man in Black" began writing songs at the age of 12. His mother took in washing to pay for singing lessons and, at 17, Cash won first prize in a local talent show. In 1955, after a stint with the Air Force and classes at radio announcer's school, he auditioned at famous Sun Studio in Memphis. Sent home to write "a weeper with a tempo," he came back two weeks later and recorded "Cry Cry Cry." A year later he cut his first million-seller, "I Walk the Line," and there was no stopping him. Other hits: "Hey Porter," "Fulsom Prison Blues," "Orange

Blossom Special," "A Boy Named Sue." A hard-living carouser with a definite dark side to his personality, Cash was once arrested trying to cross the Mexican border with a guitar-case full of pep pills and he almost died of an overdose following a Nashville car crash. Eventually his first wife divorced him. In 1967 he married June Carter, daughter of Mother Maybelle Carter of the famous Carter family. They performed together and had a hit with "Jackson." In 1983 Cash put in six weeks at the Betty Ford Clinic. A seven-time Grammy winner, Cash has also starred in two TV series: "The Johnny Cash Show" (ABC, 1969-71) and "Johnny Cash and Friends" (CBS, 1976). Movies include: *A Gunfight, The Pride of Jesse Hallam, Murder in Coweta County*. In 1975 he produced a best-selling autobiography, *Man in Black*.

Johnny Cash

ELDRIDGE CLEAVER *BLACK ACTIVIST, AUTHOR (b. Leroy Eldridge Cleaver, 8/31/1935, Little Rock, AR)* In the late 1960s, Cleaver personified in-your-face black activism. Raised in Wabbaseka

Eldridge Cleaver

("one of the smallest dots on any map of Arkansas," he has called it), Cleaver moved to Los Angeles in 1946. Sent to reform school at 14, he was later arrested in 1958 for the attempted armed rape of a nurse, and sentenced to prison. He was paroled in 1966. Two years later he burst onto the national scene with the publication of *Soul on Ice*, a book of prison essays on the African-American experience that has sold over two million copies. On April 6, 1968, Cleaver, then Information Minister of the Black Panthers, was wounded in a gun battle with the police in West

Oakland, CA. He subsequently jumped bail and fled the U.S., an international fugitive. After hiding out in Algeria and Cuba, Cleaver returned to America in 1975. His renunciation of the Panthers and his professed religious conversion cost him followers. Eventually, murder charges were dropped and Cleaver was placed on probation for assault. In 1978 he failed to recapture literary success with *Soul on Fire.* He's also had several more clashes with the law, including arrests for cocaine possession. In 1994 he reportedly suffered a debilitating brain hemorrhage.

BILL CLINTON *FORTY-SECOND PRESIDENT OF THE UNITED STATES (b. William Jefferson Blythe IV, 8/19/ 1946, Hope, AR)* Although the most famous Arkansan of them all was born "in a place called Hope," Clinton spent most of his youth in Hot Springs, where he moved at the age of six. His natural father, a WWII veteran, was killed in a Missouri car crash four months before his son's birth. In 1950 Clinton's mother Virginia, a nurse-anesthetist, married car salesman Roger Clinton, whose name young Bill Blythe would later take as his own. (Roger Clinton died in 1967.) At Hot Springs High School, Bill Clinton was an all-state saxophone player. In his senior year, he traveled to Washington as a Boy's Nation delegate and shook hands in the Rose Garden with his idol, President John F. Kennedy. After graduating in 1968 from Georgetown University in Washington (where he also worked in

J. William Fulbright's Senate office), Clinton continued his education with two years of graduate study at Oxford on a Rhodes Scholarship. Then it was on to Yale Law School, where he met Hillary Rodham of Chicago. In 1973, Clinton returned home to Arkansas and briefly taught law at the U of A in Fayetteville. The next year he was joined by Hillary Rodham, whom he would marry in 1975. It was in Fayetteville, in 1974, that he made his first run for elected office – a long-shot campaign for Congress in which he defeated three Democratic primary challengers but narrowly lost the general election to the Republican incumbent. In 1976, at age 30, he ran for attorney general, and won. Two years after that, he was elected governor – the youngest in Arkansas history. In 1980, however, his political career suffered a major setback when he lost his re-election bid to Republican Frank White. (This same year his only child, daughter Chelsea, was born.) But two years later, Clinton was back, winning the rematch handily. He won again in 1984, 1986 and 1990. As governor, Clinton moved to improve education and promote new industry. His fellow governors voted him the most effective governor in the nation. In 1988 he achieved his first moment in the sun of national TV, but got badly burned when his nominating speech for Gov. Michael Dukakis at the Democratic National Convention ran too long and he was heckled. He managed to partially defuse the incident by going on "The Tonight Show" and winning over the

Tipper and Al Gore; Chelsea, Hillary and Bill Clinton

audience with self-deprecating humor and a blast from his sax. On October 3, 1991, from the front steps of the Old State House in Little Rock, Clinton declared he was a candidate for the presidency. After a fiercely-contested primary fight, Clinton was nominated in July 1992 as the Democratic standard-bearer. Four months later, following a bruising Presidential campaign, he and running mate Sen. Al Gore of Tennessee, received 43 percent of the popular vote, swamping independent candidate billionaire Ross Perot, and ousting incumbent George Bush. On January 20, 1993, he took over the world's most powerful job. ➤ *See also:* Hillary Rodham Clinton, Vincent Foster, J. William Fulbright, Virginia Kelley.

HILLARY RODHAM CLINTON *FIRST LADY (b. 10/26/1947, Chicago, IL)* The daughter of a textile company owner, Hillary Rodham was raised in the Chicago suburb of Park Ridge. As president of her high school senior class, she earned so many honors that her parents recalled "being slightly uncomfortable at her graduation." In 1965 she entered Wellesley College, graduating with more honors. At Yale Law School, where she edited the *Yale Review* and worked in the community for Yale Legal Services, she met Arkansan Bill Clinton. (She overheard him holding court in the library and boasting about the size of Hope watermelons.) In 1973, she joined the staff of the Children's Defense Fund in Washington before serving on the Impeachment

Inquiry Staff of the Judiciary Committee of the U.S. House of Representatives during the Watergate proceedings. In 1974 she followed Bill Clinton down to Fayetteville and married him the following year. Together they taught law at the U of A. When her husband was elected state attorney general in 1976, the couple moved to Little Rock, where Hillary Rodham Clinton joined the old-line Rose Law Firm, eventually emerging as a top-dollar litigator and partner earning several times her husband's $35,000 salary. She was twice voted one of the 100 Most Influential Lawyers in America by *The National Law Journal.* Daughter Chelsea was born in 1980, named for the Judy Collins recording of "Chelsea Morning." After Bill Clinton became governor in 1978, his wife founded the Arkansas Advocates for Children and Families, and became active in public school reforms, chairing the Arkansas Education Standards Committee which created public school accreditation standards that became a national model. When Bill Clinton failed in his bid for a second term, some blamed the loss in part on voter resentment that his feminist wife had not dropped her maiden name. In 1982 she acquiesced: "I gave it up. It meant more to them than it did to me." During the 1992 presidential race, Hillary Clinton was by her husband's side through thick and thin, even to the point of having every detail of her marriage scrutinized by the national press. As First Lady, she is clearly the President's most trusted and most influential advisor. ➤ *See also:* Bill Clinton, Vincent Foster.

CARROLL CLOAR *ARTIST (b. 1/18/ 1913, Earle, AR; d. 4/10/93, Memphis, TN)* Famed for his flat, primitive paintings of life in the Mississippi River Delta, Cloar was born on a farm near West Memphis. He moved from Arkansas at 17, attended art school, served in WWII, and eventually settled in Memphis. Today his work hangs in the Museum of Modern Art, the Whitney, the Smithsonian and the Metropolitan, among many. Perhaps the most significant collection of his work resides at Arkansas State University. He died of a self-inflicted gunshot wound.

CLIFTON CLOWERS *"WOLVERTON MOUNTAIN" MAN (b. 10/30/1891, Center Ridge, AR; d. 8/15/1994, Morrilton, AR)* In 1962 the name Clifton Clowers became notorious as the fiercely protective father in the hit record, "Wolverton Mountain." Written three years earlier by Clowers' nephew, Merle Kilgore, the song became a number one country hit when performed by Claude King. According to neighbors, the real-life Clowers was nothing like the character in the song. Friendly and devout, he lived most of his life on Woolverton (sic) Mountain, a few miles south of the Conway/Van Buren county line.

IRA CORN *BRIDGE CHAMPION (b. Ira George Corn, Jr., 8/22/1921, Little Rock,. AR; d. 4/28/82, Dallas, TX)* A successful businessman, Corn organized the first professional American bridge team, "The Aces," and won three world championships.

FLOYD CRAMER MUSICIAN
(b. 10/27/1933, Shreveport, LA)

Although born in Louisiana, pianist Cramer was raised in Huttig, near El Dorado. A prodigy, he was playing piano by age five. After high school, he joined "The Louisiana Hayride," then moved on to Nashville's Grand Ole Opry. During the 1950s Cramer frequently backed Elvis Presley on concert tours, recordings and movie soundtracks. His "Last Date" in 1960 established Cramer's "lonesome cowboy" keyboard style and was one of the year's top-selling singles. Other hits: "On the Rebound," "Fancy Pants."

JOHN DALY GOLFER (b. 4/28/66,
Sacramento, CA) In 1991 Daly caused a sensation by winning the PGA Championship in his first year on the pro tour, only the second rookie to ever capture a major title. (The ninth alternate, he didn't even know he was going to play until the night before the tournament, and had never seen the course until his first round.) Now one of the sport's top draws, Daly has led a troubled life on and off the links. Professionally, Long John has been reprimanded several times and even suspended from the tour. A recovering alcoholic, he was once charged with assault by his live-in girlfriend, whom he later married. Daly played his college golf for the U of A. In July 1995, capping a dazzling career comeback, the grip-it-and-rip-it kid won the British Open.

WILLIAM DARBY MILITARY HERO (b.
William Orlando Darby, 2/8/1911, Ft. Smith, AR; d. 4/16/45, Turbole, Italy)

Darby commanded WWII's elite striking force, the Rangers. Formed in 1942, the all-volunteer unit spearheaded operations throughout the world. A soldier's soldier, Darby was wounded three times and decorated ten times by four governments. He repeatedly turned down promotions to stay with his men. Following a disastrous 1944 raid, the Rangers were withdrawn from combat. (Of the original members of the first three Ranger battalions, less than 200 made it back to the States alive.) Darby was reassigned to a desk job and ordered to take it easy. In 1945, however, he joined an inspection tour in Italy and then

William Darby

finagled himself into another fighting unit. Soon afterward, the 34-year-old Darby was killed by heavy German shelling as he returned from a routine visit to the front. Two days later, all German forces in Italy surrendered. Gen. Patton said simply, "He was the bravest man I knew." The Army named a troop transport, a camp and a Ranger Training Command in his honor. Darby was made a brigadier general posthumously. In 1958 a fellow commando wrote *Darby's Rangers*, which Warner Brothers loosely adapted into a movie starring James Garner.

DANIEL DAVIS *ACTOR b. 1945?, Gurdon, AR)* Famous as Niles, the butler on TV's "The Nanny," Davis grew up in Gurdon and Little Rock. As a child he performed regularly on the local afternoon kiddie show, "Betty's Little Rascals," for almost five years. Later, Davis appeared on Broadway and in the movies. He now lives in New York.

GAIL DAVIS *STAR OF "ANNIE OAKLEY" (b. 10/5/1925, McGehee, AR)* One of the best-remembered TV westerns of the 1950s was "Annie Oakley," starring pint-sized, pig-tailed Gail Davis, the first woman to star in an action series. Raised mostly in Texas and Pennsylvania, Davis was discovered by an agent in California. After appearances in dozens of B-movies in the 1940s, she was picked by Gene Autry to star in "Annie Oakley," which he produced. It was a huge success, running from 1953 to 1956. The feisty little Oakley could out-ride

and out-shoot any man around, but she never killed anyone, preferring to shoot the guns out of their hands instead. After the series ended, Davis predicted, "I'm going to be Annie Oakley for the rest of my born days."

HERMAN DAVIS *MILITARY HERO (b. 1/3/1888, Manila, AR; d. 1/5/23, Memphis, TN)* In 1919 Gen. John J. "Blackjack" Pershing ranked "The 100 Greatest Heroes of World War I." Fourth on his list was Davis. A farm boy who loved hunting, Davis entered the service in 1918. During the Meuse Argonne offensive, he inched across a no-man's land under withering fire and single-handedly dispatched four German machine gunners, saving his entire company. Later in the war, the 5' 3" Davis killed upwards of 30 more Germans (reports vary). Back home in Arkansas, Davis preferred not to discuss his exploits; he stored his decorations in an old tackle box. A few years later he began to suffer the lingering effects of exposure to German gas, and died of tuberculosis at age 35. In 1925 a statue of Davis was dedicated in his hometown.

WILLIE DAVIS *BASEBALL PLAYER (b. William Henry Davis, 4/15/1940, Mineral Springs, AR)* The Dodgers' starting center fielder for 13 years, Davis was among the fastest players in the game. A three-time Golden Glove winner, he also twice led the league in errors, once committing a World Series record of three errors in a game, all coming in the same inning. In 1996 he was arrested for terrorizing his parents with a samurai sword.

DIZZY DEAN *HALL-OF-FAME PITCHER, SPORTSCASTER (b. Jay Hanna Dean, 1/16/1910, Lucas, AR; d. 7/17/74, Reno, NV)* Born into a Logan County sharecropper family, Dean became one of the most colorful personalities ever associated with baseball. He entered the big leagues in 1930, when a scout pulled him off a sandlot and signed him with the St. Louis Cardinals. In his first full season with the famed Gas House Gang, Dean won 18 games and led the National League in strikeouts and shutouts. During the 1934 pennant drive, he pitched nine games in 19 days. In the World retired in 1941, never having made more than $25,000 a year playing baseball. Career stats: 150-83; 3.03 ERA. Later Ol' Diz turned to sportscasting. His fractured syntax ("he slud into third" and "the players returned to their respectable bases") generated even more fans, as well as the ire of grammarians. Despite a protest by teachers to the FCC, he refused to change his style, insisting, "I'm gonna talk like I talked in Arkansas." In 1952 Hollywood produced a bio, *The Pride of St. Louis*, starring Dan Dailey. Dean entered the Hall of Fame in 1953.
➤ *See also:* Paul Dean.

The Dean brothers – Dizzy and Daffy

Series, Dean won two games and his younger brother Paul won the other two. His 30-7 performance earned him the league's MVP award. Following an injury in the 1937 All-Star Game, his career declined. In 1938 he was traded to the Cubs and

PAUL DEAN *BASEBALL PITCHER (b. Paul Dee Dean, 8/14/1913, Lucas, AR; d. 3/17/81, Springdale, AR)* The younger half of the feared "Me 'n' Paul" Dean brothers of the 1930s St. Louis Cardinals, Paul Dean followed his brother Dizzy into the famous Gas House Gang in 1934. As a rookie he won 19 games, including the third and sixth games of the World Series against the Detroit Tigers (Dizzy picked up the other two wins). Afterward, a sportswriter tagged him "Daffy," a nickname he disliked. In 1936 he developed shoulder problems, retiring in 1943. Career stats: 50-34; 3.75 ERA.

➤ *See also:* Dizzy Dean.

BILL DICKEY *HALL-OF-FAME CATCHER (b. William Malcom Dickey, 6/6/1907, Bastrop, LA; d. 11/12/93, Little Rock, AR)* One of the top catchers ever, Dickey was raised in Kensett and Little Rock, the son of a railroad conductor. He signed with the New York Yankees in 1928 and became the team's starting catcher the following year (earning a princely $4,000). In his 16 seasons with the Bronx Bombers, Dickey played in 1,789 games, produced 202 HR and 1,209 RBI, and batted .313 lifetime. He played in eight World Series, helping win seven of them. Connie Mack called him "the greatest catcher I've ever seen." A close friend of Lou Gehrig, Dickey played himself in the movie, *The Pride of the Yankees*. After Navy service in WWII, Dickey took over as manager of the Yankees in May 1946, but quit five months later once the team had been officially eliminated. He managed the Arkansas Travelers for a time, then rejoined the Yankees as a coach. He was inducted into the Hall of Fame in 1954. Four years later, he was the first player inducted into the Arkansas Sports Hall of Fame.

WILLIAM T. DILLARD *DEPARTMENT STORE TYCOON (b. 1914, Mineral Springs, AR)* The founder of the Dillard's department store chain worked at his father's country store, graduated from the U of A in 1935, then earned his MS at Columbia. Returning home, he spent a few months with Sears before opening his first store in 1938 in Nashville, Arkansas. After a stint in the Navy in WWII, he opened a second outlet in Texarkana. In 1960, with the purchase of Tulsa's Brown-Duncan, Dillard began an amazing growth surge. Today, headquartered in Little Rock, Dillard's is one of the world's most successful retail companies, operating over 200 stores.

MELINDA DILLON *ACTRESS (b. 10/31/1939, Hope, AR)* Dillon has been nominated twice for the Academy Award for her supporting performances in *Close Encounters of the Third Kind* and *Absence of Malice*.

MIKE DISFARMER *PHOTOGRAPHER (b. Michael Meyer, 1884, IN; d. 1959, Heber Springs, AR)* Disfarmer operated a small Main Street photography studio in Heber Springs throughout the 1940s and 50s. An eccentric, reclusive alcoholic, he produced plain, unaffected portraits of country people for ten cents a picture. Upon his death at 75, the contents of the studio were saved from the trash heap by a $5 bid. Years later, the local newspaper began running the evocative portraits on a regular basis. Eventually they were collected into *Disfarmer: The Heber Springs Portraits*, hailed by the *New York Times* as one of the best photography books of the year. Today, Disfarmer portraits are highly prized. Of the photographer himself, little is known. Raised primarily in Stuttgart, he moved with his mother to Heber Springs after the death of his father, and remained there for the next 45 years, virtually friendless. Only one or two photos of him are known to exist.

David O. Dodd

DAVID O. DODD *"THE BOY MARTYR OF THE CONFEDERACY"* *(b. 11/10/1846, Victoria, TX; d. 1/8/64, Little Rock, AR)* Few events of the Civil War so stirred the emotions of Arkansans as the hanging of 17-year-old non-combatant Dodd by Union troops in 1864. Born in Texas of Arkansas parents, Dodd returned to the state with his family when he was 12. On a trip to Camden in December 1863 he was intercepted by Union soldiers, who discovered a coded notebook detailing Federal military strength around Little Rock. A military tribunal sentenced Dodd to die as a spy. Reportedly, the garrison commander believed the boy would break down and reveal his sources – but he never did. On a snowy January afternoon, the condemned boy was removed from the compound in a wagon, forced to ride atop his own coffin to be hanged. Today, Little Rock is adorned with several monuments commemorating Dodd, including those at the Old State House and MacArthur Park. He is buried at Mount Holly Cemetery.

JIMMY DRIFTWOOD *COMPOSER, FOLKLORIST (b. James Corbett Morris, 6/20/1907, Mountain View, AR)* Composer of the famous "Battle of New Orleans," which sold over a million copies in 1959, three-time Grammy winner Driftwood is also an icon of American folk heritage. Born in the hills of Arkansas, Driftwood worked many years as a teacher, principal and school superintendent. A talented musician, he collected and wrote folksongs on the side. In June 1958, Driftwood released an album for RCA that included an old tune for which he had written new lyrics as a teaching aid – "The Battle of New Orleans." Country singer Johnny Horton's follow-up version was one of the smash hits of the decade. Later, Chet Atkins scored a top-10 success with Driftwood's "Tennessee Stud." A frequent guest on The Grand Ole Opry, Driftwood has delighted audiences with his performances on the "mouth bow." As one of the founders of the acclaimed Arkansas Folk Festival, he is also a highly respected folk expert, and has served as an adviser to the Smithsonian Institute and the National Georgraphic Society.

JOYCELYN ELDERS *U.S. SURGEON GENERAL (b. Minnie Joycelyn Jones, 8/13/1933, Schaal, AR)* Feisty, tough-talking Elders was the first African-American to serve as America's top doctor. She was appointed to the post by Bill Clinton after serving as Arkansas State Health Director for five years. A staunch advocate of contraception, sex education and legal abortion, she attended Philander Smith College in Little Rock and later the U of A Medical School; her specialty is pediatric endocrinology. After a series of controversial statements in office, Elders was fired in December 1994. ➤ *See also:* Bill Clinton.

DALE EVANS *ACTRESS, SONGWRITER (b. Frances Octavia Smith, 10/31/1912, Uvalde, TX)* Evans, the cowgirl "Queen of the West" of B-movies and TV, moved at age seven to Osceola, Arkansas. A rebellious child, she suffered a nervous breakdown at age 11. Married at 14, she had a child at 15, and was then deserted by her young husband. As a Memphis secretary she started singing on the radio. Eventually she landed in Hollywood, where, after a series of low-budget musicals, she was teamed with the King of the Cowboys, Roy Rogers, in "The Cowboy and the Senorita" (1944), the first of many. In 1945 Evans divorced her second husband and

two years later married widower Rogers. In 1951 the couple switched to TV, with the popular "Roy Rogers Show." Evans' personal life has been marred by tragedy, including the deaths of several children. A born-again Christian, she has written over a score of inspirational books and composed numerous songs, including "The Bible Tells Me So" and the immortal "Happy Trails."

ORVAL FAUBUS *POLITICIAN (b. Orval Eugene Faubus, 1/7/1910, Combs, AR; d. 12/14/94, Conway, AR)* The most controversial of Arkansas' governors, Faubus in 1957 helped precipitate a constitutional crisis that blotted the state's image for years. Born the son of a poor farmer, Faubus enlisted in the Army as a private soon after Pearl Harbor, rising to the rank of major. After the

Orval Faubus

war, he was named to the Highway Commission. In 1954 he was elected governor. During his first term, Faubus established a fairly progressive agenda, but in his second term he defied a federal court order to integrate public schools, bringing in the National Guard to prevent black students from entering Central High School. When President Eisenhower sent in federal troops, Faubus was forced to back down. But the damage to the state's reputation was severe, and economic development was stalled for years. In 1958 a Gallup poll included Faubus as one of America's ten most admired men. Altogether, he served six terms, retiring in 1967 (several subsequent comeback attempts failed). He spent his later years attempting, with some success, to rehabilitate his image. He wrote two volumes of memoirs, *In a Faraway Land* (1971) and *Down From the Hills* (1980).

➤ *See also:* Daisy Bates, Ernest Green, the Little Rock Nine.

RHONDA KYE FLEMING

COUNTRY MUSIC COM-POSER (b. 1951, Fort Smith, AR) One of Nashville's top composers, Fleming began writing songs at 14. Some of the country hits she has co-written: "Roll on Mississippi," "Smoky Mountain Rain," "Nobody," "Sleeping Single in a Double Bed," "I Was Country When Country Wasn't Cool."

JOHN GOULD FLETCHER

PULITZER-PRIZE-WINNING POET (b. 1/3/1886, Little Rock, AR; d. 5/10/50, Little Rock, AR) Scion of an illustrious Arkansas family, Fletcher passed a lonely childhood inside the Little Rock antebellum mansion built by Albert Pike (and now the Decorative Arts Museum of the Arkansas Arts Center). He quit Harvard in his senior year when his father's death left him financially independent. After a European tour, he settled in London and began writing books of experimental poetry, eventually joining the Imagist movement. In the late 1920s, Fletcher grew committed to regionalism and Southern agrarianism, contributing to the famous manifesto, *I'll Take My Stand*. In 1933 he returned to Little Rock, leaving behind his first wife. Three years later he married writer Charlie May Simon. His *Selected Poems* won the Pulitzer Prize in 1939. "I am particularly pleased that the award was given to a native of Arkansas," he said. "It may be the forerunner of further cultural achievement in Arkansas." Fascinated with state history, Fletcher helped found the Arkansas Folklore Society and the Arkansas

John Gould Fletcher

Historical Society. For the 1936 centennial celebration he wrote "The Epic of Arkansas," a long, romanticized poem, as well as a later prose history, *Arkansas* (1947). In 1937 he published his autobiography, *Life Is My Song.* Fletcher, who had long suffered from depression, drowned himself in a pond near his home Johnswood, off Highway 10. He is buried in Mount Holly Cemetery. ➤ *See also:* Charlie May Simon.

JAY C. FLIPPEN *ACTOR (b. 3/6/ 1898, Little Rock, AR; d. 2/3/71, Los Angeles, CA)* Flippen started in vaudeville, then moved to Broadway where he became a leading man in the late 1920s. After WWII he hit Hollywood and emerged as a character actor. The versatile Flippen appeared in everything from musicals (*Oklahoma! Kismet*) to comedies (*The Yellow Cab Man, The Lemon Drop Kid*), but is best remembered for westerns, especially those starring James Stewart (*Winchester 73, Bend of the River, The Far Country*). He also appeared in the TV series "Ensign O'Toole." The grizzled, craggy-faced actor played his final roles in a wheelchair, following a leg amputation.

GENNIFER FLOWERS *TABLOID QUEEN (b. Eura Gean Flowers, 1/24/ 1950, Dallas, TX)* Flowers created a media sensation during the 1992 presidential race by claiming a 12-year affair with Bill Clinton. The daughter of a crop duster pilot, she grew up in Brinkley, where her family moved when she was nine. She met Clinton, then attorney general, in 1977 as a local TV reporter. A former backup singer for Roy Clark, Flowers sold her story to *The Star* for a reported $175,000, then did a spread in *Penthouse*. In 1995 she published her memoirs, *Passion and Betrayal.*

J. William Fulbright

VINCENT FOSTER *PRESIDENTIAL COUNSELOR (b. 1/15/1945, Hope, AR; d. 7/20/93, McLean, VA)* As deputy counsel to the president, Foster's puzzling suicide only months after joining the fledgling Clinton administration shocked the nation and pricked the antennae of conspiracy junkies everywhere. Foster, a childhood friend of the president, was also a former Rose Law Firm partner of Hillary Clinton. ➤ *See also:* Bill Clinton, Hillary Rodham Clinton.

J. WILLIAM FULBRIGHT *POLITICIAN (b. 4/9/1905, Sumner, MO; d. 2/9/95, Washington, DC)* Fulbright chaired the Senate Foreign Relations Committee for 15 years. Often a voice of reason amid the mob, he cast the sole vote against funding Sen. Joseph McCarthy's investigating committee in 1954 (McCarthy denigrated him as "Senator Halfbright"). A decade later he was among the first to speak out against U.S. involvement in Vietnam (LBJ quit talking to him). Fulbright moved to Fayetteville as a boy, when his parents acquired the local newspaper. He was a gifted athlete and scholar, quarterbacking the Razorbacks and later attending Oxford on a Rhodes scholarship. Returning home in 1931, he married and taught law at the U of A. In 1939 he became president of the university but was fired two years later in what poet John Gould Fletcher termed "a fit of political irritation." In 1942 he won a seat in the House of Representatives and two years later ousted Hattie Caraway to become the state's junior senator. In Washington, he established the prestigious Fulbright fellowship program in 1946, which provided for the exchange of students and teachers between America and foreign countries. During Vietnam his search for a "rational" foreign policy infuriated Democratic and Republican administrations alike, but others in Congress later joined him in opposition to the war. On the issue of civil rights, however, Fulbright's record was less than impressive; he voted against virtually every significant bill. Fulbright was defeated in the 1974 Democratic primary by Gov. Dale Bumpers. Afterward, the "Great Dissenter" joined a posh D.C. law firm. In 1993 former protégé Bill Clinton bestowed on Fulbright the nation's highest civilian honor, the Presidential Medal of Freedom. ➤ *See also:* Hattie Caraway, Bill Clinton, Edward Durell Stone.

AUGUSTUS HILL GARLAND *U.S. ATTORNEY GENERAL (b. 1832, Tipton County, TN; d. 1899, Washington, D.C.)* After stints as Arkansas governor (1874-77) and U.S. senator (1877-85), Garland served as attorney general under President Grover Cleveland (1885-89), and pushed for tariff and civil service reform.

GIL GERARD *ACTOR (b. 1/23/1943, Little Rock, AR)* A graduate of Arkansas State Teachers College, Gerard was an industrial

Gil Gerard

chemist until 1971, when he quit his job and headed for New York. There he drove a taxi while taking acting lessons. He first gained popularity in the soap "The Doctors," before starring in the TV series "Buck Rogers in the 25th Century" from 1979 to 81.

MIFFLIN GIBBS POLITICIAN (b. Mifflin Wister Gibbs, 4/17/1823, Philadelphia, PA; d. 7/11/15, Little Rock, AR) A prominent black leader of the Reconstruction era, Gibbs was nearly 50 when he arrived in Arkansas. After being admitted to the bar, he won election as a municipal judge. Later, he became American consul in Madagascar under McKinley and Roosevelt (1879 to 1910). A wealthy businessman, Judge Gibbs did not forget the less fortunate—he helped establish a home for indigents. A Little Rock school is named in his honor. His autobiography, *Shadow and Light*, was published in 1902.

NORRIS GOFF ABNER OF "LUM AND

Chester Lauck and Norris Goff

ABNER" (b. 1906, Cove, AR; d. 6/7/78, Palm Desert, CA) Goff played Abner Peabody to fellow Arkansan Chet Lauck's Lum Edwards on radio and the movies. The son of a grocer, "Tuffy" Goff moved with his family in 1911 to Mena, where he became friends with Lauck. An ad-libbed 1931 skit evolved into the long-running "Lum and Abner" radio show. In addition to Abner, Goff played several other roles on the program, including Squire Skimp, Ulysses S. Quincy, Mousy Grey and Dick Huddleston. In 1937 he built a Hollywood mansion but maintained subscriptions to several Arkansas newspapers in order to keep in touch. Forced into retirement by heart ailments, he tended his 1,000-acre ranch in California, played golf, and even served a term as a city councilman. Goff once tried to explain the show's success: "The program is restful. We never sink any battleships or flee from any thundering elephants." ➤ *See also:* Chet Lauck, and Pine Ridge entry in *Cities and Towns* section.

ELIZABETH WARD GRACEN MISS AMERICA 1982 (b. 4/3/1961, Ozark, AR) One of Arkansas' two former Miss Americas (Donna Axum is the other), Elizabeth Ward established a post-regnum career as an actress. She moved to L.A. in 1987, added the name Gracen (there was already an Elizabeth Ward in the Screen Actors Guild), and began appearing in minor movie roles. In May 1992 she appeared in an eight-page nude pictorial in *Playboy*. The issue was rushed to the stands to exploit rumors of an alleged past dalliance with then-Presidential candidate Bill Clinton, although Gracen vigorously denied the charges in an accompanying interview. Gracen has subsequently appeared as a regular on the ABC series "Extreme," as well as the syndicated "Highlander." ➤ *See also:* Donna Axum.

FRED GRAHAM *TV JOURNALIST (b. Fred Patterson Graham, 10/6/1931, Little Rock, AR)* A familiar face to millions of Americans, television correspondent Fred Graham, formerly with CBS News, has won three Emmys and a Peabody award for his coverage. A graduate of Yale, he holds law degrees from Vanderbilt and Oxford. He is the author of *The Alias Program*, an exposé of the Justice Department's witness relocation program.

Fred Graham

AL GREEN *SINGER (b. Al Greene [sic], 4/13/1946, Forrest City, AR)* When he was nine, Green moved with his family to Michigan, where he began singing gospel with his brothers. After his father kicked him out of the group for listening to the "profane" music of Jackie Wilson, Green moved into pop. His first hit was "Back Up Train." Others: "Tired of Being Alone," "Let's Stay Together," "Look What You Done For Me," "I'm Still In Love With You," "You Ought To Be With Me," "Sha-La-La." In 1974 Green was hospitalized for second-degree burns after an ex-girlfriend poured boiling grits over him, then shot herself fatally. Later, the "Prince of Love" had a spiritual reawakening and rediscovered gospel music. In 1976 he was ordained a minister and purchased a church in Memphis, preaching weekly sermons when not on tour. In 1979, after injuring himself in a stage fall, Rev. Green declared he was giving up pop completely.

Al Green

ERNEST GREEN *CIVIL RIGHTS LEADER (b. Ernest Gideon Green, 9/22/1941, Little Rock, AR)* One of the famous "Little Rock Nine," Green was the first black graduate of Central High School and the subject of the 1992 Disney feature, *The Ernest Green Story* (filmed largely at Central). In 1993 he was among the first group inducted into the Arkansas Black Hall of Fame. Today Green is an investment consultant in Washington. ➤ *See also:* Daisy Bates, Orval Faubus, the Little Rock Nine.

BETTE GREENE *AUTHOR b. Bette Evensky, 6/28/1934, Memphis, TN)* One of the best-selling children's books of all time is Greene's *Summer of My German Soldier*. Since 1973 it has sold over a million copies and was made into a TV movie. The award-winning novel was inspired by a WWII German prisoner of war camp located near Greene's hometown of Parkin, where her parents operated a general store. In *Summer* a 12-year-old Jewish girl helps a German detainee escape from an Arkansas POW camp. Now residing in Brookline, MA, Greene, a former reporter for the *Memphis Commercial-Appeal*, has written several other books for young readers, most of which take place in Arkansas: *Philip Hall Likes Me, I Reckon Maybe; Morning Is a Long Time Coming; Get On Out of Here, Philip Hall!*

JOHN GRISHAM *AUTHOR (b. 2/8/1955, Jonesboro, AR)* No novelist of the 1990s has sold more books than Grisham. One of five children, he lived in tiny Black Oak, where he attended half of the first grade. Eventually his family moved to Mississippi, where Grisham attended college at Mississippi State and law school at Ole Miss in Oxford, where he settled down for a career in the law. On the side, he started writing novels. His first, *A Time to Kill* (1989), was published to little fanfare. But his next, *The Firm* (1991), created a sensation. Others – including *The Pelican Brief, The Client, The Chamber* and *The Rainmaker* – have also been phenomenal sellers. All have been sold to Hollywood (*A Time to Kill* went for over $6 million in 1994). He once said his "best ideas come from bush hogging."

ODELL "BAD NEWS" HALE *BASEBALL PLAYER (b. Arvel Odell Hale, 8/10/1908, Hosston, LA; d. 6/9/80, El Dorado, AR)* In his nine-year major league career, Hale played second and third base for the Cleveland Indians, Boston Red Sox and New York Giants. A fearsome hitter, he twice knocked in over a 100 runs a season. Lifetime, he was .289, with 73 HR and 573 RBI.

DAN HAMPTON *FOOTBALL PLAYER (b. Daniel Oliver Hampton, 9/19/1957, Oklahoma City, OK)* An All-Pro defensive lineman for the Chicago Bears (1979-90), Hampton played high school ball in Jacksonville, then attended the U of A, where he was an All-American (and later voted to the All-Century team). He was the fourth player selected in the 1979 NFL draft. In 1986, Hampton's Bears won the Super Bowl, 46-10 over New England. After ending his career, he turned to broadcasting and real estate. Hampton now resides in Cabot.

CONNIE HAMZY *GROUPIE (b. 1/9/ 1955, Little Rock, AR)* Known as "Sweet Connie," Little Rock-based rock groupie Hamzy claims to have had sex with hundreds of famous musicians. Her celebrated nickname derives from Grand Funk Railroad's 1973 hit, "We're an American Band": "Sweet, sweet Connie, doin' her act / she had the whole show and that's a natural fact."

JOHN HANCOCK *ACTOR (b. 1941?, Hazen, AR; d. 10/13/92, Los Angeles, CA)* A tall, heavyset black actor with a booming voice, Hancock was equally adept at comedy or drama. His credits included supporting roles in films (*A Soldier's Story*), recurring guest spots on television ("L. A. Law," as a judge), as well as appearances on stage (including the lead in an all-African-American presentation of *Death of a Salesman*). At his death, Hancock was co-starring as the cantankerous bartender in the CBS series "Love and War." He died of a massive heart attack.

DONALD HARINGTON *WRITER (b. 12/22/1935, Little Rock, AR)* The author of the complex, highly praised *The Architecture of the Ozarks* (1975), Harington has written several books chronicling mythical Stay More, Arkansas. Born and raised in Arkansas, Harington, who is partially deaf from a childhood illness, taught art in the East for 25 years before

returning here in 1981. Other novels: *The Cherry Pit* (1965), set in Little Rock; *Lightning Bug* (1970); *Some Other Place, The Right Place* (1972). His non-fiction *Let Us Build Us A City* is an absorbing survey of Arkansas ghost towns.

TESS HARPER *ACTRESS (b. Tessie Jean Washam, 8/15/1950, Mammoth Spring, AR)* Oscar-nominated actress Harper grew up in Arkansas, attended Southwest Missouri State College, then spent eight years in Texas appearing in TV commercials and dinner theater productions. In 1982 she won a Dallas casting call to play Robert Duvall's taciturn wife in *Tender Mercies*. Four years later, she was nominated as Best Supporting Actress for the role of Chick, the snoopy cousin, in *Crimes of the Heart*. Other films: *Silkwood, Criminal Law*. TV: "Chiefs," "Little Girl Lost."

CLIFF HARRIS *FOOTBALL PLAYER (b. Clifford Allen Harris, 11/12/1948, Fayetteville, AR)* A standout safety for the Dallas Cowboys (1970-79), Ouachita Baptist graduate Harris went to five Super Bowls in his football career. He now resides in Dallas.

WILLIAM HARRISON *WRITER (b. 10/29/1933, Dallas, TX)* Harrison is the author of several works that have been turned into movies, including *Rollerball*, from his short story "Rollerball Murder," and

Cliff Harris

Mountains of the Moon, from his historical novel *Burton and Speke*. He has lived in Fayetteville since 1964, teaching creative writing at the U of A.

"COIN" HARVEY *"THE PROPHET OF MONTE NE" (b. William Hope Harvey, 8/16/1851, Buffalo, VA; d. 2/11/36, Monte Ne, AR)* The first Arkansan to run for President, Harvey was the standard bearer of the short-lived Liberty Party, which attracted only a few thousand votes in 1932. Born on a farm, Harvey was admitted to the bar at 19. In 1883 he moved to Colorado, where he opened a silver mine that became the second largest producer in the area. But a sudden decline in the value of silver wrecked his fortunes. Moving to Chicago, he self-published *Coin's Financial School* – an allegory advocating silver as the standard for American currency, a then-hot subject. The pamphlet sold an amazing 2,000,000 copies, second only to the Bible at the time. Harvey became famous, and his presses churned out more titles. In 1900 he relocated to Northwest Arkansas, where he developed a summer resort he called Monte Ne, supposedly meaning "mountain water." By the end of WWI it had collapsed, but another scheme soon occupied the old man – the construction of a massive "pyramid" to contain his complete writings for the benefit of future generations. Work began on the supporting amphitheater in 1926, but disaster intervened when he lost his savings in the Crash. After his failed presidential bid, Harvey's health declined. He died at age 84. Thirty years later the ruins of his pyramid were covered by a man-made reservoir, Beaver Lake.

KEN HATFIELD *FOOTBALL COACH (b. 1943, Helena, AR)* As a player for the Razorbacks, Ken Hatfield's 81-yard runback sparked a 14-13 win over Texas in the famous 11-0 season of 1964. Twenty years later he succeeded Lou Holtz as the Hogs' 25th head football coach. Friction with his boss, athletic director Frank Broyles, resulted in Hatfield's resignation after six seasons. His Razorback record: 55-17-1. ➤ *See also:* Frank Broyles, and *Arkansas Sports*.

RONNIE HAWKINS *ROCK'N'ROLLER (b. 1/10/1935, Huntsville, AR)* Generally tagged a "seminal rock'n'roll influence," Hawkins formed his first band in his 20s at the U of A. After a few years of small-town gigs, he switched to mainline rock, but barely scratched out a living. On the advice of Conway Twitty, Hawkins moved to Canada in the late 1950s and eventually made his recording debut. His first hit was "Forty Days." Among the musicians who joined his backup group, The Hawks, during this period was fellow Arkansan Levon Helm, who later split to help form The Band. Hawkins' biggest seller was the 1959 single "Mary Lou," which peaked at #26. In 1963 he recorded a widely praised version of Bo Diddley's "Who Do You Love" (which he later performed at The Band's famous farewell concert). ➤ *See also:* Levon Helm.

LEE HAYS *FOLKSINGER, COMPOSER (b. 1914, Little Rock, AR; d. 8/26/81, North Tarrytown, NY)* Co-author with Pete Seeger of folksong favorite "If I Had a Hammer," Hays was educated in Arkansas and Georgia. In 1948 he joined Seeger in forming the famous folk group, The Weavers. (He had never heard the word "folksong" until he arrived in New York in 1936.) His bass voice can be heard on their hits "Goodnight Irene" and "On Top of Old Smokey." After the group disbanded in 1963, Hays had both legs amputated because of diabetes.

LEVON HELM *ROCK'N'ROLLER, ACTOR (b. Mark Lavon [sic] Helm, 5/26/1940, near Elaine, AR)* A pivotal member of one of the world's most famous rock groups, The Band, Helm was born dirt poor in the Arkansas Delta, the son of a cotton farmer. As a child in Turkey Scratch, he performed at county fairs and 4-H meetings. In 1958 he left home to join fellow Arkansan Ronnie Hawkins' backup group, The Hawks, and performed throughout Canada. In 1963 he and other Hawks members jumped ship to form their own group, Levon & The Hawks, later backing Bob Dylan. Around 1968 they became The Band. Their debut LP, *Music From Big Pink* (named after Dylan's Woodstock house), began a string of highly successful albums. In November 1976 they put on their celebrated farewell performance, "The Last Waltz." Since the breakup, Helm has done solo work and enjoyed an acting career, first performing in *Coal Miner's Daughter*. Later films include *The Right Stuff*, *The Dollmaker* and *End of the Line* (filmed in Arkansas with Mary Steenburgen). In 1993 Helm's autobiography *This Wheel's On Fire* was released. ➤ *See also:* Ronnie Hawkins.

BARBARA HENDRICKS *SINGER (b. 11/20/1948, Stephens, AR)* One of the world's premier lyric sopranos, Hendricks attended Horace Mann High School in Little Rock, then graduated from the University of Nebraska before arriving at Julliard School of Music in New York. Her opera debut came in 1973 at the Metropolitan; she has since performed throughout the world, including the Paris Opera and La Scala. A goodwill ambassador for the U.N., she was the only classical artist to perform at President Clinton's inauguration in 1993. She now resides in Switzerland.

JOAN HESS *MYSTERY WRITER (b. 1/6/1949, Fayetteville, AR)* A former schoolteacher, Hess is the prolific author of over 20 mysteries since 1986, including two series set in Arkansas. One features sleuth Claire Malloy, a single mother who owns a bookstore in mythical Farberville (suspiciously similar to Fayetteville). The other series stars no-nonsense Sheriff Arly (short for Ariel) Hanks and takes place in the backwoods town of Maggody. A fifth-generation Fayettevillian, Hess was an art major at the U of A and has an MA in education from Long Island University. She has also written books under the pseudonym Joan Hadley. Hess' goal: "to be rich and famous."

AL HIBBLER *SINGER (b. Albert Hibbler, 8/16/1915, Little Rock, AR)* Blind from birth, Hibbler won amateur singing contests in Memphis, then toured with several bands before hitting the big time with the Duke Ellington orchestra from 1943 to 1951. His deep, rich baritone voice was mesmerizing on hits like "Don't You Know I Care?," "I'm Just a Lucky So-and-So," "Don't Get Around Much Any More," "Do Nothin' Till You Hear From Me," and "Solitude." In 1955 his "Unchained Melody" made the top ten.

FRANK D. HICKINGBOTHAM

YOGURT KING (b. 10/14/1936, McGehee, AR) In 1981, so the story goes, businessman Frank Hickingbotham sampled a frozen yogurt dessert at a Dallas Neiman-Marcus at his wife's insistence. To his surprise, he liked it – so much so that he decided to sell the stuff himself. In October he opened his first shop in Market Place Shopping Center on Rodney Parham Road in Little Rock, named This Can't Be Yogurt!! (Later, under pressure by a Texas chain called I Can't Believe It's Yogurt!, he was forced to change the name to TCBY – The Country's Best Yogurt.) Two years later he was selling franchises. A graduate of the U of A at Monticello, Hickingbotham was once a McGehee school principal, then sold insurance. TCBY has made him a millionaire many times over.

WAYLAND HOLYFIELD *COMPOSER (b. 3/15/42, Mallettown, AR)* In 1986 songwriter Holyfield, who has had over a dozen number one hits on the country charts, was tapped to write and record a tune for the state's sesquicentennial celebration. The popular result – "Arkansas You Run Deep In Me" – was designated an official state song in 1987. Holyfield, who attended Hall High School and the U of A, has lived in Nashville since 1972. His "Could I Have This Dance?" was featured in the movie *Urban Cowboy* and won a Grammy for Anne Murray. Other compositions: "Red Necks, White Sox and Blue Ribbon Beer," "Till the Rivers All Run Dry," "Nobody Likes Sad Songs."

Wayland Holyfield

REX HUMBARD EVANGELIST (b. Alpha Rex Emmanuel Humbard, 8/13/1919, Little Rock, AR) Born in a house on Cross Street in Little Rock, future TV evangelist Rex Humbard was the son of itinerant tent revivalists and grew up mostly in Hot Springs. After graduating high school in Texas, he formed a gospel singing group that performed on radio throughout the South. In 1942 he married Maude Aimee Jones. Ten years later they settled in Akron, Ohio, and Humbard began building his own church and preaching on the radio. In 1958 the folksy, nondenominational preacher opened the $3.5 million Cathedral of Tomorrow. However, the multi-millionaire man of God ran afoul of the SEC in the 1970s due to security sales violations, and ratings began slipping. At his height, Humbard (who doesn't smoke, drink or dance) reached 100 million listeners over 620 stations throughout the world and flew around in a Lockheed jet called *Love One*. "If Jesus were here today," he once said, "he'd be on the tube and radio, too."

ARTHUR HUNNICUTT ACTOR (b. 2/17/1911, Gravelly, AR; d. 9/26/79, Woodlawn Hills, CA) An Arkansas State Teachers College graduate, Hunnicutt got his first stage break in *Love's Old Sweet Song*. He then toured as Jeeter Lester in *Tobacco Road*, married his hometown sweetheart and headed for Hollywood, where he appeared in countless films, generally as a yokel. Among his movies: *Broken Arrow, The Red Badge of Courage, The Kettles in the Ozarks, Cat Ballou, El Dorado*.

He received a best supporting actor nomination for *The Big Sky* (1952).

J. B. HUNT TRUCKING TYCOON (b. Johnnie Bryan Hunt, 1927, near Heber Springs, AR) Founder of J.B. Hunt Transport Services, Hunt parlayed a rice-hull and poultry-litter business into America's largest full-truckload carrier, employing over 7,000 drivers. His Lowell-based empire was formed in 1961; today *Forbes* ranks him among America's 400 wealthiest individuals. His career is recounted in *J. B. Hunt: The Long Haul to Success*, published in 1992.

LAMAR HUNT OIL MAN, SPORTSMAN (b. 8/2/1932, El Dorado, AR) Hunt, son of billionaire H.L. Hunt, tried for years to acquire an NFL franchise. Frustrated in his attempts, he formed the rival AFL in 1959. His club played two years as the Dallas Texans, then moved to Kansas City as the Chiefs. In 1966 his successful AFL merged with the NFL; four years later the Chiefs won Super Bowl IV. Hunt, who played college football at SMU, was inducted into the Pro Football Hall of Fame in 1972, the first AFL representative from any category. He also founded World Championship Tennis in 1967.

DON HUTSON HALL-OF-FAME FOOTBALL PLAYER (b. Donald Montgomery Hutson, 1/31/1913, Pine Bluff, AR) Hutson attended Pine Bluff High School and the University of Alabama. A versatile athlete, he received offers from both the Green Bay Packers and the Brooklyn Dodgers after his Tide squad won the Rose Bowl (with Bear Bryant at end). He caught an 83-yard touchdown pass in his first play for the Packers and emerged as the NFL's dominant receiver throughout his 11-year pro career. A nine-time All-Pro, Hutson led the league eight times in receptions and five times in scoring. In 1963 he was inducted into the Hall of Fame and in 1969 was named to the NFL's all-time team.

TRAVIS JACKSON *HALL-OF-FAME SHORT-STOP (b. 1903, Waldo, AR; d. 7/27/87, Waldo, AR)* A gritty 14-year veteran shortstop (and briefly third baseman) with the New York Giants, "Stonewall" Jackson batted over .300 six times and played in four World Series during the club's glory days of the 1930s. After his career ended, he worked as a Giants coach and managed several minor league teams. He was inducted into Cooperstown in 1982.

JOHN H. JOHNSON *PUBLISHER (b. 1/19/1918, Arkansas City, AR)* The most powerful publisher in black American history, Johnson was born desperately poor, the only son of a mill worker who died in a sawmill accident when the boy was six. In 1933 he and his mother left home for Chicago so that Johnson could complete high school (Arkansas City high schools wouldn't accept blacks). There Johnson excelled – honor student, president of the senior class, editor of the school paper. In 1942 he borrowed against his mother's furniture to publish *Negro Digest*, a magazine devoted to the ordinary life of black people. It was a big success, and Johnson built on it. In 1945 the first issue of *Ebony* hit the news-stands.

John H. Johnson

Today the Johnson Publishing Company is the largest black-owned corporation in the U.S. Among America's wealthiest individuals, Johnson also owns a highly profitable cosmetics company. In 1993 he was among the first group inducted into the Arkansas Black Hall of Fame. His autobiography, *Succeeding Against the Odds*, was published in 1989.

DOUGLAS C. JONES *HISTORICAL NOVELIST (b. Douglas Clyde Jones, 12/6/1924, Winslow, AR)* Hailed by the *Boston Globe* as "our finest prose dramatist of the American West," Jones served 27 years in the Army, retiring a lieutenant colonel. After a stint in academia at the University of Wisconsin, the Fort Smith-reared Jones settled in Fayetteville in 1974 and began turning out historical novels. His best known book is *The Court-Martial of George Armstrong Custer*, which was adapted into an acclaimed 1977 Hallmark Hall of Fame television movie. A prolific writer, Jones has published over a dozen other novels, including: *Elkhorn Tavern, Arrest Sitting Bull, The Barefoot Brigade* and *Winding Stair*. Many have Arkansas settings.

FAY JONES *ARCHITECT (b. Euine Fay Jones, 1/31/1921, Pine Bluff, AR)* One of America's premier architects, Jones grew up mostly in El Dorado, where his parents owned a cafe. Both his siblings died before he was nine. As a child Jones built a tree house complete with cantilevered balconies, screened-in porch and fireplace. (A spark from the fireplace ignited a fire that burned down the tree – house and all.) He attended the U of A, quitting to serve as a Navy bomber pilot in WWII. After the war, Jones was the first student to sign up for the U of A's new architecture department. He earned his master's at Rice and taught at the University of Oklahoma. Then his idol, Frank Lloyd Wright, invited him to study at Taliesin, the master's famous workshop. In 1953 Jones became a U of A professor, a position he held until his retirement in 1988. Although houses comprise the bulk of his work, it is Thorncrown Chapel near Eureka Springs that has brought Jones his greatest recognition.

In 1990 President Bush awarded Jones the American Institute of Architects' Gold Medal for Lifetime Achievement, the most prestigious award a U.S. architect can receive.

JERRY JONES *OWNER OF THE DALLAS COWBOYS (b. Jerral Wayne Jones, 10/13/1942, Los Angeles, CA)* In 1989 Arkansas businessman Jones purchased the moribund Dallas Cowboys football franchise. In quick order he replaced legendary coach Tom Landry with his old college teammate Jimmy Johnson – and managed to offend most of Texas. In its first season under Jones and Johnson, America's Team won only one game. But by 1994 Jones was celebrating his second consecutive Super Bowl victory. According to *Forbes*, the club is now the most valuable franchise in sports (grossing $1 billion a year in licensed merchandise). Son of a wealthy insurance executive, Jones graduated from North Little Rock High School. As a senior at the U of A he played offensive guard when the Hogs won the Cotton Bowl (Johnson was a defensive lineman and Barry Switzer an assistant coach). After college Jones developed a gift for wheeling and dealing, eventually entering the oil and gas business. When he closed his big deal in Big D, he moved to Texas. An ego clash following the 1994 Super Bowl resulted in the dismissal of Johnson. Jones promptly installed ex-Oklahoma coach Barry Switzer. Jones' motto: "I believe if you work hard, you should be able to take it all."
➤ *See also:* Barry Switzer.

MAXINE JONES *THE HOT SPRINGS MADAM (b. Maxine Temple, 1917, Johnsville, AR)* A big, buxom country girl, Jones managed a pair of notorious houses of prostitution in Hot Springs during the 1950s and 1960s, before eventually running afoul of the law. Her brothels were shut down and she spent 14 months in Cummins prison. In 1983 she wrote *Call Me Madam*, an account of her "life and hard times."

PAULA CORBIN JONES *PRESIDENTIAL ACCUSER (b. 1966, Lonoke, AR)* In 1994 Jones made headlines by suing President Clinton for "intentional infliction of emotional distress" arising from alleged sexual advances made three years earlier when he was governor. Clinton denied the accusations. Nude photos of Jones, who now lives in California, later appeared in *Penthouse*.

LOUIS JORDAN *SINGER, BANDLEADER (b. Louis Thomas Jordan, 7/8/1908, Brinkley, AR; d. 2/4/75, Los Angeles, CA)* "If I could work with anyone through eternity," Chuck Berry once said, "it would be Louis Jordan." Jordan's unique jump-band party-style sound delighted the nation in the 1940s. Born and raised in Brinkley, he played for his father's band as a youngster, studied music at Arkansas Baptist College, and performed in a Hot Springs orchestra. By 1939 he had signed with Decca as "Louis Jordan and the Tympany Five" and began producing million-sellers like "Is You Is Or Is You Ain't My Baby" and "Choo Choo Ch'boogie." Other hits: "Ain't Nobody Here But Us Chickens," "Caldonia," "Knock Me a Kiss," "Let the Good Times Roll." Jordan, who earned five gold records, also appeared in movies like *Follow the Boys* and *Meet Miss Bobbysox*. By the 1950s his popularity had virtually played out and he died in relative obscurity. Today, his music is reaching a brand new audience courtesy of *Five Guys Named Moe*, a hit Broadway show inspired by his music.

GEORGE KELL *HALL-OF-FAME INFIELDER, SPORTSCASTER (b. George Clyde Kell, 8/23/1922, Swifton, AR)* In his 14 seasons as a major leaguer (for five different American League clubs), Kell hit a lifetime .306 and knocked in 870 runs. In 1949 he edged out Ted Williams for the AL batting title (.3429 to .3428). He played in ten All-Star games. He retired from active play as an Oriole, with fellow Arkansan Brooks Robinson taking over his spot at third. Since 1958 Kell has been the play-by-play announcer for the Detroit Tigers. He still resides in his hometown of Swifton, and owns a car distributorship in nearby Newport. His brother Skeeter also played in the big leagues. ➤ *See also:* Brooks Robinson.

VIRGINIA KELLEY *FIRST MOM (b. Virginia Dell Cassidy, 6/6/1923, Bodcaw, AR; d. 1/6/94, Hot Springs, AR)* A self-described "mahogany brown woman with hot pink lipstick and a skunk stripe in her hair," the gregarious Kelley was a colorful Hot Springs character long before her first-born became the 42nd President of the U.S. She grew up in Hope, the daughter of grocers. After high school she worked her way through nursing school and began a 27-year career as a nurse anesthetist. A major Elvis fan, she once said, "I'm friendly, I'm outgoing, and I like men." Married five times (twice to the same man), she outlived three husbands, including her first, William Blythe, who died in a car wreck a few months before their son Bill was born. Her autobiography, *Leading With My Heart*, was published posthumously in 1994. ➤ *See also:* Bill Clinton, Hillary Rodham Clinton.

PAUL W. KLIPSCH *INVENTOR, ENTREPRENEUR (b. 1904, Elkhart, IN)*

Generally tagged an eccentric genius, Klipsch revolutionized the audio world with his famed Klipschorn speaker. A classic tinkerer, he built a radio receiver as a boy. He graduated from New Mexico State University in 1926, then went to work for General Electric in Chile. In the 1940s he received a patent for the Klipschorn and set up shop outside Hope, AR, on the grounds of the former Southwest Army Ordnance Proving Grounds, where he had served during WWII. By 1989, when he sold Klipsch and Associates ("A Legend in Sound"), his speakers were considered the top of the line.

ALAN LADD *ACTOR (b. Alan Walbridge Ladd, Jr., 9/3/1913, Hot Springs, AR; d. 1/29/64, Palm Springs, CA)*

Concerning Arkansas, movie star Ladd once said, "I don't remember anything about the state." He and his widowed mother were forced to leave his birthplace when Ladd was only five, after he and a playmate accidentally burned down their Hot Springs apartment house while playing with matches. Ladd knocked around in various jobs in Hollywood before getting his big break in *This Gun for Hire* (1942). Drop-dead handsome, with an icy, expressionless gaze, he captivated audiences despite his small size. In all, he made over 150 films, including the great *Shane* (1954). By the 1960s, however, his career was in decline. He died of an overdose of sedatives mixed with alcohol, a year after almost being killed from a self-inflicted gunshot

Alan Ladd

wound. In 1948, at the peak of his fame, the millionaire actor made a triumphant return to his native state. "They treated me like a king," he said. "They wouldn't let me pick up a check or leave a tip or anything." Afterward, he kept a framed Arkansas Traveler certificate in his dressing room.

CHET LAUCK LUM OF "LUM AND ABNER" (b. Chester H. Lauck, 1902, Alleene, AR; d. 2/21/80, Hot Springs, AR) Lauck played Lum Edwards (pronounced *Eddards*) to his best friend Norris Goff's Abner Peabody on radio and in the movies. The pair grew up in Mena, where Lauck's family moved in 1908, and went to the U of A together, where Lauck edited the college humor magazine. After graduation, Lauck, who had yearned for a career in commercial art, returned to Mena and worked for an auto financing company. A 1931 amateur show skit launched their professional radio careers. After retiring from show business, Lauck spent over a decade as an executive for Conoco, making after-dinner speeches. He retired to Hot Springs' Lake Hamilton in 1966, but kept his hand in several business interests, and even served on the Arkansas Racing Commission.
▶ *See also:* Norris Goff and Pine Ridge entry in *Cities and Towns* section.

TRACY LAWRENCE COUNTRY & WESTERN SINGER (b. 1967, Foreman, AR) Lawrence's first single, "Sticks and Stones," shot to number one on the country charts and he's remained a top draw ever since. The

stepson of a banker, Lawrence dropped out of Southern Arkansas University in 1988 and was later signed by Atlantic Records. In May 1991, on the day he completed recording his debut album, Lawrence was shot four times at close range by three muggers in Nashville but miraculously survived.

SONNY LISTON BOXER (b. Charles Liston, 5/8/1932*, Little Rock, AR; d. 1/5/71, Las Vegas, NV) "Ever since I was born," heavyweight champ Liston once said, "I've been fighting for my life." The twenty-fourth child of a twice-married Forrest City tenant farmer, Liston grew up picking cotton and getting into trouble. He never learned to read, or write anything other than his name. By age 18 he was in Missouri State Penitentiary, where a chaplain directed him toward boxing. In 1953 he turned pro, winning his initial bout with a first-round knockout. In the ring he was a huge, intimidating presence, with a baleful glare. In 1962 Liston knocked out Floyd Patterson in the first round to win the heavyweight title, then did it again the following year, also in the first round. Everyone thought he was invincible. But on February 25, 1964, Liston failed to answer the bell for the seventh round of his bout with then-Cassius Clay, ending his 17-month reign. He lived his last years in a plush Las Vegas home, where he died reportedly from a heroin overdose. Overall, Liston won 50 bouts (39 by knockouts) and lost four, earning $3,847,272 in purses from title matches. *Sources vary.*

THE LITTLE ROCK NINE In September 1957, worldwide attention focused on the struggle of nine black students to integrate Little Rock's Central High School. They were: Minnijean Brown, Elizabeth Eckford, Ernest Green, Thelma Mothershed, Melba Patillo, Gloria Ray, Terrance Roberts, Jefferson Thomas, and Carlotta Walls.
➤ *See also:* Daisy Bates, Orval Faubus, Ernest Green.

LAURENCE LUCKINBILL *ACTOR (b. 11/21/1934, Fort Smith, AR)* Luckinbill has appeared in movies like *The Boys in the Band* and *Star Trek V: The Final Frontier*, and TV series like "The Delphi Bureau," as well as on stage. Married to Luci Arnaz, he was formerly the husband of soap opera star Robin Strasser.

LUM AND ABNER *See* Norris Goff, Chester Lauck, and Pine Ridge entry in *Cities and Towns* section.

DOUGLAS MACARTHUR *MILITARY HERO (b. 1/26/1880, Fort Dodge, AR; d. 4/5/64, Washington, D.C.)* The man Churchill called "the glorious commander" and Truman dubbed "a damned counterfeit" was born on an army post that is now part of Little Rock, where his father was stationed. He spent only the first 18 months of his long, celebrated life here. First in his class at West Point (where he later served as Superintendent), the future Congressional Medal of Honor winner held positions as Army Chief of Staff, Field Marshall of the Philippines,

Douglas MacArthur

U.S. Far East Commander, Supreme Commander for the Allied Powers, and first U.N. Commander. In WWII he led the Allied troops to victory over Japan, and then directed the occupation. During the Korean War, MacArthur was relieved of his command by President Truman for insubordination. Afterward, the five-star general briefly tested the presidential waters – which brought him home to Arkansas for his first and only trip back. In his five hours in the state on March 24, 1952, he dedicated a rose garden at MacArthur Park (renamed for him during WWII), saying: "I have always held Little Rock and the state of Arkansas in deep reverence." But years later, at a banquet, MacArthur overruled a judge who introduced him to the crowd as an Arkansas native, snapping, "I'm a *Virginian*." He died at 84 and is buried in Norfolk, VA, where his memorabilia is housed in the MacArthur Memorial Foundation. At his death, Little Rock passed a resolution declaring the city was "proud to claim it had some part, however little, in the life of this great man."

OWNEY "THE KILLER" MADDEN

GANGSTER (b. Owen Vincent Madden, 12/25/1891, Leeds, England; d. 4/23/65, Hot Springs, AR) Among the most vicious mobsters ever to fire a tommy gun, Madden moved to Hot Springs in 1935, married a postmaster's daughter and lived in "retirement" until his death 30 years later. Chased out of New York, where he owned part-interest in Harlem's famed Cotton Club, Madden was always suspected of having run the Spa City's rackets from behind the scenes.

JIM DANDY MANGRUM

ROCK'N'ROLLER (b. James Mangrum, 3/30/1948, Black Oak, AR) In the mid-1960s Mangrum formed a group called Knowbody Else, later renamed Black Oak Arkansas, after his hometown. In 1969 they moved to L.A., cut their first album and went on tour, attracting huge audiences with legendary stage shows. Later personnel changes decimated the band, until only Mangrum remained of the original members, performing occasionally as simply Black Oak. ➤ *See also:* Black Oak Arkansas.

JOHN L. McCLELLAN *POLITICIAN (b. John Little McClellan, 2/25/1896, Sheridan, AR; d. 11/27/77, Little Rock, AR)* In the 1950s, dour-faced McClellan, Arkansas senator from 1942 until his death, headed one of the most sensational congressional investigations in U.S. history. His televised hearings on labor racketeering attracted millions of viewers and earned him a reputation as a crime-fighter. (Robert Kennedy was chief counsel.)

John McClellan

Later, he helped draft a comprehensive revision of the U.S. Criminal Code. McClellan's personal life was a triumph over a long series of tragedies. Three weeks after he was born, his mother died. In 1936 his second wife died of meningitis (he and his first wife had divorced). During WWII his son Max, an Army corporal stationed in North Africa, also died of the same disease. Six years later, his son's body was finally shipped to the U.S. for burial, but on the day of the funeral, McClellan's son John Jr. died of injuries sustained in a car accident. Thereafter, McClellan turned to drink. When a close friend advised him to lay off the bottle, the senator paused, then replied: "I'm going to show you that I am the master of my own soul." He then smashed two bottles of bourbon and never touched another drop. As a boy, McClellan was once admonished by a preacher: "Know thyself, control thyself, deny thyself." It was the code he lived by until he died of a heart ailment at age 81.

KEVIN McREYNOLDS

BASEBALL PLAYER (b. Walter Kevin McReynolds, 10/16/1959, Little Rock, AR) The sixth player taken in the 1981 draft, U of A star McReynolds (who grew up in Sherwood) hit the majors in late 1983. He was the San Diego Padres' regular center fielder during their 1984 pennant drive, knocking out a three-run homer in a comeback victory over the Cubs in

the third game of the league playoff. In 1987 he was traded to the Mets, where he later set a season record for most steals without being caught. In 1988, as the Mets and the Dodgers prepared for the deciding game of the NL championship series, McReynolds told reporters there was no way he could lose: "Either I go to the World Series or I go back to Arkansas." He retired to his home state in 1995.

WILBUR MILLS *POLITICIAN (b. Wilbur Daigh Mills, 5/24/1909, Kensett, AR; d. 5/2/92, Kensett, AR)* As longtime

chairman of the House Ways and Means Committee, Mills' career soared to rarefied heights, then crashed and burned in spectacular fashion. From age 10, Mills had wanted to be a congressman. After earning a BA from Hendrix and a law degree from Harvard, and serving a stint as a county judge, he was first elected to Congress in 1938. In 1957 he became head of Ways and Means, and for almost 20 years exercised virtually dictatorial control over fiscal legislation. In the early 1970s he flirted with a run at the presidency. But it all came tumbling down early one morning in October 1974 when stripper

Kevin McReynolds

Annabel Battistella (billed as "Fanne Foxe, the Argentine Firecracker") scurried from his car and leaped into the Tidal Basin,

Wilbur Mills

leaving an intoxicated Mills in her wake. Overnight, Mills became a national joke. Although Arkansas voters elected him to a 19th term the next month, his prestige had evaporated. He relinquished his chairmanship, served out his term and joined the Washington office of a New York law firm. But despite such massive public humiliation, Mills, who had been drinking two to three quarts of vodka a day, managed to reclaim his life. He gave up booze for good

in February 1975, spending the rest of his life as a recovered alcoholic and a vocal crusader for alcohol awareness programs.

BOBBY MITCHELL *HALL-OF-FAME FOOTBALL PLAYER (b. Robert Cornelius Mitchell, 6/6/1935, Hot Springs, AR)* From 1958-61 with the Cleveland Browns, Mitchell was one of the NFL's top halfbacks (playing alongside the great Jim Brown). From 1962-68 with the Washington Redskins, he was one of the league's top wide receivers (a three-time All-Pro, he led receivers in 1962). As Washington's first black player, he also broke the team's color barrier. After ending his 11-year career, he joined the Redskins staff. He was inducted into the Hall of Fame in 1983.

MARTHA MITCHELL *WATERGATE CELEBRITY (b. Martha Elizabeth Beall, 9/2/1918, Pine Bluff, AR; d. May 31, 1976, New York, NY)* "If it hadn't been for Martha," Richard Nixon told David Frost, "there'd have

Martha Mitchell

been no Watergate." As the outspoken wife of Attorney General John Mitchell, her late-night calls to reporters during the height of the scandal embarrassed the administration. After divorcing her husband, she died of cancer. Pine Bluff renamed a thoroughfare in her honor and declared her childhood home a landmark.

SIDNEY MONCRIEF

BASKETBALL PLAYER (b. 9/21/1957, Little Rock, AR) Arguably Arkansas' most beloved sports hero, Moncrief is credited with helping turn on the state to basketball. Born in the John Barrow

Sidney Moncrief

Addition of western Little Rock, Moncrief was the child of a broken home. His mother worked as a motel maid and the family moved to the city's tough East End when he was a boy. Although Moncrief warmed the bench in junior high, he emerged a star at Hall High School under the tutelage of Coach Oliver Elders (husband of Joycelyn). In 1975, heavily recruited by colleges, Moncrief took a chance on U of A rookie coach Eddie Sutton. It paid off. Named AP Freshman of the Year, Moncrief (who played guard) went on to lead the Razorbacks to three SWC championships. In 1978, as the swing player of the celebrated "Triplets" (also including Marvin Delph and Ron Brewer), Super Sidney helped take the Razorbacks to the NCAA Final Four. Moncrief continued his winning ways at Milwaukee, where he was five times named an NBA All-Star and twice named Defensive Player of the Year. Moncrief's off-court performance has contributed equally to his legend. His thoughtful manner and unstinting public service made him one of the most popular sports idols this sports-crazed state has ever known. Today he is retired and lives in Dallas.

PATSY MONTANA

COUNTRY & WESTERN SINGER (b. Ruby Blevins, 10/30/1909, Jessieville, AR; d. 5/3/96, San Jacinto, CA)* Famed in the 1930s and 40s as "The Yodeling Cowgirl," Patsy Montana was the first woman in country music to sell a million records ("I Want To Be A Cowboy's Sweetheart," 1936). She grew up in Hope, the only sister of ten brothers. After high school she attended the University of Western Louisiana, but dropped out for a career in show business. From 1934-48 she was a headliner on the popular Chicago radio program, "WLS National Barn Dance," performing with the Prairie Ramblers. Hits: "I'm An Old Cowhand," "Singing in the Saddle," "Deep in the Heart of Texas." During her career she made over 7,000 concert appearances, produced over 250 records, and even acted in a couple of Gene Autry westerns. *Sources vary.*

CHARLES MURPHY OIL MAN (b. Charles Haywood Murphy, Jr., 3/6/1920, El Dorado, AR)

After taking over the family business at 21 when his father suffered a stroke, Murphy built Murphy Oil Corp. into an international oil empire. Self-described as a conservative on economic issues but a liberal on social issues (he was an outspoken civil rights supporter in the early 1960s), Murphy received little formal education. "I don't care a thing about business schools," he has said. Now retired, his family wealth is estimated by *Forbes* at over $385 million.

GEORGE NEWBERN ACTOR (b. 12/30/1963, Little Rock, AR)

Newbern has appeared in several movies, including *Adventures in Babysitting* and *Father of the Bride* (as the young groom), and as a regular on TV's "The Boys are Back."

K. T. OSLIN SINGER (b. Kay Toinette Oslin, 5/15/1941, Crossett, AR)

Oslin, who calls herself as "an aging sex bomb," is one of Nashville's queens of country – with three Grammys to her credit. Although she's officially from Crossett, virtually the only time Oslin spent there was the time it took to get born. (Her father wanted her brought into the world by the doctor who delivered her brother.) In all, she spent only two weeks in Arkansas before moving on to Memphis, and then Houston, which she considers her hometown.

A late-bloomer to the country scene, Oslin made a sensational arrival with her famous "80s Ladies."

ISAAC PARKER "THE HANGING JUDGE" (b. Isaac Charles Parker, 10/15/1838, Belmont County, OH; d. 11/17/96, Ft. Smith, AR)

Famed throughout the West as "The Hanging Judge," Isaac Parker was admitted to the bar in 1859, then headed west to St. Louis, where he established his practice. In 1875 he was appointed by President Grant as judge for the Western District of Arkansas, which had jurisdiction over the Indian Nations of Oklahoma – the Badlands. When he arrived in Ft. Smith, he was the youngest judge on the federal bench. His 74,000-square-mile domain was overrun with roving gangs of killers, thieves and rapists, and policed by only a handful of marshals. In his 21 years on the

Isaac Parker

bench, Parker sentenced 160 men to die on the gallows outside the courthouse (79 were actually hanged). For 14 years there was no right of appeal. While critics decried his wholesale hangings, the hardworking, incorruptible Parker was a godsend to the citizens and lawmen of Ft. Smith, and to the native Americans with whose interests the judge was sympathetic. In the 1890s, Congress stripped Parker of much of his authority. Years of ceaseless labor on the bench had taken their toll. He died at 58, a tired and haggard man who looked many years older.

DON PENDLETON *AUTHOR (b. Donald Eugene Pendleton, 12/12/1927, Little Rock, AR)* Creator of the popular "Executioner" paperback series, Pendleton has produced dozens of novels under several pseudonyms.

JOE PERRY *HALL-OF-FAME FOOTBALL PLAYER (b. Fletcher Joseph Perry, 1/27/1927, Stevens, AR)* One of pro football's greatest running backs, Perry, who grew up in Los Angeles, played for the San Francisco 49ers (1948-60, 1963) and the Baltimore Colts (1961-62). Nicknamed "the Jet" for his quick starts, the durable Perry had the longest career ever for a fullback and was one of the game's all-time leading rushers (9,723 total yards). He was the first NFL runner to have back-to-back 1,000-yard seasons (1953-54). One of the league's first blacks, Perry was inducted into the Pro Football Hall of Fame in 1969.

ALBERT PIKE *SCHOLAR, SOLDIER, POET (b. 12/29/1809, Boston, MA; d. 4/2/91, Washington D.C.)* A man of diverse accomplishments, Pike mastered nine languages, compiled Indian vocabularies, produced over 500 works of poetry, and commanded troops in the Civil War. He arrived in Arkansas in December 1832, later acquiring the *Arkansas Advocate*. In 1840 he built what has come to be known as the Pike-Fletcher-Terry mansion, today the home of the Arkansas Arts Center Decorative Arts Museum. During the Mexican War, Pike equipped a squadron of Arkansas cavalry. As a lawyer, he took part in a landmark case for American Indians, winning a $3 million judgment for the Choctaw tribe. During the Civil War, Pike recruited 800 Indian braves and fought at the Battle of Pea Ridge. (Too fat to ride, Gen. Pike charged forward in a carriage drawn by four horses.) When some of his army actually scalped Union soldiers, the incident provoked an avalanche of criticism. At the end of the war, Pike moved to Canada, eventually settling for good in Washington. Today he is perhaps best known for his work with the Masons, for whom he proselytized from 1850. In 1901 a statue of the great man was erected in Washington's Judiciary Square – the only monument in the district to honor a man who, among other distinctions, served as a Confederate general. ➤ *See also:* John Gould Fletcher.

SCOTTIE PIPPEN *BASKETBALL PLAYER (b. 9/25/1965, Hamburg, AR)* One of the NBA's premier players, Pippen labored for years in the shadow of the great Michael Jordan before finally coming into his own. The youngest of twelve children, Pippen did not blossom in basketball until his sophomore year at the University of Central Arkansas, but was overlooked by most NBA scouts. He signed with the Chicago Bulls following the 1987 draft. In 1991 the club won its first-ever world championship, with Pippen, at small forward, contributing 32 points in the decisive fifth game against the Los Angeles Lakers. In 1992 Pippen played in the All-Star game and on the U.S. Olympic "Dream Team" and helped take Chicago to its second consecutive championship. The next year the Bulls did it again, with Pippen dominating the playoffs – the first team in almost 30 years to win three in a row.

CHARLES PORTIS *WRITER (b. 12/28/1933, El Dorado, AR)* Author of *True Grit*, one of the finest novels ever associated with Arkansas, Portis was the son of a school superintendent. He joined the Marines after high school, then returned for a journalism degree from the U of A. After stints with the *Memphis Commercial Appeal* and the *Arkansas Gazette*, he moved on to the *New York Herald Tribune*, eventually becoming the paper's London correspondent. In 1964 he quit to try his hand at fiction. He shut himself up in an Arkansas fishing shack and six months later produced his first book, *Norwood*. Next was his masterful 1968 bestseller, *True Grit*, which years later the *New York Times* called "one of those rare books to deserve the extravagant praise they elicited." Both books were sold to the movies and both ended up featuring fellow Arkansan Glen Campbell. The movie version of *True Grit* was a smash hit, helping John Wayne (as Marshall Rooster Cogburn) cop his only Oscar. A sequel with Wayne and Katherine Hepburn, plus a TV movie, were also made. Other Portis novels include *The Dog of the South, Masters of Atlantis* and *Gringos.*

DICK POWELL *ENTERTAINER (b. Richard Ewing Powell, 11/14/1904, Mountain View, AR; d. 1/2/63, Hollywood, CA)* One of Hollywood's

Charles Portis

savviest stars, Powell managed several times to successfully reinvent his career. As a boy, his family moved from Mountain View to Little Rock, where he later dropped out of high school and performed in local bands. (One of his groups, the Peter Pan Orchestra, jammed after hours in the Capitol Hotel ballroom.) In 1933 a Warner Brothers talent scout discovered him in Pittsburgh, where he was a theater MC. His 1930s movies, like *42nd Street, Gold Diggers of 1933* and *Footlight Parade*, along with several hit records, established the crooner as a major star. But by the 40s, Powell had tired of his boy-next-door image and fought for better roles. His 1945 performance as tough guy Philip Marlowe in *Murder, My Sweet* turned things around. In 1952, he was one of the first stars to switch to television, appearing in the popular "Four Star Playhouse" weekly drama. His Four Star Television production company spawned hits like "The Rifleman" and "Wanted Dead or Alive." Powell's three wives included movie stars Joan Blondell (#2) and June Allyson (#3). Old friends insisted that Powell never let success go to his head and that "he was always glad to see someone from Little Rock." In 1950 he paid his last visit to Arkansas, attending the premiere of *The Redhead and the Reformer*, a benefit for the Little Rock Boys Club. "I started out with two assets," Powell once said. "A voice that didn't drive audiences into the streets, and a determination to make

money." When he died of cancer at age 58 he left an estate valued at more than $3 million.

Dick Powell, with wife, actress June Allyson

FLORENCE BEATRICE PRICE

SYMPHONY COMPOSER (b. Florence Beatrice Smith, 4/9/1888, Little Rock, AR; d. 6/3/53, Chicago, IL) One of America's first black women composers, Price's symphonic works have been performed throughout the U.S. The daughter of a concert pianist, Price began publishing compositions while still in high school. In 1906 she graduated from the New England Conservatory of Music, then later married a lawyer and lived in Little Rock, where she taught at Shorter College. In 1927 she moved to Chicago, where she remained until her death. Price's most celebrated work is her

1932 Symphony in E minor.

LEE PURCELL *ACTRESS (b. 1947*, NC)* Twice Emmy-nominated for her performances in NBC's "Secret Sins of the Father" and "Long Road Home," Purcell is a graduate of Paragould High School. The daughter of a Marine, she was born on a military base in North Carolina. Her first movie was *Adam at Six A.M.* (1970). **Sources vary.*

WILLIAM RAGSDALE *ACTOR (b. 1961, El Dorado, AR)* The star of FOX's "Herman's Head," Ragsdale grew up in El Dorado and graduated from Hendrix College. After appearing on Broadway in Neil Simon's *Biloxi Blues*, he got his big break playing the lead in the 1985 movie, *Fright Night.*

DADDY BRUCE RANDOLPH *PHILANTHROPIST (b. 1900?, Pastoria, AR; d. 3/19/94, Denver, CO)* As the owner of a Denver barbecue restaurant, Bruce won national fame for providing free Thanksgiving dinners to thousands of needy people over the years.

VANCE RANDOLPH *FOLKLORIST (b. 2/23/ 1892, Pittsburg, KS; d. 11/ 1/80, Fayetteville, AR)* For most of his 88 years, the indomitable Randolph scratched out a meager existence chronicling the tall tales, jokes and bawdy stories of the people of the Ozarks. Raised in Kansas, he earned his MA in psychology at Clark University in 1915. After

tramping around the country, he settled in the hill country, living variously in Missouri and Arkansas (specifically Eureka Springs and Fayetteville, where he remained from 1960 until his death). He once called Arkansans "the most deliberately unprogressive people in the United States." His first major work was *The Ozarks* in 1931. Other books: *Ozark Mountain Folks, Hot Springs and Hell*, the four-volume *Ozark Folksongs*, and *Ozark Folklore: A Bibliography*. Late in life, awards and recognition finally came his way. And in 1976 the mass-market paperback edition of *Pissing in the Snow and Other Ozark Folktales*, a collection of previously censured tales, became a surprise bestseller.

CHARLIE RICH *"THE SILVER FOX" (b. 12/14/1932, Colt, AR; d. 7/25/95, Hammond, LA)* After 20 years of knocking around show business, singer/pianist Charlie Rich tapped

Vance Randolph

the mother lode in 1973 with "Behind Closed Doors." Rich grew up on a small cotton plantation near Colt, exposed to a rich confluence of music. After a year at the U of A, he joined the Air Force, where he formed a jazz combo. Following an attempt at farming, he took a shot at the music business, writing songs and playing piano in Memphis bars. In 1960 Rich charted with "Lonely Weekends," a rockabilly number. A few years later, he had a rock success, "Mohair Sam," and later, "Big Boss Man," but his career stalled and he returned to playing club dates. Then came "Behind Closed Doors" – a smash crossover hit that sold a million copies and earned Rich a gold record. His follow-up, "The Most Beautiful Girl," did even better at two million. Dubbed "The Silver Fox" because of his prematurely gray hair, Rich raked in a host of honors, including a Country Music Association Entertainer of the Year award.

NOLAN RICHARDSON *BASKETBALL COACH (b. 12/27/1941, El Paso, TX)* The only basketball coach in history to win NCAA, NIT and national junior college championships, Richardson earned the undying gratitude of Arkansas fans by guiding the Razorbacks to the top in 1994. He started out as a gifted athlete at Bowie High School in El Paso, where he later coached for ten years (posting a 190-80 record) after graduating from UTEP in 1963. Richardson then switched to Western Texas Junior College (98-14), leading his teams to three national junior college tournaments,

and winning the grand prize in his final 37-0 season. Next it was the University of Tulsa in 1981, where Richardson's first Hurricane squad went 26-7 and won the NIT championship. In 1985 he arrived in Fayetteville, but got off to a rocky start. As his teams struggled on the court, he faced a family tragedy at home: the death of daughter Yvonne from leukemia. A proud and disciplined man, Richardson persevered. In 1990 he took the Razorbacks to the NCAA Final Four. Four years later, his team won the college championship, with a 76-72 defeat of Duke. In 1995 they almost pulled off a repeat, but lost to UCLA in the final game. ➤ *See also:* Corliss Williamson, Sports.

BROOKS ROBINSON *HALL-OF-FAME THIRD BASEMAN (b. Brooks Calbert Robinson, Jr., 5/18/1937, Little Rock, AR)* Considered by many the best third baseman ever, Robinson played with the Baltimore Orioles from 1955-77. He was a 16-time Golden Glove winner and a 15-time All-Star Game starter. At third, he holds virtually every lifetime record by a significant margin – most games (2,870), best fielding percentage (.971), most double plays (618), most assists (6,205), and most putouts (2,697). Big league scouts discovered Robinson in a church league (he didn't play high school ball). At Baltimore he replaced fellow Arkansan George Kell at third, and emerged as the centerpiece of the Orioles dynasty of the 1960s. In 1970 he dominated World Series play as few ever have, winning the MVP award with a .429 average. His 1983

Hall of Fame induction drew one of the largest crowds ever. A man of enormous style and grace, Robinson went on to a successful career as a broadcaster. Other career stats: .267 batting average, 268 HR, 1,357 RBI. He played in five AL championship series and four World Series. ➤ *See also:* George Kell.

Brooks Robinson

JOE T. ROBINSON *POLITICIAN (b. Joseph Taylor Robinson, 8/26/1872, Lonoke, AR; d. 7/14/37, Washington, D.C.)* The first Southerner since the Civil War selected as the vice presidential nominee of a major party, Robinson also served as a U.S. representative, Arkansas governor and U.S. senator – within the span of a few weeks. The son of a doctor, Robinson attended the U of A, then worked as a judge's apprentice. In 1895 he was licensed to practice law.

In 1902 he won a seat in Congress. Ten years later, he was elected to serve as governor. Then a curious series of events occurred: On January 2, 1913, Sen. Jeff Davis died suddenly. Robinson, who was then both a U.S. representative and the governor-elect, announced he wanted to fill Davis' unexpired term. On January 14, he resigned his House seat, and two days later was sworn in as governor. Then, on January 28, the Arkansas Legislature elected him senator. (He also holds a spot in the trivia books as the last U.S. senator to be elected by a state legislature.) He soon made a name for himself. President Wilson called him the "moral and intellectual leader of the Democrats in the Senate." In 1923 he was chosen minority leader. Five years later, New York Gov. Al Smith picked him as his vice presidential running mate. (Will Rogers noted that the Democrats "got a great fellow in Joe. He is a real two-fisted he-candidate. He comes from the wilds of Arkansaw where they are hard to tame.") But the Democrats lost in a landslide. After Roosevelt's win in 1932, Robinson became a prime mover in the New Deal, ramming many of the administration's social initiatives through the Senate almost single-handedly. Amid debate on FDR's plan to pack the Supreme Court, Robinson was felled by a heart attack, dying alone in his bed in Washington. His wife was in Arkansas, the first time in their marriage that she had ever spent the night away from her husband.

WINTHROP ROCKEFELLER

POLITICIAN (b. 5/1/ 1912, New York, NY; d. 2/22/73, Palm Springs, CA) In 1953 the playboy grandson of oil tycoon John D. Rockefeller bought a mountaintop farm in Arkansas and settled in the next year to raise cattle. At first regarded as a curiosity, Win Rockefeller came to dominate his adopted state's economic, cultural and, eventually, political life. Before arriving in Arkansas, Rockefeller had dropped out of Yale, worked as a roustabout in Texas oil fields, then joined the Army as a private. He left the service as a lieutenant colonel with a Purple Heart and a Bronze Star, having been severely wounded in the Pacific during a kamikaze attack on his troop ship. His messy 1954 divorce made front-page news. Rockefeller escaped to Arkansas, where his philanthropic activities drew attention. In 1955 he was tapped by Gov. Faubus to head the new Arkansas Industrial Development Commission. At the AIDC, he promoted Arkansas ceaselessly. (When envious fellow governors asked how they could attract a Rockefeller for their states, Faubus replied, "I don't know, but keep your cotton-pickin' fingers off mine.") But Rockefeller broke with Faubus over the 1957-58 integration crisis and began eyeing Faubus' job for himself. In 1964 Rockefeller, an awkward campaigner, made his first run for the office, and lost. But two years later, against a rabid segregationist opponent, he won with 54 percent – the first Republican governor since Reconstruction. His two terms were marked with bold initiatives largely stymied by a recalcitrant Legislature. However, he did make progress in penal reform, improving race relations, economic development and stamping out illegal gambling. In 1970 he lost badly to the previously unknown Dale Bumpers. Three years later, Rockefeller died of cancer.

Winthrop Rockefeller

PREACHER ROE
BASEBALL PITCHER (b. Elwin Charles Roe, 2/26/1915, Ash Flat, AR) "I got three pitches," Preacher Roe used to say, "My change; my change off my change; and my change off my change off my change." After he retired, he admitted to a fourth – the spitball – which he called his money pitch. Whatever he was throwing, he did well by it. Playing for Pittsburgh, the left-hander led the league in strikeouts in 1945. For the Brooklyn Dodgers (1948-54), he went 44-8 from 1951-53. He played in three

World Series, with a 2-1 record. His lifetime record stands at 127-84. Roe was raised in Viola and gave himself his own nickname at age three, when somebody asked what he was called. For no apparent reason, he replied, "Preacher," and the name stuck. He played ball for Harding College, then signed with the Cardinals. There's a chapter devoted to him in Roger Kahn's great *The Boys of Summer*.

SCHOOLBOY ROWE *BASEBALL PITCHER (b. Lynwood Thomas Rowe, 1/11/1910, Waco, TX; d. 1/8/61, El Dorado, AR)* Raised in El Dorado, Rowe was one of the best pitchers of the Depression era. He earned his nickname as a youngster when he pitched against an adult dairy company team. The next day the story of the schoolboy who beat the men made local headlines. His best year was 1934 when the right-hander led the Detroit Tigers to a pennant with a 24-8 record (his 16 consecutive wins tied the AL record). In 1940 his winning percentage led the league and helped take the Tigers to yet another pennant. Overall, he was 158-101, with a 3.87 ERA. A big, burly man, Rowe was also good with a bat, with a .279 career average as a pinch hitter. He played in three World Series.

JOHNNY SAIN *BASEBALL PITCHER, PITCHING COACH (b. John Franklin Sain, 9/25/1917, Havana, AR)* "Spahn and Sain and pray for rain"—that was the famous battle cry for the Boston Braves in 1948, the year Johnny Sain led the National League with 24 wins. (It meant that if Warren Spahn pitched one day, and Sain the next, followed by a little helpful rain to give them a rest, Boston could win the pennant, which they did.) Sain grew up in Havana, where former big-leaguer Jim Walkup was his mentor. After several frustrating attempts at breaking into the majors, Sain was finally signed by Boston, where he had four seasons with 20 or more wins. In 1951 he was traded to the Yankees, where he helped pitch New York to two pennants. After his career ended, he became a pitching coach – the greatest who ever lived, according to Jim Bouton.

BOSS SCHMIDT *BASEBALL CATCHER (b. Charles Schmidt, 9/12/1880, Coal Hill, AR; d. 11/14/32, Altus, AR)* A fierce competitor for Detroit (1906-11), Schmidt led the Tigers to three pennants. As a young man he worked in his brother's coal mine, then joined the Springfield Midgets in 1901. Detroit bought his contract in 1906. A brawler, he was celebrated as the only man to beat his cantankerous teammate Ty Cobb in a fair fight, which he did on three separate occasions. (He also boxed an exhibition with heavyweight champ Jack Johnson.) He left the big leagues in 1912. After his death, the Tigers, learning his grave had no marker, chipped in to pay for a monument.

CHARLIE MAY SIMON *WRITER (b. Charlie May Hogue, 8/17/1897, Monticello, AR; d. 3/21/77, Little Rock, AR)* A prolific writer of 27 books, Simon is best known for her children's tales, including the 1934 classic *Robin on the Mountain*. Raised in Memphis, she attended Memphis State University, Stanford, the Chicago Art Institute, and Le Grande Chaumiere in Paris. There she married artist Howard Simon, who later illustrated several of her books. In 1936 she divorced Simon and married poet John Gould Fletcher. Her award-winning works include *Bright Morning, Straw in the Sun*, and several biographies. Simon also wrote *The Sharecropper*, an adult novel about the Southern Tenant Farmers Union. In 1953, three years after the suicide of her husband, she wrote *Johnswood*, an account of their lives together and named for the Little Rock home they had shared since 1941. It was the favorite of all her books. In her honor, the Arkansas Education Department in 1970 established the Charlie May Simon Award for Children's Literature, to be decided each year by a vote of grade school students throughout the state. She is buried beside her husband at Mount Holly Cemetery in Little Rock. ➤ *See also:* John Gould Fletcher.

GERALD L. K. SMITH

HATEMONGER, DEVELOPER (b. Gerald Lyman Kenneth Smith, 2/27/1898, Pardeeville, WS; d. 4/15/76, Glendale, CA) The man responsible for the Christ of the Ozarks and other religious attractions in Eureka Springs was one of the most notorious racists and anti-Semites in American history. Smith, the offspring of three generations of ministers, was a Shreveport pastor when he fell under the sway of Huey Long, who hired him to promote his populist Share the Wealth movement. By all accounts, Smith was a mesmerizing speaker; H. L. Mencken called him "the gustiest and goriest, the loudest and lustiest, the deadliest and damndest orator ever heard on this or any other earth." When the Kingfish was assassinated in 1935, Smith delivered a fiery funeral oration, but was soon afterward forced out of the Long political machine. In 1942 he founded the Christian Nationalist Crusade, a far-far right organization that published a torrent of hate

Charlie May Simon

literature, including a monthly magazine, "The Cross and the Flag," which Smith wrote largely himself. In 1944 he ran for president on the America First ticket. In time, Smith's quick-trigger, extremist views managed to offend just about everyone – he was anti-Roosevelt ("drive the cripple from the White House") and later anti-Eisenhower ("Stop Ike the Kike") – but his printing operations made him a fortune. In 1964 Smith purchased Penn Castle in Eureka Springs, where he and his wife began spending their summers. In 1966 they dedicated a seven-story statue of Jesus on Magnetic Mountain. Eventually, their projects would include an amphitheater for presentations of "The Great Passion Play," a Bible Museum and other attractions. Smith is buried under the left arm of his Christ of the Ozarks statue.

BREHON SOMERVELL *MILITARY HERO (b. Brehon Burke Somervell, 5/9/1892, Little Rock, AR; d. 2/13/55, Ocala, FL)* As commanding general of supply services in WWII, Army engineer Somervell disbursed over $172,000,000,000. His job was to induct, feed, clothe, arm and shelter 8,300,000 soldiers. A tough, quick-tempered man who fired or demoted more than a dozen generals, Somervell is credited with the wartime expression: "The impossible we do at once; the miraculous takes a little longer."

MARY STEENBURGEN *OSCAR-WINNING ACTRESS (b. 2/8/1953, Newport, AR)* Raised in the Park Hill section of North Little Rock,

the daughter of a train conductor, Steenburgen graduated from Northeast High School, then dropped out of Hendrix and headed for New York to become an actress. There she spent six long years attending acting classes, performing in a troupe called Cracked Tokens, and scraping by as a waitress. (Throughout this period she earned a total of $50 as an actress.) Then, in fairy-tale fashion, she was plucked from a casting call by Jack Nicholson, who handed her a leading role in his 1978 movie, *Goin' South*. Next came *Time After Time*, co-starring British actor Malcolm McDowell, whom she married (and later divorced). In 1980 her performance as the scatter-brained Lynda Dummar in *Melvin and Howard* garnered best supporting actress awards from the Academy,

Mary Steenburgen

the Golden Globe Association, the New York Film Critics' Circle and the National Society of Film Critics. In the words of critic Rex Reed, Steenburgen was "the first little girl from Little Rock to make it to the big time since Lorelei Lee in *Gentlemen Prefer Blondes*." Other movies: *Ragtime, A Midsummer Night's Sex Comedy, Cross Creek, Romantic Comedy, One Magic Christmas, Dead of Winter, Parenthood, Philadelphia*. In 1987 she executive-produced a labor of love, *End of the Line*, a film about the effects of a railroad closing on the lives of its workers. Shot entirely in central Arkansas, it premiered in Little Rock. A pal of Bill and Hillary Clinton, she returns often to her home state and assists local charities, notably Arkansas Children's Hospital.

JACK STEPHENS *FINANCIER (b. Jackson Thomas Stephens, 8/9/1923, Prattsville, AR)* Stephens attended a military academy in Tennessee, then spent a few semesters at the U of A before graduating from the U.S. Naval Academy in 1946. Later he joined his older brother Witt in creating the investment firm of Stephens, Inc. Today he's chairman of the board and also serves as chairman of the Augusta National Golf Course, site of the annual Master's golf tournament. *Forbes* places the Stephens family fortune at over $1.2 billion. ➤ *See also:* Witt Stephens.

WITT STEPHENS *FINANCIER (b. Wilton Aubert [later changed to Robert] Stephens, 9/14/1907, Prattsville, AR; d. 12/2/91, Little Rock, AR)* Founder of what for many years was invariably

called "the largest investment banking firm off Wall Street," Stephens exercised extraordinary influence over Arkansas throughout his long life. Born on a farm in Grant County, he started hustling at an early age. After peddling belt buckles and Bibles door to door, he borrowed $15,000 and began selling state highway bonds, then formed W. R. Stephens Investment Co. Later, his younger brother Jack joined the firm. In 1959 *Fortune* called the charming, folksy Stephens "one of the outstanding natural wonders" of Arkansas. In his later years Mister Witt, as he came to be called, hosted celebrated weekday luncheons that featured lively discussions of current events. He died following a stroke suffered while hard at work making trades in his office. ➤ *See also:* Jack Stephens.

WILLIAM GRANT STILL *COMPOSER (b. 5/11/1895, Woodville, MS; d. 12/3/1978, Los Angeles, CA)* Hailed by Leopold Stokowski as "one of our great American composers," Still produced a remarkable yield of operas, symphonies, ballets, and film scores. As a black artist, his career encompassed a number of significant firsts, including first black composer to have a symphony played before an American audience, and first black conductor of a major orchestra. Still's father, a music teacher, died when his son was only three months old. His mother moved to Little Rock, where the boy was raised. He graduated at age 16 from Dunbar High School as class valedictorian. After dropping out of college and serving in the

Navy in WWI, Still worked as a sideman for W. C. Handy in Memphis. In the 1930s he secured a Guggenheim fellowship and concentrated on serious composition, moving to California. His 1933 *Afro-American Symphony*, perhaps his most famous work, drew inspiration from the spirituals sung to him by his grandmother. In 1939 he was commissioned to create the theme music for the 1939 World's Fair in New York and in 1949 his opera on the liberation of Haiti, *Troubled Island*, featuring a libretto by Langston Hughes, was produced by the New York City Center Opera Company.

GRIF STOCKLEY

AUTHOR
(b. 10/9/1944, Marianna, AR)
Million-selling novelist Stockley has written several legal thrillers featuring attorney Gideon Page, who practices in fictional Blackwell County, Arkansas, a place suspiciously like Pulaski County. A lawyer who represents indigents for the Central Arkansas Legal Services, Stockley creates his popular entertainments on the side. He's a graduate of the U of A law school and a former Peace Corps volunteer. Among his novels: *Expert Testimony, Probable Cause* and *Religious Conviction*.

EDWARD DURELL STONE

ARCHITECT (b. 3/9/1902, Fayetteville, AR; d. 8/6/78, New York, NY) One of America's most successful – and controversial – architects, Stone grew up in Fayetteville, the grandson of "the richest man in northwest Arkansas." Bill Fulbright was a boyhood friend. Stone dropped out of the U of A and moved to Boston, where he attended Harvard on a scholarship, and also MIT, but never earned a degree. Eventually he apprenticed with a Boston architect, and opened his own practice in 1933. An early house

Edward Durell Stone

design for publisher Henry R. Luce brought him attention and, after his 1939 design for the main building of the Museum of Modern Art, commissions began to flow. After service in WWII, Stone built one of the preeminent practices of his day, designing many important buildings throughout the world. Among them: the U.S. Embassy in New Delhi, India (1954), which many consider his finest work; Stanford University Medical Center in Palo Alto, CA (1955); the John F. Kennedy Center for the Performing Arts, Washington (1969-71). He also designed several buildings in his native state, principally in Fayetteville: the U of A Fine Arts Center (1949); Sigma Nu Fraternity House (1951); the Married Students' Housing Complex (1957). In 1953 Stone met a female fashion writer on a transatlantic flight and proposed to her before the plane landed; she became the second of his three wives. Toward the end of his life, Stone's work grew more florid and ornamental, and increasingly less popular with critics. However, his commissions never waned and, by his death at 76, he had clearly left his mark on the architecture of his time. His autobiography, *Evolution of an Architect*, appeared in 1962.

BARRY SWITZER *FOOTBALL COACH (b. 10/5/1937, Crossett, AR)* In 1994 Barry Switzer, former coach of the Oklahoma Sooners football team, was the surprise choice to ramrod the world champion Dallas Cowboys. Son of an ex-con bootlegger, Switzer grew up on the outskirts of Crossett in a shack with no electricity or running water. An outstanding athlete, he played for Arkansas on a football scholarship. In 1959 he captained Frank Broyles' first SWC championship team, then stayed on as an assistant (coaching a couple of players – Jerry Jones and Jimmy Johnson – whose lives would later intersect dramatically with his own). In 1966 he joined the University of Oklahoma football staff and seven years later moved up to head coach. In his 16 seasons at the helm, Switzer proved himself a bigtime winner, compiling three national championships, 12 Big Eight titles and a 157-29-4 record. In June 1989, however, he was forced out of his $400,000 job by the stink of bigtime scandal: NCAA probation, three players charged with rape, another charged with shooting a teammate, and a starting quarterback indicted on cocaine charges. Switzer entered private business and even wrote a bestselling autobiography, *Bootlegger's Boy*. After five years out of coaching, Switzer confessed, "I thought my time had passed." Then, in March 1994, he got the call from owner Jerry Jones and found himself the new $1-million-a-year head coach of the Dallas Cowboys, replacing Jimmy Johnson. Once again, Barry Switzer was back on top. ➤ *See also:* Jerry Jones.

JOHN TATE *BOXER (b. 1/29/1955, Marion, AR)* Raised poor in West Memphis, Tate won a bronze medal in the 1976 Olympics. Three years later, after a 15-round decision over Gerrie Coetzee, he earned the World Boxing Association heavyweight championship – but held the title only a few months. In March 1980, he was knocked cold by Mike Weaver with less than a minute remaining in their bout, after having won virtually every round to that point. Although he boxed successfully for several years afterward, Tate could never escape his glass jaw image. In recent years, as a Knoxville panhandler, he has had various run-ins with the law, including prison sentences.

BILLY JOE TATUM *WRITER (b. Billy Joe Taylor, 2/15/1933, Little Rock, AR)* Author of the bestselling *Billy Joe Tatum's Wild Foods Cookbook* (1976), Tatum was the wife of a country doctor when her interest in wild foods and herbs was first kindled by her husband's patients, many of whom still employed home remedies to cure their ailments. Tatum has appeared on the "Tonight Show" and been profiled in *People*.

GOOSE TATUM *"THE CLOWN PRINCE OF BASKETBALL" (b. Reese Tatum, 5/3/ 1921,* NJ; d. 1/18/67, El Paso, TX)* Famed Harlem Globetrotter star Goose Tatum, the son of an itinerant preacher, moved from New Jersey to Calion, AR, as a small child, then later to El Dorado. A baseball player, he didn't set his hands on a basketball until he was in the ninth grade, then became a standout player at Washington High School. (His appearances were promoted by graffiti: "Come and see Goose get a-loose!"). There are differing stories about his nickname. One says he was dubbed Goose because of his "loosey-goosey" moves; another says it was because he loved gooseliver meatloaf. Quitting high school in his junior year, he drifted to Louisville, Kentucky, where he was drafted by the Cincinnati Clowns baseball team. His on-field antics caught the attention of Abe Saperstein, who hired him for his famed Harlem Globetrotters in 1941. Tatum quickly became the number one attraction; by the 1950s he was earning $65,000 a year. Performing before millions the world over, he was probably the most popular basketball player alive. In 1954 he quit the Trotters to form his own traveling team, the Harlem Road Kings, which he led until his sudden death at age 45. **Sources vary.*

LOUISE McPHETRIDGE THADEN *PIONEER AVIATOR (b. 1906, Bentonville, AR; d. 11/9/79, High Point, NC)* A pioneer in women's aviation, Thaden grew up in Bentonville, attended the U of A, then worked as a sales agent for a Kansas aircraft manufacturer before taking up flying. In 1929 she defeated Amelia Earhart and others to win the first Women's Air Derby. In 1936 she won the Bendix Trophy Race, competing against top male pilots and setting a record transcontinental time. At one point she held the women's altitude, speed and endurance records simultaneously. In 1938 she retired from competitive flying to spend more time with her family and write her autobiography, *High, Wide and Frightened*. She is a member of the Smithsonian Institute's Aviation Hall of Fame, and Louise Thaden Field in Bentonville is named in her honor.

RICHARD THALHEIMER *FOUNDER OF THE SHARPER IMAGE (b. 1948, Little Rock, AR)* "My ambition in life," Thalheimer once said, "was to be a big success in business." He achieved his goal as founder of The Sharper Image catalog and retail store chain, which sells glitzy, high-priced gadgets that "appeal to the boy inside the man." Thalheimer had family connections with both the Blass and the Pfeifer's department stores. He graduated from Yale in 1970, then sold encyclopedias door-to-door to afford law school. He operated an office supply business in San Francisco that he renamed in 1975 as The Sharper Image. Two years later he took out an ad in a running magazine promoting a $29 stopwatch that netted him $300. The next year, Thalheimer found another watch, spritzed up the prose, and raked in $300,000. He poured the money

Louise Thaden

back into the business, eventually publishing a slick catalog featuring everything from fog-free shaving mirrors to antique cars. In 1981 he opened the first of many retail outlets.

SISTER ROSETTA THARPE *SINGER*
(b. Rosetta Nubin, 3/20/1921, Cotton Plant, AR; d. 10/9/73, Philadelphia, PA)
A gifted performer who rose to fame in the late 1930s appearing with Cab Calloway at the Cotton Club, Tharpe was the daughter of a traveling gospel singer and raised primarily in Chicago. A singer and electric guitarist, her records included: "Rock Me," "I Want a Tall, Skinny Papa," and "That's All." Gospel: "Didn't It Rain," "Up Above my Head." Her 1951 wedding drew 25,000 paying guests. Grammy-nominated in the 1960s, she suffered a debilitating stroke in 1970 that eventually required the amputation of a leg. A second stroke killed her on the morning of a planned recording session.

HARRY THOMASON *PRODUCER*
(b. 11/28/1940, Hampton, AR) Among TV's most successful producers, Thomason has helped bring to life such sitcom hits as "Designing Women," "Evening Shade" and "Hearts Afire"– all created and largely written by his wife, Linda Bloodworth-Thomason. A graduate of Southern Arkansas University, Thomason produced several cheapie in-state movies during the 1970s – including *Encounter With the Unknown, So Sad About Gloria* and *The Great Lester Boggs* – before moving on to the big time. After his award-winning TV movie, "A Shining Season," Thomason returned home to film the popular miniseries, "The Blue and the Gray." Officially, he's executive producer of Mozark Productions (the name derives from the couple's home states of Missouri

and Arkansas). Close friends of Bill and Hillary Clinton, the Thomasons created the famous "Man from Hope" biographical film shown at the 1992 Democratic convention.

PINKY TOMLIN *SINGER, ACTOR (b. 9/9/1908, Eros, AR; d. 12/12/87, N. Hollywood, CA)* Raised in Oklahoma, this red-haired songwriter's 1934 hit, "The Object of My Affection," was inspired by his future wife, a former Miss Oklahoma. Tomlin also acted in movies and appeared regularly on an early TV show, "Waterfront." His autobiography, which has the same name as his famous song, was published in 1981.

ALPHONSO TRENT *BANDLEADER (b. 8/24/1905, Fort Smith, AR; d. 10/14/59, Fort Smith, AR)* After studying music at Shorter College, pianist Trent took over a band in the early 1920s that emerged as one of the finest "territory" bands of the pre-swing era. In 1923 it became the first black band to play a prominent white hotel, the Adolphus in Dallas, where it remained until 1933, broadcasting on radio.

JIM GUY TUCKER *POLITICIAN (b. 6/13/1943, Oklahoma City, OK)* As lieutenant governor, Tucker automatically assumed the state's top job upon the resignation of Bill Clinton in 1992. Harvard-educated, he had served as attorney general and congressman in the 1970s. On May 28, 1996, Tucker announced his own resignation immediately after being found guilty of criminal charges brought by the Whitewater independent counsel. He was the tenth sitting U.S. governor indicted this century.

➤ *See also:* Bill Clinton, Whitewater.

T. TEXAS TYLER *COUNTRY & WESTERN SINGER (b. David Luke Myrick, 6/20/1916, Mena, AR; d. 1/28/72, Springfield, MO)* In 1948 a talk song called "Deck of Cards," about a soldier explaining how playing cards correspond to major points in the gospels, became a huge country music hit. The song (later covered by Tex Ritter) was written and recorded by T. Texas Tyler, a growly-voiced performer who was born in Arkansas but raised in Texas. Tyler entered show business in his teens, appeared on "Major Bowes Amateur Hour," performed on "The Louisiana Hayride," served in WWII, organized his own C&W band, hosted a popular LA TV show called "Range Roundup," appeared in several westerns, but eventually gave up performing for the ministry. Known in the entertainment world as "the man with a million friends," Tyler also charted with "Daddy Gave My Dog Away" and "Bumming."

DON TYSON *"THE CHICKEN KING" (b. 4/21/1930, Olathe, KS)* Tyson is former chairman of Tyson Foods of Springdale, the world's largest poultry producer. Kansas food hauler John Tyson founded the company in the Depression, after his only truck ran out of gas in Springdale. After deciding he liked the area and wanted to stay, he bought a hatchery to supply chicks to local chicken farmers. Today the company slaughters 29 million birds a week. Son Don became president in 1966. The next year his father and stepmother died when a train hit their car; in 1986 his stepbrother

Randal died in a freak accident, choking to death at home while snacking on cookies and milk. Tyson's office is a replica of the Oval Office (except that the doorknobs are shaped like chicken eggs). A fanatical marlin fisherman, Tyson owns homes throughout the world. He can afford it – at last count, the Chicken King's net worth was estimated at $925 million, give or take a few nuggets.

PATTI UPTON *FOUNDER OF AROMATIQUE (b. 1938, Jonesboro, AR)* In the autumn of 1982, a Heber Springs shopkeeper invited her friend, housewife Patti Upton, to create something special for her Christmas open house. Upton, a former U of A beauty queen and ex-model, strolled about her front yard and gathered some hickory nuts, pine cones, acorns, dried leaves and other natural ingredients, added cooking oils and spices, and placed the fragrant concoction in an open container at the gift shop, purely for decoration. But customers quickly demanded samples of their own. In just a few years, Patti Upton had herself an empire – Aromatique, Inc. – all built around that original mixture of potpourri, "The Smell of Christmas." By 1992, according to *Arkansas Business*, Upton's business employed almost 500 people, with offices in New York and London, and marketed more than 200 products (including decorative fragrances and candles) through 5,000 stores in 27 countries. Called "The Smell Queen of America," Upton has been featured on TV's "Lifestyles of the Rich and Famous."

ARKY VAUGHAN *HALL-OF-FAME BASEBALL PLAYER (b. Joseph Floyd Vaughan, 3/9/1912, Clifty, AR; d. 8/30/52, Lost Lake, CA)* Vaughan grew up in California, where playmates nicknamed him "Arky" after his native state. A gifted shortstop and third baseman, he was named to the NL All-Star team nine years in a row, and hit two homers in one All-Star game. As a Pittsburgh Pirate in 1935 his .385 batting average set a team record that still stands. Vaughan drowned in a boating accident at age 40. He was named to the Baseball Hall of Fame in 1985.

JIMMY WAKELY *ACTOR, SINGER, SONGWRITER (b. 2/16/1914, Mineola, AR; d. 9/23/82, Los Angeles, CA)* Wakely appeared in a number of movie westerns, including several with Roy Rogers – like *I'm From Arkansas* (1944). Later, from 1952 to 1957 he hosted his own radio program on CBS.

JAMES DEAN WALKER *PRISONER (b. 9/11/1940, Boise, ID)* One of Arkansas' most controversial criminal cases involved the 1963 shooting death of a North Little Rock policeman. Drifter James Dean Walker was sentenced to life in prison, where he later claimed a cellblock conversion to Christ. Repeated applications for parole, however, were denied. In 1975 he failed to return from a furlough and was declared a fugitive. Almost five years later, he was picked up in California on a drug charge and, despite the protestations of several Hollywood stars and demi-stars who had taken up his cause, was returned to prison in Arkansas. In

November 1986 federal courts ruled he was entitled to a new trial. An agreement was negotiated in which Walker was sentenced to time already served. Immediately after his release, he left the state in which he had resided for 17 1/2 years, never to return.

JUNIOR WALKER SINGER, SAXO-PHONIST (b. Autry DeWalt II, 1942, Blytheville, AR; d. 11/23/95, Battle Creek, MI) Junior Walker and the All-Stars first hit the pop charts in 1965 with sax virtuoso Walker's original composition, "Shotgun," which sold over a million copies for the Motown group. Other hits: "(I'm A) Road Runner," "What Does It Take (To Win Your Love)," "Do You See My Love (For You Growing)," "These Eyes."

SAM WALTON FOUNDER OF WAL-MART (b. Sam Moore Walton, 3/29/1918, Kingfisher, OK; d. 4/5/92, Little Rock, AR)
The tale of Mr. Sam and Wal-Mart is one of the great American success stories – how a small-town shop-keeper founded an empire and ended up the richest man in the U.S. The son of a farm-mortgage broker, Walton was the youngest Eagle Scout in Missouri, state champion high school quarterback, honor roll student, and president of the student body. He graduated from the University of Mis-souri and hired on at JC Penney (Mr. Penney himself once taught him how to wrap a package). After a stint in the Army he used his savings to open a Ben Franklin variety store in Newport, AR. In 1950 he lost his lease and moved to Bentonville, where he started Walton's 5 & 10. In time he and his younger brother, J. L. "Bud" Walton, added several more stores. But Sam saw the writing on the wall: the days of "buy-it-low, stack-it-high, sell-it-cheap" discounting were swooping down on his little variety stores. Sam's big idea was to take the concept to small-town America, to places bypassed by the big discounters. The Walton brothers opened their first Wal-Mart in Rogers, AR, on July 2, 1962; within a

Sam Walton, delivering on a promise to employ-ees that he would dance the hula on Wall Street if they met profit goals, 1984

year the store had grossed $1 million. "It was the retail equivalent of an oil gusher," he later said. "The whole thing just sort of blowed." In 1970, with 30 stores, he took his company public. (If you had bought 100 shares of the original offering, at a cost of $1,650, your investment would have soared to $3 million by 1992.) Ignored for many years by the business community, Walton didn't mind – he just kept adding stores. With a sharp eye on the bottom line, he built a hugely efficient distribution system and saturated small-town markets. His 7:30 a.m. Saturday morning management meetings often started by calling the Hogs ("That's one of my favorite ways to wake everybody up, by doing the University of Arkansas' Razorback cheer.") A consummately hands-on manager, Walton flew his own twin-prop Cessna to survey his kingdom. By the 1990s his company had surpassed Sears and Kmart to emerge as America's number one retailer. Despite his enormous wealth and increasing fame, Walton remained famously down to earth. He lived in a relatively plain home in Bentonville, drove an old Ford truck, loved to play tennis and hunt quail (his favorite bird dog, Ol' Roy, is immortalized on the label of Wal-Mart brand dog food). Still, business was never far from the billionaire's brain – he once rear-ended a tractor-trailer rig on Highway 71 because he took his eye off the road in order to count the cars in a Kmart parking lot. (Fortunately, it was a Wal-Mart truck.) In 1992 his autobiography, *Sam Walton: Made in America*, was published posthumously. Naturally, it was a bestseller.

WILLIAM WARFIELD SINGER

(b. William Caesar Warfield, 1/20/1920, West Helena, AR) Although famed baritone Warfield moved to Rochester, NY, at an early age, he wrote in his 1991 autobiography, *My Music and My Life*, that "I do consider myself, in some important sense, a child of Arkansas ... I was an Arkansas boy from tip to toe, from my mama's milk to the stories I learned at my daddy's knee." After extensive classical training, Warfield debuted on the New York concert stages in 1950. The next year he appeared as Joe in the movie version of *Show Boat*. Warfield, a Grammy winner, is best known for the role of Porgy in *Porgy and Bess*, in which he toured all over the world. He also played De Lawd in the famed Hallmark Hall of Fame production of *Green Pastures*.

LON WARNEKE "THE ARKANSAS HUMMINGBIRD"

(b. Lonnie Warneke, 3/28/1909, Mt. Ida, AR; d. 6/23/76, Hot Springs, AR) With his 193-121 record, pitcher Warneke won more games in the majors than any other Arkansas native, including the Dean brothers, Johnny Sain, Preacher Roe or Schoolboy Rowe. One of the great low-ball hurlers of all time, the tall, agile right-hander led the National League in 1932 in games won (22) and earned-run average (2.37). A three-time 20-game winner for the Cubs, Warneke was given his nickname by a St. Louis sportswriter, who praised the then-Cardinal pitcher's "sizzling-fast and

Southern History (1960) he redefined the history of race relations in the post-Reconstruction South. Woodward served in the Navy in WWII and wrote *The Battle of Leyte Gulf* in 1947. His most influential work is probably *The Strange Career of Jim Crow* (1955), a compilation of essays on the origins of segregation. From 1961-77 he was a Sterling Professor at Yale University.

Woodward is the editor of the prodigious *Oxford History of the United States* and, in 1982, won a Pulitzer Prize for *Mary Chestnut's Civil War*. His autobiography, *Thinking Back: The Perils of Writing History*, was published in 1986.

DID YOU KNOW?

BORN TO INFLUENCE

In 1969 the *London Sunday Times* published a popular series called the "1,000 Makers of the Twentieth Century," listing the primary movers and shakers of our time, from A to Z. Two native Arkansans made the list: five-star general **DOUGLAS MACARTHUR** and Holiday Inn founder **KEMMONS WILSON.** The Arkansas influence is question-able, however. Both men left the state as infants – MacArthur at 18 months, Wilson at only nine months.

Whooooo Pig!   Sooie!

DOWN-HOME ARKANSAS

Well slap me naked and hide my clothes!

Down-home is a state of mind and a way of life. From the way we turn a phrase to the way we cook a meal, down-home is distinctively different. Even our towns have unusual names like Hog Scald and Greasy Corner. In the following section, we pass along favorite recipes, fascinating folklore and even share a few tips on where to find great country crafts. We think you'll agree that down-home is as welcome as the flowers in spring.

DOWN-HOME TALK

Colorful, sometimes extraordinary metaphors have a marvelous way of creeping into everyday Arkansas speech. Most of these expressions are drawn from common everyday objects and situations — from barnyard animals to food, from religion to bodily functions. And then there are those ingenious, surreal descriptions that are so off-the-wall they seem to beam in directly from the Twilight Zone. But whatever their origin, down-home speech is unparalleled in its creative use of language and outrageous sense of humor. So come on and immerse yourself. You'll be talkin' down-home quicker than an Arkansas preacher can spot a counterfeit nickel!

AGE

He's so old he could have been a
   waiter at the Last Supper.
Old as Methuselah.
Old as black pepper.
Old as dirt.
He has so many wrinkles he has
   to screw his hat on.

ANGER

Madder than a sore-titted bitch.
Havin' a conniption fit.
Madder than a wet settin' hen.

APPETITE

Tastes so good it makes you want to swallow your tongue.

I'm as hungry as a moth on a nylon sweater.

I'll stir up somethin' that'll knock your hat in the creek.

BEAUTY

Pretty as a goggle-eyed perch.

Cuter than a June bug on a sow's ear.

Pretty as a bald-faced heifer.

BUSY

Busy as a bee in a bottle.

Busy as a long-nosed weevil in a cotton patch.

Busy as a barefoot boy in an ant bed.

CLOTHING

As sexy as socks on a rooster.

She's wearin' her Sunday-go-to-meetin' dress.

Her dress fits tighter than skin on a sausage.

CLUMSY

He couldn't hit a bull in the ass with a bass fiddle.

He couldn't hit the ground if he fell.

He can't walk and chew tobacco at the same time.

Graceful as a three-legged cow in labor.

COMMON

Common as dishwater.

Common as pig's tracks.

Common as a belly button.

COMPLAINTS

You'd gripe if they hung you with a new rope.

What do you want – okra in your soup?

If she went to heaven, she'd ask to see the upstairs.

CONFUSION

Like a rubber-nosed wood pecker in the Petrified Forest.

Walks around like a goose huntin' thunder.

Runnin' around like a June bug on a hot griddle.

Like a calf starin' at a new gate.

CONTRARY

If you threw him in the river, he'd float upstream.

I don't care if it harelips all the hogs in Texas.

Stubborn as a cross-eyed mule.

CRAZY

Crazier than a pet coon.

Crazy as a road lizard.

Crazy as a peach orchard boar.

CROWDED

So many folks you can't stir 'em with a stick.

Not enough room in here to cuss a cat.

So crowded you have to go outside to change your mind.

DEPRESSION

My heart's heavier than a bucket of hog livers.

Lower than a mole's belly button on diggin' day.

So low I could jump off a dime.

DIFFICULTY

Like tryin' to lick honey off a blackberry vine.

Like tryin' to push a noodle through a key hole.

Like tryin' to pick fly shit out of black pepper.

DIMWITTED

If brains were dynamite, you couldn't blow your nose.

Doesn't know diddly squat.

Doesn't know pea turkey.

If you put his brain in a blue bird, it'd fly backwards.

His head's as empty as last year's bird's nest.

DISHONESTY

He'd steal flies from a blind spider.

Sneaky as a weasel in a chicken house.

Crooked as a dog's hind leg.

So crooked they'll have to screw him in the ground to bury him.

EXCITEMENT

Feisty as a calf in clover.

Excited as a spring lizard in a hen house.

She's so excited she has to walk sideways to keep from flyin'.

Excited as a bug in a tater patch.

FEELINGS

Feel like I been sackin' wildcats and run out of sacks.

Feel like I been jerked through a knothole backwards.

Feel like I been rode hard and put up wet.

FINE

Finer than frog's hair split four ways and sanded.

Fine as split silk.

Fine as dollar cotton.

Fine as snuff.

FRUGALITY

So cheap he wouldn't pay a dime to see a pissant pull a freight train.

So tight he crawls under the gate to save the hinges.

Tight as Dick's hatband.

FUTILITY

Pointless as white-washing horse manure and settin' it up on end.

Like tryin' to sneak daylight past a rooster.

Like tryin' to nail Jell-O to a tree.

GAIT

She walks like an old hen with an egg broke in her.

Walks like he has a corncob up his rear.

He has a hitch in his git-along.

Runs like a chicken pullin' a wagon.

GENEROSITY

She has a heart soft as summer butter.

She has a heart as big as her behind.

HAPPINESS

Happy as a dead hog in the sunshine.

Happy as a possum in a cow carcass.

Happy as a dog in a slaughterhouse.

Happy as a toad frog under a drippy faucet.

HOMELINESS

So ugly he'd scare a hungry dog off a meat wagon.

So ugly his daddy had to tie a pork chop around his neck so the dog would play with him.

So buck-toothed he can eat corn on the cob through a picket fence.

Looks like he's been hit in the face with a wet squirrel.

Looks like forty miles of bad road.

HOT

Hot as the hinges of Hell.

Hotter than a Kmart parkin' lot in July.

Hotter than a billy goat in a pepper patch.

Hot enough to fry spit.

INEXPERIENCE

He just rode into town on a load of pumpkins.

She cooks peas and turnips in the same pot.

Greener than a gourd.

LAZINESS

So lazy he stops plowin' to fart.

He was born lazy and had a set-back.

Lazy as a pet coon.

He's like a blister; he don't show up 'til the work's done.

LIFE

Life is short and full of blisters.
Tomorrow's just the same soup, different bowl.
That's life – if it isn't chicken, it's feathers!
If it ain't broke don't fix it.

LOCATION

He lives in hollerin' distance.
He lives so far out in the country that sunlight has to be piped in.
He lives a tater-chunk away.

MEANNESS

Mean as a chicken-eatin' sow.
Mean as a crocodile with a gum boil.
Mean as a two-stingered wasp.
He's so mean he'd take his wife's egg money.

MEDDLING

Mind your own beeswax!
Chew your own tobacco.
Tote your own skillet.

NAKED

Naked as the day you were born.
Buck naked.
Naked as the day is long.
Naked as a scraped hog.

NERVOUSNESS

Nervous as a porcupine in a balloon factory.
Nervous as a long-tail cat in a room full of rockers.
So nervous she could thread a sewin' machine with it runnin'.
Nervous as a whore in church.

NOISE

Bawlin' like a dyin' calf in a hail storm.
Hollerin' like a pig under a gate.
Noisy as a jackass in a tin stable.
Noisy as a cornhusk mattress.

OBESITY

Spread out like Dallas.
Her rear looks like two tomcats fightin' in a gunnysack.
She's got a rear end like a forty-dollar mule.
He's two-ax-handles-and-a-plug-of-Day's Work wide.
An ass as fat as a river bottom coon.

PATIENCE

Patient as a buzzard waitin' for a mule to die.
Don't start choppin' 'til you've treed the coon.
Don't count the crop 'til it's in the barn.

POVERTY

So poor he couldn't buy a redbug a rasslin' jacket.
So poor he couldn't make a down payment on a hotdog.
Poor as Job's turkey.
Broker than the Ten Commandments.

PROCREATION

She's got enough kids to bait a trotline.
They had a generation of children.
Children: yard apes, rug rats.

QUIET

So quiet you could hear a gnat
 scratch.
Quieter than a mouse pissin' on a
 cotton ball.
So quiet you could hear your hair
 grow.

RAIN

Frog strangler.
Gully washer.
Cob floater.
Clod buster.

RELUCTANCE

Before I'd do that I'd get a tin beak
 and peck shit with the chickens.
I'd rather walk through an alley
 wearin' cheese underwear.
I'd rather shave my head
 with a cheese grater.

SCARCITY

Scarce as hog
 tracks on a linen
 tablecloth.
Scarce as horse
 manure in a
 two-car garage.
Scarce as hen's
 teeth.
Rare as a black cow
 with a white face.

SKINNY

Skinnier than a bar of soap after a
 hard day's wash.
So thin she could bathe in a gun
 barrel.
She's no bigger than the hammer
 on a .22.
Thin as a slice of boarding house
 pie.

SLOW

If they hang me, I hope they send
 you after the rope.
Too slow to catch a cold.
Slow as suckin' buttermilk through
 a straw.
So slow he couldn't catch the
 seven-year itch.

SOFT

Soft as a moth's nose.
Soft as a butterfly's belly.
Soft as a two-minute egg.

SPEED

Faster than an alligator can chew a
 puppy.
In a New York minute.
Fast as an Arkansas preacher can
 spot a counterfeit
 nickel.
 Faster than
 a scalded
 dog.

STRENGTH

So strong
 he can
 crunch
 pecans
 between his
 toes.
Stronger than an acre
 of new-mown garlic.

SURPRISE

Well, slap me naked and hide my
 clothes!
Well, I'll be a suck-egg mule!
Well, drag me in the bushes and
 leave me for ripe!

TALKATIVE

Her tongue is tied in the middle
  and waggin' at both ends.
He can cuss the gate off its hinges.
He can talk tomatoes off the vine.
He talked 'til his tongue hung out
  like a cow rope.

TROUBLE

She got her tit caught in the
  wringer.
He's in a bad row of stumps.
That's a fine how-do-you-do!

VANITY

She wouldn't go to a funeral
  unless she could be the corpse.
Proud as a dog with a hemstitched
  tail.
She's so spoilt that salt wouldn't
  save her.

WEALTH

He's got enough money to burn a
  wet mule.
She's choppin' tall cotton.
He has
  more
  money
  than
  Carter
  has
  pills.

WELCOME

As welcome as a polecat at a camp
  meetin'.
As welcome as the flowers in spring.
As welcome as a bastard at the
  family picnic.

WORRY

You'd worry the warts off a frog.
You'd worry the horns off a billy
  goat.
Fretful as a hen with one chick.

WORTHLESS

Worthless as a pinch of sour owl
  manure.
He's not fit to carry guts to a bear.
Handier than hip pockets in a shroud.
Useless as two buggies in a one
  horse town.
Ain't worth dried spit.

DID YOU KNOW?

The truck, specifically the Chevy pickup, is the most popular vehicle in Arkansas and has been for a coon's age. In 1993 there were 539,186 pickups registered in the state. The following were the top ten best-selling vehicles in Arkansas in 1994. (Note that only three of these are cars.)

1. Chevy 1500		10,366
2. Ford F150		8,418
3. Ford Ranger		4,704
4. Chevy S10		3,561
5. Honda Accord		3,301
6. Ford Explorer		2,105
7. Pontiac Grand Am		2,030
8. Ford Escort		2,026
9. Dodge Caravan		1,981
10. Dodge Dakota		1,854

SOURCE: R. L. Polk

COLORFUL ARKANSAS PLACE NAMES

As Fred W. Allsopp wrote in *Folklore of Romantic Arkansas*, "Few states can compare with Arkansas in the singularity or picturesqueness of its place names." Though some of these names and places have disappeared from our maps, take a gander at the many charming appellations we've come up with through the years.

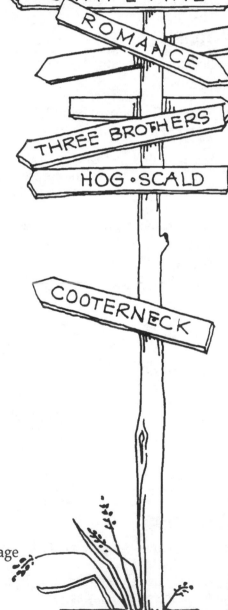

Acorn	Deep Elm
Amity	Deer
Apt	Delight
Back Gate	Denmark
Bald Knob	Dowdy
Battles	Dutch Mills
Bear	Earle
Beaver	Echo
Ben Hur	Egypt
Beverage Town	Emerson
Birdeye	England
Birdsong	Evening Shade
Birdtown	Evening Star
Bloomer	Farewell
Blue Ball	Fifty Six
Blue Eye	Figure Five
Boiling Springs	Flippin
Bonanza	Floral
Bono	Fly Gap
Bright Star	Forty Four
Budd Kidd Springs	Fox
Bug Scuffle	Friendship
Buttermilk	Gin City
Calamine	Goobertown
Calico Rock	Gourdneck
Catalpa	Granny's Gap
Chimes	Grapevine
Coldwater	Gravelly
Colt	Greasy Corner
Cooterneck	Greasy Creek
Coy	Greenwich Village
Cozahome	Grubbs
Cow Faced Hill	Guy
Cricket	Gum Springs

Hasty
Healing Springs
Health
Heart
Hector*(named for President Grover Cleveland's bulldog)*
Hogeye
Hog Jaw
Hog Scald
Hollywood
Hominy
Huff
Ink
Jerusalem
Joy
Lake Dick
Lick Skillet
Light
Little Flock
Lost Corner
Magazine
Magnet Cove
Marble
Marmaduke
Martin Box
Mist
Moccasin Gap
Morningstar
Nail
Natural Steps
Needmore
Nellie's Apron
Number Nine
Oil Trough
Okay
Old Joe
Overcup
Ozone
Pansy
Paris
Peach Orchard
Pee Dee
Peel

Pencil Bluff
Pickles Gap
Poughkeepsie
Prime
Process City
Rag Town
Ralph*(there's also a* Waldo *and* Emerson*)*
Roe
Romance
Rose Bud
Round Pond
Rule
Rush
Saddle
Sam's Throne
Scotland
Smackover
Snowball
Social Hill
Soda Bluff
Stamps
Standard Umpstead
Strawberry
Success
Sunset
Three Brothers
Three Creeks
Toad Suck
Tomato
Treat
Turkey Scratch
Ulm
Umpire
Velvet Ridge
Waldo
Weiner
Welcome
Wild Cherry
Whisp
Whistleville
Yell
Zinc

ARKANSAS FOLK REMEDIES

Long before modern medicine stretched its sterile latex-gloved fingers into the countryside, simple folk concocted their own remedies based on herbs, household ingredients, superstition and half-truths. These folk cures were handed down from generation to generation and traces of these inherited treatments can be found in almost every Arkansas family. Some of these remedies may have helped. Some remedies definitely hurt. Some did nothing at all. But belief in their curative powers was probably the strongest medicine of all. Although the following examples of are not prescribed for what ails you, they are a cinch to put a smile on your lips and possibly make you queasy all at the same time.

❖ **Thrush** To cure a baby with thrush (a mouth fungus), find a man who was born after his daddy died (so he'd never seen his daddy) and have him blow three times in the baby's mouth. A seventh son has the same powers.

❖ **To wean a nursing baby** Put soot on the mother's breast and the baby won't have anything to do with it.

❖ **Boll hives** Scarify the patient by clipping the skin under one shoulder blade, take two drops of blood in a spoon with milk and feed it to the patient.

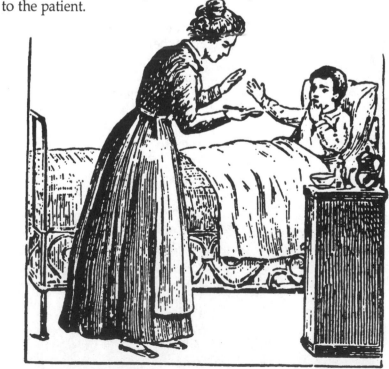

❖ **Chicken pox** Set the patient by the door of the chicken house, then go inside and scare the chickens out so they will fly over the patient and shed feathers on the person with the pox.

❖ **Whooping Cough** Feed the patient goat's or mare's milk.

❖ **Headache** Rub crushed onions on the forehead.

❖ **Earache** Warm some urine and put a few drops in the ear.

❖ **Colic** Tie a bag of asafetida (a stinky plant resin formerly used in medicines) around a colicky baby's neck. Feed the baby breast milk with a drop of kerosene and a drop of asafetida in it.

❖ **Diarrhea** Drink blackberry juice.

❖ **Diarrhea and vomiting** Put five drops of peppermint oil on a level teaspoon of white or brown sugar and eat it.

❖ **Common cold** Melt together tallow, turpentine and coal oil. Dip a flannel cloth into the mixture, wring out, tie around neck and leave overnight.

❖ **Burns** A poultice of raw white potato scrapings will draw out the fire. Or you can boil cottonseed, strain the seed out and mix the water with melted homemade lard to make a salve for the burn. Another option is to coat the burn with egg white to stop the pain immediately and prevent blistering. A third remedy is to have a man who has never seen his daddy blow on the burn and draw out the fire.

❖ **To stop bleeding** Apply a mixture of soot and lard.

❖ **Chigger bites** To stop the itch, rub the bite with chewed snuff or tobacco.

❖ **Poison ivy or oak** Make a lotion of buttermilk and salt or vinegar and salt.

❖ **Croup** Boil together an onion, some turpentine and lard. Dip a cloth in the mixture and put it on the patient's chest.

❖ **Hoarseness** Bake a lemon 20 minutes in a moderate oven. Sweeten with brown sugar and eat.

❖ **Bee or hornet stings** Cut a fresh onion and rub it over the sting.

❖ **Sprained ankle** Mix vinegar and clay into a thick paste. Apply all around the ankle and foot. Leave it on for a day or two, keeping it moist with vinegar.

❖ **Ringworm** Apply the juice of a green walnut hull to affected area.

❖ **Boil** Fill a jar half full of hot water. Place over the boil to form suction.

❖ **To keep from catching measles and whooping cough** tie some asafetida in a rag and wear it around the neck.

Arkansas Banana?

The Paw-Paw Patch

Where, O where is pretty little Susie?
Where, O where is pretty little Susie?
Where, O where is pretty little Susie?
Way down yonder in the paw-paw patch.

Pickin' up paw-paws, puttin' um in her pockets,
Pickin' up paw-paws, puttin' um in her pockets,
Pickin' up paw-paws, puttin' um in her pockets,
Way down yonder in the paw-paw patch.

Come on, boys, let's go find her,
Come on, boys, lets' go find her,
Come on, boys, let's go find her,
Way down yonder in the paw-paw patch.

If you grew up in Arkansas, at some point you probably sang this popular folk song and you most likely wondered "What the heck is a paw-paw anyhow?" Well, the paw-paw (*Asimina triloba* [L] Dunal.) is also called custard apple and Arkansas banana. This small member of the custard apple family, grows to a max of 40 feet high, more typically 15-20 feet. The leaves are large, eight to ten inches long, broad at the end. The edible paw-paw fruit is rounded, from two to five inches long and soft when ripe, greenish yellow to very dark brown. This plant is found state-wide, primarily in mountainous parts on moist northern slopes, protected gullies, coves or small stream valleys. It's usually an "under tree" found in stands of white, red and chinquapin oak, shagbark, hickory and sugar and red maples. Driving through the mountains near Jasper on Scenic Highway 7, the lush foliage of the paw-paws provides an almost tropical ambiance. If you get the urge to pick up paw-paws and put um in your pocket — good luck! The possums and raccoons usually polish off the low-lying Arkansas bananas pretty quickly after the rich fruit matures.

SOURCES: *Trees of Arkansas* by Dwight M. Moore, Arkansas Forestry Commission; *The Folk Songs of North America* by Alan Lomax.

SUPERSTITIONS

People have always had a predilection for assigning meaning to ordinary events in an effort to make sense out of the world around them, and those notions can be very persistent. It is rare to find an individual, regardless of his level of sophistication, who doesn't grow a tad uneasy when a black cat crosses his path. Many of the following bits of superstition and folklore may be familiar. Others, however, may open new avenues for anxiety.

It is bad luck to put a hat on a bed.

A horseshoe over the door brings good luck. This superstition was brought over by settlers from England. There it was believed that St. Dunstan, the patron saint of blacksmiths, shod the Devil's hoof and exacted from the Devil a pledge to stay away from any building where the horseshoe was displayed.

◆ If there's a ring around the moon, it's going to rain.

◆ The hoot of an owl means the weather is going to change.

◆ Planting a cedar tree near a house will bring death to those who live there.

If a girl takes the last piece of cake or bread off a plate, she'll never marry. A girl hoping to snag a guy should never let anyone sweep under her feet when she's sitting down, either.

If lightning strikes more than one time in the same place, it means there's gold buried there.

If your nose itches, someone's comin' with a hole in their britches.

A cricket on the hearth brings good luck.

It's dangerous to drink sweet milk when eating fish.

If it rains while the sun is shining it means the Devil's beating his wife.

◆ Spit on fish bait to bring good fishing luck.

Don't bother wetting that wiggler if you see turtles sunning themselves on logs at the water's edge. Or if the cows are lying down in the field. These are sure signs the fish aren't biting.

DOWN-HOME COOKIN'

Arkansans have always know what good eating was all about – cornbread, a mess of turnip greens, black-eyed peas and a big slab of tomato. In the world as we know it, what can equal the aroma (that's right, *aroma*) of a perfectly vine-ripened tomato? We have traditionally been partial to simple foods from the garden, nearby woods and the catfish pond. Often our choices have been based on economics. Fresh produce and line-caught fish were cheap. Some call our cuisine "soul food." And indeed it is nourishment for the soul as well as for the body for those who've been raised on down-home cooking. We also must own up to a smattering of white trash concoctions featuring Jell-O, Cool Whip and sometimes soda pop as ingredients. But we offer these recipes with no apologies. That's part of who we are. And truth be told, some of these taste pretty darned good. The following are a sampling of some Arkansas down-home favorites that'll make you yearn to get greasy around the mouth.

■ MISS LILLIAN'S CAT-HEAD BISCUITS

(So-called because they're as big as a cat's head.)
2 cups flour
3 teaspoons baking powder
¼ teaspoon baking soda (scant)
½ teaspoon salt
⅓ cup shortening
1 cup buttermilk (If you're fresh out of buttermilk, here's a quick substitute: add 2 tablespoons white vinegar or lemon juice to regular "sweet" milk to make a cup, stir it up and let it sit for five minutes until it clabbers.)

Combine dry ingredients. Cut in shortening until mixture looks like coarse meal. Add buttermilk to make dough. Turn dough onto floured surface and knead lightly. Divide into ten pieces and roll and shape each piece into 1-inch thick circle about the size of a small house cat's head (3 inches diameter). Or you can cut them out using the open end of a large jelly glass. Place on a lightly greased cookie sheet, brush tops with melted butter. Bake in preheated 450° oven for 12 minutes or until brown. These are larapin' good when dipped into a mixture of sorghum syrup marbled with warm butter.

■ MR. BILL'S HUSHPUPPIES

1 cup cornmeal	1½ teaspoon baking soda
1 cup flour	1 tablespoon sugar
1 teaspoon salt	1 egg
Buttermilk	1 tablespoon baking powder
1 bunch green onions, chopped fine	

Combine all ingredients, add enough buttermilk to make a thick batter. Drop by teaspoonfuls into hot oil or shortening. Fry until golden and crunchy.

■ JULIA GAIL'S HOT WATER CORNBREAD

2 cups cornmeal	1 teaspoon salt
¼ cup flour	Boiling water

Combine dry ingredients. Add enough boiling water to make a stiff dough. Form into patties and fry in hot oil or shortening until golden brown. Serve with a smear of butter.

■ COON 'N' SWEET POTATOES

1 raccoon, dressed	1 onion
(black tie optional)	3 cloves garlic
Vinegar	Shortening
Salt and pepper	1 medium green pepper
1 cup chopped celery	5 sweet potatoes
Flour	

Soak coon in mild vinegar and water solution for an hour. Drain, cut coon into small pieces. Sprinkle with salt and pepper; cover with water. Add minced garlic, celery, onion and green pepper and boil until coon is slightly tender. Remove from heat and drain. Brown coon in shortening, then place in roasting pan. Make a brown gravy with the flour and drippings and pour over coon. Surround the coon with peeled sweet potatoes and bake at 350° for about 45 minutes.

■ VENISON POT ROAST

3 - 4 pounds of venison (that's *deer* meat, for the hunting-impaired)

Flour	6 carrots
Shortening	6 potatoes
Salt and pepper	4 onions

Dredge meat with flour, add salt and pepper and brown in hot shortening. Braise meat for 2 to 3 hours over low heat (a little water in a covered skillet). When meat is tender, add vegetables and more hot water. Cook until vegetables are done. Make gravy from the liquid and pour over meat and vegetables. Serves about 8.

■ WILD DUCK WITH WILD RICE

2 ducks	2 tablespoons vinegar
2 cups celery, chopped	1 tablespoon sugar
2 cups onion, chopped	1 teaspoon Worcestershire sauce
2 cloves garlic, minced	2 cups water
2 teaspoons salt	Hot cooked wild rice
¼ teaspoons black pepper	

Put clean ducks in water with 1 teaspoon salt. Bring to a boil, then simmer for an hour. Put the rest of the ingredients in another pan and bring to boil. Take the ducks from the water and place them breast-down in a roasting pan. Pour hot mixture over ducks. Cover and bake for 2 hours at 300°. Uncover and turn ducks over to brown during the last 30 minutes cooking time. Serve with wild rice. Make a sauce with the mixture the ducks were cooked in. (To remove "wild" flavor from duck before you cook it, draw and pick the duck, soak overnight in the fridge in a bath of vinegar with allspice, bay leaves and onion. Drain off liquid before cooking.)

■ SOUTHERN FRIED CATFISH

Don't be turned off by the catfish's "bottom-feeder" image. Arkansas is one of the top catfish producing states and the catfish you find in restaurants and in the grocery store is farm-raised, which means their food intake is controlled. In fact, farm-raised fish convert top-feeders because that's where the food is. Catfish lends itself particularly well to frying. It is also eater-friendly as the few bones the catfish has are primarily large ones rather than those teensy ones that slip past and get hung in the throat.

Here's how to cook catfish to perfection: Put some yellow cornmeal and a generous sprinkling of salt into a brown paper bag. Place rinsed catfish steaks or filets into the bag and shake until they are coated with cornmeal. Drop fish into hot short-ening and fry until golden brown. (You know the grease is hot enough when a match dropped into it will ignite.)

■ **CRAWFISH ETOUFFEE**

Long a staple in the diet of our Cajun neighbors to the south, crawfish (a.k.a. crawdads and Arkansas lobster) is becoming more common in the state due to farming of the crustacean delicacies.

2 ½ pounds crawfish tails (frozen will do)
1 stick butter   2 large onions, chopped fine
3 tablespoons flour
½ cup fresh parsley, chopped
Salt
Freshly ground pepper, to taste

Melt butter in Dutch oven, add flour and mix well over low heat. Add onions, mix well. Cover with ½ inch water and simmer for about 45 minutes, careful not to scorch. Add crawfish tails, season to taste. Simmer 20 minutes more, adding water if needed to thin gravy. Add parsley. Serve over bed of hot rice. Serves 4 - 6.

■ **TURNIP GREENS**

Mess of fresh greens (a *mess* being a large paper bag full)
¼ pound salt pork   1 teaspoon sugar
2 cups of water (or more)   1 teaspoon salt

Boil salt pork in a couple of cups of water in a large covered pot for about 20 minutes. (If you're trying to limit your lard intake, you can substitute a splash of corn oil for the salt pork and still get a tasty pot of greens.) Wash greens thoroughly to get rid of the grit and remove tough stems. Add washed greens to the pot with the pork. Add sugar and salt. Cook on low heat for two hours or until tender. Remove lid and boil a little longer on medium until most of the liquid (pot liquor) is gone. Serves 6 - 8.

■ **SILLA'S POKE SALLET**

Poke sallet is one of those delicacies that Southerners have very strong feelings about (though their feelings are not as strong as the smell that comes from cooking the greens). The deal is that these wild greens 1) smell funny when you cook them, and 2) will make you deathly ill, if you don't parboil them first. Poke has never been cultivated like turnip greens or collards and one explanation is that in order for the seeds to germinate, they must first pass through the digestive systems of birds; therefore they sprout where they land. Right about now you are probably thinking, "thanks for sharing." Anyway, if you're partial to life on the edge, we pass along a family recipe favored by Silla Smith, who thought few things in life could compare with a mess of poke sallet.

Boil young poke greens in salt water until tender. Discard salt water and wash poke greens thoroughly in cold water. Drain greens, then slowly fry in enough bacon grease to season. If desired, beaten eggs can be stirred in while frying. Take care not to over-fry greens.

■ CHEESE GRITS

1 cup grits
4 cups water
1 teaspoon salt
1 stick butter or margarine
1 6-oz. roll garlic cheese
½ cup milk
2 eggs
1 cup sour cream
1 cup grated sharp cheddar

Cook grits in 4 cups water and 1 teaspoon salt according to directions on package. Add butter and garlic cheese to hot grits and stir to melt. Beat eggs with milk; add sour cream. Add mixture slowly to grits and stir. Pour into 2 quart greased casserole, top with grated sharp cheddar. Bake for 45 minutes at 350°. Sprinkle with paprika for a dash of color before serving.

■ AUNT WANDA'S BREAD PUDDING

2 cups scalded milk
¼ cup butter or margarine
2 eggs, slightly beaten
½ cup sugar
¼ teaspoon salt
1 teaspoon ground cinnamon
½ teaspoon nutmeg
3 cups soft day-old bread cubes
(5 or 6 slices)
½ cup raisins

* To prevent bugs from making their homes in your flour and other grains, put a few bay leaves in with the stored grains. Bugs hate bay leaves.

Combine hot milk with butter. Stir milk mixture slowly into beaten eggs; add sugar, salt and spices. Put bread cubes and raisins into 1 ½ quart baking dish that has been lightly greased with butter. Pour milk mixture over and stir gently to moisten bread. Place baking dish in a pan of hot water. Bake at 350° for about 40 minutes or until knife inserted at the edge comes out clean. Remove from hot water. Serve warm or cold. Serves 6.

■ **UNCLE EARL'S WHISKEY SAUCE FOR THE BREAD PUDDING**

> ## Let's have some more bread pudding!

2 egg yolks   ¼ melted butter
2 tablespoons sugar   Whiskey to taste

Beat yolks over medium heat until thick. Remove from heat and gradually beat in butter. Add sugar and whiskey. Drizzle over bread pudding. (Or if you prefer yours "Uncle Earl style"— *douse* it on the pudding.)

■ **CHESS PIE**
It is said that Bill Clinton has a fondness for this Southern treat. Now you, too, can eat like the ruler of the greatest nation on earth.

4 eggs, beaten   4 tablespoons cream
1 ½ cups sugar   1 teaspoon vanilla
2 teaspoons cornmeal   1 unbaked pie shell
¼ cup melted butter   dash salt

Combine all ingredients in order. Blend well; pour into unbaked pie shell. Bake 30 minutes at 350°.

■ **EARTHQUAKE CAKE**

This recipe, or variations thereof, made the rounds in 1990 when residents of northeast Arkansas prepared for a crackpot-predicted quake along the notorious New Madrid fault. Fortunately, the quake did not materialize. This recipe, however, did create a stir. (Your activities are likely to register on the Richter scale as well if you shovel in too many slices of this rich cake.) When this motley cake comes out of the oven, it looks as thought it's been through an earthquake. Not to worry, the taste remains intact.

1 cup chopped pecans
1 cup flaked coconut
1 German chocolate cake mix
1 8-ounce package cream cheese

1 stick margarine
16 ounces powdered sugar
1 teaspoon vanilla extract

Spray bottom of a 9-by-13-inch pan with nonstick vegetable spray. Mix together pecans and coconut and spread in bottom of pan; set aside. Prepare cake mix batter according to directions; pour batter over pecans and coconut mixture. In a mixing bowl, cream together the cream cheese, margarine, powdered sugar and vanilla. Drop by spoonfuls onto batter. Bake at 350° for about 50 minutes.

■ **DIRT PIE**

1 cup cold milk
3 ½ cups (8-oz carton) Cool Whip
1 4-oz package instant chocolate pudding mix
1 ½ cups "rocks" (*granola chunks, chocolate chips, chopped peanuts, etc.*)

20 Oreos crushed
1 graham cracker pie crust

Pour milk into medium bowl. Add pudding mix. Beat with wire whisk until well blended, 1 to 2 minutes. Let stand 5 minutes. Fold in Cool Whip. Stir 1 cup crushed cookies and the "rocks" into pudding mixture. Spoon into pie crust. Sprinkle remaining crushed cookies over top. Freeze until firm (about 4 hours).

■ **MEMAW'S SWEET POTATO PIE**

2 eggs
1 cup sugar
1 teaspoon salt
⅛ teaspoon ground nutmeg
1 ½ cups cooked mashed sweet potatoes (can use canned yams, drain liquid)

1 cup milk
2 tablespoons butter
1 teaspoon ground cinnamon
1 unbaked 8-inch pie shell

Beat eggs slightly; add sugar, salt , spices and milk. Add butter to mashed sweet potatoes and blend well with milk and egg mixture. Pour into unbaked pie shell and bake at 450° for 10 minutes. Reduce heat to 350° and bake for 30-40 minutes or until filling is firm.

■ AUNT MATTIE'S SNICKERDOODLES
(No actual Snickers or doodles in these.)

2 ¾ cups sifted flour
3 teaspoons baking powder
1 ¾ cups sugar, divided use
4 teaspoons cinnamon, divided use

½ teaspoon salt
1 cup soft butter or margarine
2 eggs

Sift flour, baking powder and salt and 2 teaspoons of the cinnamon together. In another bowl, cream butter and 1 ½ cups of the sugar until fluffy. Add eggs and beat. Add dry ingredients gradually and mix well. Chill in refrigerator for an hour, then shape dough into small balls using one teaspoon for each. Combine remaining ¼ cup sugar and 2 teaspoons cinnamon. Roll balls in sugar mixture then place 2 inches apart on ungreased cookie sheet. Bake at 400° about 10 minutes.

■ CLASSIC 7UP POUND CAKE

1 cup butter or margarine, softened
½ cup shortening
3 ½ cups sugar, divided use
1 teaspoon vanilla
1 teaspoon almond extract
1 teaspoon butter-flavored extract
5 eggs
3 cups all-purpose flour
½ teaspoon salt
1 ¼ cups 7Up, divided use.

Heat oven to 300°. Combine butter, shortening, 3 cups of the sugar and extracts in large bowl; beat until light and fluffy. Add eggs, one at a time, beating well after each addition. In another bowl combine flour and salt; add this to the first mixture alternately with 1 cup of the 7Up, beating well after each addition. Spoon into well-greased and floured tube pan. Bake 1 hour and 45 minutes or until done. Cool in pan on wire rack for 10 minutes. Remove from pan. In a small heavy saucepan, combine remaining ¼ cup 7Up and the remaining ½ cup sugar and bring to boil. Boil 2 to 3 minutes or until sugar dissolves. Punch holes in top of cake with a toothpick; spoon glaze over the cake. Cool completely .

■ BLUE CONGEALED SALAD

(No potluck dinner in Arkansas is complete without a congealed salad of some sort.)

1 can pineapple juice
1 can blueberries
2 packages lemon Jell-O
1 mashed banana
½ pint whipped cream

Bring pineapple juice to a boil. Add Jell-O, blueberries (don't drain) and mashed banana. Let cool completely. Top with whipped cream and chill.

■ OKRA DILL PICKLES (about 8 or 9 pint jars)

7 pounds small okra pods
8 or 9 garlic cloves
⅔ cup canning salt
4 teaspoons dill seed

6 small hot peppers
6 cups water
6 cups vinegar

Wash and trim okra. Fill hot pint jars firmly with whole okra, leaving ½-inch head space. Place 1 garlic clove in each jar. Combine salt, dill seed, hot peppers, water and vinegar in large saucepan and bring to a boil. Pour hot pickling solution over okra, leaving ½-inch head space. Remove air bubbles. Wipe jar rims. Adjust lids. Process pints for 10 minutes in a boiling water bath.

■ WATERMELON RIND PRESERVES

(We don't waste *anything!*)

2 pounds prepared rind (2 quarts)
2 pounds sugar (4 ½ cups)
1 - 2 lemons, thinly sliced
6 - 7 ½ cups water

Use *only* the white rind. Cut into 1 inch squares or oblong pieces ½ inch by 1 inch. Cover with lime water and let stand 3-4 hours. (To prepare lime water use: 2 tablespoons calcium oxide [lime] and two quarts water.) Pour off lime water and rinse well. Cover with fresh water and let stand for 2 hours. Boil lemon slices in ½ cup water for 5 minutes. Combine sugar with 7 ½ cups water and bring to boil. Drain rind and add to the syrup. Simmer until the rind becomes clear and tender and the syrup has a honey-like consistency. Add lemon when the syrup thickens. Let stand in the syrup until cold. Pack rind into hot sterilized jars. Bring syrup to a boil and pour over the rind. Adjust the lids and process in a water bath at simmering temperatures for 15 minutes.

■ FIG JAM

2 quarts figs   4 cups sugar   ¼ cup lemon juice

Wash, stem and peel figs. Crush or chop figs. Add sugar. Cook slowly, stirring often until the mixture is thick (about ½ hour). Add lemon juice and stir. Pour into hot sterilized jars. Seal immediately.

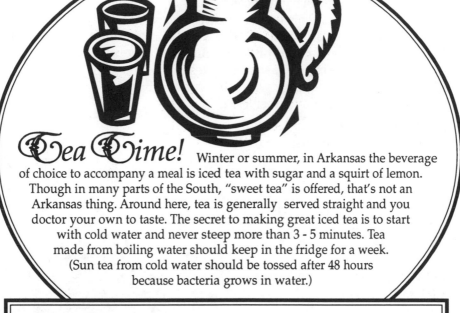

Tea Time! Winter or summer, in Arkansas the beverage of choice to accompany a meal is iced tea with sugar and a squirt of lemon. Though in many parts of the South, "sweet tea" is offered, that's not an Arkansas thing. Around here, tea is generally served straight and you doctor your own to taste. The secret to making great iced tea is to start with cold water and never steep more than 3 - 5 minutes. Tea made from boiling water should keep in the fridge for a week. (Sun tea from cold water should be tossed after 48 hours because bacteria grows in water.)

Tea Trivia!

* Iced tea was born at the 1904 St. Louis Trade Fair. Finding hot tea a hard sell in the summer, one vendor poured the beverage over ice and the fair-goers slurped it up.
* Tea is the second most popular beverage in the world, second only to water.
* A cup of tea has about 40 milligrams of caffeine (a cup of coffee about 150).
* Tea is one of the few natural sources of fluoride.
* The tea bag was a happy accident. A tea merchant sent out samples in small silk bags and customers began ordering tea packed in those bags.
* There are more than 3,000 varieties of tea.
* The terms pekoe (as in orange pekoe, pronounced *PECK-o*) refers to the size of a leaf, not to flavor or a type of tea.

SOURCE: Tea Association of the USA

ONE SMART COOKIE

During a televised debate in the heat of the presidential campaign of 1992, Jerry Brown recklessly charged that while Bill Clinton was governor of Arkansas he had funneled money to his wife's law firm. Hillary was justifiably ticked off and she responded spontaneously, with her now famous, "Well, I could have stayed home and baked cookies." (Rather than pursue a career.) Critics jumped on this like a duck on a June bug, claiming Hillary had cast aspersions on motherhood, apple pie, and "Old Glory." This media feeding frenzy made its way to the pages of *Family Circle's* July 21, 1992, issue, which featured a Bipartisan Bake-off between Hillary and Barbara Bush complete with an invitation for readers to write in and cast their votes for their favorite recipe. The following is Hillary's recipe, which beat out Barbara's cookies when the votes were tallied in November 1992.

Hillary's Chocolate Chip Cookies
1 ½ cups unsifted all-purpose flour
1 teaspoon salt
1 teaspoon baking soda
1 cup solid vegetable shortening
1 cup firmly packed light-brown sugar
½ cup granulated sugar
1 teaspoon vanilla
2 eggs
2 cups old-fashioned rolled oats
1 package (12 ounces) semisweet chocolate chips

Preheat oven to 350°. Grease baking sheets. Combine flour, salt and baking soda on waxed paper. Beat together shortening, sugars and vanilla in large bowl with electric mixer until creamy. Add eggs, beating until light and fluffy. Gradually beat in four mixture and rolled oats. Stir in chocolate chips. Drop batter by well-rounded measuring teaspoonfuls onto greased baking sheets. Bake in preheated 350° oven for 8 to 10 minutes or until golden. Cool cookies on sheets on wire racks 2 minutes. Remove to wire rack and cool completely. Makes 7 ½ dozen cookies.

FRIES WITH THAT HUBCAP?

The March 1995 issue of *Southern Living* ran a list of the best hamburger joints in Arkansas. Here are their choices and comments:

☛ **Cotham's**, Scott. Six-inch hubcap burgers, "nicely grilled and not at all greasy."

☛ **Feltner's Whatta-burger**, Russellville. Burgers that are "several cuts above the chain." Check out the fries and strawberry shakes.

☛ **Fuzzy's Restaurant and Bar**, Fayetteville. Hickory burger with barbecue sauce and cheddar. A "prototypical college-town hangout for chowing down while sipping a beer and watching a game on TV."

☛ **Hugo's**, Fayetteville. This joint is "a delightfully dim restaurant-bar in the basement of a terrific bookstore and coffeehouse."

☛ **L.V. Rogers Package Store**, Pine Bluff. Juicy burgers from fresh ground beef. Served in the backroom of the liquor store. And "don't miss the creamy, surprisingly light Velveeta cheese fudge."

☛ **Sno-White Grill**, Pine Bluff. "Variations on the classic short-order burger: crisp-crusted without being dry."

CRAFTY COUNTRY FOLK

Necessity is indeed the mother of invention. Nowhere is that more evident than in the inventiveness of those who live a rural life. Country folks understand about "makin' do" and the meaning of "waste not, want not." A prime example of native resourcefulness is the quilt. Where we once looked upon these cozy covers as a means to keep warm on chilly nights, over the past few decades hand-pieced quilts have come to be recognized as works of art. Intricate hand-pieced quilts fashioned from scraps of calico and lined with flour sacks now fetch handsome prices (many of the vintage ones go for thousands of dollars). Worn, lovable old quilts, like the ones that graced your grandmother's bed, even turn up in Hollywood eateries as table covers to evoke a "rustic" ambiance while cushioning the bottled water. Who'd a thunk it?

As country has become chic, Arkansas has gained a national reputation for the quality of its arts and crafts. At the Ozark Folk Center in Mountain View you can find a variety of marvelous hand-crafted items, including white oak baskets, rocking chairs, pottery, corn shuck dolls —

as well as quilts. The Arkansas Crafts Galleries, which sell only top-notch juried selections by Arkansas artisans, have four locations around the state. They sell hand-carved wooden bowls and walking sticks, ironworks and pottery among other wares. If you want to go treasure hunting, we offer some suggestions below. You can also happen upon some pretty intriguing stuff for sale along the side of the road, particularly in northwest Arkansas. (U.S. 65 North and Scenic Arkansas 7 are brimming with finds.)

Additionally there are a gazillion arts and crafts fairs held state-wide throughout the year, peaking in the fall. (At many local fairs and bazaars you can find some quality items, but be forewarned — you are also likely to encounter beaucoups of dolls with crocheted hoop skirts to disguise spare rolls of toilet paper, ceramic geese in every incarnation, decorative eyelet-trimmed fly-swatter covers and Razorback *everything*.)

SOME PATTERNS WORTH REPEATING

The following are some popular traditional quilt patterns you are likely to run across in your search for hand-made treasures.

LOG CABIN One of the most common designs of the Colonial days. Also known as Straight Furrow or Barn Raising, depending on the placements of units and colors.

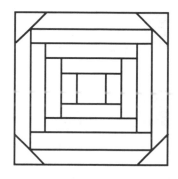

WRENCH Named in the early 1900s, the design is much older but remained un-named for years. Similar patterns are Sherman's March, Hole in the Barn Door and Shoo Fly.

SUNBONNET SUE A favorite for a child's quilt, it is seen in many variations.

ALBUM Also called Friendship Quilt. It was generally made as a gift (especially for hope chests) by friends and relatives who signed blocks they contributed.

GRANDMOTHER'S FLOWER GARDEN Also called Martha Washington's Garden, Mosaic, Hexagon and Honeycomb. (When it is called a "garden" quilt, each flower is surrounded by a row of green to represent flower leaves and then a row of white to represent the winding path through the garden.)

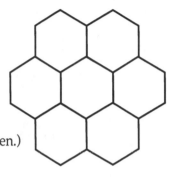

16 PATCH Named in the 1930s, this is a variation of the traditional 4 Patch, so named because each square can be broken into four patches of the same size.

DRESDEN PLATE Got its name in the late 1800s based on the popular porcelain and china from Dresden, Germany. Also known as Friendship Ring or Aster.

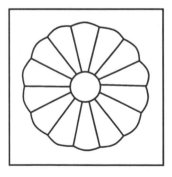

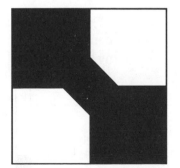

BOW TIE Also known as Neck Tie, this pattern dates from early Colonial days.

TIPS ON SELECTING A QUALITY QUILT

Since the market is currently flooded with cheap imports, here are some guidelines for choosing an authentic, well-crafted homemade quilt.

✔ Fabric should be tightly woven cotton (no polyester or loosely woven imported cotton).

✔ Quilts should have a separate binding around the edges secured with tiny, tight stitching. (Folding the top of the quilt over and stitching it to the back won't cut it.)

✔ Pieces on the quilt top should match up perfectly. Corners on squares and triangles should be sharp and in alignment.

✔ Stitches should be plentiful and compact – roughly five to eight stitches per inch.

WHERE TO SHOP 'TIL YOU DROP

➠ **Arkansas Crafts Galleries** (1-800-952-9941). With over 300 members, one of the most famous crafts guilds in the mid-south is headquartered in Mountain View (Ark. 5, 9 and 14 N). A top-of-the-line, hand-pieced quilt may run anywhere from $200 for a twin to $600 for a king size. Additional outlets:

Hot Springs, 231-A Central Avenue. (501) 321-1640.

Eureka Springs, 33 Spring Street. (501) 253-7072.

Little Rock , Excelsior Hotel. (501) 371-0841.

➠ **Ozark Folk Center** Off Ark. 5, 9, 14, Mountain View. Twenty frontier skills are demonstrated in the park's large crafts forum. (501) 269-3851.

➠ **Ozark Heritage Crafts** Junction of Ark. 7 and I-40, Russellville. (501) 967-3232.

➠ **Ozark Native Crafts** U.S. 71 near Winslow. Handiwork of more than 300 craftspeople offered through this co-op. (501) 634-3791.

➠ **Scenic Highway 7 Arts and Crafters Co-op Gift Shop** Jasper.

➠ **Artist Point** U.S. 71 North of Mountainburg. Locally-made crafts including wood carvings. (501) 369-2226.

➠ **Ferguson's Country Store** U.S. 65, St. Joe.

➠ **Hardy Old Town** U.S. 62-63, Hardy. This preserved 1920s village offers antiques, crafts, specialty stores overlook-ing the Spring River. (501) 856-3210.

➠ **Helena's Old Almer Store**

➠ **Van Buren Historic District**

➠ **Vinson Square** 107 W. Elm, Rogers.

➠ **West Garrison Historic District** Fort Smith.

➠ **War Eagle Fairs** East of Rogers off Highway 12. Affiliated with the Ozark Arts and Crafts Fair Association, two major league fairs are held each year at the scenic War Eagle Mills Farm. Crafts exhibitors must live in Arkansas, Missouri, Kansas or Oklahoma. Over 150 booths. Annual Antique Show and Heritage Crafts Fair is held each year for three days beginning the first Friday in May. War Eagle Fall Fair is held the third weekend in October. (501) 789-5398.

Top Picks For An Old-Fashioned Arkansas Flower Garden

1. Hydrangea
2. Snow Ball Bush
3. Hollyhock
4. Wisteria
5. Daffodils
6. Iris
7. Spirea
8. Cannas

9. Lantana
10. Old-fashioned roses
11. Gardenia
12. Forsythia
13. Honeysuckle
14. Azalea
15. Petunias

DID YOU KNOW?

PRETTY IN PINK

The color of the flowers of the common garden hydrangea vary depending on the pH of the soil. Acidic soil blossoms you see are blue. If you think they are prettier in pink, add lime (the chemical, not the citrus fruit) to the soil to raise the pH. (There are some varieties that have been bred to hold their original color regardless of pH factor, *Ever Blue* and *Pink 'n' Pretty* are two.)

Cannas, those vibrant plants of many varieties that can be anywhere from two to eight feet tall, are also called *Indian Shot*. This is because the black seeds of the plant are so hard that they were used as ammunition by early Colonists.

VITAL STATISTICS

The whole is greater than the sum of our parts.

Though numbers and statistics don't tell the whole story, they do give us some interesting insights into who we are, what we do, how we live and how we die. The following are some Arkansas numbers to crunch for those so inclined.

Numbers are our friends.

POPULATION (1990 Census)

Total: 2,350,725
White: 1,950,674
Nonwhite: 400,051

WHERE THE FOLKS ARE

1. Little Rock (Pulaski County)	175,795
2. Fort Smith (Sebastian County)	72,798
3. North Little Rock (Pulaski County)	61,741
4. Pine Bluff (Jefferson County)	57,140
5. Jonesboro (Craighead County)	46,535
6. Fayetteville (Washington County)	42,099
7. Hot Springs (Garland County)	32,462
8. Springdale (Benton & Washington counties)	29,941
9. Jacksonville (Pulaski County)	29,101
10. West Memphis (Crittenden County)	28,259
11. Conway (Faulkner County)	26,481
12. Rogers (Benton County)	24,692
13. El Dorado (Union County)	23,146
14. Blytheville (Mississippi County)	22,906
15. Texarkana (Miller County)	22,631
16. Russellville (Pope County)	21,260
17. Sherwood (Pulaski County)	18,893
18. Paragould (Greene County)	18,540
19. Benton (Saline County)	18,177
20. Searcy (White County)	15,180
21. Van Buren (Crawford County)	14,979
22. Camden (Ouachita County)	14,380
23. Forest City (St. Francis County)	13,364

24. Bentonville (Benton County) 11,257
25. Magnolia (Columbia County) 11,151
26. Stuttgart (Arkansas County) 10,420
27. Arkadelphia (Clark County) 10,014
28. Harrison (Boone County) 9,922
29. West Helena (Phillips County) 9,695
30. Hope (Hempstead County) 9,643
31. Malvern (Hot Spring County) 9,256
32. Batesville (Independence County) 9,187
33. Bella Vista (Benton County) 9,083
34. Mountain Home (Baxter County) 9,027
35. Osceola (Mississippi County) 8,930
36. Cabot (Lonoke County) 8,319
37. Wynne (Cross County) 8,187
38. Siloam Springs (Benton County) 8,151
39. Monticello (Drew County) 8,116
40. Helena (Phillips County) 7,491
41. Newport (Jackson County) 7,459
42. Maumelle (Pulaski County) 6,714
43. Morrilton (Conway County) 6,551
44. Warren (Bradley County) 6,455
45. Hot Springs Village (Garland & Saline counties) 6,361
46. Trumann (Poinsett County) 6,304
47. Crossett (Ashley County) 6,282
48. Pocahontas (Randolph County) 6,151
49. Marianna (Lee County) 5,910
50. Clarksville (Johnson County) 5,833

▼ Between 1940 and 1950, Arkansas' population declined by almost
40,000 people.

THE TYPICAL ARKANSAN was born in the state; is of Irish, German or
English descent; and is probably a high school graduate. Almost 68% of
us were born here. A little over 1% (24,867) were foreign born (as in
another country, not say *New Jersey*). About 66% of Arkansas residents
25 or older have a high school diploma. Around 13% have a bachelor's
degree or higher. Arkansas is still largely rural with 46.5% of the population living outside the urban areas. (The national average is 24.8%
rural.)

BIRTHS

- There were 34,744 births to Arkansas residents in 1994.
- Nearly one out of every five births (6,978) were to mothers 19 and under.
- Thirty-two percent of all births (11,245) were to unmarried women.
- More than three-fourths of the black births were to unmarried women (5,806 out of 7,855 or 73.9%).
- One-fifth of the white births were to unmarried women (5,317 out of 26,348 or 20.2%).
- About 64% of the teenage births (ages 12-19) were to unmarried teenagers.
- There were 2,846 births weighing less than 5.5 pounds (8.2 % of the total).
- Congenital anomalies (birth defects) were reported on the birth certificates of 466 newborns (1.3% of live births).

SOURCE: Arkansas Department of Vital Statistics 1994, most recent available.

WHAT'S IN A NAME?

The following is a run-down of the top ten most popular names given to children born in Arkansas in 1993 (and *no*, Bubba isn't on the list – at least not officially). Most of the names are pretty predictable: the traditional names with a good helping of biblical influence. But 178 Kaylas and 305 Codys? That Cody thing may indicate that Kathie Lee Gifford's influence is far more pervasive than we'd previously thought.

Girls		Boys	
Ashley	349	Christopher	358
Jessica	324	Michael	336
Brittany	238	Joshua	332
Sarah	231	Tyler	325
Taylor	214	James	317
Emily	206	Zachary	307
Amber	186	Cody	305
Hannah	179	Jacob	277
Kayla	178	William	269
Samantha	168	Matthew	258

SOURCE: Arkansas Department of Health

DEATHS

Infant Mortality

- The Arkansas infant mortality rate was 9.4, while the U.S. death rate was 7.9 (rate per 1,000 live births)
- Black Arkansans had an infant mortality rate of 13.4, compared to a white rate of 8.3.
- Congenital anomalies (birth defects) was the leading cause of infant deaths, claiming 67. Sudden Infant Death Syndrome (SIDS) was second with 30 deaths. Respiratory Distress Syndrome was third with 27 deaths.

Child Deaths: We're Number 9

Death rates among children due to neglect and abuse are higher in Southern and Western states. Of the ten states with the highest death rates, Arkansas ranks ninth. The other states with high death rates: Nevada, Arizona, Florida, Alaska, New Mexico, Mississippi, Georgia, Oklahoma. South Carolina followed Arkansas at number ten. Factors leading to child abuse include poor education, unemployment, poverty, lack of available health care and drug abuse.

SOURCE: Centers for Disease Control and Prevention in Atlanta; University of Missouri (1994)

How Arkansans Die

- Heart Disease – 8,329
- Cancer – 5,903
- Cerebrovascular Disease – 2,176
- Chronic Obstructive Pulmonary Disease – 1,177
- Accidents – 1,143
- Suicide – 371
- HIV – 152
- For Ages 1-34, accidents constituted the leading cause of death – 38% (459) of the deaths for this age group.

Total Arkansas Deaths in 1994 – 26,261

Twenty-two Arkansans were killed in their cars at railroad crossings in 1994.

BEE CAREFUL!

Although snakes give a lot of us the creeps, it seems the critters we ought to fear are bees, cows and the family dog. During the period from 1982 to 1993, forty-two Arkansans died from animal-related injuries. None of those deaths were from snakebite.

- Thirteen deaths from horse-riding accidents.
- One death from a fall from a mule.
- One death by bull-trampling in a rodeo arena.
- Eight cattle-related deaths.
- Nine deaths from wasps, bees or hornet stings.
- Four deaths from dogs: three from attacks, one an elderly woman who was knocked down by a dog.
- Three deaths from riding unspecified animals.
- One death of an Arkansan who stepped on a sea anemone while swimming in the ocean (obviously, while out-of-state).

SOURCE: Arkansas Dept. of Health, *Arkansas Health Counts, Vol. 1, Issue 2,* John Hofheimer, Editor

---

DID YOU KNOW?

HIV:IT'S HERE.

Arkansans are the least informed of all Americans about AIDS and HIV. According to a 1994 survey by the Center for Disease Control in Atlanta, 15% of Arkansans had never even heard of HIV. Pretty alarming since HIV, the virus that causes AIDS, has been reported in each of the 75 counties of Arkansas. Two of every 10 new cases is heterosexually acquired. Two of every 10 new cases is a woman. Four of every 10 new cases is a minority.

From 1983 (when records began) to 1993 there were 2,976 HIV positive cases reported. 1,624 cases of AIDS were reported. In 1993, 64 women were reported to have AIDS. In 1993, seven people under the age of 20 were reported to have AIDS. There were 152 HIV-related deaths in Arkansas in 1994.

SOURCE: Arkansas State Health Department

DIFFERENT STROKES

Arkansas has the highest death rate in the nation for stroke. We have long been part of the "stroke belt," a band of states where death from stroke is elevated enough to set them apart statistically from other parts of the nation. Other stroke belt states include: Oklahoma, Louisiana, Indiana, Tennessee, Virginia, West Virginia, Georgia, Alabama and Mississippi. Stroke is not necessarily a disease of old age. Almost one in four stroke victims is below the age of 65. The Southern diet which can be high in cholesterol and fat as well as smoking, heredity and lack of exercise are risk factors. The most important factor is high blood pressure which effects almost one in three American adults.

UP IN SMOKE

Arkansas has the fourth-highest percentage of smokers among the states, trailing Kentucky, Tennessee and Michigan. Twenty-six percent of Arkansas' adult population smokes. According to a State Health Department survey, Arkansans most likely to smoke are: divorced, white or Hispanic men age 25-34, those who have been unemployed for at least a year, those with an annual income of $20,000-$24,000, those who never attended college.

SOURCE: Arkansas Dept. of Health, 1993 survey.

FOURTH IN FAT

Arkansas weighs in at number four in the nation in obesity – and we're getting fatter all the time according to recent studies. Indiana tops the fatness chart, followed by Mississippi, West Virginia – and our home *sweet* home. Maybe it's time to wave bye-bye to the Moon Pies.

MORE DOUGHNUTS, MR. PRESIDENT?

Bill Clinton is the third heaviest president, at 6 foot 2 ½ and fluctuating between 215 and 235 pounds. The heaviest to date was William Howard Taft who was 6 feet tall and weighed up to 332 pounds and required a special bath tub to be built for him in the White House. Number two in tubbiness was Grover Cleveland at 5 feet 11, weighing 260 pounds.

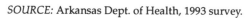

TOPS IN FUNGUS

Arkansas has the dubious distinction of being number one in blastomycosis – a fungal infection that can cause pneumonia. The fungus thrives in wet wooded areas like those in south Arkansas. Some who are exposed to the blastomyces are unaffected by the spores – in fact about 60% of people who've had the infection never know it. But the disease can cause acute and chronic pneumonia. The disease can be fatal, but is treatable. Blastomycosis is rarer than histoplasmosis which is an infection caused from the fungus that lives in blackbird and chicken guano. Though we rank number one among the states in reported cases, there are only about thirty cases a year.

MARRIAGES & DIVORCES

Looking at the numbers, it would seem that we like to get married and we like to get divorced. Arkansas has both a higher marriage and divorce rate than the national average. The most popular month to get married is June; May comes in second. The least favorite month for marriages is January. The most common day for nuptials is Saturday; Friday is second most common. Sunday is the last choice for weddings. Divorce is popular year-round.
- Marriages in 1994 – 38,339
- Median age for the bride was 27, groom 29
- Divorces/annulments – 17,294
- The Arkansas marriage rate was 16.0 compared to a U.S. Rate of 9.1 (rate per 1,000 population).
- The divorce rate was 7.2 for Arkansas and 4.6 for the U.S. (rate per 1,000 population).
- Peak times for divorces in Arkansas are during the first year of marriage and somewhere between the 6th and 10th year.

County Distinctions
- Highest rate of marriage – Carroll County, 168.3 (rate per 1,000 population) Median age of bride 31, groom 33.
- Highest rate of divorce – Independence County, 9.4 (rate per 1,000 population)
- Highest infant mortality – Prairie County (32.3 per 1,000 live births.)
- Highest overall death rate – Baxter County (17.3 per 1,000 population.)
- Highest number of illegitimate births – Phillips County (67 % of live births.)

SOURCE: Arkansas Department of Vital Statistics, 1994

Bang The Pan Loudly: The Shivaree
Derived from the French word charivari, a shivaree is a mock serenade made my blowing toy horns, beating on pans, etc.; often played as a practical joke on newly married couples. Dating from the Middle Ages, the shivaree was still a popular custom earlier this century in many rural areas including Arkansas. Friends of the newlyweds would gather on the wedding night, collect every noise-making utensil they could muster from cow bells to shot guns and make their way to where the newly married couple was hole up for their honeymoon. Then all hell would break loose. The revelers would circle the house clanging and banging and hollering until eventually the couple would open the door and they would all parade in and be treated to refreshments. It was considered a measure of the couples popularity in the community and the more the merrier.

SOURCE: Garden Sass by Nancy McDonough; Laverne Warwick of Royal

RETIREMENT IN ARKANSAS: A GREAT PLACE TO KICK BACK

Arkansas' population has the second highest percentage of elderly residents of the 50 states. Florida ranks number one. So why do so many people come to Arkansas to retire? For a variety of reasons. Natural beauty alone lures many who after a lifetime of dealing with freeways and smog and hassle yearn to get away from it all. Arkansas enjoys a mild climate with short winters so you can pretty well golf year-round. Most Arkansans don't own a snow shovel. Arkansas residents are also among the least- taxed in the country, ranking 49th in per capita state and local taxes. The national average is $2,083. Arkansas residents average $1,334. Property taxes are much lower here as well. And here you can get more bang for the buck – your money will buy more in Arkansas where the cost of living is reasonable. Of course, we like to think people relocate here because we welcome them with a generous dose of Southern hospitality. Neighbors in Arkansas not only know your name – they know your dog's name.

In addition to the numerous amenities targeted toward retirees, there are several planned resort/retirement developments scattered about the state.

- **Bella Vista Village** *210 Town Center S.E., Bella Vista, AR 72714. 1-800-228-7328.* Located on Hwy. 7 North near the Arkansas-Missouri border in Benton County. Established in 1965, this community has 12,000 residents. Six golf courses, eight lakes, three country clubs, pools and more.
- **Cherokee Village** *P.O. Box 250, Cherokee Village, AR 72525. 1-800-228-7328.* Begun in 1954 as one of the nation's first planned retirement communities. Located in the Ozark foothills of Sharp County. Two golf courses, seven lakes.
- **Diamondhead** *Box 7053, Hot Springs, AR 71913; (501) 262 4470.* Located 15 miles southeast of Hot Springs and surrounded by Lake Catherine. Development began in 1970. Golf course, Olympic-sized pool, country club.

- **Fairfield Bay** *P.O. Box 1008; Fairfield Bay, AR 72088. (501) 884 -3333.* Established in 1966 on the north shore of the 40,0000-acre Greers Ferry Lake in north central Arkansas. Two championship golf courses, ten lighted tennis courts, Olympic-sized pool, health spa, marina. Three thousand permanent residents.
- **Holiday Island** *2 Holiday Island Drive; Holiday Island, Eureka Springs, AR 72632; 1-800-643-2988.* Located seven miles north of Eureka Springs on the White River. Founded in 1970, there are about 1,000 permanent residents. Golf course, pools, Table Rock and Beaver lakes, marina and yacht club.
- **Horseshoe Bend** *P.O. Box 4083; Horseshoe Bend, AR 72512; (501) 670-5433.* Located in the foothills of the Ozark Mountains. Community offers golf, tennis, pool.
- **Hot Springs Village** *1110 Cooper Circle; Hot Springs Village, AR 71909; 1-800-228-7328.* Located 16 miles northeast of Hot Springs with about 9,000 full-time residents. Security, medical services, day care, pool and fitness center, RV campsite, community center with ball-room, banquet kitchen and meeting rooms.
- **Ozark Acres** *P.O. Box 207; Hardy, AR 72542. (501) 966-4317.* Founded in 1959 and located eight miles east of Hardy, 525 residents. Two lakes, pool, boating and fishing.

INCOME IN ARKANSAS: STILL PATHETIC AFTER ALL THESE YEARS

During the Depression in 1933, the per capita income in Arkansas was $152. (That's per year, folks!) Before the stock market crash in 1929, the annual per capita was a whopping $305. In 1941 the average income was $423, barely above Mississippi and below every other state. The national average at that time was $885. In 1955 we really surged ahead – the average household income was $1,062. In 1983, Arkansas was still 49th. We held on to our record in 1993 with an average income of $15,994 (as usual, saved from last place by Mississippi at $14,708.) The national average was $20,781.

Arkansas has been an exceptionally slow learner when it comes to teacher salaries. In 1938 the average yearly salary for a teacher in Arkansas was $570, while the national average was $1,374. As Elliott West cleverly points out in his introduction to the reprinted *WPA Guide to 1930s Arkansas*, "had a school teacher left Arkansas to work anywhere else among all the states, territories and protectorates, he or she would have made less only by a finding a job in Mississippi, Samoa, or Guam."

SOURCES: U.S. Department of Commerce; *WPA Guide to 1930s Arkansas*

ARKANSAS BORING?

So says The Boring Institute, a weird New Jersey outfit that delights in provoking the media. Based on massive media overexposure, Arkansas garnered tenth place among the institute's 11th annual "Most Boring Celebrities of the Year" honorees. (Not too shabby for a state few people had even heard of a few short years ago.) We'd like to say thank you for this award. It's an honor just to be nominated.

SOURCE: The Boring Institute, Maplewood, N.J., 1994

CRIME AND PUNISHMENT

In the early days, Arkansas had a reputation for being a lawless, violent place where murder and mayhem were the norm. Unfortunately, it would seem that history is repeating itself. The violence that permeates our society has not by-passed this small state. The number of homicides in Arkansas climbed 62% between 1987 and 1994. In 1994 there were 293 murders and 1,026 reported rapes in Arkansas.

MURDERS

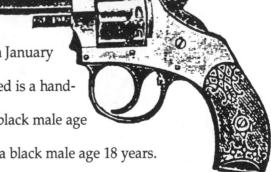

- Most murders occurred in September (34).
- Least murders occurred in January (20).
- Most frequent weapon used is a handgun (53.6%).
- Most frequent victim is a black male age 21-25 years.
- Most frequent offender is a black male age 18 years.

RAPE

- In 1994 there were 1,026 rapes reported in Arkansas.
- Fifty-three percent of the rapes occurred on the week-end, 20% of those on Saturday.
- Between midnight and 2 a.m. was the most common time for a rape to be committed.
- More rapes occurred in June. The least in January.
- Three of every five victims were white. White victims have increased 27% over a five-year period. Black victims have decreased 6%.
- Two victims were less than one year old. The oldest was 94.
- Almost three-fourths of all rapes were committed by persons known to the victim. 24% of those involved family members.
- 40% of all rapes occurred in the victim's residence.
- Most frequent victim is a white female 13-15 years old.
- Most frequent arrestee was a white male 18-20 years old.

Weapon type used in murders

- Handgun 157
- Rifle 18
- Shotgun 24
- Other firearms 18
- Knife/cutting instrument 29
- Club or blunt object 17
- Hands, fists, etc. 10
- Fire 3
- Strangulation/asphyxiation ... 7
- Other 12

Total Murders 1994 293

SOURCE: Lynn Bulloch, Arkansas Crime Information 1994

The Brady Law went into effect on February 28, 1994. Through December 31, 1994, the Arkansas State Police used the law to prevent 352 illegal handgun purchases. Most of those who were denied guns due to background checks were convicted felons. Every day 76 handguns are purchased in Arkansans.

WHERE YOU DO THE TIME IF YOU DO THE CRIME

The following is a breakdown of the facilities which are part of the Arkansas Department of Corrections. The administrative offices of the department are located in Pine Bluff.

- **Benton Unit** Established in 1874. Located five miles south of Benton off Hwy. 67 in Saline County. Minimum security. Capacity 325 inmates. Work release, pre-release, substance abuse treatment program,education, regional maintenance.

- **Cummins Unit** Established in 1902. Located 28 miles south of Pine Bluff, off Hwy. 65 in Lincoln County. Custody level: maximum-medium-minimum. Capacity 1,850. Approximately 16, 500 acres. Agricultural operations: Livestock, field crops, edible crops, feed mill, slaughterhouse, poultry. Industrial operations: vinyl products/silk screening, engraving, garment factory, furniture refinishing.

- **Varner Unit** Established 1987, 28 miles south of Pine Bluff off Hwy. 65 in Lincoln County. Custody level: maximum-medium-minimum. Capacity 1100. Acreage same as Cummins. Agricultural operations: vegetable processing plant, field and edible crops.

- **Delta Regional Unit** Established in 1990. Located 50 miles southeast of Pine Bluff in Chicot County. Custody level: Medium-Minimum. Unit capacity: 400.

- **Diagnostic Unit** Established in 1981. West of Pine Bluff off West 7th Street in Jefferson County. 137 acres. Custody level: medium-minimum. Unit capacity: 467. Industrial operations: garment factory. Special operations: Intake – all male inmates, except death row inmates, are tested and classified at the unit before being transferred to a permanent unit. Special program unit for mental health, hospital facility, regional maintenance unit, construction warehouse, central warehouse, substance abuse treatment program and education.
- **Pine Bluff Unit** Established 1976, same location as Diagnostic Unit. Medium-minimum security. Capacity 438. Industrial operations: garment factory. Special program unit for mental health.
- **East Arkansas Regional Unit** Established 1992, 17 miles southeast of Forrest City in Lee County. Custody level: medium-minimum. Capacity: 600. 2,500 acres. Special Operations: education.
- **Jefferson County Jail/Correctional Facility** Established 1990. West of Pine Bluff off West 7th Street. Custody level: medium-minimum. Capacity 400. Special operations: jail.
- **Maximum Security** Established 1983, 25 miles northeast of Pine Bluff, off Hwy. 15 in Tucker, Jefferson County. Unit capacity 432. 4,420 acres. Agricultural operations: field and edible crops. Death Row, substance abuse treatment program, education.
- **Tucker Unit** Established 1916. Located 25 miles northeast of Pine Bluff. Capacity 796: 676 female inmates, 120 male inmates. Custody level: maximum-medium-minimum. Agricultural operations: field and edible crops. Industrial operations: mattress, bus and fire truck refurbishing, school desk, chair repair, athletic equipment, graphic arts and microfilming. Women's intake and housing, work/study release, pre-release, substance abuse treatment program, education, vocational education.
- **Wrightsville Unit** Established 1981. Located 10 miles south of Little Rock off Hwy. 365 in Wrightsville, Pulaski County. Custody level: medium-minimum. Capacity 800 (includes 150 beds at the Boot Camp Program). Acreage: 3,300. Agricultural operations: beef production. Industrial operations: duplicating, furniture manufacturing.
- **Mississippi County Work Release** Established 1975, one mile west of Luxora off Meadow Road. Minimum security. Unit capacity 71. Work

release, regional maintenance unit, substance abuse treatment program, education.

- **North Central Unit** Established 1990, three miles north of Calico Rock off Hwy. 5 in Izard County. 599 acres. Custody level; medium-minimum. Capacity: 300. Substance abuse treatment program, education.
- **Northwest Arkansas Work Release Center** Established 1980. Located in the City Administration Building in Springdale. Custody level: minimum. Capacity: 16.
- **Texarkana Regional Correction Center** Established 1983. Located 100 North Stateline Avenue. Custody level: minimum. Capacity 119. Regional maintenance unit, work release center, education, substance abuse treatment program, bi-state detention center.

INMATE INFO
- Inmate population: 8,333
- Bedspace capacity: 8014
- Average daily inmate population: 8,916
- Average monthly inmate admissions: 280
- Average monthly inmate violators returned: 74
- Average monthly inmates discharged: 75
- Average monthly inmates paroled: 192
- Total inmates released: 4,043
- Sex of inmates – Male: 93.8%, Female 6.2%
- Black 57.9%, White 41.6 % Other, .5 %
- Average age of inmates 31.6 years
- Overall age of admissions: 28.4
- Security level: Maximum: 15.7%, Medium 50%, Minimum 33.7%
- Average length of sentence for admissions: 9 years, 6 months
- Average length of stay before release: 2 years, 5 months.
- Average Beta I.Q. of Inmate – 87.3
- Percentage of inmates who admitted using drugs or alcohol at time of the crime: 42%.
- Average inmate cost per day: $32.95
- Ratio of security officers to inmates 1:5

TOP FIVE OFFENSES (percent of inmate population by category)
1. Drug offenses – 16.2%
2. Burglary – 16.0%
3. Homicide – 15.7%
4. Sex Offenses – 11.8%
5. Aggravated Robbery – 10.4%

SOURCE: Dept. of Corrections, June 30, 1994

TRIPLE EXECUTIONS

Three men were executed by the state of Arkansas at Cummins Prison on August 3, 1994, between 7 and 9:15 p.m. This was the first time in 32 years that any state has executed three people on a single day. Darryl Richley, Hoyt Clines, James Holmes were tried and convicted together along with a fourth man, Michael Ray Orndorff in the 1981 slaying of Rogers businessman Don Lehman. An error in Orndorff's trial was discovered by the court of appeals earlier in the year and he was removed from death row. Richley, Clines and Holmes were put to death by lethal injection. The last time there were multiple executions in Arkansas was in 1939.

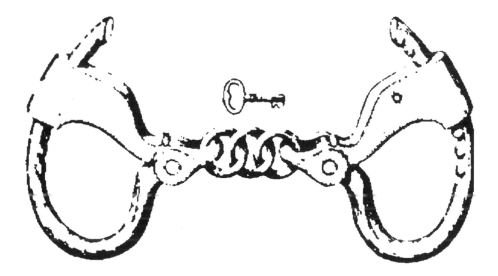

ANNUAL EVENTS

Start with a coon supper, end with a Nutcracker

Here's a sampling of the numerous fairs, festivals, events and activities held each year in the state. Yep, Arkansas has everything from a coon supper to a national documentary film festival. You can join UFO panel discussions, study soap making, chase greased pigs, tour bat caves or cheer the crowning of Miss Champagnolle Bottoms. Since we can't list them all, we've confined the entries to those events that have been around for a while and/or appear to be well-attended. Then again, sometimes we note events just because we enjoy the name – as in the case of the Strange Family Bluegrass Festival held in Texarkana. Be sure to check with local chambers of commerce for precise dates, times and fees since these often vary from year to year.

Yippee! It's coon supper time!

JANUARY

Coon Supper Gillett. What better way to ring in the new year! This annual fund-raiser is an Arkansas political tradition and never fails to attract a passel of pols. And is it any wonder? The folks in Gillett prepare quite a feast with over 1,400 pounds of raccoon meat to entice our public servants. (If you're a culinary right-winger, don't despair. There are plenty of conservative meats served as well.)

Buffalo National River Events Jasper. Eagle awareness week, elk watch.

Eagles Et Cetera Weekend Bismarck (DeGray State Park). Lake tours, art exhibit, raptor demonstrations, guided bird walks.

Thoroughbred Racing at Oaklawn Hot Springs. Live horse racing through April. The Racing Festival of the South (last week of the meet) culminates in the Arkansas Derby, a prep race for the Kentucky Derby.

FEBRUARY

Arkansas Flower and Garden Show Little Rock (Statehouse Convention Center). World-class flower show, landscaped gardens, commercial exhibits.

Hikes, Hugs and Hearts Morrilton (Petit Jean State Park). The romantic legend of the ill-fated French damsel "Petit Jean" is at the heart of this evening of guided hikes, candlelight dinner and dance. Reservations required.

Quad State Regional Toughman Contest Texarkana. Regional boxing and tough guy contests.

Valentine's Day Gala Washington (Old Washington Historic State Park). Romantic celebration at historic 1832 Williams Tavern with food and entertainment in 19th century style. Reservations required.

Winter Wings Weekend Lake Village (Lake Chicot State Park). Field trips for avid birders to explore southeastern Arkansas in winter.

MARCH

Arkansas Marathon Booneville. Twenty-six mile foot race following scenic route along Arkansas Highway 10. A fairly fast course with three small hills. Free admission.

Bass Fishing School Ashdown (Millwood State Park). Brush up on your bass angling.

Battle of Poison Spring Re-enactment Chidester (Poison Spring State Park). Re-creation of the Civil War battle that took place here April 18, 1864.

Jonquil Festival Old Washington State Park. Thousands of blooming jonquils, some of which were planted by early settlers. Arts, crafts, tours of historic structures.

Mid-Southern Watercolorists Exhibit Little Rock (Arkansas Arts Center). Competitive exhibit featuring some of the best watercolor artists in the region.

Pepsi Cola Walleye Classic Fairfield Bay (Greers Ferry Lake). Entry Fee.
Pioneer Craft Festival Rison (Pioneer Village). Craftspeople demonstrate soap making, basket weaving and quilting. Country music and wagon rides.
Professional Championship Rodeo Texarkana (Four States Fairgrounds). Professional cowboys from the four-state area compete: calf scramble, saddlebronc, bullfighting and bareback.
Red Stocking Revue Fort Smith. Follies with local talent. Songs, skits, dances.
Spring Nationals Motor Sports Truck Pull Extravaganza Texarkana (Four States Fairgrounds). The battle of the monster trucks.
Used Book Sale Roland (Pinnacle Mountain State Park). Something for everyone. Cheap.
Victorian Classic 10K Meter Run Eureka Springs. 10K race plus a two-mile fun run and/or walk through the hilly historic district.

APRIL

Arkansas Federation of Porcelain Artists Convention El Dorado. Porcelain art created by native artists; world-famous artists demonstrate their talents.
Arkansas Folk Festival Mountain View (Ozark Folk Center). This popular festival has been pulling 'em in for over three decades. Special guest performers, crafts demonstrations, guest and staff musicians. Additional activities in downtown Mountain View.
Barrett Hamilton Young Arkansas Artists Exhibition Little Rock (Arkansas Arts Center). A competitive exhibition featuring paintings, drawings and sculpture by Arkansas students in grades K-12.
Blue Sky Mule Days Fayetteville. Mule jumps and races, old-time single mule pulls.
Celebration of Birds Lake Village.
Ding Dong Days Dumas. Games, entertainment, 5K run.
Fiddle Contest and Spring Folk Music Festival Eureka Springs.
Fordyce on the Cotton Belt Festival Fordyce. Celebration of the town's railroad heritage with free train rides, parades, quilt show and sale, 5K run.
Hogskin Holidays Hampton. Greased pig races, hog calling, pig kissing and pageants for Little Miss Pig Tails and Miss Champagnolle Bottoms.
Indian Lore Days Wilson (Hampson Museum State Park). Demonstrations of Native American crafts and skills.

Invitational Fiddle Competition Mountain View.
New Shiloh Arts and Crafts Fair Magazine.
Ozark Foothills Craft Guild Show and Sale Mountain View.

Ozark Scottish Festival and Highland Games Batesville. Scottish festival with bagpipe competitions, parade, athletic competitions and more.
Ozark UFO Conference Eureka Springs. Speakers, panel discussions dealing with UFO reports from around the world; reports on unexplained phenomena like "crop circles." Testimonials from those who have had run-ins with extra-terrestrials. Admission charged.
Dulcimer Jamboree Mountain View (Ozark Folk Center). Workshops in playing mountain or hammered dulcimer, beginner through intermediate levels; nationally-known instructors, mini-concerts; competition for Southern Regional Dulcimer Championship.
South Arkansas Mayhaw Festival El Dorado (Rainey-Newton House). Day-long music and dancing. Jelly-making demonstrations, mayhaws and mayhaw jelly for sale. Country lunch served.
Spinach Festival Alma, the "spinach-canning capital of the world" and home of the world's largest spinach can. Parade featuring Popeye, a pancake breakfast, games, pony rides and a spinach drop.
Spring Tour of Historic Homes Eureka Springs. Sponsored by the Bed and Breakfast Association.
Turkey Track Pasture Pickin' Waldron. Crafts show and bluegrass jam sessions.
Wye Mountain Daffodil Festival Bigelow. Nothing but yellow as far as the eye can see. Seven acres of daffodils featuring 30 varieties. Crafts, barbecue and lots of buttercups.

MAY

Arkansas Catfish Festival Eudora. Catfish cook-off, catfish eating contest, catfish racing, industry trade show and competition for the honor of being Miss Catfish.
Arkansas Heritage Week Sponsored by the Department of Arkansas Heritage, this celebration actually lasts ten days. Activities spotlighting the state's colorful history are planned statewide. Call for a schedule: (501) 324-9150.
Armadillo Festival Hamburg. Live armadillo show, street dance, carnival, Little Mr. and Miss Armadillo crowned.

Back-in-the-Hills Antique Show and Heritage Crafts Fair War Eagle.
Belle Fort Smith Tour of Historic Restorations Fort Smith.
Boggy Creek Monster Day Fouke. Celebrate the legend of Bigfoot, the hairy six-foot monster reportedly spotted here in the early 1970s. There's food, crafts, games, live country music and carriage rides to keep those fears at bay. There's also a monster hunt for the those who dare.
Bryant Alive Bryant. Parades, food, crafts.
Christian Motorcycle Association State Rally Hatfield. Cycle games, fish fry, talent contest and two religious services per day.
Crawfish Festival Dermott (downtown). Crawfish eating contest, beauty pageants, bands, dancing, 5K race.
Free State of Yell Fest Dardanelle. Yelling contest, carnival, antique cars, ugly dog contest, fireworks and pageants.
Greek Food Festival Little Rock (Annunciation Greek Orthodox Church). Greek, mid-Eastern and Indian foods; groceries, pastries. Belly dancers.
Historic Helena Tour of Homes Helena.
Library Book Sale Little Rock (main library downtown). Sponsored by FOCAL, Friends of the Central Arkansas Libraries, this twice-yearly sale is a book lover's dream.
Loose Caboose Festival Paragould. Celebration of Paragould's railroad heritage. Street basketball, carnival, arts and crafts, three entertainment stages.
Magnolia Blossom Festival Magnolia. Sidewalk art show, live music, car show, kids carnival; archery, bass, golf, softball, bowling, and domino tournaments.
Mount Nebo Chicken Fry Dardanelle.
Old Fort Days Barrel Racing Futurity Fort Smith (Harper Stadium). This is the worlds' largest barrel racing competition. Open to registered Quarter horses, competitors come from as far away as Canada for the three races with total purses around $400,000.
Picklefest Atkins. The state's pickle capital celebrates with tours of the pickle processing plant, pickle-eating, pickle juice drinking, rodeo, music, crafts and more.
Quapaw Quarter Spring Tour of Homes Little Rock. Celebration of history, architecture and neighborhood revitalization of restored private homes built in 19th and early 20th centuries.

Regional Air Show Fort Smith. U.S. military aircraft displays and performances by national flying forces. Astounding aerobatics, music, food.

Riverfest Little Rock. Celebration of the visual and performing arts with entertainment on four stages. Food vendors.

Sidewalk Arts and Crafts Fair Eureka Springs.

Spring Tour of Homes Batesville.

Territorial Restoration Craft Show and Festival Little Rock.

Toad Suck Daze Conway (Toad Suck Lock and Dam). Three-days of food, rides, crafts, toad-jumping contest.

Wildwood Festival of Music and the Arts Little Rock (Wildwood Park). Month-long celebration of the arts that runs the artistic gamut from *The Barber of Seville* to a country hoedown. The festival draws many well-known artists and performers.

World's Championship Steak Cook-Off Magnolia. Competition for showmanship, best-looking pit, best-cooked steak (16-ounce rib eye). Celebrity judges pick the best steaks and the governor presents awards. Steak dinners with all the trimmings are served to the public (for a fee) and entertainment follows the meal.

JUNE

Antique Auto Show and Swap Meet Morrilton (Petit Jean Mountain). Antique and classic cars compete for awards. Over 1,250 vendor spaces selling body parts (automotive) and accessories.

Bradley County Pink Tomato Festival Warren. Miss and Little Miss Pink Tomato beauty pageants, talent contest, carnival, street dance music jamboree, and All-Tomato Luncheon pay tribute to Arkansas' official vegetable (though botanically a fruit).

Brickfest Malvern. Celebration of the "brick capital of the world" includes tennis tournament, concert and brick-making, brick-toss and best-dressed brick contest.

Buffalo National River Canoe Race Marshall.

Dog Show Texarkana. All-breed dog shows and obedience trials.

Lonoke Minnow Madness Lonoke.

Lum and Abner Days Mena. Celebration of Mena natives Chester Lauk and Norris Goff, stars of the popular 1940s radio show "Lum and Abner." Music, arts and crafts, pageants.

Mosquitofest McCrory. Mosquito-Swat Dash, The Great Mosquito Chase 5K Run, Shriner's parade, concessions.

Oil Town Festival Smackover. Celebration of the town's oil boom days.

Old Timers Day Van Buren.

Ozarks Native Arts and Crafts Fair Winslow.

Perch Jerk Classic Jersey. Two-person team fishing tournament for ages 10 and up.

Purple Hull Pea Festival Emerson. Crafts, games, Miss Purple Hull Pea crowned, World Championship Rotary Tiller Race.

Railroad Days Festival McGehee.

Rusty Wheels Old Engine Club Show Western Grove. Demonstrations of antique gas and steam engines, grist and saw mills, old cars, antique and classic cars.

JULY

Bat-O-Rama West Fork (Devil's Den State Park). Guided cave tours to see the bats, bat talks, bat house building demonstration.

Grape Festival Altus. Grape stomp, street dances, fresh grapes and wine tasting here in "Napa Valley East."

Johnson County Peach Festival Clarksville. Oldest outdoor festival in the state. Crafts, sports, games and lots of peaches. Princess Elberta, Queen Elberta and Miss Arkansas Valley pageants.

Rodeo of the Ozarks Springdale. One of the biggest rodeos in the country, features big-name cowboys and cowgirls.

That Dam Night Run Arkadelphia. DeGray Lake Dam 5K has run, walk and wheelchair divisions.

White River Carnival Batesville. One of Arkansas' oldest festivals. Hot air balloons, youth fishing tournament, driving tours of historic Batesville, bass classic, ski show, arts, crafts, Miss White River Pageant.

Fourth of July celebrations are held in many towns around the state. Check with local chambers for specifics.

AUGUST

Albert E. Brumley Sundown to Sunup Gospel Sing Springdale.

Arkansas Championship Grape Stomp and Wine Fest Paris. Blessing of the new wine, bluegrass music, grape stomping and wine tasting.

Great Arkansas Pig-Out Morrilton. Street dance, concert and lots of food vendors.

Great Mosquito Assault and World Championship Mosquito Calling Contest Walcott (Crowley's Ridge State Park). Insect repellent testing chamber, games and some serious bug info.

Greers Ferry and Little Red River Water Festival Heber Springs. Water ski shows, fishing contests and more.

Hammered Dulcimer Workshops Mountain View (Ozark Folk Center State Park). Reservations required.

Hang-In Dardanelle (Mount Nebo). Hang gliders from everywhere swoop off Mt. Nebo.

Hanging Dice Nationals Fort Smith. Dealers from across U.S. show off their custom rods dating from 1935-1964.

Junkfest Marshall. Arkansas' largest yard sale with over 150 independent yard sales held along U.S. 65.

Logan County Musical Convention Booneville. Oldest event of its type west of the Mississippi River. Gospel music, quartets, solos, composers, groups from Arkansas and sur- rounding states participate in this songfest.

Northwest Arkansas Bluegrass Festival Harrison.

Old Soldiers Reunion Heber Springs. Parades, carnival, fireworks and Miss Cleburne County Pageant.

Pine Tree Festival Dierks. Arts, crafts, beauty pageants, talent show, 5K run.

Possum Stampede 5K Race Hot Springs (Lake Catherine State Park). Challenging course, trophies and unique prizes.

Rodeo and Parade Crossett. Miss Rodeo Arkansas contest.

Southern Gospel Sing Cabot.

Strange Family Bluegrass Festival Texarkana (Strange Family Park). Music, crafts, social with lots of Strange family members.

Tontitown Grape Festival Tontitown. Over 6,000 pounds of homemade pasta and sauce are served at the Italian spaghetti dinners highlighting this tasty festival. Carnival, crafts and live bands add to the harvest celebration.

Watermelon Festival Hope. Watermelon-eating and seed-spitting contests, crafts, music and more in the town where Bill Clinton was born.

Wild Orchid Hunt McNeil (Logoly State Park). Guided trail walks to look for wildflowers and the Crane Fly orchid.

Zoo Days Little Rock. Food entertainment, arts and crafts and, of course, animals.

SEPTEMBER

Antique Car Show Morrilton (Museum of Automobiles). Vintage car show and competition.

Arkansas Jazz and Blues Fest Hot Springs.

Arkansas Mountain Bike Championships West Fork (Devil's Den State Park). State championship series races.

Clothesline Fair Prairie Grove Battlefield State Park. Over 200 arts and crafts exhibitors spread out over the battlefield. Gospel and country music, square dancing and tours of historic structures.

Diamond City Gem, Mineral and Jewelry Show Murfreesboro. Diamond cutting demonstration, gem dealers, crafts and flea market, barbecue and entertainment on the square.

Flintknapping Day Scott (Toltec Mounds Archaeological State Park). Guest flintknappers demonstrate techniques used by Native Americans to turn stone into tools and weapons. Films, guided tours of park.

Four States Fair Texarkana. Professional rodeo, carnival, exhibits, and more.

Frog Fantasies Festival Eureka Springs. Frog fanciers gather to share frog art and memorabilia.

Great Arkansas Clean-Up Statewide. Thousands of volunteers pitch in to clean litter from the shorelines of Arkansas' rivers, lakes and state parks. A free picnic for the volunteers is held at most sites afterwards. Contact Corps of Engineers.

Hawk Watch Roland (Pinnacle Mountain State Park). Help the Audubon Society spot migrating birds of prey. Films in the visitor center.

Jazz Festival Eureka Springs. Traditional, swing and contemporary jazz performed at various clubs, bed and breakfasts, and the Basin Park band shell.

Ouachita Indians Fall Fest and Pow Pow Mt. Ida. Indian arts and crafts, dancing, games, native foods.

Riverfront Blues Festival Fort Smith. Organized to preserve and perpetuate American blues, festival features nationally-known performers.

Solemn Ol' Judge Days Mammoth Spring. Event honors Judge George D. Hay, founder of the Grand Ole Opry. He came up with the idea while in Mammoth Spring.

Summerset North Little Rock (Burns Park). Labor Day week-end celebration to ring out the summer. Arts and crafts booths, food, music and face-painting.

Winefest Altus (Weiderkehr Village). Arts, crafts, grape stomping, German band, polka dancing, hot air balloons.

County fairs are held throughout the state this month and next. Check locally for details.

OCTOBER

American Crossbow Tournament Huntsville (Withrow Springs State Park).

Antique Show and Sale Fayetteville.

Arkansas Apple Festival Lincoln. Hootenanny, seed popping and apple core throwing competitions.

Arkansas Rice Festival Weiner. Tickle your taste buds with over 500 different rice dishes to sample for free. Entertainment, farming and crafts exhibits, beauty pageants, cooking contests.

Arkansas State Fair and Livestock Show Little Rock Fairgrounds. Giant midway, concerts with big-name entertainers, rodeo, and lots of cotton candy and funnel cakes to eat right before you climb aboard the Tilt-a-Whirl. Date varies.

Arts and Crafts Festival Bella Vista. 500 exhibitors, food vendors. Proceeds benefit charities and scholarships.

Autumnfest Fayetteville. A major event with formal ball, street dance, arts and crafts.

Bean Fest and Great Arkansas Championship Outhouse Race Mountain View. Bean cook-off, parade, talent show, free beans and cornbread lunch. Great race of outbuildings around the town square.

Boone County Quilt Show and Sale Harrison.

Civil War Weekend Lake Village. Living history demonstrations, Southern Belle Social.

Donna Douglas Arts and Crafts Festival Eureka Springs (Holiday Island). Artists and craftspeople sell their wares. Miss Douglas (Ellie May Clampett) signs autographs daily — if she's not takin' a dip in the cement pond.

Fall Foliage Color Tour Jasper. Buses leave from the gazebo on the Jasper Square for day trip. Bring sack lunch.

Great North American Bed Race Texarkana. "Homemade" beds compete for speed, showmanship and originality.

King Biscuit Blues Festival Helena (downtown historic district). The best in Delta blues is performed by many of the greats who got their start on the 1940s "King Biscuit Time" radio show. Gospel, blues, barbecue cook-off, games.

Mt. Magazine Frontier Days Paris. Log sawing, nail driving, beard contest, antique cars and more.

Mums, Music and Muscadines Festival Jacksonville. Business expo and trade show, 5K run, dog show, carnival.

Music Fest El Dorado. All kinds of music, food booths, family activities.

Octoberfest Hot Springs. German harvest celebration includes costume contest (lots of lederhosen seen around the Arlington this time of year), German food, music, games for kids, 5K race.

Ozark Creative Writers Conference Eureka Springs. For those interested in promoting and learning creative writing. Best-selling authors featured. Fee charged.

Pumpkin Fantasy Land Forrest City. Come see pumpkins (as well as their relatives squash and gourd) decked out in costumes and make-up and on display for your viewing pleasure. Conveniently located next to the pick-your-own pumpkin patch.

Sheep to Shawl Springdale (Shiloh Museum). Demonstrations of the steps involved in producing a piece of cloth from shearing to weaving.

Terrapin Derby Day Lepanto.
War Eagle Fair Hindsville (War Eagle Mills Farm). One of the most highly respected crafts shows in the country. Over 350 booths of weaving, woodworking, basket-making, stained glass and more.
Wiggins Cabin Festival Crossett. Juried arts and crafts festival on the grounds of the historic Wiggins Cabin.
Wild Turkey Calling Contest and Turkey Trot Festival Yellville. 10K race, parade, beauty pageant, Miss and Mr. Drumstick contests, turkey dinner.
World's Championship Quartz Crystal Dig Mt. Ida. Rock hounds try their luck at winning cash and trophies by digging the best crystals from area mines. Entry fee.

NOVEMBER

Arkansas Celebration of the Arts Hot Springs. Week-long celebration of the thriving arts scene in Arkansas. Features the Gallery Walk, open houses. Art and sculpture for display and sale. Poetry readings. Activities take place in the downtown Central Arts District, all within easy walking distance. Events are free and open to the public.
Buck Fever Festival Banks. Celebration of the deer hunt. Antler exhibitions and competitions.
Chili Challenge Greers Ferry. Chili cook-off, games, entertainment, celebs.
Christmas Arts and Crafts Extravaganza North Little Rock (Northside YMCA).
Christmas in Lights Eureka Springs. Downtown historic district as well as many of the Victorian homes are decorated.
Documentary Film Festival Hot Springs (Malco Theater). This is the only documentary film festival in the U. S. outside of Los Angeles. Award-winning films from around the world are shown. Many filmmakers accompany their films for informal discussions after showings. Admission is free and there's plenty of espresso for sale at the coffee shops downtown.
Festival of Trees Little Rock (Statehouse Convention Center). Black-tie preview party, style show luncheon, Tux 'n' Trees silent auction featuring some of the state's most beautifully-decorated trees. General admission viewing of trees. Proceeds go to cancer research.

Fun With Fungus Mushroom Workshop Roland (Pinnacle Mountain State Park). Learn how to identify local edible and poisonous mushrooms and take a walk to search for fungi.

Library Book Sale Little Rock (main library downtown). Sponsored by FOCAL, Friends of the Central Arkansas Libraries, this book sale offers up zillions of discarded and donated books of all kinds as well as sheet music, maps, records, old magazines. Something for everyone and dirt cheap.

South Arkansas Quartet Convention Hot Springs (Grand Avenue Baptist Church). Groups from Arkansas and Texas belt out Southern gospel.

Toys Designed by Artists Exhibition Little Rock (Decorative Arts Museum). Contemporary toys designed by artists in competitive exhibition.

Original Ozark Folk Festival Eureka Springs. This is the folk festival that started it all. Music workshops and concerts.

Wheelchair Basketball Tournament Sherwood. National championship was won in '91, '93 and '94 by The Rollin' Razorbacks.

World's Championship Duck Calling Contest and Wings Over the Prairie Festival Stuttgart. Duck gumbo cook-off, duck calling classes and contests, Sportsman's Dinner and Dance.

DECEMBER

Candlelight Carol Service Conway (Hendrix College Greene Chapel). Scripture reading and choral responses performed almost entirely by candlelight.

Christmas at the Ace of Clubs House Texarkana. Historic house built in the shape of a playing card "club" and financed by poker winnings is decked out in Victoriana.

Christmas Frolic Little Rock (Territorial Restoration). Celebration of frontier Arkansas Christmas traditions.

Christmas to Share Hot Springs. Arkansas' largest Christmas party for senior citizens. Refreshments, entertainment, door prizes.

Delta Art Exhibition Little Rock (Arkansas Arts Center). This regional competition of art and sculpture is one of the best in the South.

King Cotton Classic Pine Bluff (Convention Center). *The New York Times* hailed this event as the top high school basketball tournament in the U.S. See the cream of the high school athletes dribble toward college and pro status.
The Nutcracker There are more performances of the ubiquitous Christmas ballet than there are freckles on a turkey egg. There's bound to be a Sugar Plum Fairy tip-toeing about your neck of the woods this holiday season.
Winter Bird Seed Sales McNeil (Logoly State Park). Feeders and birdseed for sale. Held in conjunction with the Arkansas Wildlife Federation.
Christmas parades and celebrations are held statewide this month. Check your local listings.

THE NATURAL STATE

Ticks, chiggers, critters and more...

We don't call it "The Natural State" for nothing. Mother Nature has been very generous to Arkansas. We are blessed with clean air, clear water, lush forests and abundant wildlife. But Mother Nature also has her quirky side – hence ticks and chiggers. And tornadoes. And the humidity. Oh, all right, nothing's perfect. But sometimes Arkansas comes pretty darned close. In the following chapter we take a look at the good and the not-so-good that go into making Arkansas a natural wonder.

HUNTING

Sixty percent of Arkansas is forests – that's over 20 million acres. Seventy-five percent of the state is rural. That means endless cover for game of all kinds. Some of the more important game species in Arkansas are profiled below (if there's no declared season, the species is off-limits). Hunting licenses can be purchased at most sporting goods stores or from the Game and Fish Commission. For information about licensing and hunting regulations call them at (501) 223-6300. And while we're on the subject of rules, remember what your mother always told you and pick up after yourself. Get an education (hunter, that is). Mind your manners – respect the rights of other people and their property – don't go barging in uninvited and start shooting off your weapon six ways to Sunday. Don't take more than you can eat – it's wasteful. And though your mother may not have mentioned it, for heaven's sake don't shoot yourself or anyone else.

WHITE-TAIL DEER

This is the state's most important large game species. All 75 counties have deer, making Arkansas the most convenient deer-hunting state in the South. The white-tail deer is one of the Game and Fish Commission's biggest success stories. In the 1920s, fewer than 500 of this species remained in Arkansas. Proper management has brought the population back to an estimated 750,000 animals. No matter at what point you enter the state, you are never far away from deer cover. In addition to the regular Arkansas deer season, there is a special season for archers – both longbow and crossbow. With over 3,000,000 acres in national forests open to public hunting, and other vast tracts managed for timber production, there is no lack of range for deer.

TURKEY

The eastern wild turkey is the species native to the state. Because of their size, beauty and sagacity, hunters consider the wild turkey the very finest of game birds. They are wary and it takes skill and patience to call them within gun range.

BOBWHITE QUAIL

Often called partridge, this bird is distributed throughout the state. Arkansas is nearly as well known for its quail hunting as for its waterfowl shooting. Between the higher mountains and the intensively cultivated Delta, there is an abundance of the type of habitat preferred by bobwhites.

SQUIRRELS

Both gray and fox squirrels range throughout the timbered lands of the state. Hardwood trees which provide food in the form of acorns and other nuts, and hollows for dens are essential to their existence. The squirrel is the state's most important game animal in terms of the numbers who hunt them.

RABBITS

Two species of rabbit are found here. The cottontail ranges in shrubby and grassland habitat on the uplands. Swamp rabbits are found along streams and bayous.

DOVES

The mourning dove nests in and migrates through the state. During fall migrations, large numbers concentrate where grain crops are grown. They are hunted principally in the eastern part of the state.

DUCKS AND GEESE

Arkansas is probably most famous for the excellence of its waterfowl hunting. Originally, much of the eastern portion of the state was covered with lakes and swamps. Although drainage has reduced the extent of the water areas, ducks still congregate in large numbers on the lakes, overflow waters and rice fields. Stuttgart is at the center of duck country and calls itself the "duck capital of the world." During the shooting season, the mallard is by far the most numerous duck species, and the most sought after. Other species include: pintail, wood duck, teal, black duck, baldpate and gadwall. Canada, blue, snow and white-fronted geese migrate across Arkansas each fall as they move from breeding to wintering grounds.

OFF LIMITS

All wildlife in the state is protected by law unless a declared hunting season has been established by the Commission (if you aren't certain, call and ask before you shoot). There are many species that are not fair game, among them are:

- Golden Eagle
- Bald Eagle
- Great Horned Owl
- Screech Owl
- Barn Owl
- Alligator Snapping Turtle
- Elk
- Red Fox
- Turkey Vulture
- Alligator
- Red-Tailed Hawk

GET SMART!

Anyone born since January 1, 1969, is required to pass a hunter education course before hunting in Arkansas. The only exception is for those hunters under age 16 who hunt under the direct supervision of a licensed adult at least 21 years old. The course is offered free from the Game and Fish Commission. It is recommended that students be at least 11 years old. The course is a minimum ten hours of instruction. Too often parents buy a gun for a child without making sure the youngster receives proper training. Many veteran hunters have developed unsafe

hunting practices and unethical habits. Statistics prove that hunter education can help eliminate many of the tragic accidents that happen each year. To find out when the next course will be taught in your area call (501) 223-6377 in Little Rock or tollfree 1-800-482-5795 from anywhere else.

HUNTER SAFETY TIPS

- Treat every gun as though it were loaded and ready to fire.
- Never point a gun at anything you don't want to shoot; keep safety on until ready to shoot.
- Unload guns when not in use. Take down or have actions open; guns should be carried in cases to shooting area. Always unload firearms before riding in any vehicle, including ATVs.
- Be sure barrel is clear of obstructions. Take only ammunition specifically intended for the gun you are using.
- Be absolutely sure of your target and what is beyond it before you pull the trigger. Know the identifying features of the game you hunt.
- Wear hunter orange so you can be seen.
- Know the range of your gun. Even a .22 rimfire can travel over 2½ miles.
- Never climb a tree or fence or jump a ditch with a loaded gun. Never pull a gun toward you by the muzzle.
- Never shoot a bullet at a flat, hard surface or water. At target practice be sure your backstop is adequate.
- Store guns and ammunition separately. Keep beyond the reach of children.
- Avoid alcoholic beverages before or during shooting.

TURN IN POACHERS!

To report game law violations call 1-800-482-9262. Rewards up to $500 are offered for information resulting in a citation being issued for major game and fish violations. You can remain anonymous. Report what you've seen as quickly as possible, in as much detail as possible – such as license plate numbers, vehicle description, etc. and leave the rest to the wildlife officers.

GO WITH THE GLOW

It is unlawful to hunt or to accompany a hunter during a declared gun or muzzleloading deer season without wearing a hat and an outer garment above the waistline of hunter orange or chartreuse. These bright fluorescent colors are more visible than others (especially at dawn and dusk), are not found in nature, and don't blend with other colors – which is why they are so effective.

TIPS FOR THE GREAT OUTDOORS

- To waterproof canvas camping equipment, paint on this mixture: 6 cups soybean oil and 3 cups turpentine and let dry. (Caution: turpentine is toxic and flammable.)
- To waterproof matches: dip kitchen matches (about half way down the wood) into melted paraffin wax. Let cool.
- Put a dash of salt into your coffeepot to enhance the flavor of your coffee.
- Wash your hands in salt water to remove the fish odor.
- If you sprinkle salt into the frying pan before frying fish, they won't stick to the bottom.

Animal Gestation and Longevity

Animal	Gestation (days avg.)	Longevity (yrs)
Beaver	122	5
Cat	63	12
Cow	284	15
Deer (white-tail)	201	8
Dog	61	12
Fox (red)	52	7
Goat	151	8
Guinea Pig	68	4
Horse	330	20
Mouse (field)	21	3
Opossum	14-17	1
Pig	112	10
Rabbit	37	5
Sheep	154	12
Squirrel (gray)	44	10
Wolf	63	5

FISHING

Whether you're on the creek bank dunking a red wiggler from a cane pole or cruising the river outfitted in Eddie Bauer behind the wheel of a $20,000 bass boat, fishing can be great fun. With over 12,000 miles of fishable streams and over 600,000 acres of lakes in the state, Arkansas has some of the finest fishing in the nation. The following are some of the state's more important game fish, with tips on where to find them and how to snag them. Remember if you're 16 or older, you need a license. Call the Game and Fish Commission at (501) 223-6300 for details.

Get more fishing thrills with a

CATCH·EM·QUICK ®
lifelike **LURE**
WORLD'S FASTEST SELLING LURE
PROTECTED BY U. S. PAT. 2,792,662

BLUEGILL

(Lepomis machrochirus) Common names: bream, brim, perch. The bluegill varies in color probably more than any other sunfish, from pale blue to bright orange, depending on the water where it lives. The males are usually dark bluish-green with darker areas arranged in vertical bars. The females are usually lighter. A dark spot is normally found on the back part of the dorsal fin. They feed mainly on insects, but also eat microscopic plants, shrimp, crayfish and snails. More bluegills are caught in the state than any other fish.
Habitat: Bluegills are found throughout the state, but rarely in cool, swift streams.
Bait: Earthworms and crickets. Can be caught on small jigs, popping bugs and wet flies.

LARGEMOUTH BASS

(Micropterus salmoides) Common names: bigmouth bass, lineside, green trout. Usually dark green on the back and sides, shading to white on the belly. May weigh upwards of 20 pounds, but most are from one to three pounds.

Habitat: Found statewide, they are the most commonly caught bass on most lakes and stock ponds. Early spring and fall are the best fishing times.

Bait: Feed on insects, small fish, crayfish and can be caught on a variety of lures made to imitate these natural foods.

SPOTTED BASS

(*Micropterus punctulatus*) Common name: Kentucky bass. Olive green on the back with numerous dark blotches, usually diamond-shaped. Scales below the lateral line have dark bases forming lengthwise rows of small spots (hence, the name). A six-pounder is large; one to three pounds common.

Habitat: Generally distributed statewide, may be found in same waters as smallmouth or largemouth. More commonly stream fish, may also be found in deep, clear water lakes with clean rock shorelines.

Bait: Best is live crayfish. Also, small spinning lures and minnow imitations.

SMALLMOUTH BASS

(*Micropterus dolomieui*) Common names: brownie, bronze bass. Generally brown or bronze on back and sides, with vertical, dark olive-colored bars, grayish belly. Seldom exceeds seven pounds; one to two pounds most common.

Habitat: Found in Ozark and Ouachita mountains in north and western Arkansas in streams, rivers and large, clear, man-made lakes. Pound for pound, the smallmouth is said to be one of the fightingest fish around, especially on light spinning gear. According to *Outdoor Life* magazine, the Caddo River heads the list of the five top Southern streams for smallmouth bass. White Oak Lake (April through May) is also listed as one of the top Southern bass waters.

Bait: Live bait, small spinning lures and minnow imitations are best.

STRIPED BASS

(*Morone saxatilis*) Common names: ocean striper, striper, white bass, rock fish. Similar to white bass, but grows much larger, has darker side stripes. Many five to ten pounders are caught and some over 40 pounds. Excellent sporting fish and good eating.

Habitat: They have been stocked into many large reservoirs, some smaller lakes and occur in the Arkansas and Red rivers. Using radio transmitters, freshwater striped bass have been shown to cover up to 50 miles in a day.

Bait: Most are caught by trolling deep-running artificial lures or shad imitation baits; also on or near the surface while schooling or spawning.

WHITE BASS

(Morone chrysops)
Common names: sand bass, striped bass. Silvery, with dark horizontal stripes along the sides. Several three to four pound white bass are caught each year, but the average is three-fourths to one and a half pounds.
Habitat: Common in Arkansas and Mississippi

Lutz original **PORK BAITS**

THE BLACK RASCAL
Mister Bass Won't Let It Pass!

Never before such an enticing bass lure! It produces action a-plenty . . . crazy, nervous, fish-catching action that big lunkers just can't resist. Exclusive (patented) Lutz features make the Black 'Rascal the outstanding bass bait, the delight and joy of fishermen everywhere . . a record-maker at Bull Shoals, Norfork, Ouachita.

One trial will convince you! Sizes for all equipment from fly-fishing to surf-casting.

6" Size Jar of 3	9" Size Jar of 2	4" Size Jar of 3	2" Size Jar of 3
75c	$1.00	75c	75c

Also try the many other tried-and-proved Lutz Pork Baits . . . famous for fish-catching!

LUTZ PORK BAIT COMPANY
1234 Jefferson   Kansas City 5, Mo.
AT ALL LEADING TACKLE STORES

rivers and has been stocked in many man-made reservoirs across the state. Young fish eat primarily insects; adults eat insects, shad, minnows and other small fish. They are a schooling fish and can often be caught in large numbers when a school is located – usually by seeing small fish jump out of the water to elude the white bass. Best times: during spring spawning runs and during late summer and fall schooling.
Bait: Small plugs and spoons are best lures.

BUFFALO FISH

(Ictiobus spp.) Common names: gourdhead, blue rooter, razorback. Three species are found in the state: bigmouth, smallmouth and black. All are potentially large, thick-bodied weighing two to 20 pounds.
Habitat: Found in southern and eastern parts of the state in rich or turbid waters, chiefly in larger rivers, streams, natural and man-made lakes. Seldom caught on hook and line. However, thousands of pounds of this excellent eating fish are caught each year with trammel nets and other commercial fishing gear.

CHANNEL CATFISH

(Ictalurus punctatus) Common names: fiddler, willow cat, forked-tail, blue channel. Like all catfish, channel has smooth scaleless body, barbels or "whiskers" on upper and lower jaws and sharp stiff spines on the dorsal and pectoral fins. Body is usually gray to greenish-gray, shading to white under the belly. Sides and back are usually spotted. May weigh up to 30 pounds, usually two to ten. This is the type of catfish served in most restaurants, usually fried whole or in steaks.
Habitat: Found statewide, they have been stocked extensively by the Arkansas Game and Fish Commission and many private fish farmers. Naturally a stream and river fish, it has adapted well to natural and man-made lakes. Will eat almost anything including insects, fish,

crayfish and carrion.
Bait: Worms, minnows, cut bait and artificial lures.

FLATHEAD CATFISH

(*Pylodictis olivaris*) Common names: mud cat, yellow cat, shovelhead cat, Appaloosa cat. The flathead has a flat head (surprise, surprise), wide mouth and small eyes set high on the head. Mottled yellowish-brown color. Ninety to 100 pound flatheads are not uncommon; average is two to twenty pounds. Flatheads are an important commercial fish. Big, bone-free steaks can be cut from large fish.
Habitat: Found statewide, but uncommon in the mountainous headwater streams. A solitary species spending the day in deep water near cover, they move into shallow to feed at night. Natural foods include insects (for the smaller flatheads), fish and crayfish.
Bait: Live or freshly killed bait is used on trotlines, jugs and rod and reels.

BLUE CATFISH

(*Ictalurus furcatus*) Common names: white fulton, cold boarder, blue channel cat. Similar to the channel, but almost never has dark spots on the back and sides. It grows much larger than the channel, occasionally weighing more than 100 pounds. Three to 20 is more common. A valuable commercial food fish.
Habitat: They normally inhabit large rivers and reservoirs. Most common in the Arkansas River. Found in moving water, not still pools. Often caught below dams on the Arkansas River.
Bait: Trotlines and jug lines baited with fish or other live bait are favorite ways to catch blue cats.

DID YOU KNOW?

THE ONE THAT GOT AWAY

The fossil skull of a 10-foot-long 1,500-pound catfish that lived 40-45 million years ago was found in south Arkansas. The two-foot-long skull with the bone of a nine-inch dorsal fin still protruding was found in Camden in October 1983. The giant catfish had lived in the shallow sea that once covered south Arkansas. The catfish fossil, a rarity in itself, is the first one ever found in Arkansas. Most catfish fossils in North America have been found in Wyoming.

BROWN TROUT

(Salmo trutta fario) Olive brown on the dorsal surface with lower sides and belly yellowish or white. The brown trout differs from other trout in having dark and rusty red spots on the sides of its body that are surrounded by pale halos. Unlike the rainbow, the tail is not usually forked and is without spots.

Habitat: Like the rainbow, the brown trout is not native to Arkansas but has been widely stocked and can be found in same locations as rainbow. The current world-record brown trout is a 40-pound 4-ounce whopper caught in the Little Red River in 1992.

Bait: Brown trout are fond of baby rainbow trout and will bite artificial rainbow trout lures. They also love crawdad tails.

GET A GRIP!

When handling catfish, wear gloves. The spiny pectoral and dorsal fins easily puncture skin. The spines, however, are not poisonous as many people think. The sting you feel when you are poked is from the fish's slimy coating which will burn any open wound. If you get stuck, wash thoroughly to avoid infection.

SAUGER

(Stizotedion canadense) Common names: jack, jack salmon, pike. Long, cylindrical body, sharp teeth. Resembles the walleye, but does not have the large blotch on the back of dorsal fin. One to two pounds is average.

Habitat: Found in large rivers, tolerates more turbid waters than the walleye. Most commonly found in the Arkansas River, most are caught in the turbulent water below the navigation dams.

Bait: Live minnows or small fish-imitating lures. Deep-running lures and spoons are sometimes trolled for sauger.

WALLEYE

(Stizostedion vitreum) Common names: walleyed pike, jack salmon, pike jackfish. Slender, cylindrical body, large canine teeth, whitish eye. Fifteen to 18 pounders occasionally caught; average is two to five pounds.

Habitat: Found in large, cool mountain streams of northern and western Arkansas and in many large, deep cool-water impoundments. Natural food is fish. They are voracious feeders and help keep the

smaller fish thinned out.
Bait: Live minnows, large jigs or plugs. Fish at night or late evening.

WARMOUTH

(*Lepomis gulosus*) Common names: goggle-eye, mud bass. Dark olive to gray-colored fish with brownish sides and yellowish markings, large mouth, red-rimmed eye, only three anal spines.
Habitat: Commonly found in eastern and southern Arkansas in sluggish streams and lakes. Prefers slow-moving, weedy, mud-bottomed waters.
Bait: Worms, wet flies and popping bugs.

LITTLE FISHES

There are 57 species of minnows. Most minnows are small stream fishes often used by fishermen for bait and serve as a vital link in the natural food chain by converting plant material to animal material for use by larger fish and other animals. While most minnows are small, the introduced carp, goldfish and grass carp are also true minnows. There are more species of minnows than any other group of fishes.

SAY "RED WIGGLER"

The trend toward catch-and-release fishing has resulted in fiberglass fish mounts. All you do is provide a participating taxidermist with a clear photo of your trophy and exact length and girth measurements and – *Voila!* A true replica of your prize fish. The Freshwater Fishing Hall of Fame has also introduced a new program for recognizing record fish that were released. For more information: Freshwater Fishing Hall of Fame; Box 33; Hayward, WI 54843. (715) 634-4440.

FLOAT STREAMS

Many of Arkansas' float streams are calm enough so you can do just that – float. Others offer some pretty swift currents, so be sure you know which kind you're up to. The following are some of the states more prominent streams.

- Big Piney Creek
- Buffalo River
- Caddo River
- Cadron Creek
- Cossatot River
- Eleven Point River
- Little Missouri River
- White River
- Kings River
- Mulberry River
- Ouachita River
- Saline River
- Spring River
- Strawberry River
- Little Red River

WILD THINGS – KEEP OUT!

You want to discourage woodland creatures from doing lunch in your garden. You don't want to blow them away and a fence is too pricey. So what do you do?

- Plant a perimeter of marigolds, the pungent odor repels rabbits (the African variety is the most effective).
- Plant a living fence to discourage deer: thorny bushes like holly, hawthorn and Japanese barberry. Deer aren't partial to English ivy, irises or daffodils – but they are fond of fruit trees and strawberry plants.
- Slugs? Well, those marigolds and vegetables attract these nocturnal nibblers. Bury a few jars up to the rim in the soil around your plants. Fill the jars with cheap beer and the slugs will slime over, crawl into the jar and drown. And you don't even have to put up a neon sign.
- Large dogs are a good deterrent for those pesky squirrels, a.k.a. tree rats.
- For Pete's sake don't feed the animals if you don't want them hanging around your house. They'll be back with their friends.

NATIONAL WILDLIFE REFUGES

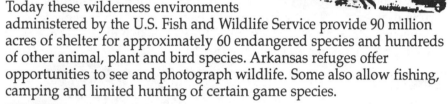

In 1903 President Theodore Roosevelt signed an executive order protecting our feathered friends on Florida's Pelican Island – birds like the egret and heron whose plumes were sought for ladies' hats. The feathered hats went out of style, but fortunately the refuge concept didn't. Today these wilderness environments administered by the U.S. Fish and Wildlife Service provide 90 million acres of shelter for approximately 60 endangered species and hundreds of other animal, plant and bird species. Arkansas refuges offer opportunities to see and photograph wildlife. Some also allow fishing, camping and limited hunting of certain game species.

BIG LAKE

11,038 acres. Located in Manila, this is the oldest federal refuge in Arkansas and one of the oldest inland refuges in America. Established in 1915.

FELSENTHAL

65,000 acres. Established in 1975, this is Arkansas' newest refuge. Located in south Arkansas near Huttig.

HOLLA BEND

6,367 acres. Near Russellville. One of Arkansas' best spots for viewing and photographing wildlife, particularly eagles and waterfowl.

OVERFLOW

6,140 acres. Near Crossett.

WAPANOCCA

5,485 acres. 15 miles north of West Memphis. Bought in 1961 with revenue collected from duck stamps.

WHITE RIVER

113,000 acres. Dewitt. Dedicated in 1935 as a sanctuary for migratory waterfowl, this is the largest refuge in the state.

GOING...GOING...GONE.

ENDANGERED SPECIES

Despite the richness of our state's wildlife, many animals like the panther that once roamed our state have disappeared from Arkansas' landscape. Many other species that were once plentiful, like the passenger pigeon, have disappeared altogether from the face of the earth. All fish and wildlife within the state of Arkansas are fully protected by the Game and Fish Commission regulations. To reiterate, if there's no declared hunting season on a particular species, then it's illegal to take it. In addition to the state regulations, the federal Endangered Species Act imposes a maximum fine of $50,000 or one year imprisonment or both for the taking or harming of any protected species. There are currently 24 endangered and threatened fish and wildlife species recognized for the state of Arkansas. Over the past ten years 11 new species have been added to the list. *Endangered* means any species which is in danger of extinction throughout all or a significant portion of its range. *Threatened* means any species which is likely to become an endangered species within the foreseeable future. The following is a list of the species in jeopardy.

MAMMALS
INDIANA BAT

(Myotis sodalis) Endangered. The decline in numbers of this insectivorous species is due mainly to commercialization of caves, desecration by vandals and disturbances causes by spelunkers. Range in northern Arkansas.

OZARK BIG-EARED BAT

(Plecotus townsendii ingens) Endangered. Same as above. Range in northwestern Arkansas.

GRAY BAT

(Myotis grisescens) Endangered. Same situation as above. Range in north Arkansas. There is a colony of gray bats inhabiting Bonanza Cave in Baxter County under the protection of the U.S. Forest Service.

FLORIDA PANTHER

(Felis concolor coryi) Endangered. Range entire state, at one time. Long thought to be extinct in Arkansas due to loss of habitat, persecution by predator control programs and a serious decline in the panther's prey, the white-tail deer, during the early 1900s. There have been no sightings of panthers in Arkansas for years.

BIRDS

BALD EAGLE

(Haliaeetus leucocephalus) Endangered. Range entire state. Loss of habitat, egg-shell thinning due to pesticide poisoning and human persecution brought the bald eagle to desperately low numbers. But through successful efforts to raise and release eagles in to the wild, the population has been steadily growing. There are currently 10 pairs of breeding eagles in the state. Lake DeGray is a favorite habitat.

ARCTIC PEREGRINE FALCON

(Falco peregrinus tundrius) Threatened. Eastern part of state (transient). A victim of pesticide poisoning, the peregrine falcon which preys upon other birds in flight, is probably only a migrant in Arkansas during the winter months. This falcon, the fastest bird in North America, is capable of speeds up to 180 miles per hour in a dive.

LEAST TERN

(Sterna antillarum) Interior population endangered. Range Mississippi River and tributaries. This small, inland-nesting seagull-like bird is having a difficult time surviving due to severe loss of its breeding areas. Man now regulates most sand-bed rivers for flood control, water supply, etc., disturbing the natural flow of the water and altering the character of the beaches. Additionally, the birds must compete with humans for beach space and are often unsuccessful rearing their young around human disturbances.

BACHMAN'S WARBLER

(Vermivora bachmanii) Endangered. Eastern part of state. This very small warbler was once found in the river swamps of the entire southeastern United States. Loss of habitat has reduced the population to near extinction. There are no verified reports since 1910.

IVORY-BILLED WOODPECKER

(Campephilus principalis) Endangered. Range northeastern and southern Arkansas and Arkansas River. A combination of early persecution and the continued destruction of the bottomland habitat of this magnificent bird has reduced the population to near extinction. The last reference to an Arkansas sighting was in 1891.

RED-COCKADED WOODPECKER

(Picoides [=Dendrocopos] borealis) Endangered. Talk about picky! This bird requires 80 - 100 year old living pines afflicted with heartwood disease for nesting purposes. Modern timber practices have eliminated most of its nesting habitat, but the U.S. Forest Service and certain lumber companies have set aside areas where this bird's special

requirements will continue to exist. Efforts to protect the woodpecker have resulted in an increase in the bird population.

REPTILES
AMERICAN ALLIGATOR

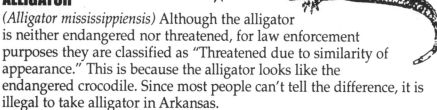

(Alligator mississippiensis) Although the alligator is neither endangered nor threatened, for law enforcement purposes they are classified as "Threatened due to similarity of appearance." This is because the alligator looks like the endangered crocodile. Since most people can't tell the difference, it is illegal to take alligator in Arkansas.

FISHES
OZARK CAVEFISH

(Amblyopsis rosae) Threatened. Benton County. These blind, white, almost translucent fish resemble catfish but are the size of guppies. They live in underground streams. Like the bats, their habitats have been disturbed by human activity in caves.

LEOPARD DARTER

(Percina pantherina) Threatened, critical habitat determined: Polk, Howard and Severe counties. This tiny fish is considered threatened because of its small numbers, restricted distribution and habitat changes. The Mountain Fork River in Polk County has been designated as Critical Habitat for the leopard darter in Arkansas.

PALLID STURGEON

(Scaphirhynchus albus) Endangered. Mississippi and St. Francis Rivers.

MOLLUSKS
FAT POCKETBOOK PEARLY MUSSEL

(Potamilus [=Proptera]capax) Endangered. St. Francis River, Cross and St. Francis counties. Extensive mussel taking and habitat modification due to channelization and siltation from agricultural runoff have been major factors in the decline of this invertebrate. Formerly common in Arkansas wetlands, this species is presently known to occur in Arkansas within the Lower St. Francis and White rivers. Other mollusks have similar habitat problems.

MAGAZINE MOUNTAIN SHAGREEN LAND SNAIL

(Mesodon magazinensis) Threatened. Logan County.

CURTIS' PEARLY MUSSEL

(Epioblasma [=Dysnomia] florentina curtisi) Endangered. Spring River, Lawrence County.

PINK MUCKET MUSSEL

(Lampsilis orbiculata) Endangered. Current River, Clay and Randolph counties; Spring River, Sharp County; Ouachita River, Clark County; Black River, Clay, Randolph and Lawrence counties.

TURGID BLOSSOM MUSSEL

(Epioblasma turgidula) Endangered. Spring River, Sharp County.

SPECKLED POCKETBOOK MUSSEL

(Lampsilis streckeri) Endangered. Little Red River, Van Buren and Searcy counties.

ARKANSAS FATMUCKET MUSSEL

(Lampsilis powelli) Threatened. Ouachita River system in the Saline, Caddo and upper Ouachita rivers.

OUACHITA ROCK POCKETBOOK MUSSEL

(Lampsilis wheeleri) Endangered. Kiamichi River and Little River.

ARTHROPODS

CAVE CRAYFISH

(Cambarus zophonastes) Endangered. Stone County. Small white blind crayfish is found in underground streams. Environmentalist have been studying and counting the remaining crayfish in Logan Cave near Springdale.

INSECTS

AMERICAN BURYING BEETLE

(Nicrophorus americanus) Endangered. Ozark and Ouachita mountains. This nocturnal species is unusual among insects because the parents work together to care for their young. The beetles hang out in carcasses of small animals and find mates. Together, they strip the carcass of hair, roll it into a ball, lay eggs on it and bury it until they hatch. Some think the decline of the beetle population is due to competition with other species for food and space. One theory links their diminishing numbers to the extinction of the passenger pigeons in the 1920s; the carcass of a pigeon would have been very attractive to a beetle family.

SOURCE: Karen Yaich, Arkansas Game and Fish Commission

Shooting passenger pigeons on a plantation near the Ouachita River in 1875. The last known passenger pigeon died in a zoo in 1914.

THE BEAR STATE - JUST BARELY

During Arkansas' early days, large numbers of black bear roamed the river bottoms and canebrakes in eastern and southern Arkansas and the western Ouachita forests. Many tales were told of hunting and trapping the abundant bear population in the state.

Consequently, Arkansas earned a reputation as "The Bear State." However, in the early 1900s, our bear population was almost wiped out due to destruction of habitat and commercial hunting for pelts and bear grease. But the nickname lived on long after the bear had disappeared. The Legislature of 1923, in fact, passed a resolution which stated that "The Bear State" led to a false

impression of Arkansas and that the expression was no longer appropriate. Finally, in 1927, the state Legislature closed the hunting season on bear.

In an effort to restore our native bear population, the Game and Fish Commission released 250 black bear in the Ozarks and Ouachitas from 1960-68. Today the bear population is thriving. A few years ago, bear hunting legally resumed in the state – under stringent guidelines. Requiring extensive forest cover for habitat, black bear range primarily in the Ozark and Ouachita mountains, White River Refuge and the Cache and Mississippi River bottoms. Although many people claim to have seen honey bears and brown bears in the state, the honey bear is just another name for a black bear, and the brown bear is just a black bear going through a brown growth phase. Black bear range in color from coal black to light brown or cinnamon.

POISONOUS SSSSSSNAKES

There are four types of poisonous snakes found in Arkansas. Three of these are pit vipers: rattlesnakes, water moccasins and copperheads. Pit vipers have a heat-sensitive pit between their eyes and nostrils which helps them locate and strike at warm-blooded prey. They also bear live young. The fourth type of snake is the coral snake. However, its occurrence in Arkansas is extremely rare. All poisonous snakes have poison glands, grooved fangs and vertical pupils. While snakebites are not common in Arkansas, if you spend much time outdoors you are likely to encounter a snake at some point. If that happens, stay calm and move away and try to remember that snakes perform a valuable function by controlling the rodent population and snacking on other vermin.

RATTLESNAKES

Four varieties of rattlesnake range in Arkansas: western diamondback, western pygmy, timber and canebrake. In general, rattlesnakes are as nervous as Barney Fife, but highly aggressive and do poorly in captivity. Their venom is extremely poisonous. They prey on small animals, including birds and lizards. The pygmy is less than two feet long and is usually gray to reddish with black blotches along its back. It is found in the woods, along streams and lakes and sometimes beneath debris. Timber and canebrake rattlers are usually brown, pinkish-gray or yellowish with dark crossbands and black tails. They can grow as long as six feet and are found in wooded hillsides, river lowlands and canebrake thickets. These are the types you usually find when clearing land. The most aggressive of the rattlers (and fortunately, the most rare) is the diamondback which grows up to seven feet long. It is brown or grayish with the distinguishing diamond pattern on its back and alternating black and white rings on its tail. They prefer rough, rocky terrain. Rattlesnakes, like all snakes, are deaf and cannot hear their own or another snake's rattle.

WATER MOCCASIN OR COTTONMOUTH

It is almost always found in or near swamps or slow-moving streams. They are fond of hiding under beached boats and draping themselves on branches over water. They will eat almost anything including fish, frogs, and other small swamp creatures. At maturity, the snake reaches about five feet. The body is covered with dark bands on a background of brown or muddy green. When aroused, it opens its mouth wide revealing the white cottony lining of the mouth and throat, hence the nickname "cottonmouth." The moccasin's poison is about as potent as that of the rattlesnake. Its bite can cause pain and death. For humans, the cottonmouth is considered the most dangerous because the snake not only injects its venom into the victim, but the snake has a mouthful of bacteria from feeding on slime-covered water creatures and that can cause an infection at the bite site. An excellent swimmer, this snake will usually move rapidly away from people. However, they have been rumored to attack.

SOUTHERN COPPERHEAD

This is the most common of the poisonous snakes found in Arkansas. It is found in forested areas where there is plenty of ground cover. It feeds on mice, insects and other small animals and it often hides in woodpiles and debris-strewn grassy areas. It has a coppery head and "hour-glass" body patches. It is thick-bodied, usually about two feet long (four feet max), and is much smaller and less poisonous than the moccasin. Its bite is painful and must be treated immediately, though the poison is rarely potent enough to kill. The copperhead probably bites more people than any other snake in North America.

TEXAS CORAL

This snake is a small cousin of the cobra and the only member of the cobra family found in the Americas. While it is the most lethal snake to range in Arkansas, it is also the rarest poisonous snake to be found. At maturity it reaches about three feet, and is found on rocky hillsides, dense woods, rock crevices, leaf piles, logs and stumps. It is a colorful snake with red, yellow and black bands. It is often confused with the harmless members of the king snake family. The coral snake is distinguished by the pattern of its colors: the red band touches the yellow band. In non-poisonous snakes, the red band touches the black band. Because the Texas coral has short fangs located in the back of its small mouth, it can't inflict a major bite, except maybe between fingers or toes.

SOURCES: *Golden Guide To Reptiles and Amphibians*; *Killer Snakes* by Russell Freedman; *Poisonous Snakes* by Seymour Simon; Little Rock Zoo.

Snakebite

The best treatment is to avoid being bitten in the first place. Look *before* you place your hand or foot in areas that may be attractive to snakes. When camping, fishing, hiking or doing yard work, protective clothing such as ankle-high boots or canvas gloves are a good idea. Seventy-five percent of snakebites occur near the ankle; most of the rest occur on the wrist or hand.

POISON GLAND

GROOVED FANGS

Children should be instructed not to play in areas known for snakes – and if they do encounter one, they should never tease or try to handle it.

What to do if snakebite occurs:

- Try to identify the type of snake. Although there are only four types of poisonous snakes in the state, even a non-poisonous snake can inflict a serious bite. Capture or kill the snake so it can be identified; try not to destroy identifying marks. Hold the snake by the tail, even when it's dead.
- Thoroughly cleanse the wound with soap and cool water and cover it with a sterile gauze. Put nothing else on the wound.
- Transport the injured person to the nearest doctor. If the snake is thought to be poisonous, have the victim lie down with the wound slightly lower than the rest of the body.
- Cutting into the wound and attempting to suck out the poison is controversial. In general, try to remain calm and seek immediate medical attention.

DID YOU KNOW?

MILK SHAKE FOR A MILK SNAKE

In Arkansas folklore there is said to be a spotted serpent called the milk snake which survives by sucking milk from cows in the pasture. A cow which has been milked by a milk snake is supposed to get all shook up when a human attempts to milk her thereafter.

SOURCE: Ozark Magic and Folklore by Vance Randolph

STOP
BUGGING ME!

July and August are peak months for stings. Here are some pointers to keep bugs from bugging you:

- Don't use scented preparations when going outdoors (perfume, aftershave, lotion, hairspray, etc.). Floral odors tend to attract bees and wasps.
- Avoid wearing dark clothing and floral prints (you don't want to be mistaken for a blossom by a hungry bee). White is said to be the *least* appealing to insects.
- Use caution when mowing the lawn, trimming hedges or cutting flowers. (Yellow jacket burrows are found in the ground.)
- Don't go barefoot outside.
- Beware of wasps that also tend to nest around boat docks and fences.
- Handle garbage cans and trash with care.
- Beware of bees around clover fields and picnic areas.
- If attacked by a hostile bee, move slowly. Don't make jerky movements.

ITSY-AND-NOT-SO-BITSY SPIDERS

There are two types of dangerous spiders in Arkansas: black widow
and brown recluse. Although all spiders are venomous, these are the
only two with venom potent enough to cause serious complications in
humans. It should be noted that any spider bite can cause an infection
simply because of the bacteria at the wound site. It's a good idea to
wear gloves when cleaning out garages, woodpiles, storage rooms or
other such areas where these spiders are likely to make their homes.

BLACK WIDOW

The female is coal black with an hour-glass shaped red mark on the
underside of the abdomen. She is much larger than the
male. (Few humans ever see a male black
widow as he is generally devoured
by the female after
mating.) Black
widows are
rather
abundant. They usually
build their webs in or
beneath objects near the
ground. Fortunately,
they are shy and do
not bite without great
provocation. A black widow's bite
causes intense pain, muscle spasm and weak pulse
and may cause death. The pain moves gradually from the wound and
concentrates in the abdomen. Medical attention should be sought
immediately.

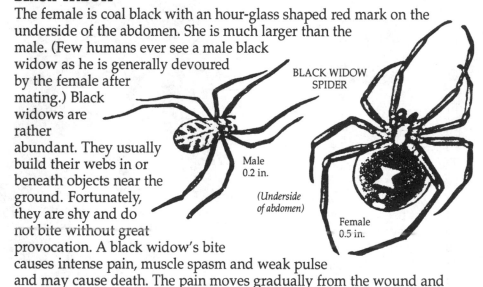

BLACK WIDOW
SPIDER

Male
0.2 in.

(Underside
of abdomen)

Female
0.5 in.

BROWN RECLUSE

Light brown to tan in color with long legs, this spider measures about
¾ inch across (including legs). The cephalthorax is marked with a
distinctive dark-colored "fiddle" shape on the back. The brown recluse
is generally found hiding out in closets or other storage areas where it
feeds on roaches and silverfish. The bite of the brown recluse may not
be immediately painful, but if not treated, tissue breaks down in the
area of the wound. As in the case of the black widow, medical attention
is imperative. If possible, save the spider for identification.

TARANTULAS

Those hairy, scary-looking spiders that crop up in horror flicks, are
victims of false media hype. Tarantulas are not actually dangerous to
humans. Of course, like any other creature, they might nip you if you

handle them roughly, but they are not venomous like the black widow or brown recluse.

SOURCES: UALR Department of Biology; *Better Homes and Gardens Medical Guide; Golden Guide to Insect Pests.*

TICKS, CHIGGERS AND SKEETERS

This unholy trinity of blood-sucking parasites can make summer in the Arkansas outdoors miserable. Here's some info on why they do what they do – and what you can and can't do about it.

TICKS

These minuscule pests are not really insects. They're arachnids – relatives of the spider. They differ from spiders in having the abdomen fused with the cephalthorax so that the body is made up of one region. Of the 15 species of ticks known in Arkansas, the most common by far is the lone star tick, which accounts for about 95% of the tick population in the state. This tick derives its name from the conspicuous white spot on the back of the female. The male is characteristically marked by the horseshoe outline on the back.

The lone star tick is a three-host species. Each of the life stages – larvae (seed tick), nymph and adult – feeds on a different animal. Adults and nymphs spend the winter in ground trash, under stones or in some cases, in the soil. Emergence begins as soon as the temperature rises. After mating, females attach to a large animal host and feed until completely engorged for a period of 6 -13 days or more. (Virgin females may remain attached for 30 or more days.) Males attach and feed for a brief period, then detach and mate. After complete engorgement, the female drops to the ground to lay from 3,000 to 5,000 eggs. After the arduous egg-laying, the female is exhausted and soon dies. The young larvae climb up on grass and plants to await the passing of a host animal.

All stages of the lone star tick attack man, deer, cattle, horses and

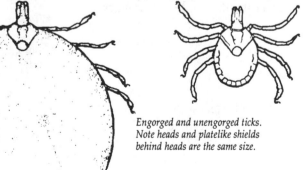

Engorged and unengorged ticks. Note heads and platelike shields behind heads are the same size.

dogs. Adult ticks don't usually occur on smaller animals, but seed ticks and nymphs are prevalent on rabbits, squirrels, foxes, raccoon, skunks and have been removed from 40 species of birds. So what do ticks do if no host is forthcoming? Well, ticks can afford to be patient. They can go an entire year without feeding. Adult ticks may live for three years. One record in tick literature tells of a male *Ixodes texanus* tick that survived 22 years waiting for his next meal to saunter by. Control of the tick population is almost impossible. Cutting the underbrush, spraying oneself and domestic animals with repellent give partial relief. Staying out of vegetation in the spring and summer is often the only answer. Or heading for the river flood plains and the Delta which are tick-free.

Is there any truth to the old remedies such as ingesting small quantities of sulfur will make you less appetizing? Or that spraying kerosene on your pants and shoes will make ticks keep their distance? Not according to Dr. J. L. Lancaster, *professor emeritus* of the University of Arkansas Department of Entomology – a man who has studied Arkansas ticks extensively. (There is also a risk of the kerosene coming into contact with the skin and causing blistering.) What does Dr. Lancaster recommend to keep ticks at bay? Permanone Tick Repellent. It comes in an aerosol can and is for clothing application only. It is available at farmers supply outlets around the state at a cost of about $5.95 for 6 ounces.

SOURCES: Dr. J. L. Lancaster, U of A Fayetteville; Arkansas Cooperative Extension Service

Tick Bites

Some ticks spread diseases such as Rocky Mountain spotted fever, tularemia and relapsing fever. A tick can often be felt before it starts to burrow under the skin, but after it begins to suck, it usually cannot be felt. Examine skin and clothing after a day in tick-infested country. The head of a tick tenaciously resists removal from skin. Don't try to remove ticks with unprotected fingers or allow crushed parts or juices to contact skin. To make a tick let go, coat it with nail polish to suffocate it, then remove it with tweezers. Wash thoroughly with soap and water. *Never* try to get a tick to let go by holding a lighted match or cigarette next to it – you might burn yourself.

CHIGGERS

As if ticks were not enough. The chigger – also called redbug or harvest mite – is the small member of the order Acarina. (The tick is a large relative of the chigger.) A chigger is a newly hatched mite that crawls around on low vegetation until it can attach itself to a passing vertebrate. The first growth stage, larvae, is the only stage in which the chigger is a parasite. The chigger stays on the host sucking blood, partially embedding itself in the flesh until it is full, then drops off. However, on humans (who are not a normal hosts) it bores through the human skin, then injects a poison that causes a great itching welt which lasts for a week or longer. The itching may be the only way of knowing you've been in an infested area because chiggers are so small most people can't see them without a magnifying glass. The more the bite is scratched, the more the welt humps up to surround and protect the chigger. In safety, the chigger drinks predigested tissue and remains embedded in the flesh where it dies, creating a painful chigger bite for the host.

To Relieve the Itch:

• Make a paste of baking soda and water, apply to bite.
• Apply diluted household ammonia to bite.
• Apply calamine lotion or rubbing alcohol.

SKEETERS

Mosquitoes do seem to be omnipresent during the evening hours of summer, and particularly bothersome in the Delta. Stuttgart with its flooded rice fields provide a perfect breeding ground. Only the females buzz (so humans can hear it) and bite. Female mosquitoes need protein from blood so that they can make eggs. Male mosquitoes don't bite because their flimsy mouth parts cannot cut into skin. The female finds her victim by sensing warm, moist air around the body. Her mouth is made up of bristles and tubes; bristles jab up and down to punch holes in the skin. Saliva flows through one tube into the skin and blood is sucked into the mouth through another. The abdomen swells with blood. Then she releases a droplet of liquid from intestines to reduce her weight for an easier get away. She flies off with a belly full of blood, usually before the victim can feel the bite. After resting for several days digesting the blood, she lays her eggs, between 75 and 500 of them. So what can you do to discourage the blood-sucking little darlings? Get rid of any standing water around your house, burn citronella candles when outdoors and spray down with your basic insect repellents.

SOURCES: "Mosquito," Encyclopedia Brittanica; 101 Wacky Facts About Bugs & Spiders by Jean Waricha

MORE OF THE ITCHY AND SCRATCHY SHOW
POISON IVY

Poison ivy dermatitis usually begins as an intense itch; soon a rash develops over areas which have been exposed. It may appear as streaks with various sizes of blisters. Blisters may continue to break out up to 72 hours after exposure. The best prevention is to learn to recognize and avoid poison ivy, oak and sumac. If you accidentally come into contact with the plants, strip down as soon as possible, briskly wash skin with soap and warm water and launder clothes. If you do develop the rash, there are various medications such as calamine lotion and cortisone cream to help relieve the itch. And don't scratch! Scratching can cause infection. Poison ivy can only be spread from direct contact with the resin from the plant. The clear fluid inside the blisters is not toxic. Aside from direct contact, here are some of the most common ways to get poison ivy:

- By contact with a pet that has been roaming about and brushed up against the plant.
- From firewood where ivy may have grown.
- From gloves or other outdoor clothing which has not been washed after contact with poison ivy. (The oily resin which produces the rash remains intact and potent for a very long time.)
- Burning leaves. If there are any poison ivy plants in there, burning them can release the resin droplets into the air – and what goes up must come down.

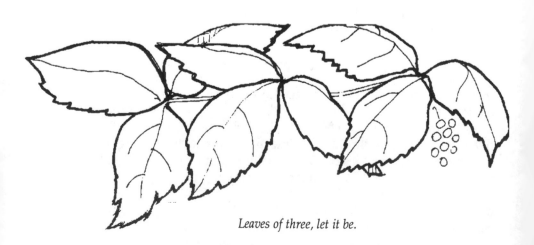

Leaves of three, let it be.

AAAACHOOOOO......
A SNEEZE GUIDE TO ARKANSAS

The downside to living in a temperate zone with a long growing season and mild winter is having lots of pollen. The chart below shows the approximate time the most common inhalants in Arkansas are prevalent. In the late spring and early summer, the grasses become more important and the weed pollens only cause difficulty in the fall. Dust and mold may cause year-round trouble depending on individual exposure.

SOURCE: Dr. Kelsy Caplinger, Little Rock Allery Clinic

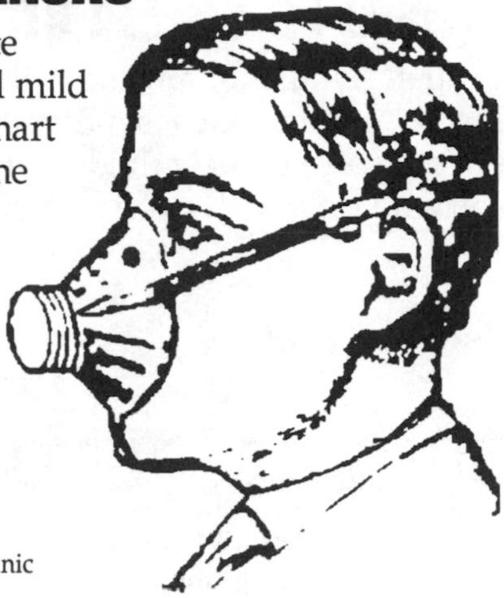

Seasonal Variations of Inhalant Allergens in Arkansas

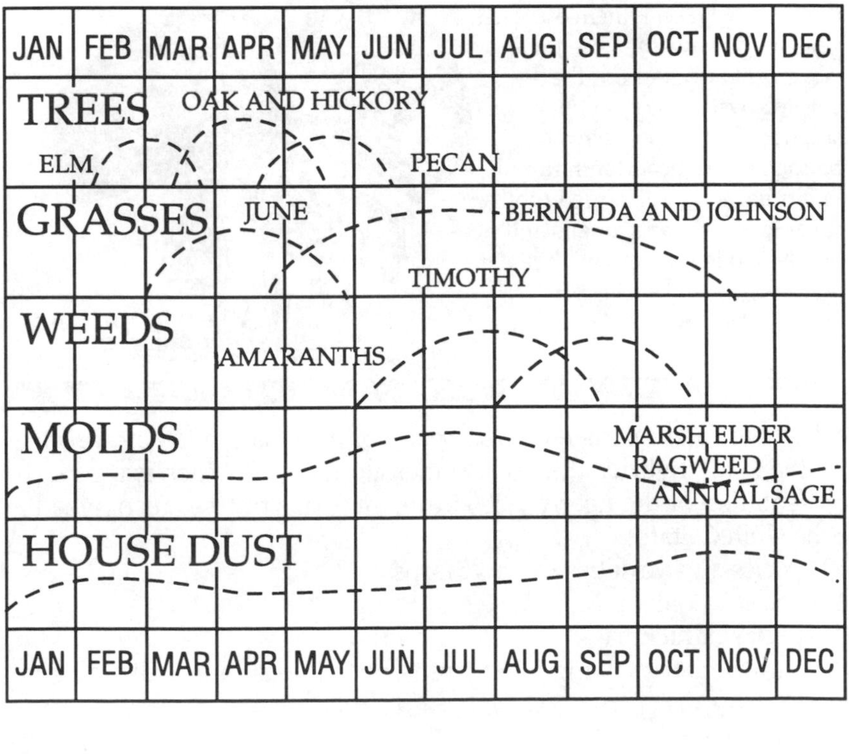

JAN	FEB	MAR	APR	MAY	JUN	JUL	AUG	SEP	OCT	NOV	DEC
TREES — OAK AND HICKORY, ELM, PECAN											
GRASSES — JUNE, BERMUDA AND JOHNSON, TIMOTHY											
WEEDS — AMARANTHS											
MOLDS — MARSH ELDER, RAGWEED, ANNUAL SAGE											
HOUSE DUST											
JAN	FEB	MAR	APR	MAY	JUN	JUL	AUG	SEP	OCT	NOV	DEC

PINE TREES -
NOTHING TO SNEEZE AT

It is extremely rare for anyone to be allergic to pine. This is because the oily resin from the pine pollen doesn't dissolve in body fluids. For those living in Arkansas, a state with a plethora of pines, this is good news!

DID YOU KNOW?

THERE'S FUNGUS AMONG US

Arkansas is no stranger to fungi. But mildew aside, many edible gourmet mushroom can be found growing in their natural state. Several varieties of chanterelles are common: the black chanterelle "poor man's truffle," as well as vermillion red and several kinds of yellow chanterelles. Black and yellow morel mushrooms also grow wild, but have a short growing season and require diligence on the part of those in the know who seek them out each year. If you have the nose for it, you might also root out the coveted oyster, inky cap, parasol, sulphur shelf, honey, pink bottom, bear's head tooth fungus, polars bears' paw, bearded tooth fungus, lion's mane fungus and hen-of-the-woods mushroom.

SOURCE: Jay Justice, President, Arkansas Mycological Society

➜ There are approximately 200 species of trees native to Arkansas. With the many hybrids, the total comes close to 300 which is a good representation of the nearly 1,200 different forms of trees recognized for the United States.
• 63 species and varieties of hawthorns
• 41 species of oaks
• 23 species of hickory
Of the saw timber growing in Arkansas, over 83% is pine, oak, and gum.

SOURCE: Trees of Arkansas by Dwight M. Moore, Arkansas Forestry Commission

REALLY BIG TREES!

Here are the five largest trees in the state as determined by the Arkansas Forestry Commission's "bigness index." The index is the total of a tree's circumference in inches, its height in feet and one-fourth its spread. The spread is determined by measuring the top or crown in feet from "dripping point to dripping point."

1. **Bald Cypress** southeast of Malvern. 37 feet 7 inches in circumference, 138 feet tall with a 60-foot crown.
2. **Water Tupelo** near Gillett. 28 feet 3 inches in circumference, 140 feet tall, 60-foot crown.
3. **Cherrybark Oak** in Bearden. 21 feet 2 inches in circumference, 144 feet tall with a 113-foot crown.
4. **Eastern Cottonwood** near Van Buren. 22 feet 10 inches in circumference, 126 feet tall, 91-foot crown.
5. **Southern Red Oak** in Lonoke. 20 feet, 10 inches in circumference, 99 feet tall, 117-foot crown.

WEEDS - NATURE'S OVERACHIEVERS

Ever wonder who or what unleashed dandelions and crabgrass on us? Well, in the 1850s, European immigrants cultivated crabgrass here like wheat and ground the seed into a breakfast gruel called "manna grits." Dandelions came over with the Puritans who ate the greens and fermented the flowers into wine (though being Puritans, they probably didn't really *enjoy* the wine). Dandelion greens were very popular in the South during the Civil War. (We'll eat anything green and leafy that resembles turnip greens.) Southerners even used ground dandelion roots as a coffee substitute.

And what about that prolific vine kudzu? Asians have been making wallpaper and tea from kudzu for ages. America was introduced to it at the Philadelphia Centennial Exposition in 1876, and then it cropped up again at the New Orleans Exposition in 1883. The plant caught on. Literally. By the early 1900s Southerners planted kudzu for shade over their porches and farmers planted thousands of acres in the fast-growing forage. The Soil Conservation Service thought kudzu would be perfect to plant on eroded land to hold the soil. Well, talk about too much of a good thing! Kudzu grows up to a foot a day and, ultimately, has the perseverance of an Arkansas tick.

ARKANSAS WEATHER: MOTHER NATURE'S MOOD SWINGS

The weather in Arkansas can be as unpredictable as her people. The weather can also be downright nasty (the metaphor stops here). When you think earthquakes, tornadoes, and floods, Arkansas probably doesn't come to mind. But we have our share. Tornadoes are Arkansas' biggest natural disaster. Our state also experienced the greatest earthquake of historical times in North America in 1811 when the New Madrid shook things up.

THE BIG ONE: WHOLE LOT OF SHAKIN' GOIN' ON

The first shocks of the New Madrid were felt December 16, 1811. The area most violently shaken by the disturbance was some 30 miles square of New Madrid, Missouri. Less violent effects of the disturbance were manifest hundreds of miles away, especially along the Mississippi. The "sunk lands of the St. Francis" river basin, situated in Craighead, Mississippi,

Poinsett and other counties of northeast Arkansas, still remain as visible evidence of the quake. One or more of the eight major shocks was felt at widely scattered points covering all of the United States east of the Rocky Mountains. Most of the felt effects were reported from cities along the major rivers or along the Atlantic Coastal Plain. This may in part be due to the location of the population centers in those areas, but that is thought to be only a partial explanation.

In much of Arkansas, even the largest shocks of the 1811-1812 quakes probably caused no damage and would not have been felt by many persons. The three major quakes caused few casualties because the area was so sparsely populated. Although there were many drownings on the Mississippi River as the result of the quakes, the reports of the day indicated that only one person could definitely be established as having died on land during these events – a woman who ran until exhausted and died of fright.

However, another new Madrid earthquake like the ones of 1811-1812 could cause $14 billion in damages in a seven-state area that includes Arkansas, experts estimate. According to John D. McFarland III, geologist with the Arkansas Geological Commission, quakes with the intensity of those in 1811 seem to occur in the region about once every 700 years. Today, a quake of that density would "devastate anything east of Crowley's Ridge." In an attempt to prepare for such an eventuality, the 78th General Assembly passed ACT 1100 in 1991: "An act to safeguard life, health and property by requiring earthquake resistant design for all public structures to be constructed or remodeled within the boundaries of this state beginning September 1, 1991." The typical school and hospital buildings built before the code was enacted in 1991 would be among the first to fall if an earthquake hit. The older structures are made of rigid concrete blocks with flat roofs that afford no flexibility.

The last New Madrid earthquake that caused damage occurred in 1843. According to McFarland, there is almost daily detectable activity along the New Madrid fault line. Seismologists have estimated that damage-causing earthquakes can be expected to occur at least once every 100 years. In that respect, the New Madrid is overdue.

Although the focus is on northeast Arkansas, a large earthquake was reported felt in western Arkansas late last century and seismic activity has been recorded in south Arkansas as well. It has been speculated that the south Arkansas tremors might have some connection to the deep brine wells in that part of the state, but that has not been verified.

The Task Force on Seismic Instrumentation reported in January of 1993 that "at the present time, there are no seismographic or strong motion stations or networks in Arkansas that report directly to anyone in Arkansas." Arkansas is essentially dependent on the information gathered and disseminated by the Center for Earthquake Research and Information in Memphis which is not set up to be Arkansas specific. It was the task force's recommendation that Arkansas needs its own motion detecting and data gathering network to learn more about how earthquakes impact on this particular state and how we can better be prepared for the coming quakes. The cost of setting up our own observatory program would run about a million and a half dollars.

SOURCES: *John D. McFarland;* Arkansas Geological Commission; *Highlights of Arkansas History* by Dallas T. Herndon.

TWISTERS: THEY CAN GET YOU AND YOUR LITTLE DOG, TOO!

Though Arkansas may not have as many tornadoes as Texas or Mississippi, for some reason the ones we have are more severe. From 1880 to 1993, tornadoes have killed a total of 1,467 Arkansans. Arkansas ranked highest of all states for the most killer tornadoes between 1916-1980. The worst killer storms in the state's history occurred March 21, 1952. That day three tornadoes killed 111 persons and injured an additional 772. In recent years, an average of seven Arkansans have died from tornadoes each year.

Arkansas is extremely vulnerable from March through September. Though tornadoes can and do occur anytime of the day or night, the most common time for a tornado to hit is from late afternoon to late evening. In Arkansas, 5 p.m. is when most tornadoes occur. The greater tornado frequency during the afternoon and evening is due to the instability of the atmosphere caused by the buildup of heated air near the earth's surface on long, warm sunny afternoons. After sunset, the layer of the atmosphere near the earth's surface begins to cool. This usually restores more atmospheric stability and reduces the threat of tornado occurrence.

Sixty-four percent of the tornadoes in Arkansas move from the southwest to the northeast. But tornadoes can come from any direction.

Some tornadoes have stopped their forward movement, turned and looped back across their path. Their average speed of advance is 30 mph, but a few move as fast as 70 mph. The wind within the tornado can vary from 100 mph to over 205 mph. The best defense against a tornado is preparation. Keep an eye out for signs of tornado activity as soon as a tornado "watch" is issued by the weather service. Be prepared. If you live in tornado country, you should develop a plan and have frequent drills so everyone in your home or business knows what do to if the time comes. Always have a radio and flashlight with good batteries handy.

Tornado Watch means the conditions are right and there is a possibility of a tornado in the area defined. Remain alert for approaching storms.

Tornado Warning is issued when a funnel has been sighted or indicated by weather radar. If you are in the path of the storm, haste is important. Move to a pre-designated place of safety. The main points to remember while seeking shelter are: keep away from windows, doors and outside walls and protect your head. Flying debris from tornadoes causes the most deaths and injuries.

TORNADO STATS FROM 1950 - 1994

- Total number of tornadoes 854
- Average tornadoes per year 19
- Average deaths per year 6
- Average injuries per year 82
- Pulaski County had the most tornadoes 40
- Faulkner and Lonoke counties tied for second place with 28 each
- Benton and Mississippi counties tied for third place with 27 each
- White County has had more tornado deaths than any other county 54
- Lafayette County has the least number of tornadoes 3
- Total deaths 279
- Total injuries 3696

NOAA WEATHER RADIO

Severe weather can be monitored over a special weather radio system that has been installed by the National Weather Service. This radio system provides round-the-clock information on all potential as well as current severe weather. Special radio receivers are needed and are available at radio shops, electronics stores, department and discount stores. Many multiband radios and scanners can also receive the frequencies. The transmitter sites and their assigned frequencies are listed below:

Fort Smith	162.4	MHz	Mountain View	162.40	MHz
Gurdon	162.475	MHz	Star City	162.40	MHz
Jonesboro	162.55	MHz	Texarkana	162.55	MHz
Little Rock	162.5	MHz	Winslow	162.475	MHz
Memphis	162.475	MHz			

IF A TORNADO APPROACHES:

• Stay away from doors and windows. Don't run around opening windows to equalize pressure in your house. That's a myth. Forget the windows and take cover.

• In homes and small buildings, go to the basement or to an interior part on the lowest level – closets, bathrooms or interior halls. Get under something sturdy. Put pillows and blankets over your head.

• In schools, nursing homes, hospitals, factories and shopping centers go to pre-designated shelter areas. Interior hallways on the lowest level are usually best.

• In mobile homes or vehicles get out and go to a substantial structure. Mobile homes, even if tied down, offer little protection from tornadoes and should be abandoned. If there is no substantial structure nearby, lie flat in the nearest ditch, ravine or culvert with your hands sheltering your head.

• Never try to outrun a tornado in your car.

• In open country, move away from the tornado's path at right angles. If there is not time to escape, lie flat in the nearest ditch.

• No matter how tempting the notion of documenting the impending disaster for "Eyewitness Video," forget the camcorder. Seek shelter for yourself and your family.

LIGHTNING: THE SHOCKING FACTS

Lightning kills more people each year in the U.S. than tornadoes or hurricanes. Lightning is a highly underrated killer. Since it generally kills only one or two persons at a time, it doesn't grab the headlines as the more spectacular hurricanes, tornadoes and floods do when they kill hundreds and cause millions of dollars in damage in a single episode. Anyone who is outdoors during a thunderstorm is highly susceptible to being struck by lightning. Lightning will normally strike the highest object in the area of discharge and is especially attracted to metal, a good conductor. Some of its more popular targets are farmers, golfers and fishermen. In 1994, there was one death and 21 injuries from lightning in Arkansas. Your chances of being struck by lightning are estimated to be 1 in 600,000, but could be reduced if you follow safety rules. The air near a lightning strike is heated to 50,000° F – that's hotter than the surface of the sun.

LIGHTNING MYTHS

MYTH: If it's not raining then there's no danger from lightning.

FACT: Lightning often strikes outside of heavy rain and may occur as far as ten miles away from any rainfall.

MYTH: The rubber soles of shoes or rubber tires on a car will protect you from being struck.

FACT: Rubber soles and rubber tires don't do diddly to protect you. However, the steel frame of a hard-topped vehicle provides increased protection if you are not touching metal. Although you may be injured if lightning strikes your car, you are much safer inside a vehicle than outside.

MYTH: People struck by lightning carry an electrical charge and should not be touched.

FACT: Lightning victims carry no electrical charge and should be attended to immediately.

MYTH: Heat lightning occurs after very hot summer days and poses no threat.

FACT: So-called "heat lightning" is actually just plain old lightning from a thunderstorm too far away for thunder to be heard. However, the storm may be moving in your direction.

MYTH: Lightning never strikes the same place twice.

FACT: Does too.

LIGHTNING SAFETY RULES

If a thunderstorm threatens, your best bet is to take shelter in a house or large building – or in an all-metal vehicle (not a convertible). Don't talk on the phone unless it's an emergency. If you are stuck outside, follow these tips:

• Don't stand on a hilltop.

- Don't stand under a large tree isolated in a field.
- Get out and away from open water. Don't stay in a boat.
- Get away from tractors and other metal farm equipment.
- Drop the golf clubs.
- Get off scooters, bikes, golf carts.
- Stay away from wire fences, clotheslines, metal pipes, rails and other metallic paths which could carry lightning to you from some distance away.
- In open areas, go to a ravine or valley.
- If you're hopelessly isolated in a level field and you feel your hair stand on end – indicating that lightning is about to strike – drop to your knees and bend forward putting your hands on your knees. Do *not* lie flat on the ground.

FLASH FLOODS: TOO MUCH OF A GOOD THING

Flash floods have recently become the number one stormy weather killer in the United States. As we become a more urbanized society, flash flood problems will increase since we will be building on flood-prone areas. Cities like Hot Springs and Harrison have suffered serious flash floods in the past. In September 1978, a devastating flash flood struck central Arkansas and caused ten deaths. Most flash flooding is caused by slow-moving thunderstorms, thunderstorms repeatedly moving over the same area, or heavy rains from hurricanes and tropical storms. Preparing individuals for the eventuality of flash floods is difficult since most people don't have a built in fear of floods. In the spring of 1927, Arkansas experienced a devastating flood when the Mississippi, Arkansas, and other rivers overflowed their banks and flood waters eventually covered more than 4,000,000 acres of land in eastern and central Arkansas. One hundred twenty-seven Arkansans died, thousands of families were left homeless, property damage ran into the millions.

SAFETY RULES:

- Know where higher ground is and how to get there quickly. Don't try to out-run a flood.
- Many flash floods occur at night. Be especially cautions, it's harder to recognize the danger.
- Above all, don't try to drive through or walk across flooded area. Nearly half of all flash flood fatalities are auto related. A mere two feet of water will carry away most automobiles.

SOURCE: National Weather Service.

MO

OK

TX

TN

MS

LA

	Interstate Highway		▲	Tourist Information Center
	U.S. Numbered State Highway		●	State Park Location
	State Highway		◆	National Park Location
	Great River Road			

CITIES AND TOWNS
From Little Rock to Lake Dick!

The following is a rundown on Arkansas cities and towns. We hit the high points like history, points of interest, industries and facilities for the 20 largest towns, plus a couple of notable exceptions – Hope (because it's Bill Clinton's birthplace) and Eureka Springs (because it's a major tourist destination). We also include, in alphabetical order, thumbnail sketches of a whole slew of smaller though equally charming Arkansas communities. (Population based on 1990 census.)

LITTLE ROCK

Capital of Arkansas.
Seat of Pulaski County.
Population: 175,795

Information: Little Rock Bureau for Conventions and Visitors (501) 376-4781.

Greater Little Rock Chamber of Commerce, 1 Spring Street; Little Rock 72201. (501) 374-4871. TeleFun: For pre-recorded info on what's going on in the Little Rock area call (501) 372-3399.

HISTORY

In 1541 Hernando de Soto became the first white man to cross into Arkansas Territory. It would be another 150 years before another white man came this way. In 1686 Henry de Tonti founded a trading center at Arkansas Post, the oldest French settlement on the Mississippi River. Then, on March 10, 1791, under orders from Governor Bienville of New Orleans, the Frenchman Bernard de La Harpe and 16 soldiers left Arkansas Post to explore the Arkansas River. On April ninth, they reached Little Rock. They proceeded up the river but were forced to return to Arkansas Post about a week later because most of their supplies were destroyed when a canoe capsized. During the course of the journey, La Harpe and his men noted the character of the land and the Indians who inhabited it. Many stories had been circulated about a large emerald rock on the river. However, when La Harpe and his men finally reached the greenish rock, they found it was not emerald at all. This legendary emerald rock was named *la petite roche*, French for "little rock," to distinguish it from the "big rock" which La Harpe encountered a short distance up the river.

Dumont, one of the members of La Harpe's expedition, made this observation: "If in this expedition, we had not the good fortune to discover the emerald rock, we had the satisfaction of traversing a very beautiful country, fertile plains, vast prairies covered with buffalo, stags, does, deer, turtles, etc. We saw rocks of jasper, marbles...others of slate...we discovered a little stream which rolled gold dust in its waters."

Although La Harpe recommended to the French government that they

Little Rock skyline

establish a trading post there, the French government thought it a bad idea. For nearly 100 years, Little Rock remained a wilderness. People crossed the river there, but no one stayed. In 1803 Arkansas came into the U.S. as part of the Louisiana Purchase. When Louisiana attained statehood in 1812, Arkansas became part of Missouri Territory. By 1819 there were 14 residents of the Little Rock community. It was not surveyed as a town until 1820 when a post office was established. In

1821 when the territorial government moved from Arkansas Post to the more centrally located Little Rock, there were fewer than a dozen houses there and no regular streets. 1821 marked the arrival of the state's first newspaper, the *Arkansas Gazette*; until it was sold in 1991, the oldest daily paper west of the Mississippi. (The *Gazette* had been founded two years earlier at Arkansas Post by William Woodruff.) Little Rock grew slowly – so slowly, in fact, that in 1822 there was talk that the capital might be moved again unless the developers took more interest in its improvement. An attempt was made at one time to rename Little Rock, and "Arkopolis" appears on some early maps. March 16, 1822, the *Eagle* was the first steamboat to ascend the Arkansas River to Little Rock.

Little Rock experienced its first period of growth in 1824. By July, about 40 families were living in Little Rock.There had only been five or six the year before. A building boom was underway. Little Rock's first church was established this year. It was a Baptist mission founded by the Reverend Silas T. Toncray, a black minister from Memphis. His congregation was composed of both black and white members. In 1827 there were about 60 buildings in the town – six brick, eight frame, the remainder log cabins. This new growth of the city brought increased attention to Little Rock. Life in the territory came to center more around the new location. But the boisterous new capital of the Arkansas Territory had its problems. In 1827 Little Rock was still covered with trees and streets were no more than trails. (A law passed in 1826 prohibited shooting in the streets on Sunday.) Even as late as 1835 the streets were deeply rutted and covered with stumps and trash. The city had no system of fire protection for many years. Flooding was a concern, as were drinking and gambling. But in spite of these imperfections, the city progressed and on October 7, 1831, Little Rock was the first city officially incorporated in Arkansas. In 1832 when Washington Irving made a stopover in Little Rock, he noted in his journal that the place was a flourishing village with two rival newspapers and three hotels. In 1834 the Little Rock Jockey Club was organized; horse racing was a popular pastime. Theatrical performances began that year on November 3. The Little Rock Thalian Society performed the comedy "Soldier's Daughter" and the following day the *Gazette* reviewed the play and found it very satisfactory and "far better than we had anticipated." After covering expenses, profits were put to charitable purposes.

Little Rock did not suffer great damage during the Civil War. In fact, during the war, the city's population grew from less than 4,000 in 1860 to over 12,000 in 1870. Little Rock flourished during the 1890s. As the city grew during the 19th and 20th centuries, a neighborhood of gracious homes developed in the area south of the Territorial Restoration. Now known as the Quapaw Quarter, many buildings are listed on the National Register of Historic Places. Arkansas attained statehood in 1836. That year, the Old State House was built (it now serves as a museum of Arkansas politics and history). Construction on the current Capitol began in 1899 and it is modeled on the U.S. Capitol.

Little Rock is, perhaps, still best remembered for the infamous integration crisis at Central High School in 1957. The admission of nine black students to the all-white school made national headlines when President Eisenhower placed the Arkansas National Guard under federal control to ensure the safety of the black students who tried to attend classes there. It was without doubt one of the nastiest episodes in not only Little Rock's history, but America's history.

Where the political elite meet to eat

Today Little Rock is not only the geographic and political center of the state, the metropolitan area is the financial and cultural hub of Arkansas as well. Many nationally-known successful business are headquartered here such as Dillard's Department Stores; Stephens, Inc., one of the largest brokerage firms outside of Wall Street; Alltel Information Systems; and TCBY, the international yogurt industry whose 40-story building in downtown Little Rock is the tallest building in the state. Our former governor and longtime resident has made rather a splash on the national political scene, as well.

SOURCES: *Living in Arkansas* by O.E. McKnight; *Historic Arkansas* by John L. Ferguson & J.H. Atkinson; Little Rock Bureau for Conventions & Visitors.

POINTS OF INTEREST

Arkansas Aerospace Education Center

3301 E. Roosevelt Rd. (501) 376-4629. Situated right across from the airport, the big attraction here is the 250-seat IMAX theater. The six-story screen, the largest film frame in motion picture history, and a 16,500 watt sound system make you feel like you're really out there in the wild blue yonder.The theater shows space and aviation-related films which run seven days a week (call for show times and admission prices). The center also has an exhibit hall with permanent and changing exhibits.There's an exact replica of the Apollo Command Module suspended from the ceiling in the rotunda, as well as three full-scale model airplanes (two suspended from the ceiling and one grounded). "The Right Stuff" Gift Shop offers high-tech fun with state-of-the art toys and games as well as aerospace collectibles and memorabilia. The East Little Rock Branch Library is also housed here with the largest collection of aviation and aerospace materials outside the Smithsonian's National Air and Space Museum.

Arkansas Arts Center *MacArthur Park, 9th* and *Commerce. (501) 372-4000.* The state's largest cultural institution and only major art museum. The six galleries display a variety of changing exhibits as well as outstanding exhibits from foundation collections. The collection of more than 750 American drawings from 1900 to the present is particularly strong. The center also houses a children's theater, museum school, gift shop and Vineyard In The Park restaurant. Free admission.

Old Paint gets a makeover

Arkansas Carousel Restoration Studio *107 Main. (501) 375-5556.* The only remaining Herschell-Spillman track carousel once delighted children of all ages in War Memorial Park. Today the trusty steeds are getting a facelift.

Arkansas Governor's Mansion *18th and Center.* Home of all Arkansas governors since its completion in 1950, including Bill and Hillary who lived there during the twelve years Bill was governor.

Arkansas Museum of Science and History *MacArthur Park.* *(501) 324-9231.* Founded in 1927, this is one of the state's oldest museums. Located in the Old Arsenal Building which was built in 1842, this was the birthplace of General Douglas MacArthur. The museum houses over 15,000 scientific and anthropological objects with hands-on exhibits featuring early Arkansas explorers and Indians.

Arkansas Repertory Theatre *601 Main. (501) 378-9405.* Top-notch professional performances at the Rep's Main Stage Theatre entertain more than 90,000 theater enthusiasts each year.

Arkansas State Fair *State Fairgrounds on Roosevelt Rd. (501) 372-8341.* Ten days each fall the fair offers entertainment, championship rodeo, livestock judging, exhibits, food and the biggest midway in the state with innards-scrambling rides to prove it. Call for exact dates.

Plum Bayou House – Territorial Restoration Dog Trot

Arkansas Territorial Restoration *200 East Third. (501) 324-9351.* This frontier history museum includes thirteen structures from territorial days. Included is the oldest building in Little Rock, the Hinderliter Grog Shop; the 1824 print shop of William Woodruff, first publisher of the *Arkansas Gazette.* Guided tours are offered with actors portraying the first residents of these historic homes. The museum store sells the work of over 200 Arkansas artisans. Admission charged.

Little Rock ranks #1 in the nation for highest per capita Velveeta consumption. We like our Rotel dip here.

Arkansas Vietnam Veterans Memorial *Southeast corner of the state Capitol grounds.* Designed by Steve Gartman to honor over 600 Arkansans who died or are missing in action as a result of the Vietnam War. The monument contains almost 700,000 pounds of granite. It was authorized by Act 394 of the 74th General Assembly and was dedicated March 7, 1987.

Barton Coliseum *W. Roosevelt Rd. (501) 372-8341.* One of the nation's finest indoor arenas, it is the site for major concerts and the Arkansas State Fair and Livestock Show each fall. 7,112 permanent seats, expands to 10,012 with chairs. Twenty acres provide space for outdoor attractions and parking.

Children's Museum of Arkansas *Union Station,W. Markham and Victory. (501) 374-6655.* One of the state's newest museums with interactive exhibits, recreated farmer's market and two-story Victorian house.

Decorative Arts Museum *Seventh and Rock Streets. (501) 372-4000.* Located in the historic Pike-Fletcher-Terry residence, the museum collections include contemporary craft objects, toys designed by artists and traveling exhibitions. Admission free; donation suggested.

Lake Maumelle *West of town off Ark. 10.* The principal reservoir for the city's water supply. Fishing, sailing. No swimming.

DID YOU KNOW?

DOG TROT

One of the more elaborate of the early Arkansas log cabin styles was the dog trot. This consisted of two separate log pens with a covered breezeway between them. Other names for this style were possum trot, turkey run, wind-sweep, and two P. The "two P" indicating perhaps the two pens and a passage. The passage or breezeway was the coolest part of the house and where most people preferred to be on a steamy dog day afternoon. The best chairs were kept out on the gallery, as were the wash basin and water bucket. The saddles and firewood were stored here and the animal pelts were stretched here to dry. It was also where the dogs ran and slept, hence the name dog trot.

The Plum Bayou Log House at the Territorial Restoration is a version of the dog trot style. Built around 1830, the log house was moved in 1976 from a plantation in Scott for display in Little Rock. Children visiting the site can see demonstrations of pioneer skills like candle-making and butter churning. The Pemberton family of North Carolina lived in the house when it was in its original location in Scott.

SOURCE: *Garden Sass* by Nancy McDonough

Little Rock Central High *14th and Park Streets (501) 324-2300.* In September 1957 world-wide attention was riveted on this imposing brick building, which emerged as a symbol of racial intolerance. Built 30 years earlier at a then-astounding cost of $1,500,000, Little Rock Central High School was celebrated as "The Most Beautiful High School in America" by the American Institute of Architects and was a great source of pride for city fathers.

That all changed at the opening of the 1957-58 school year, when nine black students sought to gain an education there, following the U. S. Supreme Court's landmark Brown vs. Board of Education ruling, which decreed that racial segregation in public schools was

Central High School

unconstitutional. When Gov. Orval Faubus allowed the situation to get out of hand, President Eisenhower was forced to federalize the Arkansas National Guard in order to ensure the safety of the students. Troops continued to patrol the school until the academic year ended in 1958. Before school reopened, the Arkansas Legislature passed a law giving the governor power to close schools that were in danger of being integrated. When the feds insisted on integration without delay, Faubus closed down all four of the city's high schools. Little Rock voters endorsed the action in a special election. The schools remained closed for the 1958-59 school year, an event that spawned several private schools for whites and kept many kids both black and white from attending school that year.

After the closings, school board members resigned and new ones were elected. Three of the new members proved rabid segregationists. There was a recall election and voters retained the three moderates and ousted the segregationists. In June 1959 a special federal court declared the school closing law unconstitutional. Little Rock schools reopened in the fall, but not without protests and violence. Three weeks into the term, three bombs went off in Little Rock, one at a school board office. The five offenders were caught and convicted. In 1959-60, a smattering of black students attended Central. Throughout this dark period, as the world watched the tragedy unfold, lives and careers collapsed in almost casual fashion. Villains – and a few heroes – abounded. The *Arkansas Gazette*, which later won a Pulitzer Prize for its coverage, lost circulation when it bucked popular sentiment. Moderate Congressman Brooks Hays was defeated by outspoken segregationist Dr. Dale Alford after an eight-day write-in campaign. Faubus, however, found himself in the catbird seat. His popularity grew immensely, even beyond Arkansas. In 1960 the National States Rights Party nominated him for president; Faubus supported John Kennedy.

It would be nice to say that race is no longer an issue in Little Rock public schools, but it would not be accurate. Today, Central High, as well as the entire school district is 65% black due to the numbers of white families who have opted for bedroom communities or the stability of private schools.

Over the years, the old, still-impressive Gothic building has served as the site of several movies and TV shows recounting this painful episode of Arkansas, and American, history. Most recently, it can been seen in Disney's *The Ernest Green Story*, which portrayed the personal experiences of one of the original black students. Due to its pivotal role in the nation's march toward equal rights, Little Rock Central High was declared the city's first National Historic Landmark by the National Park Service. It is also listed on the register of National Historic Places.

Little Rock Zoo *#1 Jonesboro Drive. (501) 663-4733.* Located in War Memorial Park, the zoo houses over 600 animals on 40 acres. Open since 1926, modern additions include a Tropical Rain Forest Display, Big Cat Display and the Great Ape Exhibit. Children's Kiddieland features a miniature train ride encircling the duck pond. Children under 12 must be accompanied by an adult. No pets in zoo.

Maumelle Park *West of town off Ark. 10.* Boating, camping, fishing, playgrounds, baseball fields, volleyball and basketball court. On the Little Maumelle River in the shadow of Pinnacle Mountain.

Mount Holly Cemetery *Located from 11th Street to 13th Street,Gaines Street to Broadway. (501) 663-3629.* "The Westminster of Arkansas." As the only cemetery in town from 1843 to 1863, this is the burial place of many prominent figures from Arkansas' territorial days up to the present.

Murry's Dinner Playhouse *6323 Asher Avenue. (501) 562-3131.* Get a generous helping of entertainment and good food at one location. Seating for 300.

Old State House *300 West Markham. (501) 324-9685.* Opened in 1836, this example of Greek Revival architecture was the state's Capitol from 1836-1911. The building now houses the Arkansas Museum of History and Archives. It is recognized architecturally as one of the most beautiful antebellum structures in the South. Construction was begun in 1833 and completed about ten years later at a cost of $125,000. In 1836, while still incomplete, the building was used as the meeting place of the first state Legislature and for the inauguration of Arkansas' first governor, James S. Conway. The building and property are owned and maintained by the state. By 1951 legislative action, the former designation of War Memorial building was officially changed to The Old State House. Permanent exhibits include Arkansas' First Ladies' gowns, an exhibit about President Bill Clinton, a Wilderness Gallery and 19th century legislative and executive chambers. In Granny's Attic, visitors can see and touch Victorian era items. The Old State House was the backdrop for President Clinton's 1992 election night victory speech. Free admission.

Philander Smith College *812 W. 13th. (501) 375-9845.* Established in 1877, this is the state's oldest private historically-black institution of higher learning. Located near I-630 on an enclosed 12-square-block campus in the Quapaw Quarter, PSC is a non-sectarian college affiliated with the United Methodist Church and the United Negro College Fund. Enrollment is around 900 students with dormitory space for 220. Facilities include a 500-seat auditorium. Dr. Joycelyn Elders, controversial activist who served briefly as Surgeon General of the United States, is a graduate.

Pinnacle Mountain State Park *West of town on Ark. 300, off Ark. 10. (501) 868-5806.* An environmental education 1,770-acre park with interpretive programs. Visitor center has displays and audio-visual program. Hiking trails lead to the summit of Pinnacle Mountain. Arkansas Arboretum is newest feature with plant life displays native to all regions of the state.

Quapaw Quarter *1315 Scott Street. (501) 371-0075.* Historic downtown area with many restored antebellum and Victorian structures on the National Historic Register. Self-guided walking and driving tours through the oldest part of the city are available from the Quapaw Quarter Association which also sponsors an annual tour of private historic homes held the first week-end in May.

Riverfront Park *La Harpe Blvd., from Arch to Commerce Streets. (501) 371-4770.* Developed along 10 city blocks of the Arkansas River, this park features the "little rock," the landmark for which the city was named by La Harpe, a history pavilion and an amphitheater.

CHEAP SKATE

During the winter of 1880, the Arkansas River froze solid enough for skating. For the first time ice skates were sold in Little Rock. For many years people dated everything from "the winter the river froze over."

SOURCE: *The Story of Arkansas* by Presson and Thomas

Robinson Center *Markham and Broadway. Box office: (501) 372-0699.* Performing arts center hosts many productions, exhibitions and conventions. It is home to the Arkansas Symphony, the Broadway Theater Series, and Ballet Arkansas.

State Capitol Building *Located on Woodlane and Capitol. (501) 682-5080.* Construction began in 1899; the General Assembly moved into the building in 1911. The rest of the state government followed by 1914. The current Capitol building is a 3/4 scale replica of the nation's Capitol in Washington D.C. The greater part of the stone used is Batesville marble and was quarried in Arkansas. Changing exhibits in the public areas. No admission charged. Gift shop on the first floor with a variety of Arkansas souvenirs. Tours available.

Statehouse Convention Center *Located between La Harpe and Markham Streets in the Statehouse Plaza on the lower level of the Excelsior Hotel. (501) 376-4781.* Little Rock's newest convention facility, with over 62,000 feet of exhibit space.

Taborian Hall *9th and State Streets.* Built in 1916 as the headquarters for the Arkansas Chapter of the Knights and Daughters of Tabor, a national black fraternity, the building was one of the anchors of 9th street which served as the black business and cultural community until the 1950s. Louis Armstrong, Count Basie, Cab Calloway and Duke Ellington all played the hall's ballroom.

Villa Marre – TV star

Trapnall Hall *423 E. Capitol. (501) 372-4791.* Listed on the National Register of Historic Places, this 1843 building was restored in 1963. Open for tours. The Governor's Reception Hall is available for rental.

University of Arkansas at Little Rock (UALR) *2801 S. University. (501) 569-3362.* The University's metropolitan branch serves more than 13,000 students. The 150-acre campus continues to grow, opening its first 306-bed residence hall in 1992. Other facilities include a theater, two art galleries, recital hall and a planetarium which has a 40-foot acoustical dome and a quadraphonic sound system and a Minolta star projector *(501) 569 3277.*

University of Arkansas for Medical Sciences *4301 W. Markham. (501) 686-5000.* Incorporates the Colleges of Medicine, Nursing, Pharmacy, Health-Related Professions, Graduate School, Child Study Center and a 375-bed teaching hospital and affiliated Ambulatory Care Center. A new family medical center was opened in 1986, the Arkansas Cancer Research Center in 1989. The eight-story, 505-bed John L.

McClellan Memorial Veterans Administration Medical Center is located on the south end of the campus. *(501) 661-1202.*

Villa Marre *1321 Scott. (501) 374-9979.* This 19th century Italianate Victorian residence owned by the Quapaw Quarter Association is authentically decorated with period furnishings with pieces dating from 1850-1910 and open for tours.The exterior was used as the establishing shot of Shugarbaker's on the CBS sitcom *Designing Women.* Admission charged. Rentable for private functions.

War Memorial Park *West Markham and Fair Park.* Ray Winder Field, home of the Arkansas Travelers baseball team (a AA farm team for the St. Louis Cardinals), seats over 8,000. (501) 664-1555. War Memorial Stadium (seats 53,000) hosts Razorback football games (501) 663-0775. A fitness complex includes indoor and outdoor pools. A golf course is also located here, (501) 663-0854.

Wildwood Park for the Performing Arts *Denny Road, 1.6 miles off Kanis Road west of Little Rock. (501) 821-0285.* 105-acre forested complex of performance theaters, where music and crafts festivals are held each year. The month-long celebration of music and the arts in May draws many notable artists and performers.

• •

NO PLACE TO RUN; NO PLACE TO HIDE

The HBO documentary "Gang War: Bangin' in Little Rock" made a lot of racket when it premiered August 2, 1994. The film was about the upsurge of gang activities in heartland cities across the U.S. and it focused on Little Rock where the murder rate per capita is higher than either Los Angeles or New York. More than 50 gangs have been identified in Little Rock and many members are affiliated with major national gangs such as the Crips from Los Angeles and the Vice Lords from Chicago. Smaller cities like Little Rock are increasingly being used by major gangs to expand drug markets and other illegal trades. The one-hour documentary was filled with drive-by shootings and brutal killings which have become routine in the capital city. It is estimated that one in eleven kids in Pulaski County are gang members. To add credence to the documentary's portrayal, a 1994 assessment by the FBI ranked Little Rock as the fourth most dangerous city in the country – a distinction we're not too proud of. Atlanta was ranked number one, followed by St. Louis. Newark, New Jersey, came in third.

• •

YES, YOU CAN GET HERE FROM THERE.

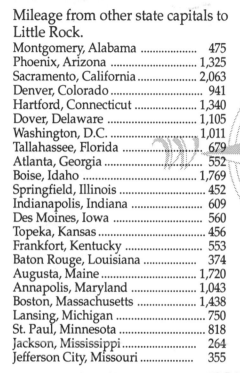

Mileage from other state capitals to Little Rock.

Montgomery, Alabama	475
Phoenix, Arizona	1,325
Sacramento, California	2,063
Denver, Colorado	941
Hartford, Connecticut	1,340
Dover, Delaware	1,105
Washington, D.C.	1,011
Tallahassee, Florida	679
Atlanta, Georgia	552
Boise, Idaho	1,769
Springfield, Illinois	452
Indianapolis, Indiana	609
Des Moines, Iowa	560
Topeka, Kansas	456
Frankfort, Kentucky	553
Baton Rouge, Louisiana	374
Augusta, Maine	1,720
Annapolis, Maryland	1,043
Boston, Massachusetts	1,438
Lansing, Michigan	750
St. Paul, Minnesota	818
Jackson, Mississippi	264
Jefferson City, Missouri	355

Helena, Montana	1,728
Lincoln, Nebraska	602
Carson City, Nevada	1,952
Concord, New Hampshire	1,550
Trenton, New Jersey	1,078
Santa Fe, New Mexico	873
Albany, New York	1,357
Raleigh, North Carolina	901
Bismarck, North Dakota	1,318
Columbus, Ohio	734
Oklahoma City, Oklahoma	344
Salem, Oregon	2,186
Harrisburg, Pennsylvania	1,091
Providence, Rhode Island	1,369
Columbia, South Carolina	759
Pierre, South Dakota	998
Nashville, Tennessee	346
Austin, Texas	477
Salt Lake City, Utah	1,438
Montpelier, Vermont	1,539
Richmond, Virginia	952
Olympia, Washington	2,303
Charleston, West Virginia	730
Madison, Wisconsin	719
Cheyenne, Wyoming	1,065

FORT SMITH

Sebastian County has two county seats: Fort Smith and Greenwood. Population: 72,798.

Information: Chamber of Commerce; 612 Garrison Avenue; P.O. Box 1668; Fort Smith, AR 72902. (501) 783-6118. Fort Smith Convention and Visitors Bureau; 2 North B; Fort Smith, AR 72901; (501) 783-8888. 1-800-637-1477.

Tours: C & C Frontier Tours; 3rd and Rogers Avenue. (501) 674-2865. Tour the Historic District on an 1880s mule-drawn covered wagon or a Victorian surrey. Tours depart in front of the Fort Smith Historic Site.

HISTORY

In 1808 a delegation of Cherokee from Tennessee visited Washington to ask for territory west of the Mississippi River. The U.S. government agreed and secured land from the Osage in today's Arkansas and Missouri. The Cherokee began moving west. By 1813 a number of them had emigrated and settled on the Arkansas and White rivers. Almost immediately the Cherokee, who in large measure had adopted the white man's ways, clashed with the Osage, a tribe that had been in contact with the whites for 100 years, but had steadfastly clung to its ancient ways.

In 1817, Bvt. Major William Bradford moved a company of the U.S. Rifle Regiment up the Arkansas River and established a military outpost in order to keep the peace between the warring tribes. On Christmas Day 1817, Bradford landed at Belle Point and put his men to work building Fort Smith, which was named for Bradford's commanding officer, Bvt. Brig. General Thomas A. Smith. In 1824, the garrison received orders to move westward because of the hostilities on the frontier. They went 80 miles up the Arkansas River and established Fort Gibson. The army abandoned Fort Smith, but occasional transient troops continued to use the old post as temporary quarters.

More Indians arrived. For some time the U.S. government had been encouraging eastern Indians to move west. When Andrew Johnson became president in 1829, the government committed itself to moving all the eastern tribes to the Indian Territory. This enforced movement of the eastern tribes became known as the "Trail of Tears." Not only did the Indians lose their homes, but thousands died on the march west.

The five eastern tribes who came to the territory were far more sophisticated that the "wild" tribes to the west. They built

Judge Parker's courtroom

villages, cotton gins, and schools and began transplanting their civilization to the wilderness. In 1834 the Choctaw assembled near present Tuskahoma, Oklahoma, to adopt their new constitution, patterned on that of the United States. Five years later, the Cherokee also adopted a constitution. They were soon followed by the others who became known as the Five Civilized Tribes, complete with their own courts, their Light Horse (an efficient mounted constabulary), and all the other departments necessary to functioning nations. While the Five Civilized Tribes were strengthening their governments, other tribes moved into the area. Alarmed by the increasing migration and by a growing feud among the full and mixed bloods of the Cherokee and Creek, Arkansas settlers demanded the re-establishment of Fort Smith. Army officers pointed out that the Five Tribes provided an effective buffer between the Plains Indians of the west and the white settlements. Presumably, intra-tribal squabbles would not affect the whites. The Army's role would be to occupy posts beyond the frontier to prevent hostile Indians from attacking the western settlements. Fort Smith was considered to be no longer on the frontier. The frontier lay on the western border of lands belonging to the Five Tribes.

But Arkansans were not impressed, and in 1838 their political pressure caused the Army to begin building a new Fort Smith near the earlier post, part of which is still standing. Although the original plans called for a large bastioned masonry fort, the Army, as expenses mounted, modified its plans; Fort Smith would be a supply depot for the more westerly posts. Late in 1842 the General Assembly incorporated Fort Smith, then a town of nearly 500 persons. Throughout the 1840s there was an epidemic of duels and fondness for horse racing. In fact, the first church in town was financed in 1844 by racing enthusiasts who raced their horses on Race Track Prairie at the edge of town.

Those with a penchant for settling differences with pistols fought it out on a sandbar on the Arkansas River in Indian Territory removed from those annoying anti-dueling laws. In 1848 one notable quarrel was between Albert Pike, author and attorney and John Selden Roane, later to be governor of Arkansas. A crowd gathered on the sandbar to observe the two first engage in the traditional formalities of bowing, shaking hands and so forth and then start blasting each other repeatedly with pistol fire with neither scoring a hit. A Cherokee named Bill Fields who was in attendance is said to have remarked that with such fine weapons he could kill a squirrel at 75 paces.

1848 was a memorable year. Gold was discovered in California and everybody and his dog lit out for riches. Fort Smith, which by 1849 was servicing only the frontier forts, was transformed overnight as a noisy supply depot and point of departure for hundreds of emigrants who took the southern route across the plains. This influx of emigrants brought with it the usual problems of revelry and rowdiness and the city saw fit in 1849 to pass ordinances to curb the offending activities. The city council reserved the right to " license, regulate, tax or suppress ... pawnbrokers, money changers ... public masquerade balls, sparring exhibitions, dance houses, fortune tellers, pistol galleries, corn doctors ... museums and menageries ... horoscopic views, lung testers, muscle developers ... billiard tables and other instruments used for gaming." While the gold rush created prosperity as well as problems in Fort Smith, the good fortune did not trickle down throughout the state. Arkansas lost 1,000 people in 1849 and 2,000 in 1850.

At the start of the Civil War, Fort Smith was taken by Confederate troops and later by Union troops. It would change hands several times before the end of the war. No major battles took place here and the commissary building was alternately used as a prison or a refuge for women and children. By 1871, the Army decided that Fort Smith had outlived its usefulness. The Indian frontier had moved so much farther west that the old post could not even serve efficiently as a supply depot. The Army moved its few remaining troops out; a year later, the U.S. Court for the Western District of Arkansas moved in.

All hell had broken loose in the Indian Territory (that sprawl of land which would not come become the state of Oklahoma until 1907). The

Invitation to a neck-tie party

Indians had their own laws, but they had no authority over whites so the Territory became a haven for lawless bands of murderers, train robbers and bandits who found the rugged terrain and legal entanglements a real plus. Desperadoes like the James Gang, Belle Starr and Cole Younger whooped it up. Only the Western District Court at Fort Smith had jurisdiction over the crimes involving persons not subject to tribal courts. A handful of U.S. deputy marshals and tribal Light Horse struggled to keep order. This was the situation when 36-year-old Judge Isaac C. Parker arrived at Fort Smith in 1875. His predecessor had resigned under a cloud. Parker, a Republican and an outsider, and the youngest member of the judicial bench, found little welcome in Fort Smith. Parker definitely had his hands full; the town had 2,500 people, 39 saloons but no paved roads, sidewalks or public schools. But he brought to the Western District Court personal dedication, incorruptibility and a sympathy for the Indian. These qualities soon won him respect at Fort Smith and in the Territory. He also brought another much-needed quality – energy. His unique court demanded it. The District Court for Western Arkansas had the normal federal jurisdiction for approximately one-half of the state, although the court's greatest influence and authority was felt in the Indian Territory. For years, Parker's court opened at 8:30 a.m. and continued until dusk, sometimes into the night.

During his 21 years on the bench he saw more than 13,000 cases docketed in his court. More than 9,000 defendants were convicted or pleaded guilty. Of these, 344 were tried for capital offenses and 160 were sentenced to hang. Only 79 were hanged, but they were cited as proof of the "hanging judge's" severity. (Ironically, he has been described as pink-cheeked, slightly rotund with a contagious chuckle that reminded one of Santa Claus.) Few detractors took notice of the tremendous load of the Western District Court, or to the savage nature of the crimes committed in the Indian Territory. Parker, in later years, said, "It was not I who hung them. I never hung a man. It is the law." In truth, he had no choice. Until 1897, the Revised Statutes of the United States specifically commanded that anyone convicted of murder or rape "shall suffer death." Only these two crimes carried the death penalty. Other felonies, such as horse stealing, brought prison terms. For the first 14 years Parker served, his court was unique in that sentences could not be appealed to higher courts – a presidential pardon was the only way out of a conviction. In 1889 and '91 Congress enacted laws that permitted the Supreme Court to review capital cases. Gradually, as more and more of the Indian country was opened, the new settlers demanded local courts. Finally, in September 1896, Parker's court lost its territorial jurisdiction.

Ten weeks later, the ailing judge died, a victim, his doctor said, of 21 years of overwork. He is buried in Forth Smith National Cemetery.

Fort Smith began the transformation from a frontier post to a city. In 1871 the military pulled out and the fort passed to the Department of the Interior. In 1879, the Little Rock & Fort Smith Railroads (now Missouri-Pacific) reached its western destination. Three years later, the St. Louis, Arkansas & Texas line would make its way down from Fayetteville. The railroads stimulated coal mining in the area and the mines increased the city's importance. In the early 1900s natural gas wells were drilled south of town and the cheap fuel brought factories. The low-cost fuel sources and the Arkansas River which provided a navigable channel to all ocean ports made Fort Smith one of the leading manufacturing cities in Arkansas. Today there are more than 200 plants producing a variety of products. Furniture is a big one, as well as air conditioning components for Whirlpool. Industry has proven to be a major economic force with accompanying cultural by-products. Even the first free public library in Arkansas was established in Fort Smith in 1908, the building donated by steel magnate Andrew Carnegie.

SOURCES: Fort Smith Chamber of Commerce; National Park Service, U.S. Department of the Interior, *WPA Guide to 1930s Arkansas.*

POINTS OF INTEREST

Alfonzo Trent Home *1301 N. 9th (Private residence).* Childhood home of this famous jazz musician who with his local band made a meteoric rise to the top playing Big Band sounds in the 20s and 30s. They became the first black band to broadcast in America, and the first to use the front entrance instead of the service entrances at clubs they played.

Belle Grove Historic District *North 5th, 6th, 7th, and 8th from North "C" to North "H."* Beautifully restored homes and buildings line the streets of the 22-block district and reflect an architectural span of 130 years. They showcase Romanesque Revival, Queen Anne, Eastlake Victorian Renaissance, Gothic Revival, Victorian Baroque, Second Empire and Transitional to Neo-Classical styles.

Bonneville House *(c.1868) 318 N. 7th. (501) 782-7854.* Victorian Renaissance home of Susan Bonneville, young widow of General Benjamin Bonneville, an explorer and commandant of Fort Smith's early garrison. Furnished with period antiques.

Chimney of Zachary Taylor's Home *Located at the east end of Garrison Avenue on the grounds of the Convent of Mercy.* At the beginning of a career which would lead to the presidency, General Zachary "Rough and Ready" Taylor took command of the unfinished fort in 1841 and moved his family to a residence here.

Clayton House *(c. 1882) 514 N. 6th. (501) 783-3000.* W.H.H. Clayton, U.S. District Attorney in Judge Parker's court, played an important role in civilizing the frontier. As State Superintendent of Public Instruction, he established over 30 public schools. The restored Victorian Renaissance Baroque home features elegant carved entrance doors, staircase and ornate fireplaces. Open for tours.

Darby House *311 General Darby Street. (501) 782-3388.* Boyhood home of General William O. Darby, famed leader of Darby's Rangers in World War II.

Fort Chaffee Established in 1941 and named after the late Maj. Gen. Adna R. Chaffee, the first chief of armed forces, the 72,000-acre post serves as the training site for the Army Reserves and National Guard. During WWII, Fort Chaffee was home to three Armored Divisions. It was here at the base barbershop that Elvis Presley received his basic training buzz cut in 1958. The event was documented by film crews and newspapers from around the country.

Fort Smith Art Center *423 N. 6th. (501-784-ARTS)* Located in the lovely Vaughn-Schaap home, a pink brick Victorian Second Empire house built around 1882 was the first house saved and restored in the Belle Grove District. It now houses a gallery of fine paintings and sculpture.

Fort Smith National Historic Site *Corner of 3rd and Rogers. (501) 783-3961.* Established in 1961, this unit of the National Park Service commemorates an important phase of American's westward expansion. The site includes :

- **Belle Point** High on a bluff overlooking the Arkansas River, this is the site of the first Fort Smith. Occupied by soldiers from 1817-1824, the original foundation remains.

- **Commissary Storehouse** Serving as a corner bastion for the second Fort Smith, this stone building was completed in 1846 and served many purposes over the years – barracks, residence for court officials, and Judge Parker's chambers.

- **Barracks/Courthouse/Jail** Rebuilt after a fire in 1851, this building was originally used as a barracks for troops stationed here. In 1972, the Federal Court for the Western District of Arkansas moved into the building. The infamous jail named "Hell on the Border" housed thousands of prisoners before a second jail was built.

- **Gallows** This reproduction of the 1886 gallows is a grim reminder of the chaotic conditions that existed during Judge Parker's time. From

1875-1896, Judge Parker heard more than 13,000 cases, and sentenced 160 to death. Only 79 criminals were actually hanged during his years on the bench. The original gallows could hang as many as six criminals, and was later replaced by one constructed on this site that could hang up to 12 at one time. It was taken down and burned in 1897.

DID YOU KNOW?

How About A Raise?

When Judge Parker was appointed to the court in Fort Smith, he was only 36 years old, the youngest judge on the federal bench. He was given only 200 marshals to police nearly 74,000 square miles and 60,000 people. Sixty-five of the marshals died in the line of duty. Parker's salary was $3,500 per year.

SOURCE: *Law West of Fort Smith* by Glenn Shirley.

Fort Smith Park This riverside park offers sandy beach, launch ramps and picnic pavilions.

Fort Smith Trolley Museum *100 S. 4th Street. (501) 783-0205.* Features restored Fort Smith Birney electric streetcars and two city buses. Railroad cabooses and other memorabilia. Offers a round-trip trolley ride from the Trolley Museum to Old Fort Museum.

Free Ferry Road Lined with outstanding "Gilded Age" homes built in the early 1900s. The road was so named because it led to the free ferry across the Arkansas River east of the city.

Frisco Railroad Station *(1904) First and Garrison,* adjacent to the Fort Smith National Historic Site.

Miss Laura's Social Club *(c. 1899) 123 Front Street. (501) 783-8888.* This celebrated bordello was built when Oklahoma was still Indian Territory and it is the only one remaining of the brothels called "The Row" that originally stood on bustling Front Street on the Arkansas River. The Fort Smith Convention and Visitors' Bureau currently operates out of this house which is the only bordello on the National Register of Historic Places and the state's only documented brothel. This Victorian Baroque style house has three oeil-de-boef (eye of the ox) cast iron dormers, set in a mansard roof. Open seven days a week and staffed by very friendly volunteers who'll fill you in on all the gossip about Miss Laura, her girls and their clientele.

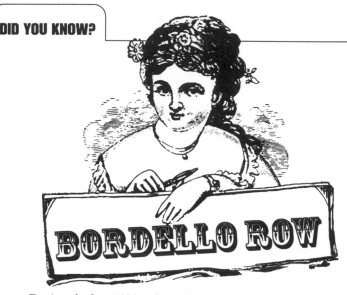

DID YOU KNOW?

During the late 1800s when adventurers and desperadoes roamed the Territory, houses of prostitution flourished openly in Fort Smith. The "Row" of seven to ten brothels originally stood on bustling Front Street (later named North First Street) along the Arkansas River. Pearl Starr, daughter of the infamous outlaw Belle Starr, worked at various times in seven of the houses. She is listed on a medical ledger in 1914 as madam of a house at 215 N. First. The Red-Light District was clearly defined by city officials and when they caught Pearl operating from an apartment on South 14th which was out of bounds for hookers, they banned her from the city during the 1920s.

The most celebrated house and the only one remaining is Miss Laura's Social Club, a Victorian Baroque two-story clapboard building with a mansard roof trimmed in wrought iron and oeil-de-boef dormer windows. Laura Zeigler bought the house at 123 Front Street for $3,000 in 1898 and sold it by 1911 to Bertha Gale Dean for $47,000. In 1924 the city fathers, after considerable nudging from the city mothers, finally outlawed prostitution. In actuality, the house continued to do a brisk business until Miss Dean sold it in 1948. Miss Laura's "daughters of joy" allegedly chilled champagne in an upstairs bathtub every Saturday night for their clientele (though their gentlemen callers probably did not frequent Miss Laura's for the beverages). Miss Laura's, still one of the most popular attractions in the Belle Grove Historic District, is on the National Register of Historic Places as Arkansas' only documented brothel. The Fort Smith Bureau of Conventions and Visitors currently operates out of the house. (They provide information and gossip *only*. No champagne in the tub.)

Old Fort Museum *320 Rogers Avenue. (501) 783-7841.* The museum features exhibits on the history of the region from 1917 to the present. Includes a collection of memorabilia and papers of World War II hero William O. Darby. Working old-fashioned soda fountain and gift shop.

Old Fort Rodeo Days Memorial Day kicks off one of the world's largest outdoor rodeos held each year at the fairgrounds. The world's richest barrel race futurity is held the week-end preceding the rodeo.

Old Town *Corner of Garrison Avenue and 5th.* A renovation of interesting and historical buildings from the late 1800s. Old Town contains shops, offices and apartments.

Patent Model Museum *400 N. 8th. (501) 782-9014.* Housed in the Rogers-Tilles House some 85 models made by inventors dated 1836-1870. The 1840s home is believed to have been built by the John Rogers family, founders of the town. It was purchased by the Louis Tilles family in 1867. Its architecture and solid brick construction is an exact copy built on a smaller scale of the barracks building of the second fort.

Miss Laura's house of ill-repute

Rogers House *904 N. 11th.* Fort Smith's most historically significant residence was built around 1865 by William Rogers, son of Captain Rogers, the founder of the town, who was appointed by the governor to be the first mayor of Fort Smith in 1842. The Victorian Renaissance style raised-cottage brick home is unusual in Arkansas.

St. Anne's Convent *Rogers Avenue, just east of the Immaculate Conception Church.* Built in 1906, this magnificent French Renaissance Chateau-style building is the only one of its style surviving in Arkansas.

Sparks House *(1887) 201 N. 14th. (501) 785-2252.* Home to Taliano's Restaurant. Built by the son of a pioneer family locally prominent in medical and financial circles. Victorian Queen Anne style has an unusual circular front window and iron flower box.

U.S. National Cemetery *South 6th and Garland.* Soldiers from Fort Smith's first garrison, Judge Parker, many of his Deputy Marshals, General William O. Darby and Civil War veterans are among those who are buried here.

Weidman's Old Fort Brew Pub *422 N. 3rd. (501) 782-9898.* A restored working brewery originally established in 1848 by German immigrant Joseph Knoble to supply beer to local pubs. The pub features made-on-the-premises beer, pasta, bread and sausages.

West Garrison Historic District Listed on the National Register, many of these old buildings in the downtown area now house restaurants, antique shops and a crafts mall.

FAMOUS LAST WORDS

When Cherokee Bill Goldsby, whom humorist H. Allen Smith called "one of the uncouthest creatures ever to come out of Oklahoma Territory," was asked on the gallows at Fort Smith if he had any final words, he replied, "Hell, no. Cherokee Bill came here to get hung, not to make no speeches."

NORTH LITTLE ROCK

County: Pulaski. Population: 61,741

Information: North Little Rock Advertising & Promotion Commission: P.O. Box 5511; NLR 72119 (501) 758-1424. Visitor Information Center: Exit 150 of Interstate 40 in Burns Park. Complete information on state and metropolitan resources, tourist attractions. Maps, restrooms, rest areas.

HISTORY

In 1839, one year after the steam ferry began crossing the river at Little Rock, a United States Army officer laid out a town on the north side and named it De Cantillon after himself. His little venture was unsuccessful, probably because most of the town site was covered by a cypress bog. The north bank was a popular area for hunting and the area became known as Huntersville and gradually was settled. The stagecoach lines operating from Fort Smith and DeValls Bluff met at Huntersville and passengers were ferried to and from Little Rock from there. A Frenchman built a hotel at the ferry landing and probably inspired by the discovery of a silver vein northeast of town, he named his business "Hotel Argenta," argenta being Latin for Silver. The settlement that grew up around the hotel took the name Argenta and was incorporated as a town in 1871. The next year the Cairo & Fulton Railroad established a terminal here. A railroad town, Argenta flourished and in 1890 Little Rock annexed part of Argenta. For 12 years, it was the eighth ward of Little Rock, a move which antagonized Argenta citizens who were trying to establish a high school there and the annexation diluted their tax base.

In the early 1900s, the small community was a boisterous town with a reputation for sleazy bars, gambling joints and cathouses. City services were almost nonexistent. In 1903, two brothers named J.C. and W.C. "Bill" Faucette set about to change things. Bill, a railroad engineer, wanted to be mayor of Little Rock. He ran in 1903 and lost. Subsequently, the Faucette brothers along with a group of citizens who were equally fed up with their community's step-child status, devised a plan to secede from Little Rock.

With the aid of some of the state's lawyers, Faucette drafted and introduced a bill to the Arkansas Legislature that had to do with districts lying between incorporated cities. On the face of it, the bill appeared to affect only the twin towns of Hoxie and Walnut Ridge. The Legislature passed the Walnut Ridge-Hoxie Bill and North Little Rock (a designation used by Little Rock Realtors) was voted back into Argenta. The name North Little Rock was officially adopted in 1917.

For many years thereafter, North Little Rock continued to be regarded as a poor relation to Little Rock. The city was known as "Dog Town" because of the Little Rock custom of dumping stray dogs there. Vestiges of the twin-city rivalry still exist, but North Little Rock has come into its own as a separate, distinct entity.

SOURCES: NLR Advertising & Promotion Commission, *WPA Guide to 1930s Arkansas*

POINTS OF INTEREST

Arkansas River Some of the best bass, catfish, and crappie fishing in central Arkansas, right in the heart of the city. Free public launch ramps in Burns Park, Murray Lock and Dam (near I-40 and I-430) and Terry Lock and Dam (near I-40 and I-440).

Arkansas Riverboat Company *Riverfront Park (501) 376-4150.* Cruises and dinner/dance excursions along the Arkansas River on the *Spirit*, a 150-passenger authentic paddle wheel riverboat. A stationary floating restaurant on an adapted Ohio-Mississippi River towboat is also located here. Private charters are available on both vessels.

Burns Park *Exit 150 off I-40. (501) 758-2400.* America's second-largest municipal park covers 1,575 acres. Activities include hiking, picnicking, golfing, baseball, soccer, archery, motocross tracks, and fishing and boating on the White Oak Bayou. The Tennis and Sports Center has six indoor and six outdoor courts. There are 37 camp sites – RV or tent. Funland play area for kids includes a 26-ton red caboose, miniature train, sandbox and slides, miniature golf.

Plane with personality at Camp Robinson

Camp Robinson *Ark. 176. (501) 751-5100.* Named for U.S. Senator Joe T. Robinson, this 32,000-acre area serves as headquarters and training base for the Arkansas National Guard and as a base for Army Reserves. It was used as a training camp for recruits during both World Wars.

McCain Mall *Off I-40.* The largest shopping center in central Arkansas (56.6 acres). The enclosed two-level mall is anchored by four major department stores.

The Old Mill *Lakeshore and Fairway Streets. (501) 758-2400.* In 1933 developer Justin Matthews contracted for the construction of a replica of an old water-powered grist mill. This authentic re-creation was

The Old Mill

ultimately filmed for the opening sequence of *Gone With The Wind.* Dionico Rodriguez, a sculptor and artist, was responsible for all the details of each piece of concrete work made to represent wood, iron or stone, as well as designing the footbridges and rustic seats. The mill was given to the city of North Little Rock on May 24, 1976, and placed on the National Register of Historic Places in 1986. Open year-round. Free admission. Available for rental, the mill is a popular site for outdoor weddings.

Toltec Mounds State Park *Located 15 miles east of NLR. (501)961-9442.* Take Exit #7 off I-440, then southeast on U.S. 165 to the park. Designated as a state park in 1979, the park preserves and interprets Arkansas' tallest Indian mounds. These mounds and earthen embankments are the remains of a large ceremonial and governmental complex inhabited by prehistoric Indians from A.D. 600 to 950. Excavations on the mounds began a century ago. Research at the site continues today and is not expected to be complete until the turn of the 21st century. A century ago, 16 mounds were located on the site. Damage during the early part of this century destroyed all but four. Guided tours are available.

PINE BLUFF

Seat of Jefferson County. Population: 57,140.

Information: Chamber of Commerce; P.O. Box 5069; Pine Bluff, AR 71611; (501)535-0110; FAX: 501-535-4593. Pine Bluff Conventions and Visitors Bureau; One Convention Center Plaza; Pine Bluff, AR 71601. (501)536-7600.

HISTORY

In the summer of 1819, the Arkansas River flooded New Gascony, a settlement of French farmers. One of the Frenchmen, Joseph Bonne, moved a few miles upstream to higher ground, striking camp in a forest of giant pines situated on a high bluff above a bend in the river. There Bonne and his family opened a trading post for trappers and hunters. Other families followed, clearing land and planting cotton. The community that grew up was called Mount Marie.

In 1829 the territorial legislature created Jefferson County, with Mount Marie as the seat. In 1832 the town was renamed Pine Bluff. John Graham, an engineer and surveyor, drew up a town of 45 blocks with a court square. The city was incorporated January 10, 1839. By 1850 the population numbered 460. Located 110 miles upstream from the Mississippi River, Pine Bluff soon became a popular port. Steamboats took on cargoes of the cotton grown abundantly in the fields south and southeast of town. In town, planters resided in majestic homes, often replete with hand-carved woodwork and imported furnishings.

Pine Bluff claims the first shot of the Civil War was fired here, and not at Fort Sumter. In April of 1861, Federal steamboats carrying supplies for garrisons at Fort Smith and Fort Gibson were halted by a warning shot fired from the riverbank by the Jefferson Guards. Cargoes were confiscated for the Confederate Army.

The battle of Pine Bluff was the only real action of the war for the town. A Federal garrison of 600 troops under the command of General Powell Clayton held the town. Confederate General John S. Marmaduke, with 2,000 cavalrymen, attacked on October 25, 1863. After furious fighting in which the courthouse was shelled, the rebels were unable to dislodge the Union troops from behind their cotton bale barricades and were forced to withdraw. For the rest of the war, Pine Bluff remained in Federal control.

During the Reconstruction era, Pine Bluff prospered. Cotton was king and the town was Arkansas' center for ginning, baling and loading cotton onto the river barges. In the 1880s railway track was laid, bringing Pine Bluff into a system that stretched from Texas to St. Louis. Huge lumber mills sprang up, chewing up trees freighted from the vast forests of eastern and southern Arkansas. By 1890 the population hovered at 10,000. Today, Pine Bluff is the state's fourth largest city and the trade, entertainment and recreation center for the entire southeastern part of the state.

Agriculture is still a major contributor to the economy of Jefferson County. Cotton, soybeans, rice and wheat are the leading crops representing approximately 279,000 acres of production and sales of over $75 million annually. Two major federal government installations are located in Jefferson County. They are the Pine Bluff Arsenal which was constructed in 1941 to manufacture and assemble incendiary munitions, and the National Center for Toxicological Research, the basic research arm of the Food and Drug Administration .

SOURCE: Pine Bluff Chamber of Commerce

POINTS OF INTEREST

Arkansas Agricultural Tours *(501) 536-7606.* Tours take you to see exactly how crops are grown, harvested, processed and delivered to the market.

Arkansas Department of Correction The central administrative offices are located west of Pine Bluff on Princeton Pike Road. *(501) 247-1800.* Correctional facilities in the Pine Bluff area are:

- **Cummins Unit** Established in 1902. Located 28 miles south of Pine Bluff off Hwy. 65.

- **Varner Unit** Established 1987, 28 miles south of Pine Bluff off Hwy. 65.

- **Diagnostic Unit** Established in 1981. West of Pine Bluff off West 7th Street in Jefferson County. All male inmates, except death row inmates, are tested and classified at the unit before being transferred to a permanent unit.

- **Pine Bluff Unit** Established 1976, same location as Diagnostic Unit.

- **Jefferson County Jail/Correctional Facility** Established 1990. West of Pine Bluff off West 7th Street.

- **Maximum Security** Established 1983, 25 miles northeast of Pine Bluff, off Highway 15 in Tucker. Location of Death Row.

- **Tucker Unit** Established 1916. Located 25 miles northeast of Pine Bluff.

Arkansas Railroad Museum *Off U.S. 65 on E. Barraque. (501) 541-1819.* Railroad memorabilia and restored railroad cars featuring Engine 819, the last 4-8-4 Northern-type steam locomotive built at Pine Bluff by the

Cotton Belt Railway. (Managed by volunteers; call before visiting to be sure it's open.)

Band Museum *423 Main Street. (501) 541-0500.* Opened in 1994 by aptly-named Jerry Horne, owner of Wallick Music Company, this museum is a celebration of the traditional American band. Highlights include an exhibit covering the Fort Smith "Smile Girls." This all-girl band sponsored by Max Wortz of Wortz Biscuits in Fort Smith marched across the country in the 1940s playing weird honking instruments. Exhibits rotate. Thought to be the only collection in the country dedicated to wind instruments. Admission free. Donations accepted.

Ben Pearson Home *716 W. Barraque. (501) 535-0463.* French Provincial design dates to 1881. Restored in 1967 by Pearson, the world-famous archer and bowhunter. (By the way, Barraque was the first paved street in Pine Bluff.)

Dexter Harding House *1104 W. 5th Avenue. (501) 536-7606.* Pine St. Exit off U.S. 65. Built in 1850 by one of the area's earliest settlers. Restored in 1976, it now serves as the official visitor center for Pine Bluff.

DuBocage Home *1115 W. 4th. (501) 536-7606.* Home of Judge Joseph W. and Frances Lindsay Bocage. This planter's mansion was built in 1866, restored in 1970 by the Optimist Club. Greek Revival style with beautiful winding staircase and period furnishings.

King Cotton Classic *Pine Bluff Convention Center. (501) 534-5464 or tollfree outside Arkansas 1-800-545-4640.* Begun in 1983 by Travis Creed, this is now the top high school basketball tournament in the U.S.

Margland Bed and Breakfast Inns *703 W. 2nd. (501) 536-6000.* Restored complex of three Victorian houses.

Martha Mitchell Home *902 W. 4th. (501) 536-7606.* Childhood home of the late Martha Beall Mitchell, the outspoken wife of the former Attorney General John Mitchell during the Watergate scandal. She died in 1977. The home was built in 1887 by her grandfather C.M. Ferguson, a wholesale grocer and native of Chester, South Carolina. Restored in 1976, the house has both Oriental and Victorian features and is furnished with period pieces from 1900-1930.

Murals on Main *(501)536-8742.* Colorful murals downtown depict the city's past and earned Pine Bluff the nickname "City of Murals."

Pine Bluff Arsenal Ten miles north, this 15,000-acre Army military reservation currently manufactures smoke munitions and provides security for about 12% of the Army's aging chemical weapons stockpile located there. Congress has ordered destruction of the weapons by 2004. The arsenal has been steadily down-sizing since 1990. During WWII the arsenal employed more than 20,000 civilians.

Pine Bluff Civic Center *200 East 8th Avenue.* Designed by Edward Durrell Stone, Arkansas native and world famous architect, completed in 1968. The center houses Arkansas' only authentic Japanese garden, a gift from Pine Bluff's "sister city" Iwai, Japan.

Pine Bluff Convention and Visitors Center *One Convention Center Plaza. (501) 536-7600.* The state's largest meeting facility includes a 2,000-seat theater, a 10,000 seat multi-purpose arena, a 12,000 square foot lobby-exhibition area and a 14,500 square foot banquet hall that seats 1,500.

One of many murals

Pine Bluff/Jefferson County Historical Museum *201 E. 4th. (501) 541-5402.* Traces the history of the area from 1830 to the present. Located in the restored Union Station depot.

Sissy's Log Cabin *2319 Camden Road. (501) 879-3040.* Sissy Jones opened an antiques business in a ramshackle log cabin in 1970. Then she designed her trademark "Victorian slide bracelets" which brought international recognition. At the 1992 inaugural festivities, Hillary wore a pendant designed by Sissy's son Bill.

DID YOU KNOW?

THE LAST MAN CLUB

In 1938, on Armistice Day, 347 Arkansas veterans of
WWI gathered in Pine Bluff to commemorate the 20th
anniversary of the end of the war. They decided to
form The Last Man Club, a tontine established around
a then-20-year-old bottle of cognac. They closed the
membership rolls and vowed to meet every year, until
one member remained. He would then inherit the
brandy. The final roll call was held July 25, 1992.
Oliver M. Williams, a former state representative from
Sheridan, opened the bottle and toasted his fallen
comrades – the surviving member of The Last Man Club.

Southeast Arkansas Arts and Sciences Center Located in the Civic
Center, includes theater, research library and two art galleries.

Trinity Episcopal Church *701 W. 3rd.* Oldest Episcopal church building
in Arkansas. Cornerstone laid 1866. Classic Gothic architecture.

University of Arkansas Pine Bluff *Highway 79N and Cedar. (501) 543-
8000.* Second oldest public institution of higher learning in the state.
Until 1973 it was called Arkansas AM & N College. 220-acre farm is
under cultivation for laboratory work in agriculture. "Persistence of the
Spirit" exhibit at UAPB chronicles the lives and struggles of black
Arkansans from 1803-1986.

JONESBORO

Seat of Craighead County. Population: 46,535

Information: Chamber of Commerce; 593 S. Madison; Jonesboro, AR
72403. (501) 932-6691.

HISTORY

The first white settler in the area was Daniel Martin, who in 1829
homesteaded with his family six miles southwest of the present city.
Almost 30 years later with an ever-growing immigrant population, it
became apparent to many members of the Arkansas General Assembly
that to govern effectively, a new county seat was needed in the
northeast section of the state. The main proponent of the move to

establish another county seat was Senator William A. Jones, who was the representative from Poinsett and St. Francis counties. Senator Thomas B. Craighead, however, representing Crittenden and Mississippi counties, was stubbornly opposed to the idea since the proposed county would include alluvial farm lands which had been providing a lucrative source of revenue to some of his constituents in Mississippi County. A master of political strategy, Jones waited until Craighead was absent from the chamber to call for a final vote on the measure.

With their leader gone, the opposing forces were unable to swing the vote in their favor and the bill passed, much to the consternation of Senator Craighead when he found out. In a spirit of good will, however, Jones moved that the new county be named after the senator who had been most opposed to its creation. So Craighead County came into being on February 19, 1859, composed of land from parts of Greene, Mississippi, and Poinsett counties. Fergus Snoddy donated 15 acres on the crest of Crowley's Ridge as a town site.

Soon afterward, the county seat was named Jonesboro in honor of the legislator who had worked so successfully in its behalf. (Jonesboro residents should thank their lucky stars that they aren't living in *Snoddyville*.) Jonesboro is nestled in the rolling wooded foothills of Crowley's Ridge and is the largest city in northeast Arkansas. It is the hub of agricultural production with Delta cotton land to the east and rice fields to the southwest. Riceland Foods has the world's largest rice mill in Jonesboro and major firms like Dupont and GE contribute to the local economy. Jonesboro is home to Arkansas State University and Debbye Turner, 1990 Miss America. Other notable natives are Hattie W. Caraway, the first woman to be elected to the United States Senate and best-selling novelist John Grisham. Jonesboro was listed in a recent publication *The Best Towns in America* by Hugh Bayless.

SOURCE: Chamber of Commerce, *WPA Guide to 1930s Arkansas*

POINTS OF INTEREST

Arkansas State University Located on more than 800 acres the University serves approximately 10,000 students and is a major presence in the city. ASU offers degrees in more than 70 major fields in eight different colleges and an independent engineering department. Write: ASU; P.O. Box 1630; State University, AR 72467. (501) 972-3024.

ASU Museum *(501) 972-2074.* Begun in 1936, this accredited 35,000 square-foot facility is located in the Continuing Education Building on campus. Emphasis is on northeast Arkansas with over 100 exhibits from

10,000-year-old prehistoric fossils to the present. Guided tours available.

ASU Convocation Center *217 Olympic Drive, ASU campus. (501) 972-3870.* Completed in 1987, at a cost of $18.6 million, this state-of-the-art entertainment and sports complex features seating for over 10,000 and 77,000 square feet of exhibition space. The center boasts the largest telescoping seating configuration in the world.

Craighead County Courthouse *S. Main between Washington and Jackson.* Completed in 1934 at a cost of $125,000, this unusual building is the only truly Art Deco courthouse in the state. Located on the grounds are two monuments: one honoring WWI soldiers and sailors; another in memory of Hattie Caraway, the first woman elected to the U.S. Senate and the first woman to head a Senate committee and to preside over the Senate.

Craighead Forest Park *307 Forest Park Loop. (501) 935-9410.* Located south of the city on Crowley's Ridge. This city-owned 612-acre park has an 80-acre lake, 26 campsites and facilities for fishing, picnicking, boating, plus an off-road cycle area and ball field.

Forum Civic Center *115 E. Monroe. (501) 935-2726.* This restored movie theater now serves as a performing arts center.

Quality Gladiolus Gardens *Highway 1B South. (501) 932-4533.* A 50-acre site for commercially grown flowers. Walking and van tours available.

Saudi Arabian Customs Training Project From 1982 to 1992 this was the only program of its kind in America. The program at ASU provided a two-year computer education program as well as training in English and administration for recently-recruited and "in service" customs agents.

Witch Hunt Jonesboro received national and international media attention in 1993 when local witches who were operating a small shop selling witch paraphernalia were practically burned at the stake by some of the locals who decided freedom of religion did not extend to their unorthodox neighbors. The witches protested and led a "religious freedom march" in downtown Jonesboro. *Newsweek* ran a piece calling Jonesboro "Fort God." Pat Robertson went ballistic on the *700 Club* ranting about Satan's influence in Jonesboro. The tabloid TV shows had a field day. CNN covered the march and footage was seen in 29 countries. The witches and an outspoken Baptist minister made the talk show rounds including *The Jane Whitney Show* which aired October 29, 1993. The show was entitled "The Great Jonesboro Witch Hunt." Terry Riley, self-proclaimed witch, filed a lawsuit in Spring of 1994 against four ministers claiming interference with his right to do business. On April 4, 1994, former Circuit Judge Gerald Pearson of Jonesboro ruled that it was within the First Amendment rights of the ministers to pitch fits over the store. Nevertheless, the Magick Moon reopened in February 1995, about a block away from its original location – right across the street from the Free Full Gospel Church and within spitting distance of three other churches. This time around, there was no organized opposition to the business, though the Rileys were harassed at home.

DID YOU KNOW?

MOVIE MAGIC

The movie made from Jonesboro native John Grisham's novel *The Client* has Arkansas connections. An important scene was shot at Snowden House, a restaurant/bed and breakfast in Hughes (St. Francis County). The house which is situated on a lake, was gussied up with Spanish moss and plants to make it look like New Orleans where the story is set. The Snowden House is the neighbor's house in the movie, and a pivotal scene takes place in the boathouse and on the pier.

FAYETTEVILLE

Seat of Washington County. Population: 42,099

Information: Chamber of Commerce; Box 4216; Fayetteville, AR 72702-4216. (501) 521-1710 or 1-800-766-4626.

HISTORY

It was nearly a decade after Arkansas became a territory in 1819 before Washington County was established on October 17, 1828. It comprised all of the present county, Benton County, half of Madison County and even some of Carroll County. (Before that, this area was included in the short-lived Lovely County.) One of the first acts of the Legislature when Arkansas gained statehood in 1836, was to create the present boundaries of Washington County, a total of 569,000 acres.

The first court convened in the newly designated county seat, called Washington Court House on May 2, 1829. Discovering that there was another Washington in the state, the name Fayetteville was selected, possibly because two of the commissioners were from Fayetteville, Tennessee. Its designation as county seat was due to its central location within its original boundaries.

Tennessee was the native state for many of the pioneers who homesteaded this wilderness and built Fayetteville. Archibald Yell, from Tennessee, became Arkansas' second governor and an outstanding citizen of Fayetteville. He had come to Little Rock by appointment as a receiver of public monies by President Andrew Jackson. A decade later, he established his law practice in Fayetteville when the population was 425.

In 1857 the Butterfield Stage Lines started and the stables were located north of the present courthouse. It formed a link in the Overland Route from St. Louis to San Francisco. The silence was regularly broken by the horn sounding on the Butterfield stage which signaled the servants at Byrnside Tavern to get a meal on the table and fresh horses harnessed.

The early settlers here were unique because they demanded schools as soon as they demanded other necessities of life. Colleges have always been at the center of Fayetteville's history. One of the most outstanding schools was the Fayetteville Female Seminary, founded by Sophia Sawyer, a Cherokee missionary. In 1850 Robert Graham, a Kentuckian, started Arkansas College, which gave College Avenue its name. The college, chartered on December 14, 1852, issued the first collegiate degrees in the state and was situated where the First Christian Church in Fayetteville is now located. The original building was burned during the Civil War, as were most of the houses, colleges and stores in town. Fayetteville being located halfway between the Federal base at Springfield, Missouri, and the Confederate positions on the Arkansas River made it a goal for both armies and it changed flags frequently. And while Prairie Grove was the only major battle fought in the area, there were many deadly skirmishes and much property destroyed in and around Fayetteville.

When Arkansas Industrial University was established under the Morrill Act, the memory of these early schools made Washington County a prime contender for the location. The county voted $100,000 in 30-year bonds and Fayetteville contributed $30,000 to secure the state university. The legislative act that established the university failed to exclude women students, so despite considerable popular disapproval the school was co-ed from the start. The university opened in a two-story frame building January 22, 1872. The first graduating class in 1876 consisted of five men and four women. The university and the town have been growing ever since. During the 1930s the population of

Fayetteville was under 10,000 people. Even through the 1960s and 70s, Fayetteville was essentially a small farming community with grain silos in the shadow of Old Main. Today, the town looks much different than it did just a couple of decades ago. (Rumor has it that all the hippies who graduated from the U of A in the late sixties became landscape architects and stayed on to practice their craft in Fayetteville.) Whatever the reason, Fayetteville is much prettier now. The town square is beautifully landscaped with flowers of infinite variety. Fayetteville is a thriving, progressive city that has gotten better with age. It is still the center of education and academic life in the state. Major industries in the area include Campbell Soup and Tyson Foods. Nestled in the rugged Ozark hills, Fayetteville is forever picturesque. Few sights can compare with the fiery fall display of sugar maples on the U of A campus. Fayetteville was included in two recent publications: *50 Fabulous Places to Raise Your Family* and *50 Fabulous Places to Retire*.

SOURCES: Chamber of Commerce, *WPA Guide to 1930s Arkansas*

POINTS OF INTEREST

Arkansas Air Museum
Drake Field, U.S. 71 South.
(501) 521-4947. A
showcase of local aviation
history where you can see vintage aircraft,
including pre-World War II racing planes in flying
condition, and actually visit a restoration workshop.
Aeronautical memorabilia, gift shop. Housed in historic white hangar.

Beaver Lake *Access east off Highway 71 north of Fayetteville.* Corps of Engineers lake with over 500 miles of shoreline. Forests, tall bluffs, meadows crisscrossed by hiking trails surround the lake. Fishing, boating, camping. Resorts, marinas, shops.

Devil's Den State Park *Highway 71 South to West Fork then follow the signs.* *(501) 761-3325.* 1,700 unspoiled acres adjoining Ozark National Forest. Cabins, hiking, camping, fishing, horseback riding in the Boston Mountains. Caves, nature programs. Cabin reservations: 1-800-264-2417.

First Family's First Home *930 California Blvd.* Small English Tudor house was the first residence Bill and Hillary lived in after they were married in 1975.

Gregg House *Dickson and Gregg Streets.* Built in 1871 by Arkansas Supreme Court Justice LaFayette Gregg.

Headquarters House *118 E. Dickson St. (501) 521-2970.* Built in 1853 by

Judge Jonas Tebbetts, the house served as a command post headquarters for both Union and Confederate officers during the Civil War. Door panels bear scars of artillery attack of the battle of Fayetteville, April 18, 1863. Currently houses Washington County Historical Society.

Historic District *Washington and Willow Streets, between Dickson and Davidson.* The site of some of Fayetteville's finest older homes. Accepted to the National Historic Register in 1979, the district includes 105 primary structures over 37 acres. Detailed guide available at Historical Society at Headquarters House.

Lake Wedington *15 miles west on Hwy. 16.* Picnicking, fishing, swimming at this scenic little national forest lake.

Mt. Sequoyah Assembly *(1922)* This Methodist facility with its lighted cross on the west side of Mount Sequoyah is a Fayetteville landmark. The conference center has housing for 360 and a great view of the city. The mountain, named for the Cherokee leader who created the Cherokee alphabet and translated the New Testament for the Indians, overlooks the city and the "Trail of Tears" that went through Fayetteville as the Indians relocated to reservations to the west.

Prairie Grove Battlefield *13 miles west on Highway 62. (501) 846-2990.* The site of a major Civil War battle in 1862. The park contains 130 acres including battlefields, monuments, museum, and several homes and buildings typical of 19th century Arkansas, park store. Battle re-enacted every other year in December. Self-guided tours.

Ridge House *Center St.* Fayetteville's oldest standing home, built by Dr. M.H. Clark in 1845.

Riverglen Feline Conservation Park *Westfork, five miles south of town on U. S. 71. (501) 839-3403.* This privately-owned sanctuary for abused or unwanted exotic cats houses around 50 felines from ocelots to Siberian tigers (and some domestic cats, as well). Tours are available.

The Old Post Office Focal point of the Fayetteville Square, this former government building now houses a restaurant and night club.

Tontitown Grape Festival This Italian settlement north of Fayetteville celebrates the grape harvest each August.

University of Arkansas *West off Hwy 71 on Maple or Dickson. (501) 575-2000.* The main campus of the state university and home of the Arkansas Razorbacks. The site was previously the William McIlroy farm. The first classes, in 1872, were conducted in the six-room McIlroy farmhouse. Visit historic Old Main, the Greek Theater built in 1930, and the sidewalks (known as the Senior Walk) bear the names of all the university's graduates beginning in front of Old Main with the class of 1876. The Fine Arts Center designed by Fayetteville native Edward Durrell Stone was built in 1949 and was the first campus fine arts center in the United States. Stone also designed the Sigma Nu House (1951) and Carlson Terrace, the married students' housing complex (1957).

- **Bud Walton Arena** *Razorback Rd. and Center St.* The newest addition to the athletic complex seats 18,000. Completed in 1993.

ONE FOR THE RECORD BOOKS!

 Bud Walton Arena houses more facilities for women than for men. Twelve public restrooms (three per quadrant). Final Score: 140 *utilities* for the women – 73 for the men.

- **Old Main Building** was begun July 4, 1873, and completed September 1, 1875. Her twin mansard towers still grace the Fayetteville skyline. Chicago architect John M. Van Osdel designed the building as an approximate copy of Illinois University's "Old Main." Stones used in the foundation were hauled 70 miles by ox-wagon over rough mountain roads. LaFayette Gregg, as Building Commissioner,

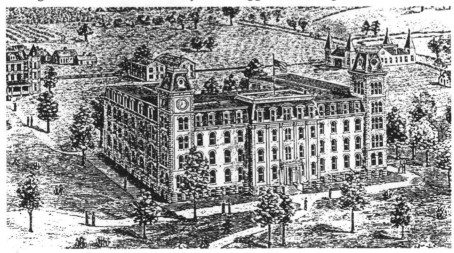

An early rendering of Old Main at the University

supervised the laying of each of the 2,6000,000 bricks in Old Main. He also wrote the legislative bill that fixed it there. Old Main underwent extensive restoration during the late 1980s and was rededicated in 1991.

- **University Museum** *Garland Ave. (501) 575-3555.* Extensive collection of exhibits not limited to Arkansas. Natural history, archaeology, and history, glassware, dinosaurs, astronomy. Gift Shop.

Walker-Stone House *Center St.* Built in 1847 by Arkansas Supreme Court Justice David Walker, this antebellum home was later the home of internationally known architect Edward Durrell Stone.

Walton Arts Center *495 W. Dickson.* Built in 1992, this is the finest cultural center of its kind in the region. A joint project between the U of A and the city of Fayetteville, it was named for Helen and Sam Walton, founder of Wal-Mart, who generously contributed to this facility. Features 400- and 1,200- seat auditoriums, rehearsal areas and an art gallery. Hosts symphonies, concerts, Broadway shows. 443-9216 (office); 443-5600 (box office).

Washington County Courthouse *Corner of Dickson and College Ave.* Constructed in 1904 of hand-cut native stone which was hauled by ox-drawn wagons from a nearby farm.

BOOMTOWN DOWNSIDE

Fayetteville is among several appealing southern cities whose population has boomed. From 1986 to 1993, Fayetteville grew by 15.9%. The downside of this growth is that in 1994, Fayetteville ranked #7 on a list of the least-affordable housing markets in the U.S. The average sale price for a home in Fayetteville was $103,753. The average family income for the area was $30,353 (1990 census.)

HOT SPRINGS

Seat of Garland County. Population: 32,362

Information: Hot Springs Convention and Visitors Bureau; P.O. Box K; Hot Springs National Park, AR 71902. 1-800-SPA-CITY

HISTORY

People have been coming to Hot Springs since the first person stumbled across the valley of the vapors as many as 10,000 years ago. Stone artifacts found near the springs give us firm evidence that Indians used the waters extensively. For them, the area became a neutral ground where the different tribes came to hunt, trade and bathe in peace. Tradition has it that the first European to see the springs was the Spanish explorer Hernando de Soto in 1541. The evidence is incomplete, for one chronicle of the expedition refers only to finding a place of hot and brackish water. It is certain, however, that French trappers, hunters and traders became familiar with the area in the late 17th century.

The United States acquired the area when the Louisiana Territory was purchased from France in 1803. The next year President Thomas Jefferson dispatched an expedition led by William Dunbar and George Hunter to explore the newly acquired springs. Their report to the President was widely publicized and stirred up interest in the "Hot Springs of the Washita." The explorers arrived at the

A group of Spa City tourists pose for a photo (c. 1895)

springs in December 1804 and "found an open log cabin and a few huts of split boards, all calculated for summer encampment, and which had been erected by persons resorting to the springs for the recovery of their health." The huts were not of Indian construction, indicating that early white settlers and trappers had built them as temporary quarters to soak their aching joints. In the years that followed, more and more people came to Hot Springs to soak in the thermal waters. In 1830, the first bathhouses were built by Asa Thompson. They were only small log cabins with plank tubs, but it was an improvement over the rocks and thickets that had previously served as bathing areas. About that time, a vapor bath was constructed by building a rock and board shelter over a water-filled niche. These improvements made the baths so popular that in 1832, the federal government took the unprecedented step of setting aside four sections of land as a reservation, the first in the country's history, to prevent exploitation. Little effort was taken to adequately identify the boundaries, and by the mid-19th century claims and counterclaims were filed on the springs and the land surrounding them. People were not eager to invest in permanent buildings when they were afraid their property might be appropriated by the feds. By 1851 when Hot Springs was incorporated as a town, it was still a crude village with two rows of hotels, bathhouses, saloons, doctors' offices and stores. The Civil War caused further decline by shutting off the flow of visitors. In spite of all this, Hot Springs was unofficially the capital of Arkansas for three months in 1862, when Governor Henry Rector, fearing capture of Little Rock by Federals, gathered up important state papers and records and fled to the spa.

After the war, as Hot Springs began to recuperate, the question of title to the land around the springs gained attention. Beginning in 1870, a system evolved over 40 years that removed lands from the four-section reservation for development of the city of Hot Springs and for satisfying suits brought before a court of claims. The government at this time also entered into a partnership with private

Where the world meets to bathe

bathhouses in which spring water from a central collection, cooling and distribution system was furnished to them and the bathhouses assumed the task of caring for the bathers. It was a partnership that prepared Hot Springs for its development as a national spa. One of the notables who was attracted to Hot Springs was "Diamond Jo" Reynolds, a Chicago capitalist who built the Diamond Jo narrow-gauge railroad between Hot Springs and Malvern with luxury coaches which offered far more comfortable transportation than the jarring stagecoach ride over the rocky mountain roads leading to the spa. Completed in 1875, the railroad was the impetus Hot Springs needed. In 1882 ten bathhouses, some of them large and costly, were already in operation. The Army-Navy Hospital was established by Congress to make therapeutic waters available to soldiers and sailors. A series of blazes swept through the wooden structures and a major one in 1913 leveled 50 blocks of stores and residences.

By 1921, the year Hot Springs Reservation became a national park, prosperity was filling Americans' pocketbooks so that they could afford more leisure time. Monumental bathhouses along Bathhouse Row built in the previous decade catered to crowds of health seekers. These new establishments, full of the latest equipment, were planned to satisfy and pamper the bather in the most artful of surroundings. Marble and tile decorated walls, floors and partitions. Some rooms sported polished brass, murals, fountains, statues, and stained glass. Gymnasiums and beauty salons helped the cure-seekers in their efforts to look and feel better.

Gambling has been going on in Hot Springs ever since there was a Hot Springs. Some folklore suggest that the early Indians played a crude game of dice there. During Prohibition, the city was a magnet for mobsters. During the 20s and 30s, Hot Springs ("Bubbles" as it was called in gangster slang) was considered a safe haven for the likes of Al Capone, Owney Madden and Lucky Luciano who often came to town to lay low. In 1935, Owney, the "Killer" Madden married an Arkansas woman he'd met while visiting. After years living in a big white house on Grand Avenue straight out of "Leave it to Beaver," Madden died in Hot Springs of old age. Hot Springs' White Front Cigar Store was an underworld hangout and was kept under surveillance by the FBI. Capone even had a regular room at the Arlington Hotel – room 442. Though betting at the racetrack was legal, casino gambling and prostitution were not. That fact didn't seem to get in the way, however. There were plush casinos and brothels all over town. The authorities were often bought off and/or simply looked the other way. From the 1880s until 1948 an amusement park called Happy Hollow was located on upper Fountain Street. The popular attraction featured a shooting gallery, 100 wild animals in cages and burro rides up the mountain trail. It is not unlikely that one might have seen Al Capone riding a donkey there with his pals on a sunny afternoon. The corner of Central Avenue and Bridge (a street only 60-feet long) was in the brothel/gambling section of town.

Ripley's "Believe-It-Or-Not" listed Bridge Street as "The World's Busiest Street For Its Size." Like Las Vegas and Reno, Hot Springs was also once known as a quickie divorce spot.

World War II slowed down the commercial activity when the armed services took over the facilities for use by servicemen. But in 1946 the bathers were back in

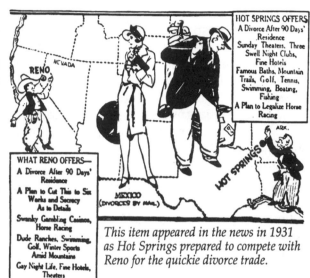

This item appeared in the news in 1931 as Hot Springs prepared to compete with Reno for the quickie divorce trade.

record-breaking numbers, taking 1.1 million baths. Since that time, however, the numbers have diminished and all but one of the bathhouses have closed. Nightclubs and casinos like the Southern Club, the Vapors and the Belvedere attracted big-name show-biz entertainers like Liberace and Sinatra and many of the rich and famous came to the Spa City to gamble and party, as well as bathe. But in 1967 when Winthrop Rockefeller took office as governor, illegal casino gambling came to a halt. As a result, the town's economy took a nose-dive, the only real industry in Hot Springs being tourism. It went from a bustling "little Vegas" to a mecca for the arthritic, though the debate over legalizing casino gambling still crops up from time to time.

Bathing continues to be a popular pastime, even though "taking the cure" no longer holds the magic it once did (people no longer have the misguided notion that thermal waters can cure syphilis and cirrhosis of the liver). Though the baths are still regarded as therapeutic for the arthritic and such, most people take the baths and massages for less clinical reasons and more for pleasure and relaxation. The Fordyce, the most elegant of the eight bathhouses on Bathhouse Row, has undergone a $5.1 million renovation and is now the visitor center for Hot Springs

National Park. Sadly, the Buckstaff is the only bathhouse offering baths these days. But bathing facilities are available at the Arlington and Majestic Hotels, Downtowner Motor Inn, Park Hilton Hotel and Hot Springs Health Spa.

Hot Springs is a strange and unique city. It's a city where bizarre and disparate elements coexist. But it has historically been this way. A Saturday in downtown Hot Springs could always find the famous and notorious wandering undisturbed and probably unnoticed by the local farmers filling their water jugs at the public fountain. On one side of the avenue one can marvel at the stunning bathhouses then cross the street and buy Bill and Hill salt and pepper shakers at a cheesy souvenir shop. Locals who would not dream of gambling in a casino, line up to place bets on the daily double at the horse races. The natural beauty of the place and the abundance of lakes and rivers make it a favorite recreation and retirement destination. The arts are thriving here as many of the older buildings are being restored and inhabited by working artists from around the world – within hissing distance of the House of Reptiles. Hot Springs boasts the only documentary film festival outside Los Angeles and the former "Sin City" is once again in the limelight as the billboards on the highway proclaim it the "Boyhood Home of President Bill Clinton."

Downwtown Hot Springs

SOURCE: The National Park Service, U.S. Dept. of the Interior; *WPA Guide to Arkansas in the 30s; The American Spa* by Dee Brown; *Encyclopedia of Crime.*

POINTS OF INTEREST

Arkansas Alligator Farm *847 Whittington Avenue. (501) 623-6172.* One of Arkansas' oldest tourist attractions, it was founded in 1902 by H.L. Campbell who imported 50 alligators that soon multiplied to several hundred. Campbell probably got the idea from Thomas Cockburn who bought 300 ostriches and opened a 27-acre ostrich farm on Whittington Avenue where tourists could ride on the big birds or watch them race. The alligator farm featured performing alligators, sold alligator-skin products and baby alligators for a dollar. The Ostrich Farm is long gone, but the Alligator Farm has survived. Subsequent owners have added a petting zoo, ostriches, goats, deer and souvenirs. The farm boasts the "Merman"(half alligator/half man) that once made Ripley's "Believe-It-Or-Not." This dusty, manufactured freak of nature is housed in a glass case inside the creepy museum part of the farm.

Arkansas Celebration of the Arts *1-800-SPA-CITY.* November. A week-long celebration of the thriving arts scene in Arkansas. Features the Gallery Walk and Documentary Film Festival. All events are free and open to the public. Activities take place in the Central Arts District – "Arkansas' little SoHo," all within easy walking distance.

Arkansas House of Reptiles *420 Central Ave. (501) 623-8516.* Over 65 exhibits of 200-plus reptiles. Gift shop and pets for sale.

Arkansas Oktoberfest The largest such celebration in the state, each October brings lots of German food and music to the Hot Springs Convention Center.

Army-Navy Hospital *Central and Reserve.* The first permanent military hospital in the country was built above Bathhouse Row at the south end. It opened in 1887 as a hospital for Civil War veterans. Its replacement, opening in 1933, cost 1.5 million dollars, and served as the Army-Navy Hospital until 1959. Now known as the Hot Springs Rehabilitation Center, it provides therapy for the mentally and physically handicapped.

Ar-Scenic Spring *103 Mt. Ida Street. (501) 623-1722.* The oldest commercial business in Hot Springs, established in 1870. See the 13-gallon bottle of water filled in 1893. Hot Springs diamond jewelry and Arkansas crafts for sale. Free Hot Springs diamond.

Bathhouse Row *Central (501) 623-1433.* Built around the turn of the century, these eight beautifully ornate houses attracted people in droves from all over the world during the Spa City's pre-WWII heyday. Named a National Historic Landmark in 1987. Baths are now available only at the Buckstaff. The Fordyce serves as the visitor center for Hot Springs

National Park. Of the remaining houses, the National Park Service is in the midst of costly exterior rehabilitation including roofing and flood-proofing, and removal of lead-based paints from interior walls. The park service plans to lease these houses in phases as they are rehabed.

Belle of Hot Springs *5200 Central on Lake Hamilton, Hwy. 7 South. (501) 525-4438.* The three-decker, 400-passenger riverboat offers daily sightseeing cruises on Lake Hamilton. Luncheon, dinner and dance cruises, tour groups and charters also available.

Central Avenue Historic District *Central (Prospect to Park Ave.).* Restored buildings dating from the late 1800s to the early 1900s now house art galleries, coffee houses, shops and restaurants. Self-guided brochure available from visitor center.

Café New Orleans *210 Central.* Built in 1889, this was originally a saloon with furnished rooms above to provide lodging for performers at the Grand Opera House which once occupied the site next door.

Castleberry Riding Stables *Hwy. 7 N. (501) 623-6609.* Scenic mountain rides, hayrides, overnight camp-outs and more.

Clinton Sites This is the town where Bill Clinton grew up. Visit the sites relating to Bill's boyhood: his homes, his high school, his favorite hang outs. Call 1-800-SPA- CITY or (501) 321-2277 for self-guided brochures.

Dryden Potteries *341 Whittington. (501) 623-4201.* Tours and demonstrations on the potter's wheel at this Hot Springs landmark. Native Ouachita Mountain clays and quartz crystal glazes are used. Gift shop.

Educated Animal Zoo *380 Whittington. (501) 623-4311.* Stage shows featuring trained domestic and wild animals. (The animals are trained by reward only, no punishment, according to the owners.) Formerly I.Q. Zoo.

Fordyce Bathhouse Visitor Center *369 Central. (501) 623-1433.* This elegant restored bathhouse serves as the visitor center and a museum for the thermal bathing industry. Orientation film and bookstore.

Gallery Walk *Central. (501)321-2277.* The first Thursday and Friday of each month, hundreds visit the art galleries and arts-related businesses that line the downtown area.

Gator Golf *2720 Albert Pike. (501) 767-8601.* Challenging 18-hole mini-golf course with life-size statues of exotic animals and a waterfall.

Grand Promenade There are two open display springs located directly behind the bathhouses. Take a leisurely stroll down the brick pathway, sit a spell, feed the pigeons and squirrels. There are park benches and viewing sites.

Hot Springs Factory Outlet Stores *4332 Central. (501) 525-0888.* Over 30 nationally known factory-direct stores.

Hot Springs Mountain Tower *Can be reached via Fountain Street off Central Avenue at Arlington Park to Hot Springs Mountain Road. (501) 623-6035.* This 216-foot observation tower with two observation decks at the summit of Hot Springs Mountain affords panoramic views of the area.

One of Bill Clinton's hometown favorites

Hot Springs Mule Trolley *264 Central. (501) 624-2202.* Fully-narrated sightseeing tours aboard a mule-drawn trolley (replicas of the ones used in 1870). Wagon and trail rides also available.

Josephine Tussaud Wax Museum *250 Central. (501) 623-5836.* The building which houses the museum was built in 1893 and thrived as the Southern Club until gambling ceased in 1967. The museum was founded by the granddaughter of the famous Josephine Tussaud of the London Wax Museum. Over 100 figures of famous people past and present, including "The Young Elvis" immortalized in beeswax and a secret ingredient to make the "skin" appear translucent. And yes, Bill and Hillary are here. Okay, they look a little like Karl Malden and Vanna White. It's not an exact science.

Maxine's International Coffeehouse *700 Central.* In 1894, J. H. McLaughlin built this corner building to house one of the most active saloons of its time. In 1912, the second floor was home to the Hot Springs Business Men's Social Club (a.k.a. Maxine Jones' bordello). Today one can indulge in the decadence of a mocha cappuccino and biscotti.

Medical Arts Building *236 Central.* Built in 1929, this magnificent 16-story tiered Art Deco structure was the tallest building in Arkansas for many years – 180 feet above street level. (As of 1987, the 40-story TCBY Tower in Little Rock is the tallest.)

Mid-America Museum *500 Mid-America Blvd., off U.S. 270 West. (501) 767-3461 or tollfree in Arkansas 1-800-632-0583.* Hands-on, self-guided tour allows you to discover the principles of matter, energy and perception as you control and work the exhibits at this state-owned museum. Also a laser show and a new exhibit documenting the region where President Clinton grew up.

Miss Arkansas Pageant Held in July at the Convention Auditorium.

Bill and Hill waxed

Mountain Valley Spring Company *150 Central. (501) 623-6671.* Home of the famous Mountain Valley Water. Originally housed the De Soto Mineral Springs when it was built in 1915. Mountain Valley assumed residence in the 1920s. Prime example of Classical Revival style. The third story was added in 1921 as a Japanese motif dance hall. Visitor center on the second floor of this historic building. Collection of antique bottles, hydroponic gardens. Enjoy free water samples. Water was first bottled at this site in 1833. The water flows (54,000 gallons a day at 65° F) from the largest cold water spring in the area. This water has been popular in the White House since the presidency of Calvin Coolidge.

Museum of Hot Springs *201 Central. (501) 624-5545.* Located in the old De Soto Hotel, the museum opened in November 1994. The exhibits focus on the city's history from 1850-1950: early barber shop, medical instruments, Civil War, Indians, gambling. Admission charged.

Music Mountain Jamboree *U.S. 270 West. (501) 767-3841.* Live country music and comedy show. Reserved seating. Gift shop, restaurant.

National Park Aquarium *209 Central. (501) 624-3474.* Native Arkansas fish in re-created natural habitat. Also colorful saltwater species exhibits.

New Ohio Club *336 Central.* Built in 1905, the Ohio Club was originally a private club and gambling saloon. Club retains the original Italian mahogany back bar.

BRUCE AND DEMI ALL WET

Hollywood superstars Demi Moore and husband Bruce Willis spend $3,000 a month on Arkansas mountain water to use for drinking, cooking and bathing. This bit of trivia from *YM Magazine's* May 1995 issue under the headline, "Are they Insane?"

Oaklawn Jockey Club *South of downtown on Central. 1-800-OAKLAWN.* Horseracing has been a popular pastime in Hot Springs since 1860. Oaklawn was built in 1905, the state outlawed horseracing in 1907 but racing resumed in 1917. The park was closed down again during Prohibition in 1919. Legal racing resumed in 1935 and has been going strong ever since. Live thoroughbred racing January through April. Satellite simulcasts May to November.

Original White and Yellow Ducks Sightseeing Tours *406 Central. (501) 623-1111.* For over 30 years these amphibious vehicles known as "ducks" have been taking visitors on tours of the city and right into Lake Hamilton. Free parking. Free pick-up at all downtown hotels.

Ouachita Scenic Railroad *Depot is located off the corner of Grand and Broadway. (501) 321-2015.* Twenty minute round-trip ride aboard 1920 Pullman passenger cars takes about 1¾ hours, winding through the Ouachita countryside along Gulpha Creek. This was originally the Diamond Jo Line built in 1876 which carried thousands of visitors to Hot Springs for many years when train travel was the only way to get to the springs.

Outdoor Adventure Tours *300 Long Island Dr. 1-800-489-8687.* Sightseeing tours in vans departing from local hotels. Also hiking, canoeing and mountain bike tours.

Panther Valley Ranch *1942 Millcreek Rd. (501) 623-5556.* Stay at an authentic Western horse ranch. Rustic accommodations and trail rides.

Off and running at Oaklawn

SCENIC DRIVES

• **Hot Springs Mountain Drive** (2.5 miles). From the Fordyce Bathhouse travel north on Hwy. 7 to the first right which is Fountain Street. Follow signs for Hot Springs Mountain. Several overlooks and the Mountain Tower at the summit offer beautiful views. Vehicles longer than 30 feet not permitted because of sharp hairpin curves. Picnic facilities. (Restrooms at summit.)

• **West Mountain Drive** (2 miles). From the Fordyce, travel north on Hwy. 7 to Whittington Avenue and turn left. Turn left again at "West Mountain Drive" sign to begin tour. After about one mile, take the side trip to the summit. Picnic tables and overlooks. Drive slowly and look out for hikers and bikers.

Short-Dodson House *755 Park Ave. (501) 624-9555).* Built in 1901, historic home was placed on the National Register in 1976. Detailed oak and maple woodwork and flooring, stained glass. Designed and built by Joseph G. Horn.

The Bath House Show *701 Central. (501) 623-1415.* Family entertainment with two-hour show featuring music and comedy. Reserved seating.

DID YOU KNOW?

Documentary Film Festival

The only documentary film festival in the United States outside of Los Angeles is held right here in Hot Springs each November. The Festival began in 1992 and has sponsored an amazing variety of award-winning documentaries. Screenings are held at the historic Malco Theatre on Central Avenue and Theartfoundation. Many of the film makers accompany their films and informal discussions are held after the viewing. Previous noteworthy participants have included Eleanor Coppola and Allen Ginsberg.

What's So Cool About Hot Water?

The most important thing about Hot Springs' thermal water is that it is naturally sterile. For this reason, the National Aeronautics and Space Administration selected this water, among others, in which to hold moon rocks while looking for signs of life. Even during the many early years that the springs were uncovered, the absence of bacteria in the water helped prevent the spread of disease. Today most of the springs have been covered to prevent contamination. There are open springs behind the Maurice Bathhouse and the public thermal water fountains at the end of Bathhouse Row at the corner of Central and Reserve where the locals can be seen filling their plastic gallon jugs with the pure water to haul home for drinking. (It is illegal to sell the thermal waters, but you can have all you want for free.) The spring water contains traces of minerals that, combined with the water's temperature of 61.6° C (142° F), give it whatever therapeutic properties it may have.

How does the water get hot? Actually, the world-famous water began warming about 4,000 years ago. It started as rain water at a time when the water and environment were pure. The rainfall percolated down through the pores and fractures in the rocks which filtered the water and conducted it deep into the earth, the increasingly warmer rocks heating it. In the process, the water dissolves minerals in the rocks. Eventually the water meets the faults and joints in the Hot Springs sandstone leading up to the lower west side of Hot Springs Mountain where it flows to the surface. The waters gush at an average rate of 850,000 gallons a day.

CHEMICAL ANALYSIS OF THERMAL WATERS AT HOT SPRINGS NATIONAL PARK
(by U.S. Geological Survey 1972 / milligrams per liter)

Silica	42.0
Calcium	45.0
Magnesium	4.8
Sodium	4.0
Potassium	1.5
Bicarbonate	165.0
Sulfate	8.0
Chloride	1.8
Flouride	.2
Oxygen	3.0
Free Carbon Dioxide	10.0

Radioactivity through radon gas emanation in 0.81 millimicrocurie per liter; analysis by the University of Arkansas.

THE SKINNY ON TAKING A DIP AT THE BATHS

Though the thermal waters do not cure kidney problems, liver ailments, syphilis or cancer as once touted, they are a wonderful way to ease muscle aches, arthritic joints or otherwise just relax and wash away the tensions of everyday life. So take the plunge and enjoy an hour or more of pure pampering. How much will all this luxury set you back? Right now the going rate for a bath is from $8 to $12.50. Massages average around $13. So what are you waiting for? It was good enough for Al Capone. (Always call for specifics on costs and hours of operation at the various locations – they vary and can change without notice.)

IT'S GOOD FOR WHAT AILS YOU!

THE TRADITIONAL BATH

1. No appointment is needed. Walk in and purchase a ticket. Leave your valuables in the personal lock box provided (you carry the key around your wrist).

2. A bathing attendant of your gender is assigned. You are escorted to a dressing room where your attendant provides you with a bathsheet to wear when padding about from one procedure to the next.

3. In the bathhalls you have a private tub which your attendant has cleaned and filled with fresh 100°F water. The tubs are big enough to stretch out and soak in for twenty minutes. You may choose to be scrubbed with a loofah (you have to buy your own mitt).

4. Full steam cabinets (two minutes) or head-out cabinets (five minutes) are available and can be helpful for lung or sinus congestion.

5. Sitz tub. This is a special tub of 108°F water for sitting in. Ten minutes here is great for relieving pain in the lower back.

6. Application of hot packs, up to four, for 20 minutes.

7. Warm shower for two minutes.

8. Massages are optional at extra cost (another 20 minutes or so).

9. Dress and retrieve your valuables.

BATHING FACILITIES

* Arlington Hotel (501) 623-7771

* Buckstaff Bathhouse (501) 623-2308

* Downtowner Hotel (501) 624-5521

* Hot Springs Park Hilton (501) 623-6600

* Hot Springs Health Spa (501) 321-9664

* Majestic Hotel (501) 623-5511

Business as usual at the Buckstaff Bathhouse

* Physical therapy using the hot spring water is available at Libbey Memorial Physical Center (501) 321-9664 and Leo N. Levi Arthritis Hospital (501) 624-1281.

HOT ROCKS!

THE HOT SPRINGS DIAMOND

These clear quartz crystals occur in abundance in the Hot Springs area. Quartz or silica is hard, usually colorless or white, insoluble mineral. Quartz crystals and veins are a very common and striking feature of the Ouachita region of Arkansas. They were formed by hydrothermal solutions of silicon dioxide and occur on sandstone. Arkansas quartz crystals are widely known for their clarity and for their habit of occurring in attractive clusters. Quartz crystals – clear, transparent and free from color or cloudiness – have assumed an important position in the construction of radio equipment, range finders, direction-finding apparatuses, periscopes, gun sights, polariscopes and other precision equipment. During World War II Arkansas quartz crystals were used particularly in radio equipment. Other crystals which are essentially free from flaws are cut and faceted to be used in semi-precious jewelry. Although not real diamonds, these "gems" are beautiful in their own right. A large chunk of crystals from nearby Mount Ida occupies a prominent position at the Museum of Natural History in New York City.

NOVACULITE

Another rock native to the Ouachita region is novaculite. The area within a 30-mile radius of Hot Springs is one of only a few locations in the world where commercial-grade novaculite is found. This region has produced the world's largest quantity of novaculite for making whetstones. The first authentic notation of whetstone in America refers to those of Arkansas. Novaculite is hard, compact, finely granulated silica rock primarily used for tool and knife sharpening. As long as 1,000 years ago, Indians mined novaculite. They did not have metal tools, but used the stone for making arrowheads, axes and scrapers. Indian Mountain is the site of several ancient quarries.

There are two commercial classes of abrasive novaculite:

Arkansas Stone A very fine-grained homogeneous rock with a waxy luster. It is usually white, and is transparent on thin edges. It is used for a fine hone.

Ouachita Stone Much more porous than the Arkansas and has the appearance of unglazed porcelain.

WAVELLITE

Also called "catseye," this stone occurs in radiating green bursts. Also occurs in yellow and blue. This mineral is sought after by many collectors.

NOTE: There are no shortage of rock shops in the Hot Springs area where you can get prospecting information. Coleman's Crystal Yard on Hwy. 7N specializes in quartz; Wright's Rock Shop on U.S. 270 West is Arkansas' largest.

SOURCE: Arkansas Geological and Conservation Commission

SPRINGDALE

Population: 29,941 (29,034 in Washington County; 907 in Benton County)

Information: Chamber of Commerce; P.O. Box 166; Springdale, AR 72765. 800-972-7261 or (501) 751-4694.

HISTORY

This small town of Tyson chicken fame is located in the Ozarks in the northwest part of the state just a stone's throw from Fayetteville up Highway 71. Truth be told, with the expansion of both towns, you can hardly tell where one stops and the other begins these days. Not so in the early days when the Osage Indians first claimed the land in the area. Later the Cherokee, Shawnee and Delaware established villages here. The Cherokee Treaty of 1828 opened the land for settlers and many families from Kentucky, Tennessee and South Carolina packed up and headed for Arkansas Territory.

A community formed about 1840 around the Shiloh Primitive Baptist Church and a post office called Lynch's Prairie was established in 1859. The little community was destroyed during the Civil War and rebuilt in 1868. In 1872 when the post office discovered there was another town named Shiloh, the town's name was changed to Spring-in-the-Dale, in reference to a spring just north of Main Street. The name eventually was shortened to Springdale. The arrival of the St. Louis-San Francisco Railway in 1881 helped re-establish the town.

From the beginning, Springdale was a trading center for fruits, vegetables and livestock. Apples, peaches, grapes and beans were the leading products until the poultry industry flew into town. Tyson Foods is the number one poultry based food company in the world with weekly production nearly equal to that of Japan and Great Britain combined. Tyson processes 25 million birds per week. Tyson is also heavy into hog raising. Internationally the company employs 55,000 people, 12,000 of those in northwest Arkansas with 1,500 working at the corporate headquarters in Springdale. In recent years, the town has attracted scores of Hispanics who have immigrated to Springdale to work in the industry. As of July 1994, the Hispanic population numbered around 5,000 in this community of 30,000. There is even a Spanish-language radio station in the area, KQXK-AM 1590, which would have been unfathomable a few years back. This change in the cultural demographics has ruffled a few feathers. But many older citizens remember when the influx of Italians to nearby Tontitown threw many people into a tizzy. Eventually, however, the newcomers assimilated and Tontitown became a valuable asset to the community.

The Springdale area is one of the fastest growing parts of the state in large part because of its solid economic base and proximity to the University of Arkansas in Fayetteville. In addition to Tyson's, another major company based in Springdale is J.B. Hunt Transport, Inc., the largest publicly-held truckload carrier in the U.S. Its corporate headquarters are in Lowell, five miles outside Springdale. A lesser known but very successful business is A. G. Russell Knives, a mail order knife business which began 30 years ago. Because it is low-profile mail order, it is better known in Japan than in Springdale. It has sales in the millions of dollars world-wide. Tourism is also a major factor in the economy, Springdale being in the midst of gorgeous Ozark country with recreational activities any way you go. Over 250 million tourism dollars were spent in this neck of the woods in 1990.

POINTS OF INTEREST

Alfred E. Brumley Sundown to Sunup Gospel Sing *Rodeo grounds. 1-800-972-7261.*This event held each August and sponsored by the Chamber of Commerce is the second largest Southern Gospel Sing in the country. Over 20,000 fans gather to hear their favorite gospel quartets and groups from dusk until dawn at this four-day event.

Arts Center of the Ozarks *U.S. 471, east on Emma, south on Blair. (501)751-5441.* This multi-purpose arts organization includes, theater, music, visual arts and crafts.

A.Q. Chicken House *Intersection of Hwy. 71B and Sanders Street. (501) 751-4633.* World-famous for

HOME COOKED

Chicken Dinners

Southern pan-fried chicken and other delights like mashed potatoes made from scratch. This is the largest restaurant in the state and has been a favorite since 1947 – that's 20 years before the Colonel came up with his secret recipe.

Chicken Capital Gifts *323 Emma. (501) 750-9600.* Chicken Chic! Antiques and collectibles with a poultry theme.

Famous Hardware Antique Mall *113 W. Emma Ave. (501) 756-6650.* A hardware store for 100 years, this 1880s building now houses three floors of antiques, glass, toys, collectibles from Victoriana to 1950s.

Orphan Train Riders Research Center *4453 South 48th St. (501) 751-7830.* A most unique museum, this center preserves the history of waifs, foundlings and half-orphans who were part of a massive placing-out of children in American history. The center was established in 1986 as a clearinghouse for information about the "orphan train era." In the mid-1800s, Charles Loring Brace came up with the idea to solve New York City's problem of homeless and vagrant children. The idea was "placing-out" children (now called foster care). Between 1854 and 1929 over 150,000 children were loaded onto trains along with supervisors and sent off to the Midwest where they were displayed on platforms for viewing and examining by prospective families wishing to take a child in. Bizarre and primitive as it sounds today, the program was quite successful according to records. By 1910 only 139 children had arrived in Arkansas from the New York Children's Aid Society. However, between 1910 and 1920 hundreds more were taken in by Arkansas families. The center houses artifacts such as clothing and toys and memorabilia and is open by appointment only. Call to arrange a tour.

Rodeo of the Ozarks One of the top rodeos in the country, held each July at Parsons Stadium with a seating capacity of 12,000. Four performances featuring big name cowboys and cowgirls draw huge crowds.

Scenic Ozark Railway Excursions *107 N. Commercial. 1-800-452-9582.* Hop aboard the Arkansas & Missouri Railroad for a scenic trip through the Ozarks on a restored turn-of-the-century passenger train. This day-long 134-mile round-trip excursion departs Springdale at 8:00 p.m. (complimentary continental breakfast on board), passes through the historic Winslow tunnel built in 1882 and arrives in Van Buren's historic district which has been featured in the movies *Biloxi Blues* and *The Blue and the Gray*. In Van Buren you can lunch, shop, tour, then catch the train and arrive back in Springdale about 5:00 p.m.

Shiloh Church *(1870) Huntsville and Main.* Located north of the museum, this two-story clapboard building on the National Historic Register is Springdale's oldest standing structure and considered the best surviving example of community architecture in the state.

Shiloh Historic District These 32 acres on the National Historic Register are bounded by Spring Creek, Shiloh, Johnson, Mill and Spring.

Shiloh Museum *U.S. 471, six blocks east on Johnson.* Located on an entire city block that was donated for a town square, this museum houses Indian artifacts, historical relics of northwest Arkansas, and the Vaughan-Applegate Collection of photography equipment which is considered by many to be the largest and finest collection in the Southwest. Other sites on the grounds: Ritter Log Cabin (c. 1855) Steele General Store (c. 1870), a doctor's office (c. 1880), Searcy House (early 1870s).

Tontitown *Off Hwy. 412 west of Springdale.* This Italian community named for Henry de Tonti was established in 1897 by an Italian priest named Pietro Bandini who was sent from Italy to investigate reports of malaria and starvation in a colony of Italian immigrants living near Lake Chicot. He purchased 1,000 acres in Washington County and relocated 35 families there where the colony immediately began cultivating grapes and making wine. Tontitown was the first community in Northwest Arkansas to grow grapes as a cash crop. The Annual Grape Festival is held each year in August following the harvest and features, grapes, of course, as well as carnival rides, raffles, music and lots of homemade spaghetti dinners. For great Italian food anytime check out Mary Maestri's or the Venetian Inn, both on Hwy. 412 West.

Tontitown Flea Market *Hwy. 412 West in Tontitown. (501) 361-9902.* Over 10,000 square feet and 130 booths of antiques, collectibles, primitives.

Wildlife Safari *(501) 736-8383.* Located 30 minutes west of Springdale in the rolling hills of Gentry, the Wild Wilderness Drive-Thru Safari is home to almost 200 species of exotic animals that you can view from your vehicle. Also a petting zoo for the hands-on experience.

Zero Mountain *U.S. 471.* First excavated in 1955, this dome-shaped mountain features caverns that are artificially cooled and can store nearly 45 million pounds of food in its 275,000 square feet.

JACKSONVILLE

Pulaski County Population: 29,101.

Information: Chamber of Commerce, 1400 W. Main; Jacksonville, AR 72076 (501) 982-1511.

HISTORY

This community located north of Little Rock is primarily known as the home of the Little Rock Air Force Base. But the LRAFB was not dedicated until October 9,1955. The town of Jacksonville had its beginnings much earlier. A North Carolinian named Nicholas W. Jackson is credited with founding the town. Jackson moved to Arkansas in 1853, settled in Prairie County and married Elizabeth Clement in 1854. In 1866 he began buying up property in Gray Township, choice acreage that completely surrounded the proposed right of way for the railroad. He moved his family there around 1867. By 1880, Jackson was considered a wealthy man. He owned one horse, eleven cows, two mules, fifteen sheep, eleven hogs and one carriage. His personal taxes for this fortune amounted to $1.75.

The town of Jacksonville dates its beginning from a deed dated June 29, 1870. For the sum of $300, N. W. and Elizabeth Jackson granted a right of way to the Cairo and Fulton Railroad Company on condition "that said railroad company establish a depot at, or near, station No. 615 of said railroad." The first official plat of the town of Jacksonville was dated January 2, 1872. Jackson built his home on the side of the right of way where the depot was to be built.

Like many other frontier towns, the early days were raucous ones. Horseracing was the biggest form of entertainment and the competition took place on the downtown streets at all hours. Eventually, a level field west of town was designated as a race track so pedestrians could walk the streets without getting trampled. Two thriving businesses of the day were saloons: William Hardcastle and Company and the J. K. P. Harbour. In 1884, the population was around 50 and the town boasted a steam grist and cotton gin, flour mill and gin, grocery store, druggist, dry goods and Methodist and Baptist churches. Fruit growing was a major segment of the economy.

In 1940 as the U.S. became more involved in World War II, nearby Camp Robinson was enlarged and made a training camp for 100,000 men. Then in 1941 Jacksonville became the site of an ordnance plant manufacturing fuses and detonators and and employing 2,900 people from the surrounding areas. At the time, Jacksonville's population was about 400. There were major housing and traffic problems as a result of all the new activity. Arkansas' congressional delegations gained the interest of the Air Force in locating a base in central Arkansas. Major lobbying took place to convince the Air Force that Pulaski County was the place to be. In 1951 and 1952, members of the Little Rock Chamber of Commerce and interested businessmen of Pulaski County sought sites that were satisfactory and were also not prime agricultural sites.

The choices narrowed down to Wrightsville, Woodson and the old ordnance plant near Jacksonville. As it turned out, Wrightsville had drainage problems, Woodson had topographical problems and Jacksonville seemed to have ample land. Ultimately, they had underestimated. The site, as finally determined, amounted to 6,359 acres held by 139 owners containing 104 houses, 44 barns, two churches, three stores and two industrial plants. The base was dedicated October 9, 1955, the same year the first jet bombers landed at another new base in Blytheville. Initially, the primary organization on base was the 825th Strategic Aerospace Division along with two SAC Wings. In 1961, the missile age arrived and the feds built 18 underground launching sites for Titan II Missiles across north central Arkansas from Morrilton toward Newport making Arkansas a prime first-strike target in case of war. No longer deemed necessary to national defense, the missile sites were destroyed in 1987. Though Jacksonville is now a town in its own right with ample services, schools, businesses and amenities, the base has a significant influence on the economy of not only Jacksonville but the entire Greater Little Rock area.

POINTS OF INTEREST

Little Rock Air Force Base *(501) 988-3131.* Home of the 314th Airlift Wing which operates the only Department of Defense formal training school for the operation of C-130 aircraft. With more than 80 of these aircraft, LRAFB is the largest C-130 base in the world. The base has 1,214 buildings spread over 6,123 acres. The permanent assigned military population is 4,361 with an additional transient population (military members undergoing training) of 2,114. The wing trains approximately 2,200 students from the Air Force, sister military services, the Coast Guard and many allied nations. Recent deployments include Operation Desert Storm/Shield in August of 1990. During the height of this military event, the wing had about 1,500 people and 38 aircraft deployed to more than 30 locations throughout the U.S., Europe and the Middle East. The 314th led the aborted assault of Port-au-Prince, Haiti in September 1994. During times of peace, global humanitarian relief efforts are a crucial facet of the airlift mission. In August 1992, the wing provided supplies, support and food to Somalia.

Vertac Chemical Corporation Long a thorn in the side of Jacksonville residents, herbicides including Agent Orange were manufactured by various owners of the now defunct Vertac site from 1948 until 1986. Agent Orange is a defoliant that was used extensively in the Vietnam War. The plant manufactured Agent Orange for Dow under a Department of Defense contract and resulting dioxin contamination has been the source of much controversy and concern. The carcinogen dioxin is one of the most toxic substances known to man and is associated with the production of such herbicides. In 1982 the site was identified by the EPA as one of the worst toxic waste sites in the country. The cleanup at the site was officially completed in January 1995, however the legacy of the toxin continues. Fish taken from the nearby Rocky Branch Creek and Bayou Meto that same month were still too contaminated to be eaten according to the state Department of Pollution Control. Though the production of the chemical ceased in 1986, the toxic wastes have been stored at the plant site for years. It is likely that the waste leached into the ground and into the creeks.

WEST MEMPHIS

Crittenden County. Population: 28,259

Information: Chamber of Commerce; 108 W. Broadway; West Memphis, AR 72301. (501) 735-1134, FAX 501-735-6283

HISTORY

Bearing nicknames such as the Shoestring Town, the Boom Town, the Frontier Town, and the Wonder City of the Wonder State, West Memphis had several beginnings. The first white men in the area were probably Hernando de Soto and his band. Records indicate that the original site of West Memphis came from a Spanish land grant. Around 1794 the Spanish governor of Louisiana, Gayoso removed a fort from Chickasaw Bluffs in Memphis and established Ft. Esperanza on the west bank of the Mississippi River to collect tribute for the use of the river. Gayoso authorized Benjamin Foy to be an agent for the Chicasaw and Foy settled north of the fort. The community grew and was called Hopefield. It would hold a prime location as the end of the line for both the Memphis-Little Rock Road and Railroad. Crittenden County was formed in 1825 and named in honor of Robert Crittenden, the first secretary of the Arkansas Territory. The Civil War followed by a yellow fever epidemic in 1878 pretty well did in the town of Hopefield.

The present city was settled by the Vance family. Settling here on 600 acres that had been bought by their father William Vance, Robert and Hope Vance built a log cabin, shortly replaced in 1875 by a frame residence. This and the railroad stations were the only buildings, and because of the flood waters, they were built on stilts. In 1884, the sons of Hope Vance – Robert, Frank and Arthur – laid out the town of West Memphis on the river bank. Robert Vance was appointed first postmaster in 1885; the population was approximately 200. By clearing the land, the lumber industry cleared the way for the city of West Memphis. Around 1904 a young logger named Zack Bragg came to this

Ladies of Arkansas City, Desha County, shopping along the Mississippi River during the flood of 1882

region because of the copious timber and the new railroads and the river to transport his logs. The mill and its surroundings were known as Bragg, but were later associated with West Memphis because of the higher price that the name "Memphis" would bring. Lumber buyers could easily identify the St. Francis River Basin lumber by the Memphis name.

Recognizing the importance of the timber, P.T. Boltz of St. Louis sent William Hundhausen in 1914 to survey timber holdings. This resulted in the establishment of Bolz Slack Barrel Cooperage Plant. The intersection of the Rock Island and Missouri Pacific Railroads near the plant offered good transportation by rail and river. In this same area Mr. George T. Kendall erected a large frame hotel for the Bolz Company employees known as the West Memphis Hotel. W.L. Johnson, an associate of Kendall's, looked from Memphis to the west side of the river and dreamed of a city there. He drew up a plat with streets and lots and called it West Memphis. Johnson and Kendall sold lots and established a post office, despite ridicule from their friends who wanted to know whether they were selling these lots by the quart or gallon. The mud, lack of drainage, and the mosquitoes created an almost unbearable situation – yet his dream of a city remained. Malaria was rampant and claimed the lives of many early settlers. Ultimately, the nucleus for the city of West Memphis was formed.

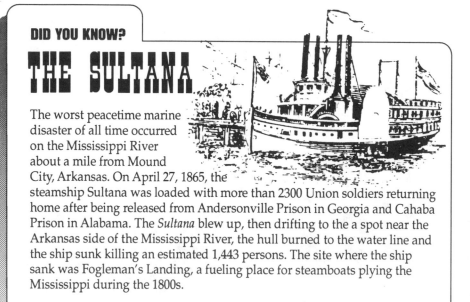

DID YOU KNOW?

THE SULTANA

The worst peacetime marine disaster of all time occurred on the Mississippi River about a mile from Mound City, Arkansas. On April 27, 1865, the steamship Sultana was loaded with more than 2300 Union soldiers returning home after being released from Andersonville Prison in Georgia and Cahaba Prison in Alabama. The *Sultana* blew up, then drifting to the a spot near the Arkansas side of the Mississippi River, the hull burned to the water line and the ship sunk killing an estimated 1,443 persons. The site where the ship sank was Fogleman's Landing, a fueling place for steamboats plying the Mississippi during the 1800s.

As early as 1859, engineers had realized that levees must control the Mississippi River floods. The Act of February 15,1893 established the St. Francis Levee District to control spring floods in the St. Francis River Basin area. However, private land owners were the first to construct levees along the Mississippi. The levees were only three or four feet high and were built with slave labor. In 1912 and again in 1913, following the New Madrid Earthquake, the St. Francis main levee broke, flooding all the area from West Memphis to Crowley's Ridge (almost 40 miles of water), causing extensive damage. Only the high ridges were out of the water. The current was so strong that steel rails were wrapped around trees. The Frisco Railway spent $150,000 repairing the tracks from Driver to Bridge Junction in 1912. People fled to Memphis or lived in houses built above the flood level, but returned when the water receded. Again a break in the levee in 1927 caused the area to flood. However, the greatest recorded flood occurred in 1937 when the river washed over the top of the levees. Because no breaks in the levees occurred, less damage was done than in 1913. Once the levees were completed and the danger of floods minimized, the population expanded. On March 21, 1927, the town was incorporated and Zack Bragg was elected as the first mayor. On April 30, 1929, the first ordinance was passed requiring men between the ages of 18 and 45 to pay $4 or work on the street one day a year. Failure to comply meant a $10 fine or jail time. Later, the council ordered all male youths to serve up to five days on road crews after floods, or pay a $4 road tax.

In the latter part of the 1920s, the first dog track located in the West Memphis area and was opened by the Mid-South Kennel Club. The race track, which was enclosed on approximately 20 acres of levee, was opened only a short time when operation was stopped by an injunction. About 1934, an act was passed by the Arkansas Legislature and approved by the governor authorizing dog racing in Arkansas. Shortly thereafter, Riverside Greyhound Club acquired the property formerly owned by Mid-South. At this track, located near the Harahan Bridge, spectators saw steeple chase races and races with monkeys riding as jockeys. The track had no mutual machines, so all figures were put on the board manually by the track superintendent's daughter. The purses for the Class A races were as small as $50. Organized dog racing came to a halt after the fire destroyed the grandstand in 1948, but dog racing was reintroduced when Southland Racing Corporation opened in 1965 with only 61 days of racing. This has expanded to 114 days of racing and is a major West Memphis attraction.

SOURCES: West Memphis Chamber of Commerce, *Arkansas Roadsides* by Bill Earngey

POINTS OF INTEREST

Southland Greyhound Park *I-40 and I- 55. 1-800-467-6182.* The world's largest greyhound racing facility. (The average visitor to Southland wagers $142.) At Southland, the dogs chase a large artificial bone around the track instead of the traditional "rabbit." Racing year-round. Call tollfree for daily schedules. No minors or cameras allowed. Group rates available.

Esperanza Trail *Off I-55 east of the city, north to Mound City.* This 10.5-mile hiking trail circles Dacus Lake, winding between the west bank of the Mississippi River and the levee. The trail passes the historic site of Hopefield, Indian mounds and the Memphis-Little Rock Road. The trail offers an opportunity to observe the terrain of the Delta as well as the levee system at work.

CONWAY

Seat of Faulkner County. Population 26,481

Information: Chamber of Commerce; Box 1492 HOA; Conway, AR 72033. (501) 327-7788. FAX 501-327-7790

HISTORY

Conway was founded by A.P. Robinson who came to the area shortly after the Civil War. Robinson was the chief engineer for the Little Rock-Fort Smith Railroad (now the Union-Pacific). Part of his compensation was the deed to a one-mile square tract of land located near the old settlement of Cadron. When the railroad was completed, Robinson deeded a small part of his land back to the railroad for a depot site. He laid out a town site around the depot and named it Conway Station, in honor of the prominent Conway family. In 1873, Faulkner County (named for Sanford C."Sandy" Faulkner, the author of the humorous dialogue and fiddle tune "Arkansaw Traveler") was created by the Legislature and Conway was designated as the county seat. With a population of about 200, Conway was incorporated in October 1875.

For many years, Conway flourished as a trade center for the large agricultural area around it. Hendrix College was established in Conway in 1890. Three years later in 1893, Central College for Girls was born. In 1907 the Arkansas Normal School was established; it would later become the University of Central Arkansas. Up until World War II, Conway's economy was built on agriculture and education. Today, the economic base is diversified with the arrival of businesses like the

Arkansas Educational Network and the Office of Emergency Services, as well as major industries like Acxiom, Frigidaire, Kimberly Clark and American Transportation located in Conway.

Being only a short hop of 30 miles north of Little Rock, many who work in the capital city call Conway home. Conway's population has been growing at a rate of 5% a year. The town has benefitted greatly from the lack of stability in the Little Rock School District which has led many Little Rock residents to look at Conway and surrounding communities as alternatives. Conway also benefits from the many tourists who pass through headed for Ozark recreational destinations.

POINTS OF INTEREST

Cadron Settlement Park Five miles west of Conway on the Arkansas River. Take Exit #125 off I-40 north of Conway. Declared a National Historic Site in 1974, this is the site of an early French trading post which flourished in the late 18th century. The settlement which grew up around around this site dates to about 1808 and was one of the first settlements in central Arkansas. Around 1815 the first post office was established at Cadron. The settlement narrowly missed being chosen as

DID YOU KNOW?

BASIC ELEPHANT 101

Riddle's Elephant Breeding Farm and Wildlife Sanctuary near Quitman in northern Faulkner County is the only one of its kind. This 330-acre farm is home to several African and Asian elephants. Scott and wife Heidi Riddle, who moved here from California in 1989, have worked with elephants for over 30 years in zoos, circuses and parks and decided to settle in Arkansas and provide a safe haven for endangered elephants. The Riddles offer a course in care and handling of elephants which is attended by zoo personnel around the country. The non-profit organization is supported by donations, grants and fund-raising efforts. For more information call (501) 589-3291.

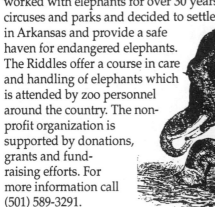

the capital of the Arkansas Territory. During the 1830s while relocating west to the Indian Territory (the infamous Trail of Tears), a large group of Indians traveling by boat on the Arkansas River were put ashore at Cadron. They camped there while combating a cholera epidemic. Many died and were buried nearby. Cadron was a station on the Butterfield Overland mail route from Memphis to San Francisco in 1858, Cadron flourished until the Little-Rock-Fort Smith Railroad was built in 1871 and bypassed the town. Facilities at the park include: boat ramp, barrier-free hiking trails, picnic areas, restored blockhouse, historical mural, markers and interpretive signs. Admission free.

Central Baptist College *1501 College Ave. (501) 329-6872.* Formerly Central College, it was established in 1893 and sponsored by the Baptist Missionary Association. Offers two-year associate degrees and four-year degrees in church ministry and music. Around 270 students.

Faulkner County Courthouse *U.S. 65B.* English Regency Revival, 1936. A 20-foot granite monument to Confederate soldiers on the grounds.

Greathouse Home/Museum Located on the grounds of the Faulkner County Courthouse, this home was built in 1830 and restored in 1966. An excellent example of dog-trot style of architecture. Furnished as an 1870s pioneer home with hooked rugs, loom, spinning wheel, cannon-ball bed. Open for tours spring through fall.

Hendrix College *1601 Harkrider. (501) 329-6811.* This co-educational, four-year, liberal arts college was founded in 1876 in Altus, Arkansas, purchased by the Methodist Church in 1884 and moved to Conway in 1890. An undergraduate community of approximately 1,000 students, the college is a recognized leader among independent colleges in America. Hendrix offers a Bachelor of Arts degree in 23 majors. *Money* magazine's 1994 *Best College Buys Guide* listed Hendrix College as 25th on their list of 100 American colleges and universities that offer a quality education for the money. Hendrix is the only Arkansas school on the list, ranking above pricey schools such as Harvard, Columbia and Dartmouth. Yearly tuition at Hendrix runs $8,800.

Lake Conway This 67,000-acre lake is the Game and Fish Commission's largest. Great fishing for catfish, crappie, bass and bream. Free public boat launches. Boat rentals available.

Pickles Gap Village *Hwy. 65N. (501) 329-9049.* This simulated Ozark village features gift and souvenir shops, guitar shop, kiddie zoo, antiques, Pickle Barrel Restaurant and soda fountain.

Toad Suck *U.S. 60 about 4 1/2 miles south at the Arkansas River.* This is the place with the unforgettable name. From 1820 unto 1970 a ferry operated here on the Arkansas River a few miles west of Conway. Today, you can see one of the early metal boats that used to pull the barge across the river as well as a conjoined pecan and chinquapin oak tree growing from a single trunk. A bizarre twist of nature, the tree produces both pecans and acorns. At Toad Suck Ferry Park across the river there are 49 campsites, picnic sites, pavilions, basketball courts, boat ramps and much more. The Toad Suck Lock and Dam was completed in 1969 as part of the 445-mile McClellan-Kerr Arkansas River Navigation system (from near Tulsa to the Mississippi River). The 100-by-60-foot lock can accommodate pleasure boats or barges by raising or lowering the water 16 feet inside the lock.

Toad Suck Daze Festival Held the first week-end in May, this unique event features three days of non-stop entertainment, crafts, runs, rides, food and infamous toad-jumping contests. You may have glimpsed Bill jogging in his Toad Suck Daze T-shirt – one of his many jogging ensembles that is ragged on by the

Double your pleasure – Toad Suck's conjoined oak and pecan tree

nation's fashion police. The Toad Suck One-Stop just west of the bridge can outfit you in similar presidential style.

TOAD SUCK?

Yes, it *is* a weird name. So where did it come from? Inquiring minds want to know. According to the lore and the inscription on a marker at Old Ferry Landing Park the story is this: A tavern once stood on the west side of the river. Riverboat workers, taking breaks from their labors, would drop in and belly up to the bar. The tavern keeper observed that his customers sucked on the bottles until they swelled up like toads.

Down-home chic

University of Central Arkansas *201 Donaghey Ave.; Conway, AR 72035.* *(501) 450-5000.* This school has undergone many name changes. Originally established as Arkansas Normal School in 1907; then Arkansas State Teachers College; 1967 it became State College of Arkansas; in 1975 it gained university status and was renamed University of Central Arkansas. This co-ed, four-year, liberal-arts university has an enrollment of about 10,000.

ROGERS

Benton County. Population: 24,692

Information: Chamber of Commerce; P.O. Box 428; Rogers, AR 72757; (501) 636-1240.

HISTORY

Originally a stop on the Butterfield Stage route in the mid-1800s, this northwest Arkansas town really got its start when it became a stop on the St. Louis & San Francisco Railroad line. In 1881, the town was incorporated and named for Captain W.C. Rogers, a general manager of the Frisco line. Rogers, the largest town in Benton County, developed into a commercial center with the poultry industry playing a major role in the economy. This was also an important shipping point for the "Land of the Big Red Apple." In the 1920s the elaborate parades and Apple Blossom Festivals drew huge crowds.

Industry thrives here right alongside tourism. Three big entrepreneurial companies in the area, Wal-Mart, J.B. Hunt Transport and Tyson Foods are at the heart of the boom that Rogers is experiencing. Other businesses that contribute to the stable economic base include Emerson

Electric, Scott Paper, Hudson Foods, Rogers Tool Works, First Brands. As even more companies relocate here, Rogers continues to experience record growth – 40% population growth in

Remnants of the stone amphitheater at Monte Ne

the past ten years. Daisy Manufacturing (as in B.B. guns and air rifles) is headquartered here, the largest such business in the world. The numerous recreational opportunities in the Ozarks make Rogers a popular vacation and retirement spot. Rogers has had its moments in the limelight. Betty Blake, wife of humorist Will Rogers was born here. And William "Coin" Harvey, one of America's true eccentrics established Monte Ne just south of town.

POINTS OF INTEREST

Beaver Lake *Hwy. 12, 62 or 94. (501) 636-1210.* Nearly 500 miles of shoreline for swimming, water-skiing, boating, camping. Several full-service marinas.

Daisy International Air Gun Museum *2111 South 8th. (501) 636-1200.* Daisy's claim to the world's largest display of non-powered guns, some dating back to the late 1700s, is housed in a museum adjacent to the manufacturing plant. Daisy was originator to the famous Red Ryder B.B. Gun.

Historic Downtown A participant in the Main Street Arkansas Program, many structures are on the National Historic Register. Brick streets in the district were laid in 1923. Applegate Drug Store, 116 S. First Street, designed by A.O. Clark in 1905 and restored in 1987, today houses Poor Richard's Gift and Confectionery Store with the original fixtures intact. Exotic ice cream creations prepared at the solid marble soda fountain.

Frisco Park *First and Walnut.* Site of an historical marker commemorating the first stage of the Butterfield Overland Mail in 1858. In 1981 in celebration of Roger's Centennial, the Frisco Railroad gave the city an old caboose as a symbol of the relationship between the town and the railroad.

Pea Ridge National Military Park *Hwy. 62 E. (501) 451-8122.* One of the largest battles west of the Mississippi was fought here in 1862. Self-guided tours with audio devices, historical markers.

Rogers Historical Museum *322 South Second. (501) 621-1154.* Preserves the history of the Rogers area. Visitors can experience First Street, a re-creation of three late 19th century stores, explore the Attic, a "hands-on" exhibit for kids, and step into the turn-of-the-century with a tour of the historic 1895 Hawkins House attached to the museum.

War Eagle Arts and Crafts Fair *War Eagle Mills Farm in Hindsville. (501) 789-5398.* Two fairs are held yearly in the spring and fall. These crafts fairs are biggies.

DID YOU KNOW?

A Penny For His Thoughts

In 1893, William Hope Harvey wrote a pamphlet called *Coin's Financial School* that advocated free coinage of silver as a solution to the U.S. money crunch. Astonishingly, the little book sold over a million copies. One of its admirers was a young politician, William Jennings Bryan, who sought Harvey's counsel. When Bryan lost his bid for the presidency after running on a free silver platform, a dejected "Coin" Harvey retreated to north Arkansas. In 1902 he built Monte Ne, a resort that featured the world's largest log hotels (one was 305-feet long, made of 8,000 logs). Monte Ne, however, was beset by problems, one being that the testy Harvey would become annoyed when guests stayed up late. By the end of WWI, the resort had gone belly-up. Later, Harvey founded the Liberty Party and ran for president himself in 1932. After this failure, Harvey was certain the world was going to hell in a hand basket. He began construction of a quixotic 130-foot pyramid, which was planned to serve as a repository for his own inspired writings. Old age and the Depression thwarted his designs, however. When Harvey died in 1936 only a stone amphitheater and pavilion were standing. For a time, the site was used by girls from nearby Camp Joyzelle. Later, in the 1960s, it was flooded when Beaver Lake was created. Today, when the water is low, remnants of the stone steps can be seen. It is ironic that on a summer's day at Monte Ne one can occasionally see teenage girls, Diet Cokes in hand, sunning in aluminum lawn chairs on the gravel shore of Beaver – clueless that "Coin" Harvey's dream lies just a few yards away beneath the water's surface.

War Eagle Cavern *Near War Eagle Mill (501) 789-0913.* This beautiful cavern is noted for its spectacular natural entrance.

War Eagle Mill *13 miles east on Hwy. 12. (501) 789-5343.* A working, water-powered grist mill which was once the hub of the rural community. Restaurant, gift shop. Fourteen wholegrain flours and meals made on-site.

EL DORADO

(Pronounced El-duh-RAY-doe, See <u>The American Heritage Dictionary, Third Edition.</u>*) Seat of Union County. Population: 23,146*

Information: Chamber of Commerce; P.O. Box 1271; El Dorado 71730. (501) 863-6113

HISTORY

Legend has it than an adventurer named Matthew F. Rainey became the first resident of El Dorado by accident. It is said that one day in 1843 his wagon broke down in the rugged country and being unable to get replacement parts, he held a sale of his possessions. He was so impressed with the neighboring farmer's eagerness to buy that he obtained more goods and put up a store, becoming the first to set up business in El Dorado.

Whether Rainey called the place "El Dorado" (Spanish for *place of gold*) in recognition of his good fortune, is not certain. The name was in use, however, the following year when Union County officials, seeking to move their county seat from the Ouachita River Bluff (now called Champagnolle) accepted Rainey's donation of 160 acres for the new townsite. In 1851, the town, then one square mile in area, was incorporated. Cotton growers came up the Ouachita by steamboat and cleared plantations in the neighborhood.

In 1890, there were 455 people in El Dorado. For many years it was an agricultural and timber community, reaching a population of only 3,887 by 1920. On January 10, 1921, however, the Busey-Armstrong #1, a well drilled by physician-turned-geologist Samuel Busey, blew in one mile west of the city. The gusher was reportedly so powerful that it soaked people two miles away. This discovery transformed the quiet settlement into a boomtown, complete with fancy women, city slickers and noisy night spots. According to one account, the town "thronged with a seething mass of conglomerate humanity...diamonds and costly furs rubbed elbows with oil-soaked khaki." Legitimate businessmen were joined by an influx of gamblers, moonshiners, dope-sellers, prostitutes, cut-purses and murderers who transformed parts of the city into enclaves with colorful names like: Pistol Hill, Shotgun Valley, Chicken Farm and the infamous Hamburger Row. The search for oil was immediately directed north towards the village of Smackover and the nearby Ouachita River fault line. On July 29, 1922, Smackover saw the Richardson #1 explode onto the scene and within a year the 40-square-mile Smackover field was producing oil in abundance and by 1925 it ranked first among the nation's oil fields for a brief five-month period.

On El Dorado's unpaved streets, as well as those of sister oil town Smackover, mules and oxen were said to drown. Pictures taken during this time document mules trying to drag heavy equipment through the quagmire. Tales are told of misguided waterfowl landing in the rivers of oil that coursed through low-lying areas, mistaking these sludgy tributaries for rivers and lakes.

Twenty-two trains a day were soon running in and out of El Dorado. The population skyrocketed to an estimated 30,000 people who ate and slept when they could, using empty freight cars, tents, hotel lobbies jerry-built shacks on vacant lots and rotating bed space. Feeding the hordes was a major problem. Hamburger stands cropped up everywhere. A newspaper of the day said "the sidewalks became one great dining room, crowded and jammed, beautifully scented from the 'Hamburger With,' burned waffles, fried fish and boiling donut grease, looking like a great midway." By the end of October, about 460 producing wells had been taken from a 5,000-acre area. Recovering from the first impact of the boom, El Dorado steadied and soon transformed itself from an oil camp into a city. New buildings were erected to house firms, machine shops and foundries. Refineries were built and new homes constructed. The countryside is still dotted with derricks, many of them seemingly having sprouted up as randomly as dandelions. This is the result of the wildcat speculators who came to make their fortune and would routinely approach homeowners, offer to buy mineral rights and subsequently sink a well right in the back yard.

Todays, El Dorado is well-known as the oil center of Arkansas. The

DID YOU KNOW?

H.L. HUNT SLEPT HERE

H.L. Hunt, at one time one of the wealthiest men in the country, got his start in the oil business in El Dorado during the boom. Hunt opened a gambling house in town and tried his hand at wildcatting. In 1925, Hunt bought a lot that covered a full block in the city and had an impressive three-story house built for his family. He would subsequently go broke and move on to Texas where he would make a killing. During the 1960s, the vacant, deteriorating Hunt mansion loomed as a haunted house for curious teenagers. Where the magnificent house once stood, there is now a vacant pine-covered lot off East 8th and Calion Road.

headquarters of the Murphy Oil Corporation remains in El Dorado. Other industries that contribute to the area's economy include timber, poultry processing and chemical plants. El Dorado has been called the last of the boomtowns.

SOURCES: Chamber of Commerce, *The WPA Guide to 1930s Arkansas; Early Louisiana and Arkansas Oil* by Kenny Franks & Paul Lambert

Evidence of another gusher – south Arkansas field crew drenched with oil

POINTS OF INTEREST

Arkansas Oil and Brine Museum *Between El Dorado and Smackover on Hwy. 7. (501) 725-2877.* This state museum collects, preserves and exhibits examples of Arkansas' changing oil technology and brine industry. The museum focuses on the 1920s oil boom in south Arkansas. Working outdoor exhibits include an oil well, pumping rig and three derricks. Two video presentations depict the discovery of oil in Arkansas. Brine is the salt-saturated water which is a by-product of oil production. For years it was considered useless. Now its applications vary from gasoline additives to flame retardants. South Arkansas leads the world in the production of bromine which is extracted from brine. The bromine industry got its start during the fifties. Free admission.

El Dorado Main Street Beautifully restored 1920s and 30s businesses; ornate county court house; restaurants, specialty shops; nine structures listed on National Register of Historic Places.

Felsenthal National Wildlife Refuge *U.S. Hwy 82, 40 miles east of town. (501) 364-3167.* This 65,000-acre tract established in 1975, half of which is in Union County, the rest in Ashley and Bradley counties, is the world's largest greentree reservoir, under management of the U.S. Fish and Wildlife Service. Terrific resource for nature study, hunting and fishing. Boat ramps and the newly constructed Gran Maris Campground with RV pads, are conveniently located on and near the refuge.

Moro Bay State Park *Ark. 15, 22 miles east of town. (501) 463-8555.* Peaceful park located on the Ouachita River. Picnicking, fishing, boating, hiking.

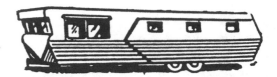

Musicfest *Downtown on the square. (501) 863-0008.* El Dorado Main Street program hosts this annual celebration the second weekend in October. Myriads of entertainers, food, arts and crafts and exhibits.

Rainey-Newton House *510 N. Jackson (501) 862-9890.* This handsome 1848 home is the oldest in the community, a well-preserved example of provincial mid-19th century Arkansas architecture. Built by Matthew Rainey, the house has stood as an El Dorado landmark for over 100 years. Tours by appointment.

Rialto Theatre *113 E. Cedar (501) 862-2162.* Built in 1929 in response to oil boom demands for cultural opportunities. This stunning Classical Revival movie theater is on the National Register of Historic Places. Its state-of-the-art heating, cooling, sound and projection systems were considered among the most modern in the Southwest. It closed in the mid-70s, but was restored and reopened in 1987. The expansive balcony is now divided into two small theaters. The first floor remains virtually unaltered.

South Arkansas Arts Center and South Arkansas Symphony *110 E. 5th. (501) 862-5474.* Arts Center has three divisions: Visual Arts,

Performing Arts and Allied Arts. Hosts monthly art exhibits, theatrical performances, artist-in-education program, children's programs. Symphony stages regular performances with a full orchestra and a variety of chamber concerts (501) 862-0521.

South Arkansas Community College Offers two-year associate of arts degree as well as degrees in business, health and a wide-range of technical fields.

DID YOU KNOW?

HAMBURGER ROW

Following the discovery of oil, El Dorado's only paved roads were around the square and down South Washington to the railroad. Mayor Frank Smith authorized the rental of spaces along South Washington between the sidewalk and the street to vendors to feed the oil rig operators, field hands, drillers, roughnecks, geologists, leasehounds and others who descended upon the city. This area became the notorious "Hamburger Row." Described then by a Little Rock journalist, "Hamburger Row is El Dorado's Broadway, its Rialto and its Bowery. It is the most cosmopolitan section in the whole state, containing under its dingy roofs, every specimen of humanity possible to conceive."

BLYTHEVILLE

Seat of Mississippi County. Population: 23,002

Information: Chamber of Commerce; 124 W. Walnut; P.O. Box 485; Blytheville, AR 72316-0485. (501) 762-0551. Tourist Information Center is located north of the city at Interstate 55. Staffed and operated by the Arkansas Department of Parks and Tourism. Restrooms, picnic tables, free maps, literature about the area.

HISTORY

Blytheville was founded in 1853 by Henry Thomas Blythe, a Virginia-born Methodist preacher who traveled about the region holding camp meetings. On high land well back from the Mississippi he built his home and a small church as a base for his ministry. The community that grew up here was called Blythe Chapel. In 1880 Blythe divided some of his land into town lots, but the community grew slowly because it was inaccessible due to boggy roads. On May 19,1891, Blytheville incorporated and Reverend Blythe became the first postmaster. In 1888, L.W. Gosnell installed a cotton gin and a smattering of cotton buyers from Memphis and Jonesboro began to come to town each fall. Subsequently, an artesian well was built bringing a good water supply to the town. During the 1890s, timber had been the a lure to lumber companies and railroads. Efforts to extend railroads to the town began in 1893 and in 1900, with a population of 302, Blytheville became the county seat for North Mississippi County. In 1901 and 1902, the rails made their way to Blytheville. For the first few years thereafter Blytheville was largely dependent on lumbering for its income. As the timber was cleared away, the residents came to see how rich the soil was. So in 1902 the first drainage district was organized and the land emerged from the stagnant water and became productive. With the establishment of Blytheville's first compress with storage space for 25,000 bales in 1911, the town began to take its place as a shipping point for cotton.

Blytheville is located five miles from the Missouri state line and eight miles from the Mississippi River. Today the alluvial soil of Mississippi County produces a quarter of a million bales of cotton and over six million bushels of soybeans annually. The naturally fertile soil is the county's greatest asset. The alluvial soil is distributed over the 578,304

Steamboat loaded with cotton bales (1870s)

acres in the county from countless overflow water by rivers and streams. In certain locations, the soil ranges to nearly 100 feet deep.

The now-defunct Eaker Air Force Base opened in 1942 and the population mushroomed to 16,221 by 1950. As the largest city in Mississippi County, Blytheville is recognized as one on the leading trade centers and markets of the Delta, particularly in northeast Arkansas and the bootheel of Missouri. Manufacturing employees make up 35% of the total employment in the area. Industries process an assortment of products from tin cans to high density discharge ballasts.

POINTS OF INTEREST

Big Lake National Wildlife Refuge Sixteen miles west of town. Private recreational facilities available. Lunker bass fishing on Mallard Lake.

Eaker Air Force Base Three miles northwest of the city, the base was once home of the 97th Bombardment Wing. It was closed in December 1992 in a military cutback.

Chickasawba Mound Northwest of town, this 13-acre site is an example of 16th century Indian culture is thought to have been occupied as early as A.D. 700. During WWII it briefly served as a German POW camp.

Mississippi County Community College U.S. 61. Opened in 1975, the nation's first solar-powered school offers career and liberal arts associate (two-year) degrees and certificate programs.

Mississippi County Courthouse Neo-Classic 1919 style featuring white marble floors, walls and stairs.

Ritz Civic Center This Art Deco facility located downtown was built in the early 1930s, purchased and renovated in 1980. Displays local and regional art and sponsors local and road-show theaters and concerts.

TEXARKANA

Seat of Miller County, Arkansas. Population: 54,287 (22,631 on the Arkansas side; 31,656 Texas). Texarkana is named for three states: TEXas, ARKansas and LouisiANA.

Information: Chamber of Commerce; P.O. Box 1468; Texarkana, Tex/Ark 75504. (903)792-7191. Tourist Information Center on I-30 has free maps and literature.

HISTORY

Legend has it that in 1542 Hernando de Soto ordered a mutinous follower hanged from an oak tree near an artesian spring in the territory of the Grand Caddoes. Less than a half hour march to the south was the site which would later be known as Texarkana.

Before the arrival of the white man, this territory was traversed by the Great Southwest Trail which, for hundreds of years, had been the main trunk line of travel between the Indian villages of the Mississippi Valley and of the West and Southwest. The heavily wooded, level lands were a natural camping ground. There, the peaceful, sedentary Caddoes tilled their rich fields of maize, beans, pumpkins and melons in their villages on the banks of the river.

The Caddoes were hosts to the worn survivors of the ill-fated La Salle Expedition in 1687. By 1719, the French had infiltrated the territory and set up a fort and trading post. During the years that followed, the Indians migrated slowly westward. Yet evidence of the Caddoes occupation and culture are to be found within a 30-mile radius of Texarkana, in not less that 70 Indian mounds which suggest considerable thought, care and technical knowledge went into their construction.

As early as 1840, rudiments of a permanent settlement in the old Caddo territory began to take form. Railroads were quick to see the possibilities of this vast new territory, and in the late 1850s, the builders of the Cairo & Fulton Railroad were pushing their railhead steadily across Arkansas to eventually meet up with the Texas & Pacific line. The Red River Bridge was opened on March 20,1874, and from that date trains have run directly from Texarkana to St. Louis. (The Cairo & Fulton is now part of the Missouri-Pacific Railway Company.) It was only logical that the point at which the two railroads converged would be ideal for a city. Consequently, the Texas & Pacific Railroad sold the first town lots on December 8, 1873; the first of which was bought by J.W. Davis and on which the shabby, now-vacant Hotel McCartney stands, directly opposite Union Station.

Although many have contended for the honor, it is not known who officially gave Texarkana its name. One popular version credits Colonel Gus Knobel who, surveying the Iron Mountain Railroad right-of-way from Little Rock to this section, came to the state line, marked the name "TEX-ARK-ANA" on a board and nailed it to a tree with the statement, "this is the name of the town which is to be built here." It was believed at the time that the Louisiana boundary was just a few miles to the south (actually it is only 25), and Colonel Knobel, in selecting the city's name, derived it from TEXas, ARKansas, and LouisiANA. Late in 1874 the Arkansas Legislature established Miller County and made Texarkana its seat. The town incorporated on October 17,1880, seven years after the Texas side (June 12, 1874).

This unique town lying in two states and divided by a survey line has had to negotiate areas of jurisdiction since the beginning. The city governments have to iron out matters of law, licensing, arrest warrants and taxation. In the early days of the raucous town, the state boundary line could hamper a lawman's attempt to pursue a criminal from one state to the other. A frequent notation on Arkansas warrants was "G.T."– Gone to Texas. It is, however, unlikely that private citizens with a bone to pick came to a screeching halt at the border.

Businesses that contribute to the economy of this schizoid town include Cooper Tire & Rubber Company, Georgia-Pacific and International Paper mills, Red River Army Depot where tanks are repaired and Lone Star Army Ammunitions Plant .

SOURCES: Chamber of Commerce; *The WPA Guide to 1930s Arkansas*

POINTS OF INTEREST

Ace of Clubs House *420 Pine Street.*
(903) 793-7108. Legend has it that entrepreneur James H. Draughon built the 22-sided house with the winnings from a poker game, and that the winning card was the ace of clubs. Architecturally unique, the 1885 Italianate Victorian home has a central octagonal stairhall with three octagonal wings and one rectangular wing, which gives it the distinctive shape of the playing card. Group tours available.

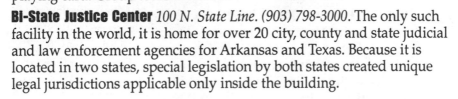

Bi-State Justice Center *100 N. State Line. (903) 798-3000.* The only such facility in the world, it is home for over 20 city, county and state judicial and law enforcement agencies for Arkansas and Texas. Because it is located in two states, special legislation by both states created unique legal jurisdictions applicable only inside the building.

Discovery Place *Pine Street, downtown. (903) 794-3466.* Large scale "hands-on" and permanent exhibits focus on science, history and human perception. A state-of-the-art theater where learning comes alive through lectures, lab demonstrations and audio-visual presentations.

Millwood Reservoir *Located 27 miles north of Texarkana on U.S. 71, 59 to Ashdown.* There are 87 miles of wooded shoreline. Lake Millwood is best know for its bass fishing and is considered by some to be the finest bass lake in the South. Red ear bream is also a principle sport fish. Facilities available for fishing, picnicking, camping and boating.

Perot Theatre *221 Main Street. 1-800-333-0927.* The historic theater first opened in November 1924 as the Saenger Theatre. Designed in Italian Renaissance style by Emil Weil, it was the "most opulent link" of the Saenger Amusements chain. It attracted performers such as Orson Wells and Will Rogers as well as vaudevillians and movie stars. The theater closed in 1977 but was later bought by the city and restored through the persistence of the citizens and the generosity of H. Ross Perot ($800,000). The $1.9 million restoration involved gold leaf, refurbished original theater seats and a British reproduction of the 1924 carpeting. The theater is home to one of the nation's major performing arts series. Features year-round entertainment – symphony, ballet, pop music and Broadway shows. Box office: (903) 792-4992. To tour the theater: (903) 792-8681.

How to be in two places at the same time

Post Office and Photographer's Island Texarkana is one of the unique cities in America in that it straddles a state line which also passes directly through the center of the downtown post office. Tourists are fond of having their photos taken at Photographer's Island in front of the post office with one foot in Arkansas and the other foot in Texas. The post office's official address is listed Texarkana, U.S.A., 75501.

Scott Joplin Mural *Third and Main.* Colorful outdoor tribute to the Texarkana native, who was a Pulitzer-Prize winning composer and ragtime pianist.

Texarkana Historical Museum *219 State Line Avenue. (903) 793-4831.* Located in the oldest brick building in Texarkana (erected in 1879), the museum collects and interprets artifacts and materials from the area including Caddo Indian artifacts; the Period Room exhibit which includes a Victorian parlor and doctor's office and the "Touch Table" which lets children look through a Victorian stereoscope to examine a homemade rabbit trap.

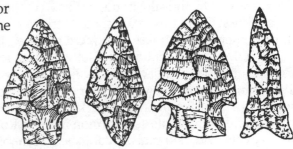

DID YOU KNOW?

JIM BOWIE: ADVENTURER

Most people know that Jim Bowie was the inventor of the bowie knife, a lethal weapon whose prototype has been copied in varying forms. But there's more to the story. Bowie was the Texas hero for whom Bowie County was named and in which lies the western half of Texarkana (the Texas side).

Bowie, a native of Logan County, Kentucky, early in life felt the urge of the frontiersman. Venturing into the Arkansas Territory, his first knife was made in what is now Washington, Arkansas. After a bloody battle with river gangs on the Mississippi near Natchez, Mississippi, he went southward to lower Louisiana. There, for a time, he engaged in slave trade with the colorful Jean Lafitte, the hero of the Battle of New Orleans.

Some time later, Bowie journeyed westward and met and married Señorita Ursula de Veramendi, daughter of the wealthy Juan de Veramendi, vice-governor of Mexico. His adventuresome spirit uncurbed by matrimony, Bowie soon found himself in active support of the Texans in their conflicts with Mexico. He later joined David Crockett and others and was among those slaughtered at the Alamo. It was this battle at the Alamo which galvanized the Texans and brought them to final grips with Santa Anna at San Jacinto on April 21, 1836, and which resulted in the rout of the Mexican army and creation of the Republic of Texas. Today, in Texarkana, there is a large statue of Bowie gripping rifle and bowie knife, facing southwest.

SOURCE: Chamber of Commerce

RUSSELLVILLE

Seat of Pope County. Population: 21,260.

Information: Chamber of Commerce; 800 East Main Street; Russellville, AR 72801. (501) 968-2530.

HISTORY

This area was historically important as a crossing on the Arkansas River. Before Russellville was established, there were other communities here at the center of a Cherokee settlement in the early 1800s. Dwight Mission, west of present day Russellville, was reportedly the first Protestant mission west of the Mississippi. In 1820 Rev. Cephas Washburn and his fellow missionaries set out from Savannah, Georgia, to set up a Cherokee mission in Arkansas. Washburn is said to have delivered the first Protestant sermon in Little Rock on his way to Russellville. Washburn also established a school for the Cherokee children that was well-attended. At one time there were seven assistant teachers at the mission and about a hundred Cherokee children enrolled.

The mission was pretty well cut off and the sense of isolation took its toll. Washburn wrote in his journal. "Hitherto we have been as entirely excluded from intercourse with the Christian world as if we were in the Japan Isles. We have heard of the arrival of letters in the Arkansas territory for us, but we have been unable to locate them." But things improved as river travel became common and a post office was established there in 1823. The *Eagle*, the first steamboat to make it up river to Little Rock in 1822, continued on with supplies to Dwight. The mission continued until 1828, when the Cherokees ceded their Arkansas lands and were removed to Oklahoma. The most distinguished of the Indians who gathered at the mission was Sequoya, also known as George Guess. Born in Tennessee, son of a Dutch trader and Indian mother, he came to Arkansas after the Cherokee Treaty of 1817. Intrigued by the white man's ability to communicate with written characters, he developed a simple Cherokee alphabet. Subsequently, literacy spread quickly throughout the Cherokee Nation. Sequoya is said to have completed work on the alphabet at the mission and at nearby Galla Rock.

In 1834 the first house was built in present-day Russellville. The traditional double log dog-trot house belonged to British born and educated Dr. T.J. Russell who, with his wife Mary Ann Graham, moved to the prairie (as it was called) where the town is now situated. As Russellville grew, Dwight and other smaller towns around it faltered. Russellville was not incorporated until 1870 and didn't really hit its stride until a few years later with the construction of the Little Rock &

Fort Smith Railroad (now Missouri-Pacific). Russellville became the county seat in 1887. Affording rail and river access and being the largest town between Little Rock and Fort Smith, Russellville was a natural trading and transportation center. The town suffered a setback in 1906 when a fire destroyed 21 businesses, but the town rebuilt and by 1919 the population was 5,000 with the "largest horse and mule market in the state. . . " according to an ad in the *Arkansas Gazette*.

Located in the heart of the Arkansas River Valley at the intersection of I-40 and Scenic Highway 7, recreational opportunities abound with water sports on the Arkansas River, Lake Dardanelle, and numerous float streams. Russellville is home to Arkansas Tech University and Arkansas Nuclear One which supplies electricity. Eight Fortune 500 companies have operations in the Russellville area, which is becoming a center for the food distribution industry. Poultry, beef and dairy cattle, swine and row crops provide the agricultural base.

SOURCES: Chamber of Commerce; *The WPA Guide to 1930s Arkansas; Arkansas Roadsides* by Bill Earngey

DID YOU KNOW?

THAT'S A MOUTHFUL

Russellville was the longtime residence of Jeff Davis (1863-1913), United States senator and three times governor, noted for his colorful down-home rhetoric. He once shouted to a political opponent, "You threatened to kill me. I am not afraid of you. I can take a corncob with a lightning bug on the end of it and run you into the river." Also from his lips: "When I licked that gang in Little Rock during the last campaign they went around on the streets with faces as long as a saddle blanket."

POINTS OF INTEREST

Arkansas Nuclear One (ANO) *U.S. 64, 6 miles west; south on CR 333.*
Clearly the most visible structure in the vicinity, the concrete cooling tower is 447 feet high and 396 feet wide at its base. Apart from the cooling tower, the primary nuclear systems are housed in cylindrical

structures 200 feet tall and 120 feet in diameter with walls from three to nine feet thick built to withstand tornadoes, floods and earthquakes. The stuff that looks like smoke billowing from the cooling tower is actually steam. Total output from this facility is 1,694 megawatts. That's enough power to light 16,940,000 hundred-watt light bulbs (or to possibly power the Jennings Osborne Christmas display for a couple of hours). Tours of ANO are available with advance notice. Contact the superintendent at Lake Dardanelle State Park for details. For a spur-of-the-moment peek, just use the visitor's parking lot at the intake canal.

Arkansas River Valley Arts Center *"B" and Knoxville Streets. (501) 968-2452.* Rotating local and regional art exhibits as well as theater and band performances.

Arkansas River Visitor Center/ Lock and Dam *Located at Old Post Road Park in Russellville. (501) 968-5008.* "Renaissance of the River" exhibits and audio-visual presentations trace the history of the Arkansas River Valley from the Indians to the present day. Also an overlook of the river, lake, lock and dam.

Arkansas Tech University *(501) 968-0389.* In 1909 the General Assembly established four district agricultural high schools in Jonesboro, Russellville, Magnolia and Monticello. The Russellville school opened its doors in 1910 with 99 boys and 77 girls. Present name was adopted in 1925 when the school became a junior college. In 1948 it became a four-year college.

Arkansas Tech University Museum of Pre-History and History *(501) 968-3941.* Located on the ATU campus, exhibits on the events of the Arkansas Ozarks and the Arkansas River Valley from prehistoric times to the present.

Bona Dea Trails and Sanctuary *Ark. 326, off Ark 7.* Managed by the Corps of Engineers, 186 acres of wetlands and wooded lowlands that provide habitat for 200 species of birds plus other wildlife like deer and coyote. Five and a half miles of winding trails for hiking or jogging. Two of the four trails provide a physical fitness "parcourse" whose 18 stations range from chin-up bars to balance beams.

Illinois Bayou Possibly the only bayou in the country with class II/III white water. Rugged scenery including the unusual Pedestal Rocks.

Lake Dardanelle State Park 34,000-acre lake with great bass-fishing, visitor center, campground, marina, miniature golf. *(501) 967-5516.*

Mount Magazine *Ark. 309, Paris. (501) 963-3076.* Highest peak in the state at 2, 753 feet. Popular for primitive camping, rappelling, hang gliding, hiking. Provides access to the Cove Lake hiking trail.

Mount Nebo State Park *Ark. 155, south of Dardanelle. (501) 229-3655.* Another jumping off place for hang gliders, this park was built by the CCC. Fourteen miles of trails that afford outstanding views. Cabins, tennis courts, pool, campground, visitor center.

Norristown Now a suburb of Russellville, this community located on a ridge near the Arkansas River was founded in 1829 by Samuel Norris. It was the last stop for the Butterfield Overland Mail before crossing the river. Around 1858, Painter Edward Washburn (Cephas' son) painted "The Arkansas Traveler" here. This widely-known painting of the country fiddler and the visitor on the white horse became the state's trademark and lithographs abound. The original painting hangs in the Arkansas History Commission offices in Little Rock.

Park-O-Meter (POM) The world's first parking meters were manufactured here in 1935.

Pontoon Bridge *Ark. 7 at Arkansas River.* Reportedly the longest pontoon bridge in the world was built on the Arkansas River in 1889-91, and not replaced until 1929. In 1912, then-president Teddy Roosevelt lumbered across. This 2,343-foot wooden bridge with a capacity of 9,000 pounds was floated on 72 boats using 11 spans with six boats under each span and a "draw-span" of nine boats. It measured 12 feet across with a few 16-feet passing lanes. The five cement pyramids used to anchor the bridge are visible on the downstream side of today's bridge.

Pope County Courthouse *Jct. of U.S. 64 and Ark. 7.* Featuring extensive interior marble, this example of Mission Deco was built in 1932. Because the county records were hidden during the Civil War, they escaped destruction and are continuous from 1829.

SHERWOOD

County: Pulaski. Population: 18,893.

Information: Sherwood Chamber of Commerce; 3901-B East Kiehl Ave.; Sherwood, AR 72120. (501) 835-7600.

HISTORY

Incorporated on April 22, 1948, the population the following September was 714. Between 1980 and 1990 the population grew at 52.5%. Though the population shot up, business development has not kept pace. Sherwood's proximity to Little Rock and North Little Rock has been a mixed blessing. While Sherwood residents get the benefit of the amenities of the metropolitan area, such as shopping, entertainment and universities, the smaller community usually loses out when it must compete with the big cities for new business and industry. Consequently, Sherwood has traditionally been a bedroom community with more than half of its residents working outside. In March of 1995, Sherwood went on the offensive and hired a professional industrial recruiter to try to rustle up some businesses that might find attractive such things as the town's low crime rate, family environment, recreational facilities and absence of property tax. Additionally, there is no charge for home garbage pickup or ambulance service for Sherwood residents. The city is putting the finishing touches on a multimillion-dollar sports complex. Sherwood is home to the Rollin' Razorbacks, the National Wheelchair Basketball Champions for 1991, 1993 and 1994. Four team members won gold medals at the 1992 Paralympic Games in Barcelona, Spain.

PARAGOULD

Seat of Greene County. Population: 18,540.

Information: Chamber of Commerce; 111 E. Poplar; P. O. Box 124; Paragould, AR 72451. (501) 236-7684.

HISTORY

In 1811-12 the New Madrid Earthquake laid waste a large portion in this Northeast portion of the state which would later become Greene County. The total devastation created sunk lands 15-20 feet deep and steep ridges. This upheaval destroyed the channel of the St. Francis River. The federal government had awarded Bounty Certificates to veterans of the War of 1812 for their services and, as luck would have it, the land set aside for their use was the uninhabitable aftermath of the earthquake.

The feds reissued New Madrid Certificates which allowed them to seek out undamaged land. In 1821, a 65-year-old surveyor who held a certificate left his home in Kentucky with two sons and some slaves searching for a place to relocate with his wife and eight kids. He crossed the ridge which now bears his name and settled on a spot near a large spring, now located in Crowley's Ridge State Park, 12 miles from Paragould. Soon other relatives and friends followed to make their homes on the ridge. The first post office was in Crowley's home.

The natural drainage pattern was so disturbed by the natural disaster that it would be years before crops could be grown. In the meantime, the stands of timber on the ridge provided a lucrative lumber industry for the growing community. Paragould was established in 1883 at the intersection of two railroads that crossed the state: the St. Louis & Iron Mountain (later the Missouri Pacific) headed by the famous railroad magnate Jay Gould who already controlled some 5,000 miles of track in Arkansas and the Southwest – and the Texas & St. Louis (later the Cotton Belt), a narrow gauge line with J.W. Paramore as its president. The unique name of the town evolved by combining "Para" from Paramore and "Gould" from Jay Gould's name, creating the only town in the country with this name. Legend has it Gould objected to being a second syllable and for a time refused to use the name on his train schedules, instead he used the name "Parmley" the name of a nearby town. They finally compromised on "Para-Gould" which later became a non-hyphenate. The town incorporated on March 3, 1883, and was voted county seat that same year although the town was still an uncultivated tract of timber. The lumber industry boomed, and by 1890 the population was 2,528. But by the 1920s the timber industry had pretty well denuded the landscape and there wasn't much left to cut. The vast treeless landscape did at last lend itself to cultivation and agriculture took over as the most important industry and remains so today. In addition, there are 14 industrial plants located in Paragould.

POINTS OF INTEREST

Crowley's Ridge College *100 College Drive; (501) 236-6901.* Private college. Two-year associate degrees. Enrollment 90.

Crowley's Ridge State Park Nine miles west of town, situated on Crowley's Ridge. Cabins, campgrounds, fishing, pavilions, hiking trails. *(501) 573-6751.*

Engine 303 *Hammond Park, U.S. 49B, north of town.* A reminder of the old days, this steam engine is the last one that ran on the Little Dummy Line, "The World's Shortest Railroad." Abandoned in 1958.

Greene County Courthouse Victorian Renaissance Revival. Built in 1888, restored in 1918. On the National Register of Historic Places. A 90-by-90 foot bomb shelter was built on the grounds in 1978. Also a bronze Statue of Liberty and a replica of the Liberty Bell.

Loose Caboose Festival

Annual event held in May to celebrate the town's railroad heritage. Carnival, street basketball, arts and crafts, food, entertainment.

Paragould Mural *Between Court and Emerson Streets.* Two-hundred-foot mural depicts early transportation in this railroad town.

BENTON

Seat of Saline County. Population: 18,177

Information: Chamber of Commerce; 607 N. Market Street; Benton, AR 72015. (501) 778-827

HISTORY

De Soto first explored what is now known as Saline County back in 1541, but settlement did not take place until almost 300 years later. In the spring of 1815 William Lockhart of North Carolina settled with his family four miles southwest of Benton, at the point where the road between Little Rock and Hot Springs crossed the Saline River. By 1819 there was a community of nine or ten families. In 1823 Ezra M. Owen began a settlement near the geographic center of the territory. He planned a school, which he hoped to make the state university, and so named his settlement Collegeville. His plans never materialized. Many settlers from Kentucky migrated here and began farming; the area was given the name Kentucky Township. A water mill was erected about 10 miles northwest of Benton in 1825. Up until then, the settlers either ground their corn by hand or made the trip to the small trading post of Little Rock 23 miles away. The first post office was established early in 1831 at the Saline crossing; it was named Saline and Lockhart was the postmaster. Not long thereafter, the residents moved to higher ground to avoid flooding and established a new settlement they named Benton, after Missouri Senator Thomas H. Benton.

Pioneers continued to come and by 1835 the population had expanded so that a new county was needed. Saline County was created on November 2, 1835, carved from parts of Pulaski and Hemstead counties. Benton was chosen as county seat due to its central location and population. The first courthouse and jail were erected in 1838. The jail was built of logs at a cost of $975. Benton had a racetrack in 1838, long before Hot Springs laid claim to one.

The Saline River and the area surrounding it take their names from the rich salt deposits found there (*saline* meaning salty). The first known industry was a salt factory which was in business as early as 1827. During that time, the salt works supplied the bulk of the salt used in the Territory, as well as to neighboring states. Other industries that followed included pottery and brick-making. The Niloak Pottery marker on Military Road marks the spot where fine pottery was once produced from richly colored native clays. In 1887 bauxite, an essential ore in the making of aluminum, was discovered and at one time Saline County produced 97% of the nation's bauxite. This industry formed the economic base for this area for decades. Saline County is one of Arkansas' faster growing counties, showing an increase of 46.5% from 1970 to 1980. Although Saline County is considered rural, more than half its resident live in urban areas, making it a bedroom community for many who work in Little Rock.

POINTS OF INTEREST

Collegeville Named in 1823 as a site for a proposed state college that never materialized. A sign erected here in 1936 by the Daughters of American Colonists states: "The Geographical Center of Arkansas Is A Few Steps North of This Highway." The marker still stands, but the ladies were a tad off. *I-30. Alexander exit, to Pine Crest Cemetery.*

Gann Museum *118 N. Market St. (501) 778-5513.* Originally the office of Dr. Dewell Gann, Sr., where he treated patients who worked for the railroads and industrial plants in the area, in addition to his regular practice. The building was built in 1893 by patients who could not afford to pay for his services. It is the only known structure in the world to be constructed of bauxite. The stone was dug from a nearby farm, hand-sawed into blocks, and allowed to harden. Dr. Gann gave the building to the city in 1946 to be used as a library (1944-66). In 1980 the museum was established to preserve the history of Saline County.

Hurricane Creek Battle Site This was the only Civil War skirmish to take place in the area. Marker on Ark. 5, northeast of Benton.

Saline County Courthouse On the square. Built in 1900 in Romanesque Revival style, it's renowned for its beautiful woodwork and striking architecture. Features two-story towers, round colored floor tiles and a four-story clock tower.

Shoppach House Built in 1853, this house was occupied by both Confederate and Union troops at various times during the Civil War. The house is restored and furnished with period antiques and historical displays.

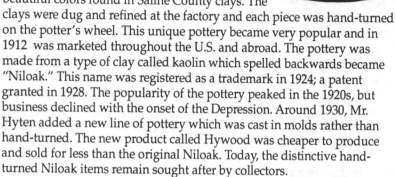

DID YOU KNOW?

NILOAK POTTERY — WHAT'S IN A NAME?

Niloak pottery was originated by C.D. "Bullet" Hyten in 1910. Bullet was inspired by the many beautiful colors found in Saline County clays. The clays were dug and refined at the factory and each piece was hand-turned on the potter's wheel. This unique pottery became very popular and in 1912 was marketed throughout the U.S. and abroad. The pottery was made from a type of clay called kaolin which spelled backwards became "Niloak." This name was registered as a trademark in 1924; a patent granted in 1928. The popularity of the pottery peaked in the 1920s, but business declined with the onset of the Depression. Around 1930, Mr. Hyten added a new line of pottery which was cast in molds rather than hand-turned. The new product called Hywood was cheaper to produce and sold for less than the original Niloak. Today, the distinctive hand-turned Niloak items remain sought after by collectors.

SEARCY

Seat of White County. Population: 15,180.

Information: Chamber of Commerce; 200 S. Spring Street; Searcy, AR 72143. (501) 268-2458.

HISTORY

The town was first called Sulphur Springs for the therapeutic waters that made the town a mid-19th century health resort. The springs that once attracted crowds to City Park on Spring Street, disappeared when wells were drilled to supply the town's water system and the springs dried up. The town was named in honor of Richard Searcy who migrated to Arkansas from Tennessee. In 1823, President Monroe appointed Searcy to be a judge on the Arkansas Territory superior court.

The community grew steadily as settlers made their way on the Arkansas, White and Little Red rivers into White County in the new state of Arkansas. Several settlements such as Georgetown, West Point, Judsonia and others were formed along the river and Searcy became the major trading center and county seat in 1837. By the time of the Civil

War, the population was around 700. Searcy became the county recruiting center for the Confederacy. After the war, Searcy and White County experienced a rebirth with the construction of the Cairo & Fulton Railroad, the Kensett-Searcy Line and further construction of roads to outlying areas in the county during the 1870s. The C&F Railroad did not run through Searcy, so city residents and business owners built a wooden tramway between Searcy and Kensett. The four-mile wooden tramway was later replaced by a railroad spur which is still in use today. During this time of reconstruction, the White County Courthouse was built in 1871. This architectural landmark is said to be the oldest functional courthouse in Arkansas. Searcy is home to Harding University and businesses such as Yarnell's Ice Cream, Land O' Frost of Arkansas and Wal-Mart Stores Distribution Center.

POINTS OF INTEREST

Dime House *504 E. Vine.* In 1926 Mady Armstrong was employed doing odd jobs. She insisted on being paid in silver. Ten years later, having saved 90% of her dimes – all 16,000 of them, she was able to have a small house built and find herself and her "Searcy Dime House" immortalized in Ripley's "Believe-It-Or-Not" in 1936. Today the house is used for storage.

Georgetown *Sixteen miles east on Ark. 36.* Known in the early 1800s as Negro Hill, the community was settled by a group of escaped slaves.

Harding University *900 E. Center. (501) 279-4000.* Affiliated with The Church of Christ, the liberal arts co-ed university has a student body over 3,000. Originally on this site was the Methodist-supported Galloway College for women, built in 1888.

Spring Park *Jct. U.S. 67B and Ark. 36.* This is the site of the town's original spring. Picnic tables.

White County Courthouse Downtown on the square. Built in 1871, the oldest functional courthouse in Arkansas has undergone many renovations and an addition in 1912. The building has streaked marble wainscoting and iron columns supporting the courtroom roof. The elaborate clock tower houses an 1855 bell that strikes on the hour.

HOPE

County: Hempstead. Population: 9,643

Information: Hope Advertising & Promotion Commission; P.O. Box 596; Hope, AR 71801. (501) 777-7500. Hope Chamber of Commerce; 108 W. Third Street, Hope, AR 71801. (501) 777-3640.

HISTORY

The city of Hope was founded in 1875 by railroad entrepreneur James M. Loughborough, and named in honor of his daughter. Hope remains a railroad and transportation center as well as an agricultural community. The top industries here are Hudson Foods (poultry products) Meyer's Bakery, Klipsch (loudspeaker systems) and tourism. Since the 1920s Hope has been know as the "watermelon capital," growing some of the largest and tastiest melons in the world. The first whopper melon was a

136-pounder; it was sent to President Calvin Coolidge in 1925. It doesn't take a rocket scientist to figure out that Hope is proud of its melons. The green and red motif is everywhere, from trash barrels to mail boxes. With the election of native son Bill Clinton to the presidency and his oft-quoted "I still believe in a place called Hope," this small town has garnered its share of media attention for something besides melons. In 1993 Hope's Tourist Center counted 9,014 visitors, which is almost equal to the number of residents in the small town, some from as far away as Zimbabwe.

POINTS OF INTEREST

Hunting and Fishing Millwood State Park is 20 miles west of town via Hwy. 73. Camping, bass fishing, nature trails. Bois D'Arc (pronounced *bo*

dark) Wildlife Management Area is noted for seasonal hunting of deer, waterfowl and other game and largemouth bass fishing.

Memory Lane The 42nd president of the United States, William Jefferson Clinton, was born at Hope's Julia Chester Hospital August 19, 1946. He lived in Hope until he was six. You, too, can visit these now historical sites and follow in the president's little footsteps. First, stop by the Chamber of Commerce Tourist Center on W. Third to get directions and pick up a map to the Clinton landmarks.

• **First home.** Until the age of four, Bill lived at 117 South Hervey with maternal grandparents Eldridge and Edith Grisham Cassidy. Bill's grandfather owned a small grocery store on North Hazel Street.

• **Second home.** Bill's family lived at 321 East 13th, a modest three-bedroom home, until Bill was six.

• **Kindergarten.** Bill attended "Miss Marie Purkins' School for Little Folks" on East Second Street, 1951-1952.

• **Elementary school.** Bill attended first grade at Brookwood Elementary on Spruce Street, 1952-1953.

• Bill's family moved to Hot Springs in 1953.

Old Washington Historic State Park Located nine miles northwest of town, on Ark. 4, this 19th century museum village includes Arkansas' Confederate Capitol, blacksmith shop, gun museum, restored homes and the steam-powered Goodlett Cotton Gin. Williams Tavern Restaurant in a restored 1832 home features cooking from the period. *(501) 983-2890.*

Watermelon Festival Held the third weekend in August when the melons are at their peak, the festival is a time for the natives to show off their monster melons, slurp up a few slices and participate in the annual seed-spitting competition. In 1985 Ivan Bright made the Guinness Book of World Records with his 260-pound melon. The center of commercial watermelon growing in the state is actually in northeast Arkansas near Leachville in Mississippi County. But Hope hangs on to its reputation for the biggest melons. Mr. Bright's record still stands.

HOW TO PICK A RIPE MELON

Unlike bananas, watermelons don't continue to ripen when you get them home. The following are some tips for selecting a ripe melon so you don't tote home a green one (green on the *inside* that is.)

- Slap it, don't thump it. A slap to the side should result in a taut vibration sort of like a drum. A dull thud means too ripe. No vibration means it isn't ripe enough.
- The bottom where the melon made contact with the ground should be pale yellow, not white or pale green.
- The skin should barely yield to pressure.
- The melon should feel heavy for its size.

DID YOU KNOW?

Scratchin' & Splashin'

Tuesday, August 17, 1941, fifteen thousand soldiers came to Hope to participate in army maneuvers. Camping in the woods without tents, these New York boys came face to face with snakes, poison ivy, ticks and chiggers. By way of hospitality, Hope provided entertainment rooms with games and music, ice water and free showers established at Fair Park and James Embree's private lake south of town. The American Legion Post helped raise money to build the showers and the city furnished the water pump. One hundred sixty men could bathe each hour; 20,000 bathed the first three days.

EUREKA SPRINGS

County: Carroll. Population: 1,980

Information: Chamber of Commerce; Box 551; Eureka Springs, AR 72632. (501) 253-8737.

HISTORY

Long before the white men came to these parts, the Indians discovered the many springs flowing from these hillsides. It was here they made their camps, both for a steady water supply and for the healing powers they believed the springs to have. Dr. Alvah Jackson was the first white man to try the curative powers of the springs, using the water to treat his son's chronic eye ailment. For years he carried small bottles of water labeled "Dr. Jackson's Magic Eye Water." Dr. Jackson recommended the water to his friend, Judge J.B. Saunders of Berryville, for an ailing leg and Saunders moved to the area and built the first house in what would some day be Eureka Springs. It is Saunders' son C. Burton "Buck" Saunders who is generally credited with naming the springs "Eureka" meaning "I have found it!"

The word spread about the miraculous healing waters that flowed from 63 mineral springs gushing from a rocky wilderness and people began flowing into the area. Basin Springs, so named because of its natural basin, became the most popular and was the focal point of the rapidly growing town. The earliest settlers came by horse or horse-drawn wagons and carriages. The stagecoach followed soon after, but the thing which really breathed life into the city was the coming of the Iron Horse. Founded in 1883, the Eureka Springs Railway at one time unloaded as many as six trains a day. During the Victorian Era, Eureka Springs became one of the most fashionable health spas in the nation, attracting vacationers with a taste for elegant hotels and bathhouses, electrified trolleys and band concerts in the park.

Eureka Springs is the largest collection of authentically-preserved Victorian structures in the central United States. The pastel paint and ornate "gingerbread" trim on the exteriors are painstakingly preserved.

The limestone buildings and walls that ramble all over town were built

"America's Little Switzerland" – quaint and twisty

from native stone. Some of the building blocks are 16 to 22 inches thick –
the Victorian answer to fireproofing. The Eureka Springs Carnegie
Library is one of two municipal libraries in the United States originally
financed by early 1900s millionaire industrialist-philanthropist Andrew
Carnegie.

With the coming of cars came a new business to Eureka Springs – the
tourist court. Motels, hotels, bed & breakfasts, cottages and inns make
up a large segment of the city's business community. The natural beauty
of the city combined with the Victorian charm and the abundance of
romantic hideaways have made the city the wedding and honeymoon
capital of the south. (The Chamber of Commerce even has a
comprehensive directory for wedding services in the city.)

In the 1930s and 40s, the city gained a reputation as an artists' colony
and continues to attract artists and
craftspeople. The streets are lined with
quaint shops and galleries. Long
known as the "Little Switzerland of
America," Eureka Springs clings to the
Ozark hillsides like an Alpine village.
Its 230 winding streets never cross at
right angles and the lowest street is
more than a thousand feet below the
highest. There are no traffic lights in
Eureka Springs. Because of its rich
past, the entire town is on the National
Register of Historic Places.

SOURCE: Chamber of Commerce; *WPA Guide to 1930s Arkansas*

POINTS OF INTEREST

Abundant Memories Heritage Village *Ark. 23 North. (501) 253-6764.*
Representation of American village life from Colonial through Victorian
era. Twenty-five picturesque buildings and thousands of fine antiques,
guns, tools, carriages, furniture. Gift shop. Crafts. Antiques.

Bank of Eureka Springs *70 S. Main. 501) 253-8241.* This working bank
recreates the turn-of-the-century with brass teller's cages and vintage
equipment.

Belle of the Ozarks *Starkey Marina, just off U.S. 62 West. (501) 253-6200.*
Beaver Lake sightseeing aboard a 49-passenger excursion boat. Cruise
takes an hour and 15 minutes and covers nearly 10 miles. Departs daily
May-October.

Cosmic Cavern *18 miles east on Hwy. 21N. (501) 749-2298.* One-hour guided tour through one of the Ozarks' prettiest caves. Holds the region's largest underground lake with depth and boundaries still a mystery.

Country Music Shows Eureka has three, all on U.S. 62 East: Pine Mountain Jamboree *(501-253-9156)*; Ozark Mountain Hoe-Down *(501-253-7725)*; Swanee River Boys Country Review *(501-253-6011).*

Crescent Hotel *75 Prospect Street. (501) 253-9766 or 1-800-342-9766.* This five-story hotel overlooking the city was a first-class accommodation when it was built in 1886. Powell Clayton, governor of Arkansas from 1868-1871, was a principal investor. The mammoth cut-stone hotel boasted 27-acres with bridle paths and walkways. But the big hotel had big money problems. From 1902-1907, it was rented out to the St. Louis & San Frisco Railroad. In the tourist off-seasons of 1908 to 1933, it was rented to the Crescent College for young women. Then in 1936 it was bought by an ex-convict con man named Norman Baker who billed

Rosalie House (1880s) – delicious Victorian gingerbread

himself as a doctor, transplanting goat glands to perk up the sex life and touting cures for cancer. The hotel was vacant after a couple of years of Norman's occupation, but it reopened in 1946. This imposing Victorian landmark has recently undergone major renovation and has been restored to her former glory.

Dinosaur World *Ark. 187. (501) 253-8113.* Several of the older dinosaurs

A tourist sticks her neck out at Dinosaur World

in this, the world's largest dinosaur park (65 acres), were sculpted by Emmet Sullivan, an artisan at Mount Rushmore. Sullivan also created Christ of the Ozarks. The dinosaurs were his last work. Ola Farwell, the brains behind the attraction opened the park in 1967 with six replicas. (He had originally intended his site to house a giant statue of General Douglas MacArthur, but local authorities vetoed the idea.) Dinosaur World was created in its place. Some of the original dinosaurs have old bulldozer parts welded into them. In 1983, 40-foot tall, four-story King Kong entered the scene, built by a man in Texas and brought to the park in three trucks. More than 100 life-sized dinosaur replicas. Miniature golf, fishing lake, RV park.

Elna N. Smith Foundation Site *Statue Road off U.S. 62 East. (501) 253-9200.* Location of the seven-story-high Christ of the Ozarks statue; The Great Passion Play; the Sacred Arts Center; the Bible Museum; the New Holy Land; the Smith Memorial Chapel; a ten-foot section of the Berlin Wall; Inspirational Woodcarving Gallery.

Eureka Springs Duck Tours *Jct. U.S. 62 and 23N. (501) 253-7879.* Amphibious vehicles tour the city and countryside then splashdown in Lake Leatherwood.

Eureka Springs Gardens *Five and a half miles west on U.S. 62. (501) 253-9244.* Arkansas' premier botanical gardens. All gardens are handicap-accessible.

Eureka Springs & North Arkansas Railway *Located at the historic depot on N. Main. (501) 253-9623.* Vintage steam locomotives and passenger cars, restored to original condition. Travel the same scenic route Victorian tourists took through the Ozark hills. About four miles round-trip (45 minutes). Route lighted at night. New animal conservatory features lions, tigers and bears. Oh my! Railroad memorabilia. Lunch and dinner served aboard the dining car. Gift shop.

Frog Fantasies *151 Spring Street. (501) 253-7227.* Frogs of every shape, color, size and fabrication collected for over 50 years.

Hammond Museum of Bells *Spring and Pine. (501) 253-7411.* More than 1,000 bells of every size, age and description.

Hatchet Hall *35 Steele Street.* Carry Nation, famed suffragette and temperance advocate, struck terror into the hearts of drinkers from this house, her last home. The house operated as a boarding house for the families of alcoholics from 1908 until her death in 1911, following a rousing lecture at Basin Circle Park. See the hatchet she used to destroy casks of demon rum. (Carrie named the house herself.)

Historical Museum *95 S. Main. (501) 253-9417.* Relics from the city's historic past. Clothing, mementos, photographs, furniture.

Inspiration Point Fine Arts Colony *U.S. 62, seven miles west of town. (501) 253-8595.* Workshops for talented students in opera, dance and orchestral music. Performances for the public at the end of the session in July. Outdoor theater.

Miles Musical Museum *U.S. 62 West. (501) 253-8961.* Extensive collection of musical instruments from nickelodeons to calliopes. Boasts the world's smallest playable zither.

Miracle Mansion Wedding Chapel *U.S. 62 East. (501) 253-9744.* Architecturally unique, the interior creates a romantic background for weddings. On the second floor is the "Wonderful World of Miniatures" featuring the Presidents and First Ladies in inaugural gowns.

Nel-Vic Tour Home *U.S. 62 East, 6 miles. (501) 253-8588.* Picnic areas with a view of the Kings River, association croquet, horseshoe courts and garden mini golf. Rooms display vintage clothing and furnishing.

Onyx Cave *Three miles east of Eureka off U.S. 62 East. (501) 253-9321.* Radio guided tours of underground rooms, unique formations, ramp access to the cave. **Gay Nineties Button & Doll Museum** located here exhibits button mosaics and dolls collected over many decades. Gift shop.

Palace Hotel and Bath House *135 Spring St. (501) 253-8400.* The Ozarks' only historic operational bathhouse, furnished throughout with period antiques for Victorian atmosphere. Hydrotherapeutic baths, steam

Unwind at the historic Palace Hotel and Bath House

treatments, massages, body wraps.

Pivot Rock & Natural Bridge *U.S. 62 West, then Pivot Rock Road.* *(501) 253-8860.* Fascinating geological formations in a tranquil wooded area with nature trails.

Queen Anne Mansion *U.S. 62 West.(501) 253-8825.* Built in Carthage, Missouri, in 1891, this magnificent home was taken apart and moved to Eureka Springs, then reassembled, piece by piece. Handcrafted woodwork, seven fireplaces.

Quigley's Castle *Ark. 23 South.* *(501) 253-8311.* Bills itself as "the Ozarks' strangest dwelling." Extensive collections of butterflies, moths, rocks, arrowheads and flowers. One woman's folk art using native stone and butterflies. Suspended rooms with flowers and shrubs growing inside the house.

Red Bud Stables *U.S. 62 East, then Rock House Road. (501) 253-6556.* Scenic trail rides on horseback through the Ozarks.

Rosalie House *282 Spring Street. (501) 253-7377.* Lovely gingerbread Victorian house built in the 1880s of handmade brick. Restored with period furnishings. Guided tours.

St. Elizabeth's Catholic Church *Crescent Drive. (501) 253-9853.* Listed in Ripley's "Believe It or Not" as "the only church you enter through the bell tower."

Thorncrown Chapel *Two miles west of town off U.S. 62. (501) 253-7401.* Designed by noted Fayetteville architect Fay Jones, it has been called the most beautiful little chapel in the world. This exquisite creation of glass and natural wood integrates beautifully with it's woodland setting. Non-denominational.

Turpentine Creek Wildlife Foundation and Ranch *Ark. 23 South, six miles. (501) 253-5841.* Animal shelter for carnivore. Specializes in large cats – lions and tigers. They pick up animals in distress anywhere in the U.S. Open all year. Admission charged.

Wings *U.S. 62 West. (501) 253-8825.* One of the Ozarks' newest and most unusual attractions, a year-round, Christmas-decorated Victorian tour home featuring exotic birds housed in beautiful atriums designed by noted aviculturist Paul Puckett.

DID YOU KNOW?

BELIEVE IT OR NOT!

Beginning in 1918, Robert Ripley fascinated the readers of his comic strip with tales of the unexplained, the illogical and the unbelievable things he found as he traveled the world. Arkansas provided great material, and Eureka Springs in particular was one of his favorite stops. At one time it was said that Eureka Springs was the most frequently cited city. That claim may not hold up today, but certainly Eureka Springs has enough unique and unusual oddities to make it much more interesting that the average town. Eureka Springs owes much of its uniqueness to the geography. The following are a few of Ripley's favorite observations:

• The lowest street is more than a thousand feet below the highest. There are 230 streets in the town and no two ever cross at right angles.

• St. Elizabeth's Catholic Church is the only church in North American where the street level entrance is through the top of the bell tower. (This, too, dictated by the steep terrain of the town.)

• Pivot Rock & Natural Bridge both caught Ripley's attention. Pivot Rock is a giant granite boulder which balances like a sculptured top on its tiny point. This oddity, as well as Natural Bridge, are the products of countless years of erosion.

AND MANY MORE. . .

As promised, here are brief sketches of a bunch of other noteworthy Arkansas towns (listed alphabetically).

ALMA Claims the title of "Spinach Capital of the World" canning 56% of the Popeye Spinach consumed worldwide. Tons of the nutritious green stuff is packed here under the Popeye brand. A statue of the well-known sailor man can be seen keeping watch outside the Alma Chamber of Commerce on Main Street. (And don't miss the world's largest spinach can located on Mountain Grove Road!) Alma celebrates its famous crop with a spinach festival each April.

© *Hearst Corp.*

ALTUS Founded by immigrants in 1875. Irish and Slavic miners worked in nearby coal mines. The Swiss and Germans established vineyards here. The first wine was sold to passengers on the old Iron Mountain Railroad when they pulled in to re-fuel. Several of the family wineries are still in operation and offer tours, free tasting and, of course, wine for sale.

ARKADELPHIA A landing on the Ouachita River during the early 1800s. The Indians were the first to make salt here, then white men followed and established the Hemphill Salt Works, one of the first industries in the state. In 1843, the town became the Clark County seat. Henderson State University and Ouachita Baptist University are located here.

ARKANSAS CITY Became Desha County seat in 1881, this town was established at the site of an early steamboat landing by former inhabitants of nearby Napoleon, a flourishing port on the Mississippi River that was washed away after several serious floods. The levee overlooking the Mississippi is the world's highest (32 feet) and longest (1,608 feet).

ASHDOWN Little River County. This early sawmill town at the intersection of three railroads was originally named Turkey Flats. Of interest nearby: Caddo Mound dating back to A.D. 1000, and 150-foot limestone cliffs that provided the cement used in building the state Capitol.

ATKINS The town got its start in the early 1870s when the Little Rock and Fort Smith Railroad was routed this way. But it's pickles that put this town on the map as "Pickle City U.S.A." The one-time little gherkin of a pickle plant in this Polk County town was bought out a dozen years ago by Green Bay Food Co., a division of Dean Foods of Illinois. Atkins is one of nine pickle-packing plants that puts Green Bay right up there as number two, right behind Vlasic. Each May the small town goes all out for the Picklefest celebration. Also, mark your calendar for International Pickle Week which has been celebrated with relish ever since comedian Sam Levenson noted the observation many years ago and remarked, "there's only one day for mother, but a whole week for pickles." Now that's a dilly! Atkins is also home to the fried dill pickle, an Arkansas specialty.

FRIED DILL PICKLES:
Poetry For The Palate

The Loner Drive-In Cafe in Atkins is known far and wide for its fried dill pickles (and for keeping the recipe a secret). After stopping by the Loner on his way through Arkansas in 1983, poet Allen Ginsberg is said to have remarked, "There's no other taste in the world quite like a fried dill pickle."

SOURCE: *Arkansas Times,* July 1983.

AUGUSTA Woodruff County. Located on the White River, the town became a trading center for lumbermen who transported logs down river to New Orleans to make ship masts. In 1852 Thomas Pough (a wealthy Quaker from Maryland) established the town at the site of the Indian village Chickasaw Crossing. Pough named the town for his daughter. During the Civil War, Union troops camped on the courthouse lawn. The town built its own one-mile rail line to connect it to the railroad. This pint-size line was called the Little Dummy after a mule-drawn street-car that was utilized when the line first started operating.

BALD KNOB This small White County town was established on the railroad line in 1878. Most of the early population relocated here from nearby Stevens Creek. The town was named for a large chunk of rock on the northeast side of town. The bald rock has since been quarried.

BATESVILLE Independence County seat. Once known as Poke Bayou, a ferry crossing on the White River. With access to the river and rails, the town was a thriving commercial center during the 1800s. Famous Batesville marble from nearby quarries was used in the construction of the county courthouse, the state Capitol building as well as other public buildings in the U.S. The town is home to nationally recognized Lyon College (formerly Arkansas College). The Pioneer Cemetery downtown is the oldest recognized and preserved cemetery in the state.

BAUXITE In 1887 the state's first geologist discovered huge deposits of bauxite, the essential ore in making aluminum, here and in the surrounding area in Saline and Pulaski counties. Bauxite quickly became an extremely profitable venture. In 1903 the Pittsburgh Reduction Company of Pennsylvania (later known as Alcoa) established a company town and named it Bauxite. During the 64 years the company was in business, all inhabitants of the town were employees. Arkansas once produced 97% of the nation's bauxite and the Gann Museum of Benton is the only building in the world made out of bauxite. Bauxite is no longer produced and the pock-marked land is now being reclaimed.

BEEBE Established in 1872 when residents of neighboring Stoney Point packed up and moved five miles east to be on the route of the new Cairo & Fulton Railroad. Town named for Roswell Beebe, first president of the railroad. A branch of Arkansas State University is located here.

BELLA VISTA Benton County. A summer resort established in 1917. Real estate promoters bought 600 acres and sold lots to wealthy oil tycoons in Texas and Oklahoma so they could enjoy the "beautiful view" at Bella Vista. The resort grew its own wine, advertised swimming, tennis, horseback riding and nationally-known orchestras who performed in Wonderland Cavern while the vacationing elite danced the night away. The resort was bought by Cooper Properties in 1963 and made a part of Bella Vista Village.

BENTONVILLE Benton County. First known as Osage, its 1836 post office name, the town was renamed in 1837 for Thomas Hart Benton, Missouri politician. But the town is best known as the hometown of the late Sam Walton, founder of Wal-Mart and headquarters for the discount-store chain that made him the richest man in America in 1987 and continues to keep his heirs at the top of the mega-bucks ladder. Wal-Mart Visitor Center is located here so you can learn all about the store's rise to fame and fortune.

BERRYVILLE Founded in 1850 by B.H. Berry, the uncle of Governor James H. Berry. Incorporated in 1876 and made seat of Carroll County in 1875.

Located here is Saunders Memorial Museum containing possibly the best collection of small arms in the U.S.; collected by Col. C. Burton Saunders (1863-1952), international award-winning sharpshooter.

BLACK ROCK So-called because of the beautiful black rocks found in the area. Established in 1884 on the Black River, this town's brush with greatness came from the discovery of a 14-grain pink pearl that was found in a Black River mussel. A short-lived pearl boom ($31,000 in 1901) led to the establishment of what is claimed to be Arkansas' first button factory in 1900. For 70 years the factory made "blanks" from mussel shells that were shipped to New York for finishing. When the button business declined, so did the town.

BOONEVILLE Settled in 1828 by Walter Cauthron as a trading post and named for his friend Capt. Benjamin Bonneville. The town was officially incorporated in 1878 under the name *Booneville* – probably through a spelling error. 1901 made a dual county seat of Logan County. In 1910 the Arkansas Tuberculosis Sanatorium opened and was described as the finest of its kind in the world. On the outskirts of town is Golden City, a gold mining town that boomed and fizzled when the state geologist reported that the veins had been salted with iron pyrite and copper percussion caps.

Wal-Mart Visitor Center – Sam's first store

BRINKLEY Originally dubbed Lick Skillet (meaning to do a thorough job – lick the skillet clean) in reference to the diligent Irish immigrants who built the Memphis & Little Rock Railroad. The town was named for the railroad's president Robert C. Brinkley. In 1909 a tornado hit this tiny town of 1,600 killing 60 people and leaving only a church and half dozen homes standing.

BRYANT Saline County sawmill town near Benton was incorporated in 1892 with a population of 132. Another bedroom community that has flourished as a result of migration from the big city life in Little Rock, many Bryant residents work in Pulaski County.

CABOT Lonoke County. Settled in the early 1870s as a stop on the Cairo & Fulton Railroad, the town has experienced tremendous growth in recent years as people relocate here from nearby Little Rock.

CADDO GAP This site marks the farthest westward point reached by De Soto in 1541 in his journey from Florida. He was most likely turned back by the Caddo Indians.

CALICO ROCK Named for the colorful rocks in the area, the site was a former steamboat landing on the White River. Located on a steep bluff, the downtown area is on three different levels.

CALION The name is a combination of two counties' names: CAL-houn and Un-ION. Historically, it was a crossing point on the Ouachita River and a steamboat port called El Dorado Landing. When the Camden & Alexander Railway joined El Dorado to the St. Louis, Iron Mountain & Southern in 1891, the landing diminished in importance. Modern Calion cropped up in 1903 with the arrival of the Little Rock Southern Line. The site is thought to be an old Indian Village, Utiangue, where De Soto wintered in 1541 after being turned back at Caddo Gap. In the 1930s, a series of dams and locks on the river made the town a shipping center. Beyond Calion Lake to the south is the site of Champagnolle Landing, one of the oldest settlements in the state, dating back to the early 1800s. It was briefly the Union County seat, but lost out to nearby El Dorado in 1840.

CAMDEN About 1783, a French trading post called Ecore a Fabre (Fabre's Bluff) grew up here at the crossroads of several Indian and pioneer trails. In 1842 it was chosen Ouachita County seat. McCollum-Chidester House here served as headquarters for Union General Frederick Steele during the Civil War. Several battlesites of the Union Army's Red River Campaign are in the area.

DID YOU KNOW?

IN GOD WE TRUST
All Others Pay Cash

Back in the 1950's Camden citizen Matt H. Rothert, businessman and coin collector, was distressed because "In God We Trust" appeared only on coins and not on paper currency. He figured paper money not only passed from hand to hand in this country but was circulated abroad. What better way to proselytize to the heathens? He convinced Senator J. William Fulbright and Rep. Wilbur Mills to introduce legislation calling for the placement of the words on paper money as well as coins.

Public Law 140 was signed by President Eisenhower on July 11, 1955, stating that "at such times as new dies for the printing of currency are adopted with

the current program of the Treasury to increase the capacity of the presses used by the Bureau of Engraving and Printing, the dies shall bear, at such place or places as the Secretary of the Treasury may determine to be appropriate, the inscription, "In God We Trust." Two years later, beginning with the $1 silver certificates, the motto began to appear on bills. Today it is on all money being produced.

SOURCE: *The Coin Wholesaler*, July 1985

CANE HILL First called Hillsboro, later Cane Hill for the dense cane growing in the area. One of the oldest settlements in northwest Arkansas (1827). The town was pretty well wiped out by the Battle of Prairie Grove. Cane Hill College, a school for young ministers was founded here in 1852 (now College of the Ozarks in Clarksville).

CARLISLE Located in the middle of the Grand Prairie Rice Belt, the state's first rice crop was harvested here in 1904. Humorist Opie Read author of *On a Slow Train Through Arkansas* and other novels, came here in the 1870s and published *The Prairie Flower*, the first of a series of newspapers. The masthead motto: "If you have to walk, be sure to start in time."

CASS Settled by Elias Turner and called Turner's Bend until the 1850s, this little community is said to have produced more wooden wagon wheels than anywhere else in the world between 1915 and 1920. Today, the community's canoe outfitters accommodate those heading out to float the Mulberry River.

CAVE CITY One of the oldest tourist stops in the state (1933). In 1889 Loyal Post Office was relocated a mile south to Horn's Cave and renamed Cave City. Legends and mysteries abound about the cave itself. The underground stream supplies the city's water and the depth of the stream is said to be affected by the fluctuations of the Mississippi River.

CENTER POINT Ebenezer Campground is the site of one of the oldest Methodist camp meetings in the South started here in 1837.

CHARLESTON Originally called Charles Town after Baptist preacher Charles Kellum, the name changed in 1874 when the town was incorporated. The town got its start around 1843 as a stop of the Butterfield Overland Mail route. The Cherokee Prairie north of town is 280 acres of the largest remaining tallgrass prairie in the state.

CHEROKEE VILLAGE Begun in 1954 as one of the nation's first planned retirement communities. Located in the Ozark foothills of Sharp and Fulton counties, there are over 4,000 residents.

CLARENDON This prehistoric Indian site was called Mouth-of-the-Cache early in the century, then changed to Clarendon in 1837. It was an old White River port and ferry crossing. The town was almost destroyed during the Civil War in retaliation for sinking a Union ship *Queen City*. The town was reincorporated in 1898.

CLARKSVILLE Called Johnson County Court House in 1836 when it was made the county seat. Incorporated in 1848 as Clarksville, this was an important coal mining town. Today it is known as the peach-growing capital of the state. Home of College of the Ozarks and the Clarksville Institute, the state's first school for the blind.

COAL HILL One of the earliest sit-down strikes in America took place in the coal mining town in 1886. The striking workers were convicts that had been leased from the state by the private mining contractors. To protest the harsh treatment and long hours, the convicts barricaded themselves in the mine, made pipe-cannons using blasting powder, and slaughtered the coal-car mules for food. After two weeks, the workers' terms were met and the state eventually abandoned the practice of leasing prisoners.

CORNING This railroad stop on the Cairo & Fulton line was incorporated in 1873, and named for the civil engineer who built the line. Dual seat of Clay County with Piggott sharing the honor.

CROSSETT Built in 1902 as a company town by the Crossett Lumber company whose employees were logging 920 square miles of Southern pine. The company had all the houses painted "Crossett gray" inside and out. Today Georgia-Pacific (and the accompanying smell of paper processing) dominates the town. GP manages 5000,000 acres of pine forests in the area and employs 3,000 workers in its mills.

DARDANELLE Established as a Cherokee trading post in 1819 and platted in 1847 by J.H. Bearley. Made dual Yell County seat in 1875 (Danville shares the honor). The 300-foot rock that juts into the Arkansas River here has long been a landmark. The origin of the town's name is uncertain. One legend has it that it derives from the Indian "dardonnie" said to mean to sleep with one eye open – perhaps referring to the Indians stationing a lookout on the top of the bluff.

DERMOTT Settled in 1832 by Dr. Charles Mc Dermott, Yale graduate, who spent a fortune trying to invent a flying machine and eventually patented one in 1872. Nearby post office Bartholomew was replaced by Bend a few miles away, and Bend was renamed Dermott in 1877. Incorporated in 1890, the arrival of the railroad in 1887 made this a prosperous crossroads town. "Arkansas lobster" (crawdads) are raised here and shipped world-wide.

DEWITT Serves with Stuttgart as Arkansas County seat since 1852. The name of the town was picked out of a hat – literally. The site surveyor Adam McCool and site selection committee members put their names in a hat. McCool's name was drawn and he got to name the new town. He named it after New York politician DeWitt Clinton whom he admired.

DUMAS In 1851, W.B. Dumas bought land here for $1.25 an acre. He built a general store and a cotton gin and the site was incorporated in 1904. The town adopted as its city's anthem the 1920s ragtime tune "Ding Dong Daddy from Dumas." The Ding Dong Days festival is held each July.

EVENING SHADE This tiny town's name became a household word when Linda Bloodworth Thomason tagged her CBS sitcom starring Burt Reynolds "Evening Shade." Hillary Clinton is said to have suggested the name. The Sharp County town's fame has brought scores of tourists to the town necessitating the opening of a visitors center. (Prior to 1848, the townsite was called Plum Spring – not quite as poetic.) A smaller and lesser-known Evening Shade lies just south of Hope in Hempstead County.)

FORDYCE Railroad town named for railroad executive Samuel W. Fordyce, the town was incorporated in 1885 an made Dallas County seat in 1906. The world's first Southern pine plywood plant was built here. Home of famed University of Alabama coach Paul "Bear" Bryant.

FORREST CITY Laid out in 1869 on the western slope of Crowley's Ridge, and named for Confederate general Nathan Bedford Forrest, the contractor who finished the Memphis & Little Rock Railroad here. Incorporated in 1871. Made St. Francis County seat in 1874.

FOUKE (Rhymes with *talc* without an "l." Sort of.) This small town got its start as a sawmill town on the Texas & Pacific Railroad in the late 1880s; the townsite was laid out in 1911. The town is best known for the legendary Fouke Monster or Bigfoot. In 1971 and again in 1973 Fouke folks reportedly encountered a large, hairy six-foot monster near Boggy Creek.

GILLETT The site of Arkansas Post, the first European settlement in Arkansas, is located a few miles southeast of this small community. The town is known for hosting a fine coon supper each year.

GREEN FOREST First called Scott's Prairie when the location was settled in 1855; incorporated with the new name in 1895. This is the home of Helen Gurley Brown, publisher of *Cosmopolitan.* This is also the home of the Quindell, the only patented apple in Arkansas. It was developed in 1942 – a cross between an Old-Fashioned Winesap and a Red Delicious.

GREENWOOD Once the main coal-shipping point of Sebastian County which in the 1930s was called the "Coal Capital of Arkansas." Just south of town the roadcut in Devil's Backbone Ridge exposes three major formations including a bed of coal in one. The formations date back 300 million years.

GURDON The town was laid out beside the Cairo & Fulton Railroad, incorporated in 1880 and named for a railroad official. The International Order of Hoo-Doo, said to be the oldest industrial fraternal organization in the world, was founded here in 1892 by a bunch of forest products association conventioneers who were stranded by a delayed train. A museum and monument are located here on Main Street. A popular Arkansas ghost story involves the Gurdon Light. The legend has it that just outside Gurdon, a train wreck resulted in a decapitated crewman whose spirit haunts the tracks, lantern in hand, searching for his head. Could the Hoo-Doo be somehow connected to the Voo-Doo?

HAMBURG When Ashley County was created in 1849, this site was chosen as county seat. The town had no name at the time. In 1850, the name Hamburg appears in court records without explanation. Local tradition has it that the origin has to do with "deer" hams that impressed the site selection committee. Hamburg is smack in the middle of deer hunting country.

HARRISON The seat of Boone County, the town was founded in 1870 at the site of a wagon road to Springfield, Missouri. Surveyed by M.L. Harrison, in lieu of payment, the town was named for him. Incorporated in 1876. In 1836 Bellar & Harp Brothers quarried a 2,000-pound block of marble and shipped it to D.C. for use in building the Washington Monument. Harrison has a thriving historic town square and offers access to many recreational opportunities including the Buffalo National River to the south.

HEBER SPRINGS First called Sugar Loaf, the town was incorporated in 1882 at the site of seven "medicinal" springs. Visitors to the spa town barely trickled in by the 1920s, but tourism flowed again when in 1962 when the Greers Ferry Lake was created. This is now one of the major recreation areas in the state.

HELENA "Helena occupies one of the prettiest situations on the river," Mark Twain wrote in *Life on the Mississippi*. He was not the first to think so. In 1797, North Carolina immigrant Sylvanus Phillips settled here, where in 1541 De Soto first crossed the river into Arkansas. The town of Helena was established in 1820 and made the county seat in 1830. Mr. Phillips named the county for himself and the town for his daughter. A thriving riverport, in 1858 Helena was described as the "garden spot of Arkansas." When the Civil War began in 1861, the plantation system was going strong. The homes of several antebellum cotton planters still stand in Helena. (The prestigious homes were located on the ridge where people were safer from the spread of diseases associated with standing water.) Helena produced seven Confederate generals, the most notable being Patrick Cleburne who is buried here.

As sharecropping replaced slavery more settlers came to Helena to work in the fields, railroad yards and loading docks. Helena became the cradle of Delta blues, the music that symbolizes rural life along the Mississippi. Helena was home to some of the greatest bluesmen, including Robert Johnson, Robert Jr. Lockwood and Sonny Boy Williamson. Today the annual King Biscuit Blues Festival, named for the historic radio program broadcast from Helena, attracts thousands of fans. Helena remains a prosperous agricultural shipping center. The land around Helena produces soy beans, rice, wheat and other crops and Riceland houses a large plant in Helena. Helena boasts many grand restored homes on the National Register of Historic Places. In the style of sister cities such as Natchez and Vicksburg, Helena has retained its colorful antebellum river-city charm. The *Delta Queen* and *Mississippi Queen* steamboats make regular stops. Phillips County Community College is also located here.

JASPER Seat of Newton County which claims to be the only county in Arkansas that has never had a mile of railroad track run through it. Site of Diamond Cave, a 1930s-style attraction discovered in 1832 by Uncle Sammy and Andy Hudson. Also here, Natural Bridge, a stunning 130-by 20-foot rock formation once traversed by wagons and log trucks.

JEROME Formerly called Blissville, town was renamed around 1916 for the main business, the Jerome Hardware Lumber Company. This was the site of 3,535 acres bought by Resettlement Administration for an experimental New Deal agricultural program for poor tenant farmers.

In the summer of 1942 approximately 120,000 Japanese-Americans (75% of whom had been born in America) were relocated at nearby Rohwer because of their suspected sympathies with Japan during WWII. About 8,500 were detained here. From 1944-45 German POWs were held here.

JUDSONIA Originally Prospect Bluff, it was a prosperous steamboat landing on the Red River in the mid-1850s. Incorporated in 1874, the town lured residents from the North with promotional brochures touting Judson University's recruitment program. As the town was settled by Yankees, many Union soldiers are buried here and a Union Civil War monument is located here as well.

LAKE CITY Serves as Craighead County seat along with Jonesboro. Originally known as Old Town, a trading post and steamboat landing on the St. Francis River in the late 1840s. Although the river is no longer navigable at this point, the town boasts the only drawbridge (built in 1934) in the world that has never been raised. Lake City's lake was actually a pond or pool of the St. Francis River. The "lake" is no longer in existence.

LAKE DICK This community with the unfortunate name, located across the river from Pine Bluff, was established as an experimental farm co-op in 1936 by the Farm Security Administration. Encircling the lake were 80 houses, syrup and feed mills, a school, retail store and gin. All buildings and equipment were leased by the cooperative and members were paid according to their tasks, profits divided at the end of the year.

LAKE VILLAGE Founded in 1856 and made Chicot County seat in 1857 after the two county seats before it were washed away. Nearby Lake Chicot, a false arm of the Mississippi River, is the largest natural body of water in the state, measuring 20 miles long. This area may be what La Salle referred to in 1886 as the Isle de Chicot, translated as "island of the teeth of the river." The "teeth" being the cypress knees that protrude from lake in this swampy refuge, frequently snagging boats. Stuart's Island near the lake's upper end was a stronghold for the infamous John Murrell and his gang of outlaws. In 1923, Charles Lindbergh stirred up quite a fuss when he made an emergency landing in a resident's yard here, four years before his record-setting nonstop from New York to Paris.

Old Man River Gets High

The land along the Mississippi River in southeast Arkansas is prime pot-growing land and the summer of 1994 was a bumper year for marijuana crops in Chicot County. On July 7, deputies seized more than 17,00 plants, one of the state's biggest hauls.

LEPANTO Settled around 1894 and incorporated in 1909, this flood-prone town's first post office was a houseboat and the city boardwalk was raised on piers.

LONOKE Incorporated in 1872 and named for the only significant landmark in the area, an exceptionally tall red oak tree, a "lone oak." Seat of Lonoke County, the only seat in the state that has the same name as the county it serves. Home of Senator Joe T. Robinson, the town was once the site of Eberts Field, a WWII aviation training center that ranked second among all aviation schools in the U.S. and France.

MAGNET COVE Settled in 1835 around what is believed to have been a volcano, no spot in the world of the same size (5.1 square miles) has as many varieties of valuable minerals including the nation's largest concentration of novaculite (whetstone). A town with magnetism, compasses go wacky here where there is lodestone in the roadbed of U.S. 270. Many tons of magnetic ore were once shipped from here to Chicago and New York and sold as love charms. The small town attracts geologists from all over the world.

MAGNOLIA Settled in 1835 and chosen seat of Columbia County in 1853. The town was named by Miss Elizabeth Harper during dinner with the commissioners at her father's home. She proposed the name Magnolia because of her love for the native trees and the name was promptly adopted. Incorporated in 1855.

MALVERN Founded in 1873 as a stop on the Cairo & Fulton Railroad, the town was also a transfer point for stagecoach service to Hot Springs. Incorporated in 1876 and selected as seat of Hot Spring County in 1878. In 1887, the treacherous coach ride was replaced by a narrow-gauge railroad known as the Diamond Jo Line, built by Chicago industrialist "Diamond Jo" Reynolds. Many of the country's elite traveled on the Diamond Jo to take the waters in the Spa City. Today Malvern is known as the "Brick Capital of the World," celebrating the town's industry with the annual Brickfest.

MANILA Originally founded as Big Lake Island in 1852 by Ed Smith. The railroad's arrival here established it as a lumber town. The name was changed in 1901 in honor of the naval victory at Manila Bay, Philippines during the Spanish-American War in 1898. Manila native Herman Davis was cited by General John L. Pershing in his list "100 heroes of WWI," and called "Arkansas' greatest hero." Private Davis was credited with single-handedly saving an entire company. There is a monument here in his honor.

MARIANNA The Lee County seat is recognized as the birthplace of the first white child born on Arkansas soil. John Patterson was born here in 1730. His grave marker bears this riddle: "I was born in a Kingdom,/ Raised in an Empire,/ Attained Manhood in a Territory,/ Am now a citizen of a State,/ And have never been a 100 miles from where I now live."

MARION Settled in 1803 by Spanish Sergeant Augustine Grande from Ft. Esperanza and known as Grande until 1836 when local landowner Matthew Talbot donated 95 lots for its site as seat of Crittenden County. Talbot ended up destitute, a resident of the county's poorhouse in 1861.

MARKED TREE The town began in 1881 as a construction camp for the Kansas City, Ft. Scott and Memphis Railroad. Located at the confluence of the St. Francis and Little rivers, the town was named by surveyors for the blazed oak that marked a ford. The outlaw John Murrell and his band of 1,000 men operated a base camp here in the 1830s and are credited by some as marking the spot so they could make an easy escape from the law.

MAYFLOWER One of the many railroad towns, the construction superintendent for the Little Rock & Fort Smith Railroad made his office in a converted Pullman car. His office-on-wheels was named Mayflower, then the name became attached to the town that grew from that spot. James Miller, Arkansas' first territorial governor, made his home here. Nearby Palarm Creek is considered the geographic center of the state.

MCGEHEE A railroad town named for a local planter Abner McGehee (pronounced Magee). Incorporated in 1906.

MENA Founded as a stop on the Kansas City Southern Railway in 1896. The line was financed by Dutch investors and the town was named for chief financier John DeGoeijen's mother. Seat of Polk County, the town was home to Chester Lauck and Norris Goff of the popular "Lum and Abner" radio program.

MONTICELLO Seat of Drew County, the town was incorporated in 1852 as a cotton trading center and was one of the most prosperous towns in Arkansas at the turn-of-the-century. Thought to be named for Thomas Jefferson's home in Virginia as many of the Drew County settlers had family ties to Virginia. The last skirmish of the Civil War in Arkansas took place near here on May 24, 1865, more than a month after Lee's surrender.

MORRILTON Established as a stop on the Little Rock & Fort Smith Railroad in the 1870s and made seat of Conway County in 1884, the railroad town absorbed nearby river port Lewisburg. The town was laid out on the property of E.H. and George Morrill, hence the name. Winrock International, a nonprofit organization established in 1985 to improve agricultural productivity and nutrition. In 1953, the seeds of this organization were sown by John D. Rockefeller III at the same time Winthrop Rockefeller came to Arkansas.

MOUNT IDA The seat of Montgomery County, the town was incorporated in 1854. Mount Ida is known as the "Quartz Crystal Capital of the World" and was for over 100 years a center of extensive mining. The town's name is attributed to Granville Whittington who came here in 1835, later being appointed the first postmaster. Whittington is said to have come from Boston where there was another Mount Ida that he was reminded of.

MOUNTAIN HOME Founded in the early 1850s by Orin L. Dodd who had a plantation here. The name supposedly originated with Dodd's slaves who were shuttled between Dodd's other plantation in Augusta and this, their "mountain home." Made seat of Baxter County in 1873, incorporated in 1888. The proximity of Norfork and Bull Shoals lakes and the White River makes this a popular recreation area.

MOUNTAIN VIEW Established in 1873 as the Stone County seat, the town has become recognized as an arts and crafts community as well as a nationally noted center for traditional Ozark Mountain music. The popular Ozark Folk Center State Park is located here. Great trout fishing on the White River.

MURFREESBORO Seat of Pike County, the town was laid out in 1836 by Tennesseans. In 1906 John Huddleston discovered diamonds on his farm. The only diamond mine in North America is today part of the Crater of Diamonds State Park. For a fee you can dig for diamonds and keep what you find.

NASHVILLE Settled by a Baptist preacher in 1835 and selected Howard County seat in 1905. In 1983 hundreds of dinosaur footprints were found at an open gypsum mine here. These 110-million-year-old fossils are displayed outside the courthouse.

NEWPORT Settled in the early 1830s the town became an important river port and railroad town. Voted Jackson County seat in 1891. Factories here made buttons from the mussels taken from the White and Black rivers. It was here that Sam Walton got his start in retail managing a Ben Franklin store. The White River Monster (a creature described as being as long as three or four pickups, gray,

peeling skin) has allegedly been sighted up and down the river with most of the sightings occurring on Towhead Island. In 1973 the Arkansas Legislature created the White River Monster Sanctuary and Retreat wherein no monster may be molested, killed or trampled.

NORFORK One of the oldest continuously inhabited towns in Arkansas, it was founded in the early 1800s by Jacob Wolf who established a trading post there at the confluence of the North Fork and White rivers.

OSCEOLA Originally called Plum Point, this site was a refueling and supply stop for steamboats on the Mississippi River. The town was incorporated in 1838 as Osceola, allegedly named for the Indian chief. This is the home of Kemmons Wilson, founder of Holiday Inn, People's Insurance Company, Arkansas' first fire insurance company, and Roy Roger's singing cowgirl wife Dale Evans (born Francis Smith). Osceola and Blytheville share dual county seat status for Mississippi County.

OZARK Incorporated in 1838, this port on the Arkansas River successfully made the transition to railroad town in the 1870s. Lumber and coal mining were once major industries. Now it's poultry processing. Since 1837 it has served as Franklin County seat along with Charleston.

PARIS Settled in the 1820s on a site which in the late 1880s spawned a dozen coal mines. Named for the Paris in France, the town became Logan County seat in 1874. Cowie Winery established here in 1967 is known for its unique and fruity Lavacaberry wine.

PARKIN Founded in the 1880s at the site of an Indian Village said to have been called Casqui by De Soto. Twenty mounds built between A.D. 1400 - 1650 have been found in the area.

PEA RIDGE Settled in 1850s as little more than a post office community. On March 8, 1862, the Battle of Pea Ridge was fought east of here (Pea Ridge National Park). This battle was arguably the most significant Civil War battle west of the Mississippi. The streets in Pea Ridge are named for Union and Confederate soldiers. North-south streets for Yankees; east-west for Confederates.

PERRYVILLE Settled in the 1830s, and in 1841 made seat of newly formed Perry County which was named for Commodore Perry of War of 1812 fame. The town was incorporated in 1878. Heifer Project International's Learning and Livestock Center is located here.

DID YOU KNOW?

All I Want for Christmas is a Heifer!

Heifer Project International is a nonprofit world hunger organization that operates on a simple premise: an underprivileged family is given an animal and required to pass on a share of the creature's offspring to another selected family who continues the process. The families are taught to care for the animals and by doing so they increase their food supply and income. The project has been very successful because it doesn't just feed people for one day, it helps them achieve self-reliance. Sometimes the recipients get bee hives or chickens or goats —whatever best benefits them. Since the organization began it has provided 21 kinds of animals to more than one million families in 110 countries and 35 states. Founded in 1944 and headquartered in Little Rock, HPI supports 290 projects that help people in 37 countries. HPI publishes a free gift catalogue for anyone who wants to give a gift that truly does keep on giving. You can give a needy family a flock of chicks for about $20. (A much better choice than those Salad Shooters.) For information or a catalog, call 1-800-422-0474 or (501) 376-6836 in Little Rock.

PIGGOTT Named Houston in 1882 when it was a railroad stop, later named after Dr. J.A. Piggott in 1883. Ernest Hemingway married Piggott native Pauline Pfiefer and it was here that he wrote much of *A Farewell to Arms*. The 1933 movie based on the novel, starring Helen Hayes and Gary Cooper, held its world premiere here.

PINE RIDGE The community founded here in the 1900 was known as Waters. In the 1930s, the popular radio show "Lum and Abner" was based on the goings on here, but the comedians called the town Pine Ridge. The tiny town received so much attention and publicity that in 1936 it officially changed its name to Pine Ridge. Jot 'em Down Store and Museum are here.

LUM AND ABNER

One of the most popular and enduring programs of radio's golden age (it never dropped out of the top ten) was "The Lum and Abner Show." It was written – ad-libbed, mostly – and performed by two Arkansans, Chester Lauck and Norris "Tuffy" Goff. Close boyhood pals, the pair grew up in Mena and attended the U of A together. After college, they returned home and found work, but liked to perform blackface comedy routines at talent shows on weekends. One night in 1931, on a Hot Springs amateur radio program, they discovered that a similar act was already on the bill and they made a last minute decision to ditch their usual routine. On the spot, without script or rehearsal, they created the crackerbarrel characters of Lum Edwards (Lauck) and Abner Peabody (Goff), who worked at Dick Huddleston's Jot 'em Down Store in mythical Pine Ridge, Arkansas. (The skit was based on characters they had observed in the real-life town of Waters, near Mena.) The boys were the hit of the evening.

Soon they had a local radio show of their own. Later, they traveled to Chicago for a network audition and the "storekeepers sketch" went national, to immediate acclaim. The rambling, easy-going "Lum and Abner Show" ran from 1931 to 1955. Lauck, a superb mimic, and Goff, a natural comedian, wrote and performed almost all of them, playing all the characters. The program achieved a number of notable radio firsts – the first major network broadcast from New York's Radio City (1933), the first marathon broadcast for charity (more than 12 hours), and the first international broadcast by a radio team. (Only Amos and Andy surpassed the duo as longest running comedy team.) They also made several movies, among them:

Radio days nostalgia in store at the Jot 'em Down

Bashful Bachelor, Dreaming Out Loud, So This Is Washington, and *Lum and Abner Abroad.* (In later years, Lauck bought the rights to the films and today they are rarely seen.)

In 1936, the town of Waters, Arkansas, officially changed its name to Pine Ridge. There the original Jot 'em Down Store remains to this day, attached to a museum housing Lum and Abner memorabilia. In Mena, a statue of Lauck and Goff was dedicated in 1979. Goff's 1978 funeral eulogy was delivered by Lum himself: "Tuff, you might look around and find a good location up there if I ever have the privilege of joining you. We might even consider opening up the old Jot 'em Down Store again. I saved the old checkerboard and I believe it's my next move." (*See also:* Norris Goff, Chet Lauck in *Famous Arkansans.*)

POCAHONTAS Originally a French trading post overlooking the Black River, the town was established around 1815 and known as Bettis Bluff, a layover for traders and a relay station on the postal road from Illinois to Louisiana. It was also a steamboat port. In 1835 the town became the Randolph County seat.

PRESCOTT First settled as Moscow on an Indian trail, in 1873 platted as a stop on the Cairo & Fulton Railroad. Made seat of Nevada (Nuh VAY duh) County in 1877, this was one of the first in Arkansas to operate its own utilities (1899).

RAVENDEN SPRINGS First settled in 1809, the town didn't take shape until 1880 when reports of curative waters at this site made it a flourishing health spa until 1910. The ailing pitched tents here and drank the water which according to analysis had an excess of oxygen.

READER For many years billed as the oldest all-steam, standard gauge railroad operating in North America, the daily Possum Trot Line ran from Reader to the old logging camp of Camp De Woody. The Reader Railroad is no longer operational.

RISON Once a stop on the Texas & St. Louis Railroad in 1882, the town is located at the center of an estimated 15-by-6-mile iron deposit which wreaks havoc with a compass. Seat of Cleveland County.

ROMANCE This tiny town was named by a local school teacher, J.J. Walters, who reportedly thought the location very romantic. The local post office does a booming business in "Love" stamps and postmarking letters on Valentine's Day.

SHERIDAN Established during the Reconstruction era by Union sympathizers, the town was named for Union general Philip Sheridan. Seat of Grant County (*named for Ulysses S.*). Grant County Museum here is called the best small historical museum in the region. It features Indian artifacts as well as relics from the Battle of Jenkins Ferry, a Civil War battle fought near here in April of 1864.

SILOAM SPRINGS Established in 1880 as a health resort touting curative waters from nearby springs, the site was once an Indian trading post called Hico. Home of John Brown University.

SMACKOVER When oil gushed here in 1922, this hamlet of 100 mushroomed into a boomtown of 30,000 with wildcat oil speculators slopping through the mud, leasing oil rights and sinking wells in a frenzy. By 1925, the 40-square-mile field ranked #1 in the U.S. in oil production for a five-month period. Like its neighbor boomtown El Dorado, Smackover was a wild and woolly place with joints like Smackover Sal's and Dutch's Place complete with gambling, drinking and prostitution. Four or five murders a night were not uncommon. The Oil and Brine Museum which documents the oil industry in the 1920s and 30s is located here. The town's name has been the topic of

A casualty of Smackover's boom days

amused debate for years. Favorite local versions have the oil well gushing "smack over" the town, etc. The name probably came from the French. One theory is that the area being covered by sumac was called by the French *Sumac Couvert* (SUE-mack COO vair), and bastardized by the local tongue to Smackover. More likely it comes from the French *chemin couvert* meaning "covered way." The name Bayou de Chemin Couvert (referring to Smackover Creek) appears in a letter dated April 5, 1789. It is likely that after the native tongue wallowed this around a few decades it came out "Smackover."

STUTTGART Seat of northern district of Arkansas County (Dewitt is the county seat for the southern.) The Rev. Adam Buerkle, a Lutheran

minister, is considered to be Stuttgart's founder. He immigrated from Stuttgart, Germany, and came to Arkansas in 1877. On April 30,1880, he became the local postmaster and named the post office Stuttgart. The town was incorporated some nine years later. "The duck and rice capital of the world" owes its success to the soil here. The prairie is composed of topsoil over a layer of clay. Rice was first grown successfully on the

Grand Prairie in the early 1900s. In 1901 W.E. Hope planted a 9 by 27 foot plot of rice, but in 1904 William H. Fuller, who learned rice culture in Louisiana, plunged in with both feet planting 70 acres near Hazen. Rice mills appeared in Stuttgart and Lonoke, and acreage jumped from 27,000 in 1909 to 143,000 ten years later.

German-American farmers migrated from Illinois and Iowa to help develop the new crop. During the next fifty years, production and processing of this grain became the basis for the city's economy. Today there are more than 103,500 acres of rice grown in Arkansas County. Riceland Foods employs over 1,000 people. Rice is followed in importance by soybeans, which were originally introduced simply to replenish the soil. Wheat, oats, milo and corn are also produced. Sportsmen find the world's best duck hunting a by-product of the rice and soybean fields and flooded timber that surround the area. Thirty-seven varieties of congregating ducks come through the Mississippi Flyway each year. The award-winning Stuttgart Agricultural Museum, one of the largest museums in the state depicts the history of agriculture and homelife of the German pioneers who farmed the Grand Prairie from the 1880s until 1921. World Championship Duck Calling Contest is held during the Wings Over The Prairie Festival during the Thanksgiving Holiday.

TONTITOWN This Italian settlement named for De Tonti was established in 1897 by an Italian priest who was sent to investigate reports of starving, malaria-stricken Italian immigrants sharecropping near Lake Chicot. The priest relocated the immigrants on the Tontitown site, they planted vineyards and became the first community in Northwest Arkansas to grow grapes as a cash crop. Several wineries operate here.

VAN BUREN In 1830 Phillips Landing was established as a steamboat port on the Arkansas River as well as a stop on the Butterfield Overland Mail route. In 1836 the name was changed to honor presidential candidate Martin Van Buren. The frontier town's location on the river and across from Ft. Smith made it a jumping off point for those heading west. Incorporated in 1842, the town saw even more prosperity as a result of the California gold rush in 1849. The downtown historic district with more than 70 restored buildings, most dating from the 1870s, was used in the TV mini-series *The Blue and the Gray* as both Gettysburg and Vicksburg. Bob Burns, the enormously popular radio comedian during the 1930s and early 40s, brought his hometown of Van Buren much attention. Burns invented a wacky musical instrument called the bazooka. The homemade horn made from several gas pipes welded together, was said to sound like a cross between a moose and a wounded tuba. The anti-tank weapon invented during WWII was named for Burns' bazooka. A permanent exhibit of Bob Burns memorabilia is located in the old Frisco Depot. Seat of Crawford County.

VARNER The Varner, Rice and Douglas families settled here in 1844. The Little Rock, Pine Bluff & New Orleans Railroad passed this way. Though the town incorporated in 1907, the original town is no longer in evidence. Cummins Prison was established here in 1902.

PAPER OR PLASTIC?

Long before Sir Henry Morton Stanley uttered the famous words, "Dr. Livingston, I presume," he clerked in a little store in south Arkansas. Stanley was born John Rowlands into a poor Welsh family. Escaping from an English workhouse, he made his way to New Orleans as a cabin boy and was adopted there by his namesake. In 1860, he was invited by a Saline River planter to visit his estate in Arkansas. The visit was unpleasant and Stanley was so indignant over the brutality displayed by the plantation overseer, he took to the road. Stanley walked 40 miles overland to the Arkansas River and got a job clerking at Louis Altschul's store at Cypress Bend near Varner. At the outbreak of the Civil War, he enlisted in the 6th Arkansas Volunteers, survived a cholera epidemic and was ultimately captured at the Battle of Shiloh in 1862. He managed a release by joining a Union artillery company, but being in poor health, he was discharged and returned to England. Stanley would ultimately become an explorer/reporter and roam the world as a correspondent. Around 1870 he was sent to Africa by the New York *Herald* to look for the missing Dr. Livingstone, whom he did meet up with and greet with the immortal line, "Dr. Livingstone, I presume." Stanley went on to live an exciting life trekking about Africa before returning to England to be knighted and serve in Parliament. In his autobiography published in 1909, Stanley related that "Arkansas malaria was worse than African fevers."

WALDRON Incorporated in 1875, made seat of Scott County in 1845. Named for the town's surveyor John P. Waldron.

WALNUT RIDGE Laid out by the Cairo & Fulton Railroad in 1873, incorporated in 1880. Seat of Lawrence County.

WARREN Home of the illustrious Bradley County Pink tomato, this cotton and lumber town was established and chosen for the county seat in 1843. The town was named for one of the founder's slaves – the only town in the state with that distinction. The Warren Prairie southeast of town is an odd-looking place said to be reminiscent of the Serengeti Plain in East Africa. The area may be the bed of a former alkali lake or a playa. It supports unusual vegetation of limited distribution and many that occur nowhere else in the state.

WASHINGTON This stop on the Southwest Trail was reportedly laid out in 1826 and is referred to as the birthplace of Texas. It was at a tavern here that Sam Houston is said to have plotted the Texas Revolution and recruited the likes of Jim Bowie and Davy Crockett. Stephen F. Austin lived here before he left for Texas. James Black, a local blacksmith, is credited with forging the bowie knife.

WYNNE Town reportedly named for prosperous merchant J.W. Wynne of nearby Forrest City. Incorporated in 1888, made Cross County seat in 1889.

YELLVILLE Whites took over this Indian settlement, called Shawneetown, when the Indians were removed to the reservations around 1828. They changed the name in honor of Archibald Yell (territorial judge, congressman and governor) in 1836 when they applied for a post office. Seat of Marion County.

THE LOST CITIES OF ARKANSAS

One of the most delightful books on Arkansas is Donald Harington's Let Us Build Us A City, published in 1986. Hailed by William Styron as "an original and unique work of Americana,"LUBUAC recounts the author's visits to eleven lost Arkansas towns. All were, in Harington's words, "places that had once aspired to be cities." Harington made the journey with a researcher named Kim, with whom he fell in love and later married. If you'd like to recreate the author's journeys, here's a listing of the eleven sites. However, we strongly urge you to read the captivating book first. For one thing, you'll need specific directions to find some of these long-lost towns. (For more information on Harington, see the entry in *Famous Arkansans*.)

- ◯ Sulphur City (southeast of Fayetteville)
- ◯ Cherokee City (north of Siloam Springs)
- ◯ Marble City (between Jasper and Harrison, beneath the defunct "Dogpatch" theme park)
- ◯ Buffalo City (south of Mountain Home)
- ◯ Cave City (north of Batesville)
- ◯ Lake City (east of Jonesboro)
- ◯ Mound City (across the Mississippi River from Memphis)
- ◯ Arkansas City (east of McGehee)
- ◯ Garland City (southeast of Texarkana on the Red River)
- ◯ Bear City (west of Hot Springs near Royal)
- ◯ Y City (northeast of Mena)

TOP ATTRACTIONS

Hey! There's more to do than whittle!

Arkansas has a variety of unique places to go and things to do that are enjoyed by natives and visitors alike. Take your pick from an eclectic menu of diversions from horse racing to wine tasting. Here's our selective list of top attractions. Though the state parks also draw many visitors, with a couple of exceptions, we do not include them in this list

since we cover them in detail elsewhere. (We number the entries for no particular reason other than we know people find comfort in numbers.)

1. HOT SPRINGS NATIONAL PARK

Hot Springs Convention and Visitors Bureau; P.O. Box K; Hot Springs National Park, AR 71902. 1-800-SPA CITY.
The Hot Springs area is probably the state's top tourist destination. People have been coming to Hot Springs since the first person stumbled across the "valley of the vapors" as many as 10,000 years ago. Hot Springs was named the country's first national reservation in 1832. By 1921, the year Hot Springs Reservation became Hot Springs National Park, prosperity was filling Americans' pocketbooks so that they could afford more leisure time. Monumental bathhouses along Bathhouse Row built in the previous decade catered to crowds of health-seekers. These new establishments, full of the latest equipment, were planned to pamper the bather in the most artful of surroundings. Some houses

were lavishly appointed with polished brass, murals, fountains, statues, and stained glass. Gymnasiums and beauty salons furthered the efforts to look and feel better. Hot Springs was also the hot spot where those in pursuit of pleasure and amusement found gambling casinos, horse racing, and big name entertainers. While the city is much tamer now, it still has a unique flavor that keeps people coming back. There is now the additional curiosity about the city that is Bill Clinton's hometown.

Historic Quapaw Bath House

The scenery is gorgeous; the architecture charming. Aside from the thermal waters that still flow downtown, there are major lakes – Catherine, Hamilton and Ouachita – for water recreation. Numerous touristy attractions: lake cruises on a riverboat, a wax museum, go-cart tracks, mule trolleys, sight-seeing amphibious ducks, aquariums, an observation tower, and, of course, the bathhouses. People do still come for the waters – for less than $30 you can treat yourself to a relaxing bath and massage. Though the Buckstaff is the only bathhouse still offering baths, bathing is available at these downtown hotels: Arlington, Downtowner, Park Hilton, Majestic and Hot Springs Health Spa. And people still come to play the ponies at Oaklawn Park and eat barbecue at McClard's. The arts have become a major attraction and monthly Gallery Walks are held which coincide with the openings of new exhibits at the galleries. In November, the city also hosts an international documentary film festival, one of the best kept secrets in this state and beyond. Hot Springs is a strangely exotic place still struggling for a clear notion of itself. It is a retirement destination, a tourist trap and a fascinating example of living history where stately marbled bathhouses sit right across the street from tacky souvenir shops. You've got to love a place like Hot Springs. For more information see the Hot Springs entry under *Cities and Towns.*

2. OAKLAWN PARK

Oaklawn Jockey Club, Inc.; P.O. Box 699; Hot Springs, AR 71902.
1-800-OAKLAWN.
This is one of the top thoroughbred race tracks in the country and was a favorite haunt of the late Virginia Kelley, President Clinton's mother. This colorful landmark located south of downtown Hot Springs has been in operation since 1904, with a few interruptions during which betting was banned. Oaklawn beckons to out-of-town visitors who come a couple of times during the live season, and to those die-hard locals who are sometimes seen in their house slippers at the two-dollar window. Live race meets are held at the park from the end of January through April, the season capped by the Racing Festival of the South. After the live season, they switch to big screen summer simulcasts by satellite every weekend from the Kentucky Derby through early fall, including such racing spectaculars as the Triple Crown and Breeder's Cup. Oaklawn also has fine restaurants and a tavern. And the concession stands serve up a darned tasty corned beef sandwich.

3. CRATER OF DIAMONDS STATE PARK

Route 1, Box 364; Murfreesboro, AR 71958. (501) 285-3113.
Finders Keepers is the name of the game at the only diamond field in North America open to the public. Located two miles southeast of Murfreesboro on Ark. 301, this is the eighth largest diamond deposit in the world. For a small fee you can prospect on a 35-acre field (the eroded surface of an ancient, gem-bearing volcanic pipe), and keep what you find. The first diamond was discovered here in 1906 by farmer John Huddleston who owned the property. Since that time, more than 70,000 diamonds have been uncovered at the crater. In 1972, the property was purchased for development as a state park and since then visitors have carried home over 18,000 diamonds. 1983 set a record for the most diamonds found in one year – 1,501.

Although diamonds are the main attraction, other semi-precious gems and minerals share the territory. Amethyst, agate, jasper, peridot, garnet, quartz, calcite, barite and many others including over 100 different rocks and minerals make this area a rock-hound's paradise. The state regularly plows the field to unearth new stones and digging tools can be rented. You enter the park through the visitor center which includes exhibits and an audio-visual program explaining the area's geology and tips on recognizing diamonds in the rough. The park has 60 campsites with water and electricity, laundry, restaurant, picnic areas and gift shop. Each September the Murfreesboro Gem, Mineral and Jewelry Show is held in the Municipal Building. Thousands of gems, rocks, minerals and jewelry are on display and for sale at the show and you can watch artisans design custom jewelry. There's also musical entertainment, door prizes and barbecue.

THE BIG ONES

- **Uncle Sam** (1924) 40.23 carats. Cut to emerald shape, 12.42 carats, sold in 1971 for $150,000.
- **Star of Murfreesboro** (1964) 34.25 carats. Value uncut at that time was $45,000.
- **Searcy** (1926) 27.21 carats. Found in a cotton field near Searcy by a ten-year-old girl. Speculation was that it may have been dropped there by an Indian.
- **Nameless diamond** (1911) 17.85 carats.
- **Amarillo Starlight** (1975) 16.37 carats. Discovered by a visitor from Amarillo, Texas. This is the biggest find since the crater became a state park.
- **Star of Arkansas** (1956) 15.31 carats. Found by a Dallas resident and cut to 8.27 carat marquise.
- **Star of Shreveport** (1981) 8.82 carats. Found by a visitor from Shreveport.

4. BUFFALO NATIONAL RIVER

P.O. Box 1173, Harrison, AR 72602-1173.
(501) 741-5443.

This free-flowing pristine river meanders 135 miles through the Ozark Mountains before it meets up with the White River in the northwest portion of the state. The Buffalo became America's first national river in 1972 through the efforts of Justice William O. Douglas

Diamond Prospecting Pointers

◆ Look for a small, well-rounded crystal. A diamond weighing several carats may be no larger than a marble. Most stones found at the park are smaller than one carat.
◆ Diamonds have an oily, slick outer surface that dirt or mud will not stick to, so look for clean crystals.
◆ The best time to prospect is after a rain when the surface area is eroded and diamonds may be exposed.
◆ Always walk with the sun in front of you so you can see the crystals sparkle.
◆ If you think you have a diamond, hold it carefully in your hand. Experience has shown that once a diamond is dropped, it is usually not found again that day.
◆ Diamonds vary in color and opacity and may be clear, pink, yellow, blue, green, gray, brown, black, white; transparent, opaque, or translucent. The most common found at the crater are brown, yellow and clear white.
◆ Bring any stone you think may be a diamond to the visitor center for free weighing and certification. Anything you find is yours! (You don't have to pay taxes on your find, regardless of the value – unless you sell it. Then the IRS nails you.)

and local preservationists who persevered. The river remains undammed and unpolluted and "floating the Buffalo" is a favorite pastime for many natives. The upper river generally requires a more experienced canoeist and is floatable in the spring and fall and after a generous rainfall in the summer. The lower part of the river is usually floatable year round and is quite docile, but it's always a good idea to call ahead to check on the river conditions.

The river is accessible from many points along U.S. 65 or Ark. 7, 14 and 21. There are numerous outfitters and accommodations in the area. Buffalo Point off Ark. 14 and Tyler Bend off U.S. 65 are the only fully-developed recreation use areas, but campgrounds are scattered along the river side and gravel bar camping is permitted. Depending on which part of the river you choose to float, the time of year and the rainfall, you can row, row, row your boat through some pretty frothy white water, or simply sit back and go with the natural flow of the river between the towering bluffs where the river has cut its path. There are plenty of spots along the banks to park your canoe and picnic, swim, hike or just sit a spell and enjoy the scenery. You can fish if you wish. In fact, you can practically reach out of the canoe and grab a goggle-eye swimming right below the surface.

DID YOU KNOW?

Elks Initiate New Members

Once native to our state, the elk vanished around 1840 due to the extensive farming and clearing by the early settlers. In 1981 and 1982, the Arkansas Game and Fish Commission worked deals with Colorado and Nebraska to swap largemouth bass for the Rocky Mountain subspecies of elk. The imported elk were released along the Buffalo in a remote section of Newton County. The elk are wilderness animals and have a low tolerance for man's intrusion. The National Parks Service controls access to the river, providing hundreds of acres of protected land along the river corridor where the elk can prosper. Today the elk population is estimated at 300 to 350 animals. If you'd like to get a glimpse of one of these magnificent creatures, drive a few miles north from Jasper on Arkansas Scenic Highway 7, turn west on the road leading to the Erbie access area on the Buffalo River. Drive slowly and look closely in the fields and forests adjacent to the river and you just might spot one. (There is no hunting season on the few elk we have and poaching is considered a serious offense.)

5. OZARK FOLK CENTER

P.O. Box 500; Mountain View, AR 72560. (501) 269-3851.

This popular and unusual state park is located one mile north of Mountain View near the junction of Ark. 66, 9 and 14. The 80-acre park provides a home to the area's craftspeople and musicians. The center is a living museum where the people are the displays. During the season (mid-April through first week in November) craftspeople demonstrate over 20 homestead skills as they were done in the Ozark Mountains before 1920. Musicians perform folk songs and ballads on traditional instruments such as the pickin' bow and dulcimer. There are festivals in the spring and fall and special contests, workshops, music shows and crafts exhibitions throughout the year. The center has a free tram service, Heritage Herb Garden and gift shop which sells authentic Ozark handmade items: toys, quilts, white oak baskets, jams and jellies. The park also has comfortable lodging, a full-service restaurant, and a convention center that can accommodate up to 1,000. For lodging information or conference scheduling, call tollfree 1-800-264-3655.

6. SOUTHLAND GREYHOUND PARK

1550 North Ingram Blvd.; West Memphis, AR. 1-800-467-6182.
The world's largest greyhound racing facility is located on 140 acres
where Interstates 40 and 55 meet. Racing is year-round with matinees
on some days. The park reportedly has the largest average daily pari-
mutuel handle of its kind anywhere. It has seating for 10,000 (indoors
with air-conditioning, or outside) and standing capacity of approximately 20,000. They have wide-screen television and close to 300 closed-
circuit monitors. The park has restaurants and concessions in case you
get hungry watching the dogs run. Incidentally, the greyhounds chase a
large artificial bone around the track instead of the traditional "rabbit."
Call tollfree for daily schedules. No minors are allowed inside the park.

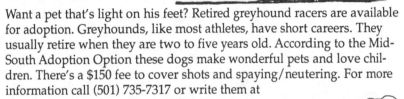

SURE BET FOR A PET.

Want a pet that's light on his feet? Retired greyhound racers are available
for adoption. Greyhounds, like most athletes, have short careers. They
usually retire when they are two to five years old. According to the Mid-
South Adoption Option these dogs make wonderful pets and love children. There's a $150 fee to cover shots and spaying/neutering. For more
information call (501) 735-7317 or write them at
P.O. Box 2088; W. Memphis, AR 72303.

*Sharing a craft
at the Ozark Folk Center*

7. GREERS FERRY LAKE AREA

This 50-mile long, 48,000-acre lake impounded behind a Corps of Engineers dam is the focus of one of the state's most popular recreational sites. The Greers Ferry area is also a popular resort and retirement destination with many planned communities nearby. The dam

was dedicated on October 3, 1963, by President John F. Kennedy shortly before his assassination. The lake created by the dam is known for its clean water and it usually ranks as one the top 20 most-visited Corps of Engineers lakes in the nation. This lake located in north-central Arkansas offers a wealth of recreational opportunities from scuba diving in the clear waters to fishing. Bass abound in the warmer water of the lake, while record-setting brown and rainbow trout have been pulled from the icy water just below the dam and in the Little Red River which feeds into the lake. Trout were introduced to the lake after the dam was built and have flourished in these frigid waters. Shortly after the dam was built, the Greers Ferry National Fish Hatchery was established along the banks of the Little Red River. The hatchery, operated by the U.S. Fish and Wildlife Service, produces about 750,000 nine-inch rainbow trout each year.

If camping is your thing, there are about 1,300 campsites operated by the Corps. There are also private campgrounds, marinas and resorts. The Greers Ferry area hosts a variety of festivals each year, the most famous being the Greers Ferry Lake and Little Red River Cleanup. This highly successful program began in 1970 and has been a role model for other cleanups across the U.S. and for legislation mandating cleanups on other federal properties. After the cleanup comes food and entertainment. The second weekend in August brings the Water Festival which draws thousands for water-ski performances, parasailing, sky-diving, rodeos, hot air balloons and the cardboard boat races which are always good for a chuckle. For festival information call 1-800-774-3237.

The current world-record brown trout was caught by Rip Collins on May 9, 1992, on the Little Red River. The 40-pound 4-ounce whopper was snagged by a marabou jig.

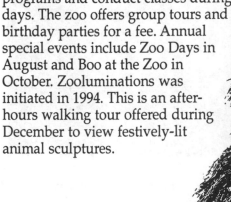

8. LITTLE ROCK ZOO

#1 Jonesboro Drive; Little Rock, AR 72205. (501) 666-2406.
Located in War Memorial Park, this is one of the finest in the country. The 40-acre zoo houses over 600 specimens of 200 species of mammals, birds, reptiles, amphibians and fish. (Unfortunately, polar bears are not among them. The Arkansas heat proved fatal. But there are four other bear varieties that are more acclimated.) There's also a Kiddieland featuring a miniature train ride encircling the duck pond.

The zoo has been open and growing since 1926 with many of the distinctive rock structures being built during the Depression by the WPA. Modern additions include the Tropical Rain Forest Display and Great Ape Display. Some of the zoos best assets are its docents (volunteer teachers and guides) who participate in ongoing educational programs and conduct classes during summer, spring break and holidays. The zoo offers group tours and birthday parties for a fee. Annual special events include Zoo Days in August and Boo at the Zoo in October. Zooluminations was initiated in 1994. This is an after-hours walking tour offered during December to view festively-lit animal sculptures.

9. BLANCHARD SPRINGS CAVERNS

P.O. Box 1279; Mountain View, AR 72560. (501) 757-2211.

Located 14 miles northwest of Mountain View, these stunning caverns are ranked among the ten most outstanding in North America. This is the only cave system in the nation developed and operated by the U.S. Forest Service. The caverns were formed from the continuous flow of water on limestone over eons and are believed to contain almost every type of calcite formation found in a limestone cave. This amazing underground spectacle, which opened to the public July 7, 1973, offers two guided tours during the warm season and one in the winter. The Dripstone Trail winds through about 0.7 miles of the uppermost level and is open year round. The longer, more strenuous Discovery Trail at 1.2 miles takes you deeper into the caverns through water-carved passages, beside the cave stream and under the natural entrance, where explorers first entered Blanchard. The Discovery Trail is only open during the summer and with nearly 700 stairsteps, this trail is not for the faint-hearted or breathing-impaired.

Pathways throughout the caverns are paved and lighted, but they also tend to be damp since the relative humidity in the cave is nearly 100%. So wear comfortable non-skid walking shoes – pumps are a *faux pas*. And take a light jacket, cave temperatures average around 58° year-round. An exhibit hall features a "Life in the Dark" display and a free screening of a fascinating film, *The Amazing World Below*. All facilities at the visitor center are fully accessible and the Dripstone Trail is accessible to wheelchairs and strollers, but some of the ramps are steep and you need a strong assistant to control a wheelchair. (You must provide your own wheelchair and brawny assistant.)

Blanchard Springs Caverns is home to five species of bats: the big brown bat, the little brown bat, the eastern pipistrelle bat, and two endangered species – the gray bat and the Indiana bat. Great care is taken not to disturb their fragile habitat. The bats hibernate in the middle section of the caverns which is not open to the public when the bats are hanging around. The Ozark National Forest which surrounds the caverns offers abundant outdoor recreation. Blanchard campground has 32 sites with flush toilets, hot showers and paved roads. There are scenic hiking trails and picnic facilities. You can take a dip in the clear waters of North Sylamore Creek or fish for rainbow trout in Mirror Lake.

OTHER ARKANSAS CAVES...

In addition to Blanchard Springs Caverns, there are two to three thousand other caves around the state with new ones being discovered all the time. Many of these are little more than a modest hole-in-the-wall, while others are spectacular cavern systems. Caves have been many things to many people. They were shelter for early cultures and refrigerators for the first Arkansas settlers. Frontier outlaws hid out in them. During Prohibition, the Blue Moon Cave north of Eureka Springs was a dance hall. In 1931, a special session of the Arkansas Legislature enjoyed air-conditioned comfort while convening in Wonderland Cave near Bentonville (which seems somehow strangely appropriate). Some subterranean life to be found in caves: blind white crayfish, grotto salamander, blind cave fish, orange-red cave salamander, mottled dark-sided salamander, blind millipedes and eight of the 16 species of bats found in Arkansas. Except for Blanchard Springs, which is operated by the government, the other commercial show caves around the state are privately owned and listed below.

- **War Eagle Cavern**
  Route 5, Box 748; Rogers, AR 72756. (501) 789-2909. Located a half mile off Scenic Hwy. 12 midway between Rogers and Eureka Springs, this secluded site in the Ozark Mountains was once used by the Indians. The cavern was opened to the public in 1978. Lots of fossils, no tight passages, underground stream. Forty-minute guided tour covers 1/4 mile. Open May to October.

- **Onyx Cave**
  Route 4, Box 420; Eureka Springs, AR 72632. (501) 253-9321. Located six miles east of Eureka Springs, this cave was accidentally discovered in 1891 when the Madison County Sheriff was chasing a bank robber. The thief was never found, but a tourist attraction

was. Open daily year-round. Radio headphones guide you on a non-strenuous half-hour tour. Easy access ramp to the cave entrance. Free admission to the Gay Nineties Button and Doll Museum on premises.

• **Bull Shoals Caverns**
P.O. Box 444; Bull Shoals, AR 72619. 1-800-445-7177. Located just off Hwy. 178 in Bull Shoals. All level concrete walkway. Underground rainbow trout stream. Guided 45-minute tours. Open March-December. First opened in 1961 in conjunction with the Mountain Village 1890, an authentically restored Ozark town.

• **Cosmic Caverns**
Route 4, Box 392; Berryville, AR 72616. (501) 749-2298. Located on Hwy. 21 northeast of Berryville, halfway between Eureka Springs and Branson, Missouri. Guided tour takes about an hour and 15 minutes. The cave was first discovered by a lead prospector in 1845. The caverns opened to the public in 1927. The January 1993 discovery of the newest section, Silent Splendor, made the "CBS News." This new find was opened for tours February 1994. Cosmic Caverns has the Ozark's largest underground lakes.

• **Hurricane River Cave**
P.O. Box 240; Pindall, AR 72669. 1-800-245-2282. Accessible from U.S. 65 north of Conway. The cave, carved out by an ancient river, has been open to the public since 1932. The tour follows a level walkway by the riverbed and crosses over a remaining cold spring that once fed into the river. One-fourth mile walk. Open March through October.

• **Mystic Caverns**
P.O. Box 13; Dogpatch, AR 72648. (501) 743-1739.
Located on Scenic Hwy. 7, eight miles south of Harrison. The older part of the caverns has been open since the 1920s. The Crystal Dome Caverns, discovered in 1968, was opened to the public in 1982. The guided tour takes you through both. Also a mineral museum. Open March through November and Christmas season, weather permitting.

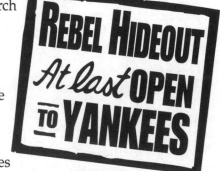

• **Civil War Cave**
Route 3, Box 28; Bentonville, AR 72712. (501) 795-2406. Located three miles west of Bentonville on Hwy. 72. This cave was used by the Confederates for ammunition storage and water source. Tour takes visitors down 340 feet alongside an underground river.

DID YOU KNOW?

THEY'RE NOT BLOODSUCKERS!

All eastern United States bats are insectivorous, thereby performing a
valuable and necessary service, especially in buggy
Arkansas. A single bat can consume
about 3,000 insects a night – a fact that
one can truly appreciate on a sticky
summer evening when the mosquitoes are dive-bombing. Many pet
stores even sell bat houses to encourage
these nocturnal flying mammals to
make their homes near your home.
Some bats can live as long as 30 years,
so we're talking long-term pest control here. And although there are such
creatures as vampire bats (which *lap*, not *suck* the blood of their warm-
blooded prey), there are *no* vampire bats in or near the United Stares
borders. So relax.

10. THE MUSEUM OF AUTOMOBILES

Route 3, Box 306; Morrilton 72110. (501) 727-5427.
Located on Highway 154 on Petit Jean Mountain, this museum was
originally built in 1964 to house the private collection of classic cars
belonging to Governor Winthrop Rockefeller. Following Rockefeller's
death in 1973, the collection was sold. The museum was later given to

the state of Arkansas
and is now leased to a
private operator. The
museum displays
privately owned
antique and classic
automobiles from
collectors throughout
the United States and
abroad, and at least
one-third of the cars
displayed are changed
annually. The museum
houses 50 restored

Arkansas Climber

vintage vehicles including the Arkansas-made Climber. The current star of the show is Bill Clinton's 1967, six-cylinder light blue Mustang convertible with the white canvas top. It is believed that the Mustang has been in the Clinton family since it was bought new by Bill Clinton's late stepfather. The Mustang is on indefinite loan to the museum and rumor has it that Bill will return for his 'Stang when he leaves office so he can tool around the state once more. The museum is open year-round. Admission is charged. There's an old-fashioned ice cream parlor and gift shop on the premises. In June, the Antique Auto Show and Swap Meet is held here. Over 100 antique and classic cars compete for awards in various categories from turn-of-the century to 1969 models. 1,250 vendor spaces are filled with cars, parts and accessories, as well as arts and crafts exhibits.

DID YOU KNOW?

The Arkansas Climber

From 1919 to 1923 the Climber Motor Corporation of Little Rock produced more than 200 automobiles and small trucks at a plant at 1800 E. 17th Street. The company bought components throughout America and assembled the cars in state. The Climber's selling point was toughness; it was built to withstand the rigors of driving unpaved roads in the South. According to the *Arkansas Gazette*, "The Climbers were touring cars. They came in four and six cylinders with cloth hoods that folded down. They had walnut paneled dash boards with wind-up clocks, leather interiors, snap down windows and ah-ooo-gah horns. The advertising slogan was 'the car you will buy.' " Only two of the rugged vehicles are known to exist today and both are at the Museum of Automobiles — one is on display, the other in storage.

THE CLIMBER FOUR

The "CLIMBER" climbs
OVER THEM ALL

You believe in Arkansas.
You live in Arkansas.
The Climber Four is made in Arkansas for Arkansas roads.

BUY A CLIMBER FOUR
AND SAVE THE FREIGHT

Limited Amount of Capital Stock For Sale

THE CLIMBER MOTOR CORPORATION
LITTLE ROCK, ARK.

TEAR OFF AND MAIL

Send me free descriptive matter and catalog CLIMBER MOTOR CORP.,

11. WINE COUNTRY

Okay, when you think of great wine, Arkansas is probably not the first place that comes to mind. But the times they are a changin'. Today Arkansas wineries are turning out some very respectable offerings, including a dry merlot, a chardonnay, a fruity sweet muscadine, and cynthiana, a hearty dry wine made from native Arkansas grapes. Though Arkansas wineries have been producing wine since the late 1800s, they are only now getting serious attention. The first wines produced here were sold to passengers on the Iron Mountain Railroad (later the Missouri Pacific) when the trains stopped for fuel and water. Even today, the price is nothing to whine about. A good bottle of native wine will only set you back about $5 or $6 – a tony vintage wine from private stock goes for around $175. Our "Napa Valley East" is located around Altus. (Altus gets its name because it was the highest or "altus" point surveyed in the Arkansas River Valley by the Little Rock & Fort Smith Railroad.) There is an annual Grape Fest held in July to celebrate the harvest.

Wiederkehr Wine Cellars *Hwy. 186 near Altus (Exit 41 off I-40).* Established by Swiss immigrant Johann Andreas Wiederkehr, the winery is the oldest and largest in mid-America and it is still family owned. It has gained international recognition and won over 300 awards since 1977. Wiederkehr's best seller is Niagara, a fruity, medium-sweet white wine. Their latest offering is a light-flavored sweet wine called Arkansas Natural. The rock-walled Weinkeller Restaurant is located on the site where Wiederkehr hand-dug his first wine cellar. Old-world German-Swiss cuisine is served in this romantic restaurant listed on the National Historic Register. Banquet service, dance area and patio dining are available.

The Swiss Chalet Gift Shop has imported gifts such as clocks and music boxes. Open seven days a week. Free tastings and tours. (501) 468-3551.

- **Post Famille Winery** About a mile south of Wiederkehr, this winery has been run by the Post family for five generations. Free tastings and tours. Gift shop featuring wine, of course, as well as juices and jellies. *(501) 468-2741.*

- **Mount Bethel Winery** U.S. 64 east of Ark. 186 in Altus at the foot of St. Mary's Mountain. Run by a different branch of the Post family tree, this is the smallest of the wineries. Free tastings and tours, gift shop. Mount Bethel's calling card is Big Daddy, a potent grape wine that's 19-21% alcohol. *(501) 468-2444.*

12. THE ARKANSAS ARTS CENTER

9th and Commerce Streets; Little Rock, AR 72201. (501) 372-4000.
The state's largest cultural institution and only major art museum is located in MacArthur Park. The six galleries display a variety of changing exhibits as well as outstanding exhibits from foundation collections. The collection of more than 750 American drawings from 1900 to the

present is particularly strong. The center also houses a children's theater, museum school, gift shop and the Vineyard In The Park restaurant. The Decorative Arts Museum on East 7th and Rock Streets occupies the historic Pike-Fletcher-Terry House. Opened in 1985, this adjunct to the Arts Center is three blocks from the main facility and displays permanent collections and traveling exhibits. It features European and American decorative arts and contemporary crafts. Toys Designed By Artists is a popular annual exhibit that runs for six weeks during the Christmas season. Admission is free for the museums, though donations are accepted.

13. PEA RIDGE NATIONAL MILITARY PARK

Site of the largest Civil War battle west of the Mississippi River, this 4,300-acre park is located ten miles northeast of Rogers on U.S. 62 at Pea Ridge. A decisive battle was fought here March 7-8, 1862, saving Missouri for the Union. The battle, which resulted in the deaths of three Confederate generals (McIntosh, McCulloch and Slack), was a strange one. It saw the South attacking from the north using French-speaking Louisianians and over 1,000 Cherokees (Pea Ridge was the Civil War's only major battle in which Indian troops were used). The Union soldiers came from Missouri, Iowa, Illinois, Indiana and Ohio and many spoke German as their first language. Moreover, the Missouri State Guardsmen, who fought for the Southern cause, were not yet officially in the Confederate service. The park furnishes a brochure for a seven-mile self-guided tour with 11 stops through the historic area, which includes the restored Elkhorn Tavern. There are displays and recorded messages at each stop. The original building was the center of fighting that marked the start and finish of the Battle of Pea Ridge. The visitor center has exhibits of Civil War artifacts, a 12-minute film presentation and a bookstore. The park is wheelchair-accessible and there's a picnic area nearby. *(501) 451-8122.*

14. THORNCROWN CHAPEL

This striking wood-and-glass masterpiece can be found tucked away in the woods high on an Ozark mountainside just two miles west of Eureka Springs off U.S. 62. The celebrated little chapel was designed by one of America's premier architects, Arkansas' own Fay Jones. The narrow, rectangular, 48-foot high chapel boasts 425 windows with over 6,000 square feet of glass. Completed in 1980, it is built of ordinary 2-by-4 beams, plate glass and garden-variety hardware. It has a gable-roof system and 22 pews. To preserve the un-spoiled woodland setting, no heavy machinery was employed and materials had to be small enough so that two men could carry them along the narrow hillside path. The result is a structure that is beautiful in its simplicity – Jones used no decorative ornaments. The building cost only

$152,000 for labor and materials, a miracle in itself.

 In 1990 President Bush awarded Fay Jones the American Institute of Architects' Gold Medal for Lifetime Achievement, the most prestigious award a U.S. architect can receive. In 1991, the AIA voted Thorncrown the best American building since 1980. Non-denominational religious services are held here on Sunday mornings. The chapel has also become a favorite spot for weddings. There is no charge to view Thorncrown; there is a collection plate at the door for donations. *To find out what hours the chapel is open or to get information about wedding rentals call (501) 253-7401.*

15. CHRIST OF THE OZARKS, THE PASSION PLAY AND RELATED RELIGIOUS ATTRACTIONS

This assortment of Christian projects initiated by Gerald L. K. Smith and his wife Elna M. has made Eureka Springs a mecca for motor coaches. In fact, the "Passion Play" pulls 'em in year after year and is consistently the #1 motor coach destination in Arkansas.

○ **The Christ of the Ozarks** This seven-story, 70-foot tall statue on Magnetic Mountain off U.S. 62 East was sculpted by Emmet Sullivan (an artisan at Mount Rushmore who also created some of the older works at nearby Dinosaur World). This is the second largest statue of Christ in the world (the biggest is in Rio). Completed in 1966, the statue could reportedly support three cars from each arm without toppling. At an altitude of 1,500 feet it can be seen for miles, therefore there is no charge. It is lighted for night viewing.

○ **Great Passion Play** Atop Mount Oberammergau off U.S. 62 East, the play is performed in a 4,400-seat amphitheater. This is the #1 outdoor drama in America based on attendance records of the Institute of Outdoor Dramas in Chapel Hill, North Carolina, which keeps up with such things. (Branson, Missouri's "Shepherd of the Hills" runs a distant second.) Since the first presentation in 1968, this reenactment of Christ's last week on earth – last supper, crucifixion, resurrection – has been seen by more than five million people. There are 250 actors plus live camels, doves, donkeys, horses and sheep. Yogurt, pizza and all-you-can-eat buffet on the premises. 1-800-882-PLAY for reservations.

○ **Sacred Arts Center** Over 1,000 works of Christian art.

○ **Berlin Wall** A 10-foot section is displayed on the "Passion Play" grounds.

○ **Gift Shops** Two of them, filled with Christian gifts.

○ **Bible Museum** One of the world's largest collections of rare Bible volumes and ancient manuscripts.

○ **New Holy Land and Tabernacle Tours** Guided tours of biblical re-creations from the Old and New Testaments. Visit the world's only complete full-scale reproduction of Moses' Tabernacle. Ten Commandments Memorial, Sea of Galilee, Manger Scene and more. This endeavor is a work in progress.

C^What better way to spend a sultry summer night than with a carload of friends, a defective audio speaker hooked over the window and a mosquito coil on the dash, taking in a double feature at the drive-in? Unfortunately, the drive-in theater has gone the way of the vinyl record album. But like the old LPs, there are a few theaters still hanging in there. So before it's too late, load up the kids, stock up on Junior Mints and head to the big screen nearest you. Be sure to call ahead for dates

and times before stuffing ten of your closest friends into the trunk.

○ **The DeQueen Drive-In**, DeQueen. (501) 642-2023.

○ **The 112** on Ark. 112, Fayetteville. Broadcasts in stereo through the FM radio transmitter to your car radio. Cool. (501) 442-4542.

○ **The Kenda**, U.S. 65 North, Marshall. (501) 448-2393.

○ **The Stone**, Ark. 87, Mountain View. (501) 269-3227.

○ **Howard Auto Theater**, Ark. 27, Nashville. (501) 845-4400.

ALL ABOARD!

If you miss the romance of train travel, or if you're like most Americans and have never known the joys of travel by passenger train, you can still get a taste of what it was like. Several companies around the state have resurrected and restored railroad cars and offer excursions.

○ **Boston Mountains Rail Excursion Company** *P.O. Box 924; Rogers, AR 72757. (501) 631-2828.* Over the Ozarks in a vintage train with breathtaking scenery and a run through the unique Winslow Tunnel. Choice of two routes departing from the historic depot in Rogers.

○ **Arkansas & Missouri Railroad** *107 Commercial; Springdale, AR 72764. (501) 756-0400.* Restored turn-of-the-century passenger cars. Tour Van Buren's historic district and the scenic Ozark countryside. Trains depart from Van Buren and Springdale.

○ **ES & NA Railway** *P.O. Box 310; Eureka Springs, AR 72632. (501) 235-9623.* Excursion rides and dining aboard vintage trains. Departs from the depot on North Main Street. Hwy. 23 North.

○ **Ouachita Scenic Railroad** *P.O. Box 879, Dept. ATG4; Hot Springs National Park, AR 71902. (501) 321-2015.* 1920 Pullman passenger cars wind through the Ouachita Mountains following the original Hot Springs "Diamond Jo" line built in 1876. Twenty miles round-trip takes about 1¾ hours. Live entertainment on board. Depot is located in restored Freight House off corner of Grand and Broadway.

STATE PARKS AND MUSEUMS

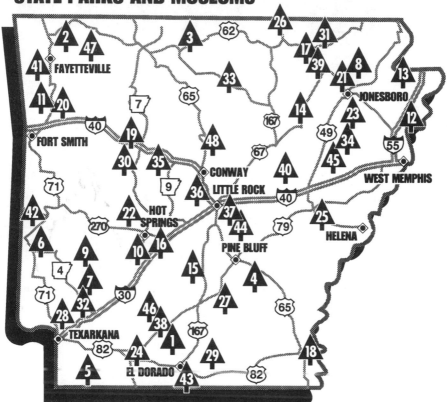

1. Arkansas Oil and Brine Museum
2. Beaver Lake
3. Bull Shoals
4. Cane Creek
5. Conway Cemetery
6. Cossatot River
7. Crater of Diamonds
8. Crowley's Ridge
9. Daisy
10. DeGray Lake
11. Devil's Den
12. Hampson Museum
13. Herman Davis
14. Jacksonport
15. Jenkins' Ferry
16. Lake Catherine
17. Lake Charles
18. Lake Chicot
19. Lake Dardanelle
20. Lake Fort Smith
21. Lake Frierson
22. Lake Ouachita
23. Lake Poinsett
24. Logoly
25. Louisiana Purchase
26. Mammoth Spring
27. Marks' Mills
28. Millwood
29. Moro Bay
30. Mount Nebo
31. Old Davidsonville
32. Old Washington
33. Ozark Folk Center
34. Parkin
35. Petit Jean
36. Pinnacle Mountain
37. Plantation Agriculture Museum
38. Poison Spring
39. Powhatan Courthouse
40. Prairie County Museum
41. Prairie Grove Battlefield
42. Queen Wilhelmina
43. South Arkansas Arboretum
44. Toltec Mounds
45. Village Creek
46. White Oak Lake
47. Withrow Springs
48. Woolly Hollow

STATE PARKS

Kick back and relax!

Created in the early 1930s, Arkansas' state park system has grown to 44 parks and four state museums which offer a wide variety of diversions. You can dig for diamonds, fish for bass, explore history, or simply kick back and do nothing at all. The parks are open year-round and uniformed staff are on-call 24 hours to keep an eye on things, help visitors and enforce the rules. Entrance to most parks is free, but there is a wide range of fees charged at some parks for many of the facilities and programs. Some facilities are closed seasonally or daily so always call ahead. For general information call Arkansas State Parks (501) 682-1191 or contact the individual parks for specifics.

PARK RULES

The rules are posted throughout the parks. These are the basics:
- **Pets** must be on a leash, caged or otherwise restrained to protect the pets and avoid disturbing other visitors. No pets allowed in cabins or lodge rooms.
- **Disorderly conduct**, indecent attire and abusive language are prohibited.
- **Quiet** is observed from 10 p.m. to sunrise. Any undue disturbance will result in ejection from the park and loss of unused fees.
- **Destruction** of state property is unlawful including the injury or defacing of trees, removal of plants, or destruction of signs, buildings or equipment. State parks have been designated as wildlife sanctuaries. All hunting, killing or capturing of any wildlife (except fish) is prohibited. You must have a license to fish if you are 16 or older.

■ ARKANSAS OIL AND BRINE MUSEUM

3853 Smackover Highway, Smackover, AR 71762. (501) 725-2877.
The museum focuses on the 1920s oil boom in south Arkansas. There are exhibits depicting Arkansas' changing oil technology and brine industry. Working outdoor exhibits include an oil well, pumping rig and three derricks. Temporary and traveling exhibits are displayed inside the museum and two video presentations about the discovery of oil and brine in Arkansas. Brine is the salt-saturated water which is the by-product of oil production. Once thought to be worthless, brine is now used in applications such as flame retardants and gasoline additives. South Arkansas leads the world in the production of bromine (BRO-meen) which is extracted from brine. Admission to the museum is free. Located on Ark. 7, one mile south of Smackover.

■ BEAVER LAKE STATE PARK

Route 5, Box 900; Rogers, AR 72756. (501) 789-2380.
The 11,646-acre Hobbs State Management Area (HSMA) is open for limited outdoor recreation and nature study, and offers undeveloped access to 28,000-acre Beaver Lake. Arkansas Sate Parks, the Arkansas Natural Heritage Commission and the Arkansas Game and Fish Commission jointly manage the HSMA property located in northwest Arkansas near Rogers. The area includes a firing range and limited seasonal hunting opportunities. Five primitive campsites are located along the hiking trail. This is one of our newer parks with approximately 2,400 acres planned for future facilities including camping and picnicking. HSMA lies on the southern shores of Beaver Lake and north of the War Eagle River.

FERRY INTERESTING...

Only one ferry remains in Arkansas – Peel Ferry across Bull Shoals Lake on the Missouri-Arkansas state line on State Highway 125 in northern Marion County. According to Garland Land of the Arkansas Highway & Transportation Department, Peel is alive and well and should be around for many years to come. It is one of the prettiest crossings in the state, according to Land, and one of his personal favorites. The water is crystal clear, there is scuba diving nearby and a new dock is under construction. And it is free.

In 1970 there were 17 ferries in the state. In 1984, five ferries were functional. Since that time we have lost Moro Bay in Union County, Guion across the White River between Mountain View and Melbourne, and Point Ferry across the Black River between Jacksonport and Newport. The latest casualty was Spring Bank Ferry across the Red River in extreme southwestern Arkansas, which connects Doddridge (Miller County) over Highway 160 with points in Lafayette County. Spring 1995 saw the opening of a two-lane, 1,422-foot bridge just north of the crossing and the ferry was no longer needed.

SOURCE: Arkansas Highway & Transportation Department

■ BULL SHOALS STATE PARK

P.O. Box 205; Bull Shoals, AR 72619. (501) 431-5521.
Curling around the towering Ozark Mountains of northern Arkansas and southern Missouri is Bull Shoals Lake. The lake is formed by the

White River which is famous for its record rainbow and brown trout. A dam forms the 45,440-acre lake where anglers enjoy lunker bass, trout, catfish, crappie and bream filled waters. Situated below the dam, Bull Shoals State Park shares the lakeshore and riverside. The park features 105 campsites along the river – 85 with water and electricity; 20 with no hookups. Park facilities include: picnic area, pavilions, playground and trails. A trout dock offers boat, motor and canoe rentals; supplies, equipment, gifts. Scenic float trips on the White River and party barge tours on the lake are available. From Mountain Home, travel six miles north on Ark. 5, then eight miles west on Ark. 178 to the park.

CANE CREEK STATE PARK

P.O. Box 96; Star City, AR 71667. (501) 628-4714.
One of the newer parks, it was developed by Arkansas State Parks and the Soil Conservation Service. This 2,053-acre park, situated on 1,675-acre Cane Creek Lake, is rich in flora, fauna and recreational opportunities. Facilities include 30 campsites, picnic sites, pavilion, launch ramp, barrier-free fishing piers, trails, visitor center with exhibits. From Star City, go four miles east on Ark. 293 to the park.

CONWAY CEMETERY STATE PARK

This 11-acre historic site preserves the grave of James Sevier Conway, Arkansas' first governor after the state was admitted to the Union in 1836. The cemetery is the family plot on the former Conway homesite and cotton plantation, Walnut Hill. Forty graves lie within the graveyard. There are no camping or visitor services available. From Bradley, travel two miles west on Ark. 160 to the community of Walnut Hill, turn south on the county road and go a half mile to the park.

COSSATOT RIVER STATE PARK-NATURAL AREA

Route 1, Box 170-A; Wickes, AR 71973. (501) 835-2201.
This park and natural area extends 11 miles along the Cossatot River, one of Arkansas' wildest streams. The river forms the rugged Cossatot Falls where only the most experienced canoeists and kayakers dare to take the plunge. Floatable river levels are usually limited to fall, winter and spring. (For river stage information from the Highway 246 access, call 501-387-3141.) Development at this primitive area is limited to the Brushy Creek Recreation Area adjacent to the Highway 246 Bridge. Day-use facilities include picnic sites, a nature trail, river access point for floating. A pedestrian walkway crosses the river and offers barrier-free access on the west side. The park is south of Mena in west central

Arkansas. The northern route is via Ark. 246 between Vandervoort and Athens. The southern route is via Ark. 4 between Wickes and Umpire.

■ CRATER OF DIAMONDS STATE PARK

Route 1, Box 364; Murfreesboro, AR 71958. (501) 285-3113.
This park offers a one-of-a-kind adventure – the chance to hunt for and keep real diamonds. Search a 35-acre field for diamonds in their natural matrix (the eroded surface of an ancient, gem-producing volcanic pipe). This unique park is the only diamond site in the world where you can search for and keep any gems you find. Prospectors enter the field through the park visitor center which includes exhibits and an A/V program explaining the area's geology and tips on recognizing diamonds in the rough. Diamonds were first discovered here in 1906, and since then over 80,000 have been found including the 40.23-carat "Uncle Sam," and the 34.25-carat "Star of Murfreesboro." Since the crater became a park in 1972, over 17,000 diamonds have been carried home by visitors. Amethyst, garnet, jasper, agate, quartz and more can also be found. Digging tools are available for rent and the park staff provides free identification and certification of diamonds. The park encompasses almost 900 acres of land along the Little Missouri River. Facilities include: 60 campsites with water and electricity, laundry, gift shop, restaurant. The park is two miles southeast of Murfreesboro on Ark. 301. Admission to mine area: Adults $4, Child 6-12, $1.50.

DID YOU KNOW?

Ringing In The President

The 4.25 carat Kahn Canary has been immortalized by Hillary Clinton who wore it during her husband's inaugurations. The flawless uncut stone is a rare intense yellow color and set in dramatic 14K gold and platinum. The natural stone was found by a logger in 1977. He later sold it to the Kahn family, Pine Bluff jewelers who own the stone. Hillary wore the diamond in the rough to two gubernatorial inaugural balls: in 1979 as part of a Victorian necklace and in 1983 in a contemporary ring setting. After catching the eye of the media in 1992, the ring was the subject of magazine articles and talk shows. Following a tour of the country, the ring returned to Kahn's Main Street location in Pine Bluff, where it is proudly displayed.

CROWLEY'S RIDGE STATE PARK

P.O. Box 97; Walcott, AR 72474-0097. Park/Campsite Reservations: (501) 573-6751. Cabin Reservations: 1-800-264-2405.

Left as an erosional remnant from the natural forces of rivers long ago, Crowley's Ridge stands 100-200 feet above the fertile plains of eastern Arkansas. The park occupies the former plantation of Benjamin Crowley whose family first settled the area. The ridge forms a narrow arc of scenic rolling hills extending from northeast Arkansas to the Mississippi River at Helena. Facilities include four fully-equipped cabins with kitchens, a group cabin area with rental kitchen and dining hall, 26 campsites, picnic areas, snack bar, trails, pavilions, baseball field, 30-acre fishing lake (electric motors only), fishing boats, canoes. The park is 15 miles north of Jonesboro on Ark. 141; or nine miles west of Paragould on U.S. 412, then two miles south on Ark. 168.

DAISY STATE PARK

HC-71, Box 66; Kirby, AR 71950-8105. (501) 398-4487.

Located on the northern shores of beautiful Lake Greeson in southwest Arkansas, this 7,000-acre park is surrounded by the Ouachita Mountains. Fishing enthusiasts have a chance for large catches of striped bass, crappie, catfish and bluegill. The Little Missouri, which forms the lake, is stocked with fighting rainbow trout above and below the lake. Facilities include: 118 campsites (97 with water and electricity, 21 tent sites), picnic areas, launch ramps, hiking trails, motorcycle trail, bicycle rental. Many visitors to the Crater of Diamonds, which is only 23 miles south, camp at Daisy. The park is one-fourth mile south of Daisy off U.S. 70.

■ DEGRAY LAKE RESORT STATE PARK

Route 3, Box 490; Bismarck, AR 71929-8194. Park/Campsite Reservations: (501)865-2801. Lodge: 1-800-737-8355 or (501) 865-2851.

Arkansas' premier resort park lies on the northeast shore of a 13,800-acre fishing and water sports paradise. *Better Homes and Gardens* magazine named DeGray one of America's 30 favorite family resorts for 1993. Camping (113 sites), swimming, tennis, golf, hiking, bicycling. Full-service marina with tackle, dock space, fuel, boat rentals of all kinds. A causeway takes you from the mainland to the island lodge and convention center offering scenic views of the lake and the Ouachita foothills. The Shoreline Restaurant overlooking the lake and pool and offers a full menu, plus banquet catering services. Meeting rooms and a 500-seat convention center are also available. The park has an 18-hole public championship golf course and driving range, Pro Shop with the works, store, laundry and tennis courts. Interpreters offer scenic boat tours, slide presentations, movies and outdoor workshops. Each January the popular Eagles Et Cetera Weekend celebrates the migration of bald eagles to DeGray Lake. Take Exit #78 off I-30 at Caddo Valley/Arkadelphia and go seven miles north on Scenic Ark. 7 to the park.

➤ *Between November 1994 and February 1995, 28 bald eagles were found dead in the DeGray area. This was the nation's largest single concentration of eagle deaths. Though natural toxins are suspected, authorities have not been able to determine the cause of these mysterious deaths.*

■ DEVIL'S DEN STATE PARK

11333 West Arkansas Highway 74;
West Fork, AR 72774.
Park/Campsite Reservations: (501) 761-3325.
Cabin Reservations: 1-800-264-2417.
The caves and crevices of this spectacular box canyon provided a perfect hideout for outlaws and renegades during Arkansas' rowdy frontier days. Hidden in some of the most rugged terrain of the Ozarks, Devil's Den is a collage of deep green forests, massive gray limestone cliffs and gurgling streams. Bridle paths and hiking trails wind through the 1,765-acre wilderness park into one of the finest scenic areas to be found anywhere. The mountain stream forms a small eight-acre lake before cascading over a native stone dam. There are numerous trails including the 14-mile Butterfield Hiking Trail. There are 13 fully-equipped cabins with kitchens and fireplaces and a restaurant and pool open in the summer. Facilities include a park store, 154 campsites, mountain bike trails, a horse camp area and riding trails (bring your own horse – the park does not provide them). To reach the park, go eight miles south of Fayetteville on U.S. 71 to West Fork, then go 18 miles southwest on Ark. 170; or exit U.S. 71 at Winslow and go 13 miles west on Ark. 74. (Trailers longer than 26 ft. should use caution on the mountainous Ark. 74.)

■ HAMPSON MUSEUM STATE PARK

P. O. Box 156; Wilson, AR 72395. (501) 655-8622.

In 1927 Dr. James K. Hampson began a painstaking study of the physical remains of an early native population which had inhabited the lands encompassed by Nodena, his family plantation. Dr. Hampson and his family, plus other professional archaeologists, have excavated and studied the Nodena site over the years. The Nodena, a Late Mississippi Period culture, inhabited the area from A.D. 1350 to 1700. They were farmers who supplemented their food resources by hunting and fishing. The Hampson collection of Indian artifacts was donated to the state in the 1950s, and today is displayed at the state park. Adjacent to the museum are picnic sites and a playground. Hampson Museum is located in northeast Arkansas in the community of Wilson at the junction of U.S. 61 and Lake Drive (five miles east of I-55).

■ HERMAN DAVIS STATE PARK

This one-acre park surrounds the monument to Private Herman Davis, an Arkansas farm boy and World War I hero. Fourth on General John J. Pershing's list of World War I's one hundred greatest heroes, he received the Distinguished Service Cross, the Croix de Guerre and the Medaulle Militaire awards from the American and French governments. The monument is in Manila on Ark. 18 (16 miles west of Blytheville).

■ JACKSONPORT STATE PARK

P.O. Box 8; Jacksonport, AR 72075. (501) 523-2143.

During the 1800s, Jacksonport thrived as a river port town in northeast Arkansas on the Black and White rivers where steamboats carried cargoes of manufactured goods, timber and cotton. The town became the county seat in 1854, and in 1869 a two-story brick courthouse was constructed. Though an important riverport, Jacksonport began to decline in the 1870s when bypassed by the railroad. By 1891 the county seat was moved to Newport and the town's mercantile stores, wharves and saloons slowly vanished.

Today, the park is dominated by the restored courthouse which houses exhibits telling the history of Jackson County. The landscaped courthouse square leads to the river's edge where *Mary Woods II*, a reconstructed 1840s White River paddle wheeler is permanently docked and available for tours. Facilities include: 20 campsites, swimming beach on the White River, pavilion and picnic sites. The park is on Ark. 69 at Jacksonport, three miles north of Newport off U.S. 67.

■ LAKE CATHERINE STATE PARK

1200 Catherine Park Road; Hot Springs, AR 71913. Park/Campsite Reservations: (501) 844-4176. Cabin Reservations: 1-800-264-2422.
A popular destination between Malvern and Hot Springs, this park covers 2,180 acres of Ouachita Mountain landscape on the shores of Lake Catherine, one of three lakes located around the resort city of Hot Springs. Shades of the past can be seen in the park facilities which were initially built by the CCC in 1937. Facilities include: 17 fully-equipped cabins, 70 campsites, rental boats (year-round), marina with bait and fuel (summer only), launch ramp, picnic sites, playground, laundry, store, swimming area and nature center (summer), boat dock, hiking trails, scenic party barge tours. Take Exit #97 off I-30 at Malvern and go 12 miles north on Ark. 171 to the park.

■ LAKE CHARLES STATE PARK

HCR-67, Box 36; Powhatan, AR 72458. (501) 878-6595.
Rambling, wooded landscape surrounds 645-acre spring-fed Lake Charles in the Ozark foothills. Beneath the surface of this crystal lake lurk crappie, bream, fighting hybrid bass and channel catfish. Close to a wide variety of historical and natural attractions such as the Ozark Folk Center, Powhatan Courthouse and Blanchard Springs Caverns, the park is a perfect home base for exploring northern Arkansas. Springtime float-fishing trips on area rivers are popular, and hunting is available in nearby wildlife management areas. Facilities include: 93 campsites, picnic sites, launch ramp, sandy swimming beach and hiking trails. From Hoxie, go eight miles northwest on U.S. 63, then go six miles south on Ark. 25 to the park.

■ LAKE CHICOT STATE PARK

Route 1, Box 1555; Lake Village, AR 71653. Park/Campsite Reservations: (501) 265-5480. Cabin Reservations: 1-800-264-2430.
Lake Chicot (*CHEE-ko*) State Park, located in southeast Arkansas on the Mississippi Delta, is secluded in a grove of native pecans and ringed by towering cypress trees. This is Arkansas' largest natural lake, a 20-mile long oxbow lake cut off centuries ago when the Mississippi River changed course. This is a peaceful site for boating and fishing. Fishing for crappie, bass and bream is popular, especially on the upper end of the lake during the spring and fall. Catfish bite year-round. Facilities include: 14 cabins (many with lake-view and fishing dock), 127 campsites, pool, picnic sites, laundry, playground, store, marina, launch ramp and visitor center with exhibits. Located within the Mississippi Flyway,

the park offers outstanding bird watching. Each September the park hosts party barge tours of the lake, levee tours and programs for viewing rare storks, ibis, egrets and ducks. The park is eight miles northeast of Lake Village on Ark. 144. (If you go in the summer, don't forget the mosquito repellent.)

■ LAKE DARDANELLE STATE PARK

Route 5, Box 358; Russellville, AR 72801. (501) 967-5516.
The park offers three lakeside areas on Lake Dardanelle, a 34,000-acre lake on the Arkansas River. Each location – Russellville (main park), Dardanelle and Ouita – has campsites, launch ramps, picnicking and restrooms. A visitor center, marina, miniature golf course, bike rental and hiking trail are located at the Russellville area. To reach the Russellville area: Take Exit #81 (Ark. Hwy. 7) off I-40 at Russellville. Turn south, then immediately turn west on Ark. 326 and go four miles. Dardanelle area: Four miles west of Dardanelle on Ark. 22. Ouita area: Take Exit # 81(Ark. Hwy. 7) off I-40 at Russellville. Turn south, then immediately turn west on Ark. 326 and go 3/4 mile.

LAKE FORT SMITH STATE PARK

P.O. Box 4; Mountainburg, AR 72946. Park/Campsite Reservations: (501) 369-2469. Cabin Reservations: 1-800-264-2435.
The Boston Mountains, surrounding 900-acre Lake Fort Smith, boasts some of the most beautiful scenery in the state. Visitors are greeted year-round with a kaleidoscope of colors from the bright blossoms of spring to the flaming reds of fall. The park covers 125 acres below Lake Fort Smith Dam with scenic backpacking opportunities (the 178-mile Ozark Highlands Trail begins here). Facilities include: 12 campsites, eight cabins, Olympic-size pool, tennis courts, launch ramp, rental canoes, fishing boats and motors, a group dormitory with kitchen and dining hall. The park is at the northern edge of Mountainburg. Watch for park access sign on U.S. 71, then go a half mile east to the park.

LAKE FRIERSON STATE PARK

7904 Highway 141; Jonesboro, AR 72401. (501) 932-2615.
On Crowley's Ridge in northeast Arkansas, this park is known for its year-round fishing and springtime blaze of wild dogwoods. The lake's 335-acres provides catches of bass, bream, crappie and catfish. Facilities include: seven campsites, tables and grills, restrooms, playground, boat rentals, launch ramp and barrier-free fishing pier. The park is 10 miles north of Jonesboro on Ark. 141.

■ LAKE OUACHITA STATE PARK

5451 Mountain Pine Road; Mountain Pine, AR 71956. Park/ Campsite Reservations: (501) 767-9366. Cabin Reservations: 1-800-264-2441.
Arkansas' largest man-made lake, Ouachita (*WASH-uh-taw*) stretches across 48,000 acres and has 975 miles of impressive mountainous shoreline dotted with quiet coves and rocky beaches. The lake is known for its clear water and great fishing for bream, crappie, catfish, stripers and trout. Boating, scuba diving, swimming and water skiing are also big pursuits. The park is located at the eastern tip of the lake and includes historic Three Sisters' Springs, once thought to have curative powers. (The springs are accessible through a modern spring house.)

Facilities include: 102 campsites, cabins, a marina with boat, party barge, motor and slip rentals, bait and supplies, swimming area, trails, store and snack bar. To get there, go three miles west of Hot Springs on U.S. 270, then 12 miles north on Ark. 227 to the park.

■ LAKE POINSETT STATE PARK

Route 3, Box 317; Harrisburg, AR 72432. (501) 578-2064.
Situated among the forested hills of Crowley's Ridge in northeast Arkansas, the shallow 640-acre lake makes for excellent catches of bass, bream and crappie. Facilities include: 30 campsites, launch ramp and boat rentals, picnic area, playground and hiking trail. From Harrisburg, go one mile east on Ark. 14, then three miles south on Ark. 163 to the park.

■ LOGOLY STATE PARK

P.O. Box 245; McNeil, AR 71752. (501) 695-3561.
At Logoly (*LOW-go-lie*) Arkansas' first environmental education state park, interpreters present workshops on ecological topics. The park's natural resources provide a living laboratory for students and nature lovers. Most of Logoly's 345 acres comprise a State Natural Area with unique plant life and numerous mineral springs. Facilities include: six group tent sites (no hookups), bathhouse with hot showers, picnic sites, trails, visitor center with exhibit area and indoor classroom. From U.S. 79 at McNeil, go 3/4 mile on County Road 47 (Logoly Road) to the park.

■ LOUISIANA PURCHASE STATE PARK

At the junction of Lee, Monroe, and Phillips counties, this park preserves the 1815 benchmark used to survey the Arkansas area of the
Louisiana Purchase. The park includes 36 acres within a headwater
swamp, a fast-disappearing ecological setting in eastern Arkansas. A
boardwalk with exhibits provides access to a monument in the swamp's
interior marking the survey's point-of-beginning. From I-40 at Brinkley
take U.S. 49 and go 21 miles south, then go two miles east on Ark. 362 to
the park.

■ MAMMOTH SPRING STATE PARK

P.O. Box 36; Mammoth Spring, AR 72554. (501) 625-7364.
One of the largest single natural springs in America, Mammoth Spring
emits nine million gallons of cool clear water every hour. The spring
forms a scenic 10-acre lake, then flows south as the Spring River, a
popular trout and float stream. Near the spring, a beautifully-restored
1886 Frisco depot houses a collection of railroad memorabilia. The
baggage room displays local history exhibits and outside is a Frisco
caboose. Facilities include: information center with exhibits, picnic sites,
ball field, trail. The park is on U.S. 63 at the town of Mammoth Spring.

MILLWOOD STATE PARK

Route 1, Box 37AB; Ashdown, AR 71822. (501) 898-2800.
One of the South's hottest fishing areas is 29,500-acre Millwood Lake. A
series of boat lanes lead anglers among timber to marshes and oxbow
cutoffs – a tree-filled fishing paradise. Famous for bass tournaments, the
lake abounds in largemouth, white and hybrid bass as well as bream,
catfish and crappie. Bird watching is popular with a wintering bald
eagle population, flocks of migrating pelicans and ducks in the fall, and
a variety of year-round inhabitants. Facilities include: 117 campsites,
picnic sites, swimming area, marina with groceries, bait, gas. Fishing
boats, pedal boats, slip rentals. From junction I-30 and U.S. 71 at
Texarkana, go 16 miles north on U.S. 71 to Ashdown, then nine miles
east on Ark. 32 to the park.

MORO BAY STATE PARK

6071 Highway 15 South; Jersey, AR 71651. (501) 463-8555.
This quiet, wooded park in south central Arkansas is located where
Moro Bay and Raymond Lake join the Ouachita River is excellent for
fishing and boating. Adjacent timberlands offer outstanding deer and
squirrel hunting. Park facilities include: 20 campsites with water and

electricity, picnic sites, pavilion, playground, trail, boat, motor and slip rentals. The park is 29 miles southwest of Warren on Ark. 15; or 21 miles northeast of El Dorado on Ark. 15.

■ MOUNT NEBO STATE PARK

Route 3, Box 374; Dardanelle, AR 72834. Park/Campsite Reservations: (501) 229-3655. Cabin Reservations: 1-800-264-2458.
A flat-topped mountain plateau, Mount Nebo looms 1,350 feet above the Arkansas River Valley offering spectacular views and is a favorite jumping-off point for hang gliders. The mountain began attracting travelers and settlers over 100 years ago when a hotel was operated on the mountain top for steamboat travelers. In 1933, a portion of the mountain was chosen as a park site, and logs and stones from the mountain were used to construct many of the park facilities. These facilities include: 35 campsites, 14 cabins, 14 miles of trails, pool, tennis courts, picnic areas, playgrounds, ball field, bike rental, pavilions, exhibits and store. Many private homes are also on the mountain. The park is seven miles west of Dardanelle on Ark. 155. Please note that this highway zigzags up the mountain and includes hairpin curves. Trailers over 15 feet should not attempt it.

■ OLD DAVIDSONVILLE STATE PARK

7953 Hwy. 166 South; Pocahontas, AR 72455. (501) 892-4708.
The park preserves the locale of historic Davidsonville established by French settlers in 1815, the site of the Arkansas Territory's first post office, courthouse and land office. Bypassed by the Old Military Road, an overland route from St. Louis southward, the river port's days as a major trade center faded by the 1830s. Indoor and outdoor exhibits provide information on this important frontier town. Today fishing is the main activity at Old Davidsonville. The park borders the Black River (boat launch ramp) and an 11-acre fishing lake with boat dock, barrier-free fishing pier, bait shop, fishing boat (trolling motors only) and pedal boat rentals. Other facilities include 50 campsites, picnic area, pavilion, playground and trails. Spring and Eleven Points rivers are nearby. From Pocahontas, go two miles west on U.S. 62, then nine miles south on Ark. 166 to the park. Or from Black Rock take U.S. 63 to Ark. 361, then go six miles north.

■ OLD WASHINGTON HISTORIC STATE PARK

P.O. Box 98; Washington, AR 71862. (501) 983-2684.
Established as a county seat in 1824, Washington became an important stop for pioneers heading for Texas along the Southwest Trail. Sam Houston, James Bowie and Davy Crockett passed this way, and James Black, a local blacksmith, is credited with forging the legendary bowie knife here. Later, the town became a major service center for area planters, merchants and professionals. During the Civil War, Washington served as the Confederate capital of Arkansas from 1863-1865. The park was established in 1973 and interprets Washington from 1824-1875. Tours include visits to the Confederate Capitol, Tavern Inn, Blacksmith Shop, Weapons Museum and several residences. The 19th-century restoration town also includes a print museum, steam-powered cotton gin and dining at the Williams Tavern Restaurant. The 1874 courthouse serves as the visitor center and houses the Southwest Arkansas Regional Archives, a resource center for historical and genealogical research. Take Exit #30 off I-30 at Hope and go nine miles northwest on Ark. 4 to Washington.

DID YOU KNOW?

ARKANSAS TOOTHPICK

In 1830, James Bowie ordered a hunting knife from James Black, a noted blacksmith in Washington, Arkansas. The knife was made from the finest steel and had a long pointed blade and a keen cutting edge. The bowie knife quickly became world-famous and constant companion of the early frontiersman. Times were wild and lawless and a settler looked upon any stranger to the Territory as a possible outlaw or cutthroat. Legend has it that whenever a stranger appeared and began getting nosy, the Arkie would remain silent for a moment while his hand slid quite naturally into his pocket and brought forth his bowie knife. Then he casually began picking his teeth with the point of the blade. The very sight of this notoriously lethal weapon would send a shiver up the spine of the stranger and make him think twice about making a suspicious move. This dramatic gesture apparently made quite an impression on those folks passing through the Arkansas Territory who went on their ways to spread the story of the "Arkansas toothpick."

SOURCES: *Living in Arkansas* by O.E. McKnight, *The Story of Arkansas* by Hazel Presson and David Y. Thomas.

■ OZARK FOLK CENTER

*P.O. Box 500; Mountain View, AR 72560. Park:
(501) 269-3851; Lodge: 1-800-264-3655 or (501) 269-3871.*
The Ozark Folk Center brings the past to the present. It
captures the simple beauty of Ozark life and lets you
experience firsthand the music, crafts and dance in this
unique mountain setting. During the season (first two
weekends in April; daily April 15 – November 7)
artisans demonstrate over 20 homestead skills and
crafts from 10 a.m. to 5 p.m. The 1,025-seat auditorium showcases the best in Ozark pickin', singin'
and jig dancin'. Special musical performances and
craft fairs celebrate the holidays. Music is played as
it was before 1940 with acoustic instruments only.
The Folk Center's gift shop offers handmade
items including toys, rocking chairs, shuck dolls,
quilts, white oak baskets, jams, jellies and much
more. Facilities include a comfortable 60-room
lodge, full-service restaurant, free tram service
and Heritage Herb Gardens. Check with the center
for complete schedule of events. To get there go one mile north of
Mountain View on Spur 382 off Ark. 5, 9 and 14.

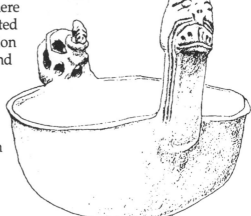

■ PARKIN ARCHEOLOGICAL STATE PARK

P.O. Box 1110; Parkin, AR 72373-1110. (501) 755-2500.
This park in eastern Arkansas which opened in 1993 encompasses a
large prehistoric Indian village representative of the late
Mississippian culture located here
from A.D. 1350 to 1550 and visited
by Hernando de Soto's expedition
in 1541. Arkansas State Parks and
the Arkansas Archeological
Survey manage the site as a
research station, museum and
interpretive center. The park is
located in Parkin at the junction
of U.S. 64 and Ark. 184.

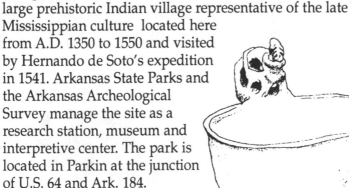

The Legend of Petit Jean

The Legend of Petit Jean is one of the stories associated with French rule in Arkansas. It goes something like this:

When Arkansas was governed by France, a group of French explorers organized an expedition to the New World to check out the French land holdings there. One of the explorers was a gallant young gentleman named Cheves. Cheves planned to go to the New World, see the sights, make his fortune, then return to France to marry his sweetheart, the lovely Adrienne. Being very much in love with Cheves, Adrienne could not bear the thought of being left behind. But times being what they were, women were not allowed on these explorations. However, Adrienne was a spunky young woman and was not easily dissuaded. It occurred to her that if she could not go as a girl, she could disguise herself as a boy. And so she did. The resourceful Adrienne, carefully decked out in boy's clothing, went to the captain and booked passage as a cabin boy on the same ship as her lover. She told the captain her name was Jean. Due to her small size, the crew fondly called her "Petit Jean"– French for Little Jean.

The ship landed in New Orleans and made its way up the Mississippi to Arkansas Post. From there they traveled up the Arkansas River to the beautiful mountain now called Petit Jean, near Morrilton. The crew made friends with the Indians of the region and because of Petit Jean's charm and disposition, she became as popular among the Indians as she had become among the Frenchmen.

One day Petit Jean became very ill. The Frenchmen and the Indians were distraught and did everything they knew to speed her recovery. Cheves stayed by her side, still ignorant of her true identity. As he sat by her, he told her of his plans to go back to France soon and marry his beloved Adrienne. When he had finished his story, Petit Jean could stand it no longer. Tearfully, she told him who she really was. Cheves was filled with joy, but his joy was short-lived. For Adrienne was very ill and growing steadily worse. Cheves nursed her tenderly, but a few days later Little Jean died. The heartbroken Cheves took her to the top of the beautiful mountain she loved and buried her under the spreading branches of a tree. The Indians who loved her said Petit Jean's spirit hovered over and guarded her grave. From that time forth, the Indians called the mountain Petit Jean.

■ PETIT JEAN STATE PARK

Route 3, Box 340; Morrilton, AR 72110. Park/Campsite Reservations:
(501) 727-5441. Lodge/Cabin Reservations: 1-800-264-2462 or (501) 727-5431.
Created in 1923, Petit Jean was Arkansas' first state park. Located between the
Ouachitas and the Ozarks, Petit Jean Mountain stands 1,100 feet above sea
level and offers panoramic views of the Arkansas River Valley. The focal point
of the park is Mather Lodge (24 rooms) and restaurant that hug the bluff of an
impressive canyon. Nearby are 31 cabins. The canyon is the work of
Cedar Creek, which cascades as a spectacular 95-foot waterfall. Upstream, a
rock dam on the creek forms Lake Bailey, 170 acres for fishing and pedal
boating. Other facilities include a boathouse with snack bar, boat rentals
and fishing supplies during summer, 127 campsites, playgrounds, picnic sites,
pool, tennis courts, launch ramps, pavilions, recreation hall, and numerous
hiking trails.

Petit Jean Mountain is also home to the Museum of Automobiles, a
showcase of antique and classic cars. Bill Clinton's classic Mustang is
here, as well as the only surviving examples of the Arkansas Climber.
Take Exit # 108 off I-40 at Morrilton and travel nine miles south on Ark.
9, then go 12 miles west on Ark. 154; or from Dardanelle, go seven miles
south on Ark. 7, then go 16 miles east on Ark. 154 to the park.

■ PINNACLE MOUNTAIN STATE PARK

11901 Pinnacle Valley Road; Roland, AR 72135. (501) 868-5806.
Pinnacle Mountain, located in a forested region near Little Rock, is a
day-use park dedicated to environmental education, recreation and
preservation. The diversity of habitats, from high uplands peaks to
bottomlands along the Big and Little Maumelle rivers, provide many
outdoor opportunities for study. The park features a visitor center with
exhibits, A/V programs, meeting room, gift shop, picnic sites, launch
ramps, pavilion and hiking trails (including a barrier-free trail). The
Ouachita Trail which begins next to the visitor center goes all the way to
Oklahoma. Camping is available at Maumelle Park, just two miles east
on Pinnacle Valley Road and there are interpretive canoe float trips in the
spring and fall. The newest addition to the park is the Arkansas Arboretum.
This 71-acre site exhibits examples of native flora representative of
Arkansas' six natural divisions: Ozark Mountains, Ouachita Mountains,
Arkansas River Valley, Mississippi Delta, Crowley's Ridge and Gulf Coastal
Plain. Situated below Pinnacle Mountain along the banks of the Little
Maumelle River, this arboretum includes a .6-mile barrier-free trail. Open to
the public, this phased project is under development. Take Exit #9 off I-
430 at Little Rock and travel seven miles west on Ark. 10, then go two
miles north on Ark. 300 to the park.

■ PLANTATION AGRICULTURE MUSEUM

P.O. Box 87; Scott, AR 72142. (501) 961-1409.
The museum focuses on cotton and the role it played in Arkansas' history and economy from statehood to World War II. Exhibits tell of plantation life in an era when equipment was mule-and-man-powered. Admission is free. The museum is located in Scott, a small Delta town southeast of Little Rock, at the junction of U.S. 165 and Ark. 161 (30 minutes from Little Rock/ North Little Rock).

■ POWHATAN COURTHOUSE

P.O. Box 93; Powhatan, AR 72458. (501) 878-6794.
During the mid-1800s, Powhatan was a busy river port shipping "mother of pearl" button blanks to markets worldwide. Powhatan served as county seat of western Lawrence County from 1869 to 1963. In 1888, a stately two-story courthouse with delicate woodwork and a classic cupola was built from red bricks made on-site. Restored in 1970, the courthouse is a regional archive containing some of the oldest records in Arkansas – many predate statehood. Powhatan is on Ark. 25, one mile south of the community of Black Rock in northeast Arkansas.

■ PRAIRIE COUNTY MUSEUM

P.O. Box 543; Des Arc, AR 72040. (501) 256-3711.
This museum tells the story of the White River community from 1831-1931. Exhibits depict how steamboating, commercial fishing, the White River mussel trade, trapping, logging and other lumber industries played important roles in life along the river. No admission charge. The museum is in Des Arc at the western end of Main Street.

■ PRAIRIE GROVE BATTLEFIELD STATE PARK

P.O. Box 306; Prairie Grove, AR 72753. (501) 846-2990.
On December 7, 1862, Union and Confederate forces clashed on a field
in northwest Arkansas, leaving more than 300 dead and over 1,600
wounded. Today, the park serves as a memorial to those soldiers.

Visitors can follow a self-guided
driving tour or walk the one-mile
Battlefield Trail. Guided tours
are offered through structures
typical of a 19th century hill
community, and the life of a
Civil War soldier is emphasized
at the park's Battlefield Museum.
A re-enactment of the battle is
hosted the first weekend of December on even-numbered years. The
park is on U.S. 62 in Prairie Grove (10 miles southwest of Fayetteville).

■ QUEEN WILHELMINA STATE PARK

*HC-07, Box 53A; Mena, AR 71953. Park/Campsite Reservations:
(501) 394-2863. Lodge Reservations: 1-800-264-2477 or 394-2863.*
Overlooking the breathtaking scenery of the Ouachita Mountains in
western Arkansas is Queen Wilhelmina State Park. Nearly 3,000 feet
above sea level atop Rich Mountain, Arkansas' second highest peak, the
park is located on the 55-mile long Talimena Scenic Highway which
winds past a succession of splendid panoramas into Oklahoma. The
first lodge, built in 1896 by the Kansas City, Pittsburg & Gulf Railroad,
was designed as an unusual resort retreat for passengers on the line.
The three-story lodge became known as the "Castle in the Sky." Since
the railroad was largely financed by Dutch interests, the new resort was
named in honor of Holland's young Queen Wilhelmina. A royal suite
was set aside for her use, in the vain hopes she would pay an official
visit. Didn't happen. Only three years later the lodge was closed and
eventually fell into ruin.

In 1958 the area was acquired for the development of a state park and
the lodge restoration completed in 1963. The lodge was very popular
until it burned in 1973. Today a modern lodge built from native stone
offers 36 guests rooms plus two "Queen's Rooms" with fireplaces, and a
restaurant with Southern fare. This is a favorite destination for viewing
the fall foliage. Other facilities include: 40 campsites, picnic areas, trails,

miniature scenic railroad, animal park, miniature golf (open seasonally), laundry and store. Go 13 miles west of Mena on Ark. 88 to the park.

■ RED RIVER CAMPAIGN

In the spring of 1864, three Civil War battles took place in south central Arkansas. Part of the Union Army's "Red River Campaign," these battles are commemorated as state historic sites.

The first battle occurred near Camden at **Poison Spring** (April 18) when Confederate troops captured a supply train and scattered Union forces. On April 25 at **Marks' Mills**, Confederate troops captured another Union supply train. With the loss of two supply trains and the on-slaught of wet spring weather, the Union Army retreated from Camden toward Little Rock. On April 29 and 30, Union troops fought off an attack by the Confederates and crossed the flooded Saline River on a pontoon bridge at **Jenkins' Ferry** and retreated to Little Rock. Today these parks offer outdoor exhibits and picnic sites. Jenkins' Ferry has restrooms, a pavilion(no electricity) and launch ramp on the Saline River. Poison Spring is 10 miles west of Camden on Ark. 76; Marks' Mills is at the junction of Highways 97 and 8 just southeast of Fordyce; and Jenkins' Ferry is 13 miles south of Sheridan on Ark. 46.

■ TOLTEC MOUNDS ARCHEOLOGICAL STATE PARK

#1 Toltec Mounds Road; Scott, AR 72142-9502. (501) 961-9442.
Just southeast of Little Rock is the site of Arkansas' tallest prehistoric Indian mounds. Inhabited from 600 to 900 A.D., these mounds and earthen embankment are the remains of a large ceremonial and govern-mental complex. Today this interpretive center is managed by Arkansas State Parks and the Arkansas Archeological Survey. Facilities include a visitor center with exhibits, an A/V theater and archeological research laboratory. Site tours are available. From Little Rock/North Little Rock, take Exit #7 off I-440 and go nine miles southeast on U.S. 165 to the park.

■ VILLAGE CREEK STATE PARK

Route 3, Box 49B; Wynne, AR 72396. Park/ Campsite Reservations: (501) 238-9406. Cabin Reservations: 1-800-264-2467.
Village Creek slices a long, flat valley through the middle of Crowley's Ridge in northeast Arkansas. On either side of the meandering stream, steep narrow ridges rise at right angles. This unique area, crossed by the Old Military Road, was settled during the early 1800s and includes the homestead of William Strong, one of Arkansas' early leaders. Most of

the park's facilities center around the two fishing lakes. Facilities include: 104 campsites, 10 cabins, boat rentals, picnic areas, sandy beach and sun deck, four pavilions, playgrounds, hiking trails, baseball and multi-use fields. Visitor center includes an A/V theater, store, gift shop. A new interpretive center offers a large meeting facility and The Discovery Room with exhibits of prehistoric artifacts and wildlife of Crowley's Ridge. Take Exit #242 off I-40 at Forrest City and go 13 miles north on Ark. 284 to the park.

■ WHITE OAK LAKE STATE PARK

Route 2, Box 28; Bluff City, AR 71722. (501) 685-2748 or (501) 685-2132.
In the midst of the Poison Springs State Forest of southwest Arkansas is 2,765-acre White Oak Lake. An excellent spot for bass, bream and crappie fishing. Abundant in wildlife, the park has regular sightings of great blue heron, egret, osprey, green heron, and bald eagles are often spotted in winter. Trails wind through the park's woodlands. Facilities include: 42 campsites, store, boat and bike rentals, launch ramp, picnic sites, playground, pavilion, beach and swimming area. From I-30 at Prescott go 20 miles east on Ark. 24, then go 100 yards south on Ark. 299, then go two miles southeast on Ark. 387 to the park.

■ WITHROW SPRINGS STATE PARK

Route 3; Huntsville, AR 72740. (501) 559-2593.
Withrow Springs is a tranquil setting for camping and quiet floats along the War Eagle River here in the heart of the Ozarks. Campsites, canoes and shuttle service are available. Other activities include: swimming, tennis, hiking, picnicking, baseball, crossbow range, river fishing for catfish, bream, perch and bass. There's also a snack bar and gift shop. The park is five miles north of Huntsville on Ark. 23; or 20 miles south of Eureka Springs on Ark. 23.

■ WOOLLY HOLLOW STATE PARK

82 Woolly Hollow Road; Greenbrier, AR 72058.(501) 679-2098.
This peaceful retreat is tucked away in the Ozark foothills of central
Arkansas. The park covers 370 acres of deep woods in the rolling
mountains. Forty-acre Lake
Bennett is a prime swimming
and fishing hole. Canoes,
pedal boats, fishing boats
and motors (electric) are
for rent. There is a
launch ramp, but bring
bait and other supplies
with you. Other facilities
include 32 campsites,
snack bar, bathhouse,
picnic area, gift shop and trail
encircling the lake. Woolly Cabin,
the log home of the area's first settlers, offers an historic perspective to
the beautiful hollow. Take Exit # 125 off I-40 at Conway and go 12 miles
north on U.S. 65, then six miles east on Ark. 285 to the park.

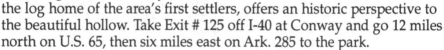

☘ SOUTH ARKANSAS ARBORETUM Adjacent to the

El Dorado High School, this 17-acre site is part of the Arkansas State Park
System. Native plant species indigenous to south Arkansas as well as
flowering azaleas and camellias can be found here. There are walking trails
and plenty of parking. (The state is also developing the new 71-acre
Arkansas Arboretum located at Pinnacle Mountain State Park.)

ARKANSAS TOURIST INFORMATION CENTERS

The state operates 14 Tourist Information Centers where you can get
detailed information about The Natural State. Thirteen of these are located
at entry points on Arkansas' borders and provide restrooms and picnic
tables. Another center is located at the offices of the Department of Parks
and Tourism directly behind the State Capitol.

1. Bentonville, U.S. 71 North
2. Harrison, U.S. 65 North
3. Mammoth Spring, U.S. 63 North
4. Corning, U.S. 67 North
5. Blytheville, I-55 North
6. West Memphis, I-40 West
7. Helena/West Helena, U.S. 49 Bypass

8. Lake Village, U.S. 65-82
9. El Dorado, U.S. 167 South
10. Texarkana, 2222 I-30
11. Red River, U.S. 71 North
12. Fort Smith/Van Buren, I-40 West
13. Siloam Springs, U.S. 412 West
14. Little Rock, One Capitol Mall

ARKANSAS HISTORY

We're small but feisty!

One thing's for certain – our state's history has been colorful from the git-go. Arkansas was forged by pioneers who weren't afraid to take risks or stand their ground and that attitude has endured. Our ancestors refused to accept our state's lot as the bastard at the family picnic. As our grandmothers might have said, "We may be small, but we're feisty!"

HAVE YOU A HOME OF YOUR OWN?

IF NOT

COME TO ARKANSAS.

Is there a spot on God's green earth that you own; that you, your wife, your children, can truly call home? is a question that interests more people to-day more than all others combined. This inquiry comes home to the heart of every true man and woman who feel that their children—penned up in tenement houses in large cities—do not and cannot breathe the pure air of heaven and feel the warm sunshine, so much enjoyed by those more fortunate. All cannot live in cities, nor all be mechanics. Then why not embrace the opportunity of securing a home for yourself and family, and give your children a chance to secure homes while young, and settle near you to be a help and comfort in your declining years. To-day the government has over 5,000,000 acres in the State of Arkansas, subject to be located for homesteads under the United States homestead law, one-fourth, or more, of which is believed to be unfit for cultivation; and to accurately ascertain which is good, tillable land, is one of the principal objects of the Homestead Company. The Homestead Company is a corporation chartered under the laws of the State of Arkansas, and has its principal place of business at Little Rock, Arkansas.

1860s circular advertising lands available to immigrants

WHAT HAPPENED WHEN

1541-42 De Soto and his band of plundering Spanish conquistadors cross the Mississippi somewhere around Helena and explore the Arkansas region which is inhabited by Indian tribes, chiefly Osage, Caddo and Quapaw. De Soto's group treks as far as Hot Springs, but fails to find the gold they seek. De Soto dies in 1542.

1673 French explorers Marquette, a Catholic priest, and Joliet, a fur trapper, descend the Mississippi River to the mouth of the Arkansas.

1682 La Salle, another French explorer, claims the Mississippi Valley for France, naming the area Louisiana for Louis XIV.

1686 Henry de Tonti, one of La Salle's lieutenants, establishes Arkansas Post for trading on the lower Arkansas River. This is the first white settlement in Arkansas and the entire lower Mississippi Valley.

1718 John Law, a Scottish financier with delusions of grandeur, attempts to establish a colony on the north bank of the Arkansas River near Arkansas Post and his company takes possession of Louisiana territory. His company goes belly-up in 1720, but Arkansas Post continues as a small trading station.

1719-22 Frenchman Bernard de la Harpe explores the Red and Arkansas rivers. The French map out much of Arkansas, hence the many French place names. La Harpe is the first to spell "Arkansas" in its present form.

1762 The French king gives to Spain all of Louisiana west of the Mississippi River, Arkansas included.

1769 Spain takes possession of Arkansas region, renaming Arkansas Post "Fort Charles III".

1800 Following more European wars, Spain secretly returns Louisiana territory, including Arkansas, to the French. Cotton is first grown commercially about this time.

1803   With the Louisiana Purchase, France sells all of Louisiana, including Arkansas, to the United States.

1804   Ouachita River is explored; U.S. Army takes over Arkansas Post.

1805   Louisiana Territory is created; includes Arkansas.

1811-12 Arkansas experiences the greatest earthquake of historical times in North America. Centered in Missouri, the New Madrid Quake creates the "sunk lands" of the St. Francis River in Arkansas. Many people drown in the Mississippi River, but because the land is sparsely populated only one death on land is recorded – a woman who runs till exhausted and dies of fright.

1812   Arkansas included in new Missouri Territory.

1813   Missouri Legislature changes the District of Arkansas to Arkansas County. It includes most of the present state of Arkansas.

1817   Cherokee granted land for reservation in western Arkansas.

1818   Quapaw cede large area to U.S.

1819   Congress creates Arkansas Territory with the capital at Arkansas Post. James Miller is appointed governor. The Territory has about 14,000 people, not including Indians.

The *Arkansas Gazette*, the state's first newspaper, established at Arkansas Post by William E. Woodruff.

1820 Homesteaders flock into Territory. Choctaw granted land in western Arkansas. *Comet*, first steamboat on Arkansas River, reaches Arkansas Post.

1821 Little Rock chosen capital. The Legislature moves there from Arkansas Post in 1821, as does the *Gazette*.

1822   The *Eagle* is the first steamboat to make it up the Arkansas River as far as Little Rock. The trip takes eighteen days from New Orleans.

1825   Choctaw cede land to U.S.

1828   Cherokee removed to Oklahoma. Dwight Mission site sold to U.S. government.

1829   Andrew Johnson becomes president and the government commits to transplanting all the eastern tribes to the Indian Territory. This movement is known as the "Trail of Tears" because thousands die on the march west from 1830-40.

1831   Because Arkansas has no adequate Capitol building, Congress gives the Territory ten sections of public land to be sold and the proceeds to be used to build a state house.

1832   Hot Springs is designated as the first national reservation.

1833   Construction begins on what is now called The Old State House.

1836   Arkansas is admitted to the Union as the 25th state on June 15. James S. Conway is elected first governor.

1837   During the first meeting of the Arkansas State Legislature, the speaker of the house stabs a colleague to death on the floor of the chamber. The killer is released for "excusable homicide."

1841   Nine hundred passenger pigeons are picked off by two
shootists in less than an hour just south of Little Rock. By
1914 the species is extinct.

1849   Fort Smith, established in 1817, becomes outfitting point for
California gold seekers. Three thousand emigrants leave
Fort Smith for California following the Gregg Trace which
leads west from Fort Smith to Santa Fe.

1857   The Mountain Meadows Massacre; the killing of 123
immigrants from Arkansas and Missouri by a group of
Mormons and Indians in Utah.

1858   Butterfield stage line passes through state.

1861   Civil War erupts. State troops seize Federal arsenal at Little
Rock and Fort Smith. Arkansas secedes from the Union.
Arkansas provides at least 60,000 men for the Southern
army.

1862   The most significant Civil War battles in Arkansas occur. In
March, the Battle of Pea Ridge (Elkhorn) is the first battle
fought in Arkansas (site dedicated as national military park
in 1963). The following December the Battle of Prairie Grove
is fought near Fayetteville.

1863   Federals capture Arkansas Post and Little Rock. Governor
Flanagin moves the state government to Washington in
Hempstead County and makes it the Confederate state
capital.

1864   Unionists frame new state constitution. David O. Dodd, a teenager accused of being a Confederate spy, is hanged in Little Rock at what is now MacArthur Park with an audience of approximately 6,000 spectators.

1867   Arkansas is put under military rule.

1868   Arkansas readmitted to Union.

1871   University of Arkansas is chartered at Fayetteville. The first classes are held the following year in the McIroy farmhouse. The U of A is first known as the Arkansas Industrial University.

1874   Joseph Brooks ejects Governor Elisha Baxter from office, beginning the Brooks-Baxter War. President Ulysses S. Grant declares Baxter the lawful governor. Present state constitution adopted.

1875   Judge Isaac Parker, at 36 the youngest member of the judicial bench, arrives in the rowdy frontier town of Fort Smith with his work cut out for him – the town has 2,500 residents, 39 saloons and no paved roads. During his 21 grueling years on the bench he sees more than 13,000 cases docketed. He becomes known as the "hangin' judge," though only 79 men are actually hanged during his tenure.

1879   Cotton plantation owners in Jefferson County import Chinese laborers to work the fields, offering them a half-pound of opium per month as inducement.

1885   President Grover Cleveland appoints Arkansan Augustus Garland attorney general.

1887   Deposits of bauxite discovered near Little Rock. At one time Arkansas produced 97% of the nation's bauxite, an essential ore used in making aluminum.

1889   Suffragette Susan B. Anthony lectures on women's rights at Fort Smith and Helena.

1896   Bee A. Dillard is the first woman to graduate from the U of A Medical School.

1903   Paperback jokebook about our much-maligned state *A Slow Train Through Arkansaw* by Thomas W. Jackson is a runaway best seller. Over nine million copies are sold in the 50 years following its publication.

1904   William H. Fuller raises the first successful rice crop near Hazen.

1906   Diamond deposit is discovered by John Huddleston on his farm near Murfreesboro. This remains the only diamond mine in North America.

1915   Present state Capitol completed.

1916   One of the biggest threats to the state, and the entire South, is hookworm disease which results from poor sanitation. Ironically, Arkansas is the first state in the Union to require smallpox vaccination for school children, teachers and other school personnel.

1918   Influenza epidemic kills more than 7,000 Arkansans, over three times as many Arkansans as died in World War I.

1919   Elaine Race Riot. Violence erupts between black sharecroppers and white planters. Governor Brough declares martial law and sends National Guard to Phillips County to restore order.

1920   William Hope "Coin" Harvey announces his plan to build a pyramid at Monte Ne, Benton County.

1921   Oil discovered near El Dorado. The Busey-Armstrong #1 blows in one mile west of town and reportedly soaks people two miles away. Hot Springs' designation becomes national park rather than national reservation.

1923   Broadway Bridge completed connecting Little Rock and North Little Rock, the first concrete automobile bridge to span the Arkansas River.

1927   Mississippi River floods about one fifth of state.

1928   Ernest Hemingway temporarily moves to Piggott, the hometown of second wife Pauline Pfeiffer, where he works on *A Farewell to Arms*. The 1933 premiere of the movie based on his novel is held in Piggott.

1929   The Great Depression begins with the stock market crash.

1932   Hattie Caraway becomes the first woman ever elected to the U.S. Senate. Following a distinguished career, she is defeated in 1944 by J. William Fulbright.

1934   Sharecroppers organize Southern Tenant Farmers Union in east Arkansas.

1935   John Tyson founds Tyson's, a small trucking concern that ships fruit and live chickens from northwest Arkansas to big cities in the Midwest. World's first parking meters (POM, Park-O-Meter) manufactured in Russellville.

1937   Cotton is king. Mississippi County produces 1.7 percent of the world's cotton. The 50,000 acre Wilson Plantation is the largest in the world.

1939   The opening sequence of *Gone With The Wind* is shot at the Old Mill in North Little Rock.

1942   World War II fears about the Japanese lead to about 110,000 Japanese-Americans on the west coast being shipped off to relocation centers in mid-America. Arkansas has two of these camps – Jerome in Chicot County and Rohwer in Desha County, with about 8,500 in each.

1950   Over the past decade Arkansas loses about 40,000 residents.

1952   The worst tornado day for the state. On March 21, three tornadoes touch down killing 111 people and injuring 772.

1957   Little Rock is in the national limelight when resistance to desegregation at Central High necessitates calling up the National Guard. In 1958 all of Little Rock's high schools are closed for the school year.

1958   Elvis Presley gets his basic training buzz cut at the base barbershop at Fort Chaffee. The event is documented by film crews and newspapers from throughout the country.

1961 Eighteen Titan II missiles with nuclear warheads are tucked away in silos dotting north-central Arkansas.

1962 Sam Walton opens the first Wal-Mart discount store in Rogers. Arkansas Arts Center opens in MacArthur park at a cost of over one million bucks.

1964 Orval E. Faubus wins an unprecedented sixth term as governor. El Dorado's Donna Axum becomes the state's first Miss America.

1966 Winthrop Rockefeller becomes first Republican governor since Reconstruction period. Senator J. William Fulbright of Arkansas, chairman of the Senate Foreign Relations Committee, becomes the leading congressional critic of the Vietnam War.

1967 Soybeans dethrone King Cotton as the state's biggest cash crop.

1969 The Big Shoot-out in Fayetteville where long-time football rivals, Texas and Arkansas, both undefeated, go head to head on national television December 3. Texas wins 15 to 14. President Richard Nixon is deposited by helicopter to witness the episode.

1971 McClellan-Kerr Arkansas River Navigation System dedicated; Arkansas and Verdigris Rivers in Arkansas and Oklahoma now navigable to the Mississippi River.

1972 The Buffalo River is designated the first national river.

1973 Arkansas' population finally tops the two million mark.

1975 *Rolling Stones* Keith Richards and Ron Wood are arrested in Fordyce en route to a concert in Dallas. Richards is cited for weapon possession (a hunting knife). The arrest makes international news and draws hundreds to City Hall. The charge is later dismissed. The *Stones* post bond and fly out of the local airport in a private jet. In other news, following the Vietnam War, over 50,000 Vietnamese refugees flee South Vietnam and are housed at

Fort Chaffee near Fort Smith during processing and orientation before they are relocated in communities throughout the U.S.

1978   Bill and Hillary Clinton with their friends Susan and James McDougal jointly purchase a 230-acre tract along the White River for about $203,000.

1979   Bill Clinton becomes governor at age 32, the youngest governor in Arkansas history.

1980   Clinton loses the governorship to Republican Frank White. Many attribute the loss to Hillary not dropping her maiden name and Clinton raising the price of car tags. Never a dull moment at Fort Chaffee – almost 19,000 Cuban "boat people" are confined here while the powers that be decide if the refugees qualify for political asylum.

1981   Arkansas becomes the butt of national ridicule when the controversial so-called "creation science" act is signed into law by Republican governor Frank White mandating that biblical precepts on creation be taught in public schools along with the Darwin's theory of evolution. The law is later ruled unconstitutional following a federal court trial in Little Rock where the nation's leading scientists testify against it.

1986   Arkansas celebrates its 150th birthday, a.k.a. the Sesquicentennial.

1988   The U.S. government reveals that chemical weapons are produced at Pine Bluff Arsenal.

1990   A hare-brained self-proclaimed prophet predicts another earthquake along the New Madrid Fault. Though many panic, the quake does not materialize. Recipes for an earthquake cake with an unsettled appearance make the rounds.

1991   *Arkansas Gazette*, the oldest newspaper west of the Mississippi, loses the newspaper war and goes out of business. Governor Bill Clinton declares for the presidency.

1992   Bill Clinton is elected president.

1993   Bill Clinton inaugurated as the
42nd president.

1994   The Arkansas Razorbacks win
NCAA Basketball Championship,
coached by Nolan Richardson. Arkansas is the first state to
designate all malls smoke-free. *Rolling Stones* Voo Doo
Lounge Tour plays War Memorial Stadium in Little Rock.

1996   Governor Jim Guy Tucker and former Clinton business
partners James and Susan McDougal found guilty on
charges brought by special Whitewater prosecutor. Republican Mike Huckabee takes oath as governor following
tumultuous day at state Capitol provoked by Tucker's
short-lived decision not to resign as promised.

"... I went down to the Old State House, a handsome Greek-
revival structure. It's now a museum devoted to Arkansas
history. This history being a straightforward affair: Arkansas
was all mountains and swamps. Indians lived there. Rednecks
took it. Yankees whupped 'em. And Tyson Foods moved in."
P. J. O'Rourke, *Rolling Stone*, 1994

FIRSTS IN ARKANSAS HISTORY

First Child in Arkansas Born of
English-American Parentage (1800)

Early in the year 1800 William Patterson, Sylvanus
Phillips and Abraham Phillips moved from Kentucky to
Arkansas and settled three miles south of the St. Francis River, at a
point known as the Little Prairie, on the bank of the Mississippi River.
Patterson's son, John Patterson, was born here during the year and is
believed to be the first white child born in Arkansas.

First Manufacturing Industry (1811)

John Hemphill's Salt Works established at Blakeleytown, Clark
County, was probably the state's earliest factory. Blakeleytown was a
small settlement on the Ouachita River just below Arkadelphia. Salt
was made here by Indians for many years before the first white
settlements were established in Arkansas. It is thought that it was here
that De Soto made salt in the winter of 1541-42. Hemphill continued
the business until his death in 1825 and his heirs carried it on until
about 1850.

First Protestant Sermon Preached in Arkansas (1811)

The Rev. John P. Carnahan, a minister of the Cumberland Presbyterian faith delivered the first sermon at Arkansas Post. Rev. Carnahan subsequently became a resident of the Pyeatt settlement at Crystal Hill, some 12-15 miles up the Arkansas River from Little Rock. This pioneer preacher also conducted the first camp meeting in the state. It was opened on Friday, May 24, 1822, and continued for five days.

First Post Office (1817)

Established at Davidsonville in June 1817. Adam Richie was the first postmaster.

First Quapaw Treaty (1818)

In a treaty concluded at St. Louis, August 24, 1818, the Quapaw Indians for whom Arkansas was named, ceded to the United States all lands claimed by them in the present state of Arkansas, except a triangular tract south of the Arkansas River.

First Newspaper (1819)

On Saturday, November 20, 1819, William E. Woodruff issued at Arkansas post the first copies of the *Arkansas Gazette.*

First General Election (1819)

Held on Saturday, November 20, 1819, the same day the first *Arkansas Gazette* appeared. Voters of the Territory chose a delegate to Congress, five members of a legislative council and nine members of a house of representatives.

First Duel (1820)

The first duel between Arkansans was fought by William C. Allen and Robert C. Ogden on March 10, 1820. Allen was a member of the Legislature and Ogden was a young lawyer. There are two versions of the story. One version is that Allen, who was some 25 years older than Ogden and was lame, became incensed because Ogden took his cane and would not return it, playfully retreating as Allen advanced. This continued until Allen became angry, limped to his room and wrote the challenge to a duel. The other version is that the two men were at dinner together when Ogden offered some criticism of a speech Allen had made in the Legislature. As the argument progressed, Ogden accused Allen of disputing his word, seized the latter's cane and struck him with it. The duel followed, Allen firing first and the bullet striking a button on Ogden's coat and inflicting a serious but not fatal wound. As he was falling, he semiconsciously discharged his pistol; the bullet struck Allen in the head, killing him instantly. Though the grand jury of Arkansas County indicted Ogden and the two men acting as seconds, through technicalities, the men were found "not guilty as charged in the indictment." The following October, the Legislature passed a law declaring that death resulting from a duel was murder. This put an end to dueling in Arkansas.

First Steamboat to Ascend the Arkansas River To Little Rock (1822)

The *Eagle* commanded by Captain Morris, was the first steamboat to make it up river as far as Little Rock. It arrived there on March 16, 1822, "seventeen days from New Orleans," the *Gazette* reported.

First Church Building (1825)

The first regular church building was erected in Little Rock by the Baptists. It was situated on the south side of Third Street between Main and Scott streets. It was built of logs. The pastor who organized it was Rev. Silas T. Toncray.

First Steam Sawmill (1826)

The first sawmill propelled by steam began cutting lumber at Helena, July 27, 1826. It was built by two men named Porter and King.

First Stage Line (1826)

Before the advent of the railroad, the most popular mode of overland travel was by means of the stage coach. The first stage route in Arkansas was that established by Wright Daniels between Little Rock and Arkansas Post in the fall of 1826. Daniels had the contract for carrying the mail between the two points and put on coaches for the conveyance of passengers. The coach left Little Rock every Tuesday at noon and arrived at Arkansas Post the following Thursday in the evening. The fare one way was $8 and each passenger was allowed 14 pounds of luggage.

First Bathhouse (1830)

Asa Thompson leased the springs at Hot Springs in 1830 and put up the first bathhouse for the accommodation of visitors. This first bathhouse was primitive and the facilities were described in 1832 as follows: "Directly in front of what is now the site of the Arlington House, and below one of the hot springs, there was a cavity cut into the rock, into which the water flowed. This was used as a bathing pool and had no covering except the bushes with which it was surrounded."

First Theatrical Performance (1834)

November 3, 1834, the Little Rock Thalian Society performed the comedy "Soldier's Daughter" in Little Rock. The following day's *Arkansas Gazette* reviewed the play and found it very satisfactory and "far better than we had anticipated." After covering expenses, profits were put to charitable purposes.

First State Election (1836)

As provided by the constitution, the first state election in Arkansas was held August 1, 1836, the year Arkansas became a state.

First Steam Ferry-Boat on the Arkansas River (1836)

The *Little Rock*, 86 feet long and 33 feet wide, was built in Cincinnati for the express purpose of serving as a ferry on the Arkansas River. According to the *Arkansas Gazette*, the ferry, one of the strongest built boats on the western waters, had sufficient room for two of the largest wagons and teams, three or four smaller carriages, 20 or 30 head of horses or cattle, with sufficient other room for more than 200 passengers.

First Theatre for Professionals (1839)

The Little Rock Theatre opened January 22, 1839, with the performance of "Charles the Second" and "Young Widow." According to the *Arkansas Gazette* the following day, "the new theatre, under the management of Mr. Walters, opened...with a respectable audience. We are somewhat surprised that so few of our country friends visit the theatre. The nights are now moonlit and pleasant; the performances close at an early hour, and a ride of six or eight miles on a brisk pony would not be unpleasant, particularly if there were a lot of lively girls in the company."

First Public Library (1843)

Established in Little Rock by *Arkansas Gazette* publisher William E. Woodruff. It was not a free library, but the books were intended for circulation among those willing to pay a small annual fee. Each book carried the following label: *Little Rock Circulating Library. Established by William E. Woodruff in the year 1843. Please read and return in two weeks. Price $2 per year.* The library contained histories(ancient and modern), standard novels, travel books, biography, scientific works and poetry. Not much in the way of "light reading."

First Railroad Company (1853)

The Arkansas Central Railroad Company, incorporated by an act of the General Assembly which was approved January 10, 1853, was formed for the purpose of building a railroad from Memphis to Little Rock.

First Geological Survey (1857)

First survey of the state was made by Dr. David Dale Owen in 1857-58. A report of this survey or "reconnaissance" as it was called, was published at Little Rock in 1858.

First Cotton Factory (1857)

A factory for the production of cotton and woolen goods was established in 1857 at Royston, Pike County, by the Arkansas Manufacturing Company. The principal promoters of the enterprise were Henry Merrill, a Georgian, and John Matlock of Camden. The factory turned out yarn and thread until 1863, when it was removed to Texas by order of the Confederate government. After the Civil War, the factory was brought back to Royston.

First Trains To and From Little Rock (1862)

The Memphis and Little Rock Railroad Company announced February 20, 1862, that on and from that day the company would run a train daily both ways between Little Rock and DeVall's Bluff.

First Civil War Engagement (1862)

On March 7, the Battle of Elkhorn, or Pea Ridge, was fought.

First Street Car Company (1870)

Incorporated at Little Rock, June 17, 1870, the first "mule car" appeared in Little Rock in 1876.

First Weather Bureau Station (1879)

July 1, 1879, the U.S. Weather Bureau opened at Little Rock the first station in the state for observing and recording weather conditions.

First Telephone (1879)

Western Union Telegraph Company installed telephone service at Little Rock in 1879. The Little Rock Exchange, put into service November 1879, appears to be the third oldest exchange in the U.S.

Something to phone home about!

In 1994, 56,000 Southwestern Bell telephone directories were collected and recycled in Central Arkansas. This saved 426 cubic yards of landfill space. It is the equivalent to almost 2,200 mature trees. About 20% of the 1995 directories were made of recycled materials. Other uses for the old directories included processing them into pulp for making roofing shingles. Contact Southwestern Bell for the recycling spot nearest you when the new phone books land on your doorstep.

First Municipal Waterworks (1884)

A waterworks company was organized at Little Rock in 1884 and a standpipe was erected near the foot of Cross Street. Water was turned on May 4, 1888.

First Electric Lights (1888)

Installed in Little Rock in September 1888, by the end of the year there were 70 street lights in operation.

First Pearls Discovered (1897)

Dr. J.H. Meyers discovered pearls in mussel shells along the Black River launching a booming pearl-button industry on the White and Black rivers that lasted until the late 1920s.

First Woman to Graduate from the University of Arkansas Medical School (1896)

Bee A. Dillard.

First Diamonds Discovered (1906)

August 1, 1906, diamonds were discovered in Pike County near the mouth of Prairie Creek by farmer John M. Huddleston.

First Free Public Library (1908)

Located in Fort Smith in a building donated by steel manufacturer Andrew Carnegie.

First Discovery of Oil (1920)

Oil first discovered in the state at the Hunter Well near Stephens on July 17, 1920.

First Radio Station (1921)

WOK in Pine Bluff began broadcasting.

First Concrete Automobile Bridge Across the Arkansas River (1923)

Broadway Bridge was completed March 14, 1923, connecting Little Rock and North Little Rock.

First Arkansas State Park (1923)

Petit Jean State Park was created. It is located between the Ouachita and Ozark mountains near Morrilton.

First Woman Elected in Own Right to U. S. Senate (1932)

Hattie W. Caraway was elected to the Congress November 9, 1932, after previously being appointed to fill out her husband's term in office after his death in 1931. In 1944 she lost to J. William Fulbright. Her career was marked by firsts: first woman to preside over the Senate, first woman to chair a Senate committee, first woman senior senator.

First Arkansas Annual Livestock Show (1938)

September 1938, the show was held at a temporary showgrounds in North Little Rock.

First TV Station (1953)

KRTV in Little Rock.

First Governor to Serve Six Terms

Orval E. Faubus was the first and only governor in Arkansas history to be elected to six consecutive terms in office. He served from 1955-1967.

First Arkansas Woman Crowned Miss America (1964)

Donna Axum from El Dorado.

First Republican Governor Since Reconstruction (1966)

Winthrop Rockefeller.

First Woman Mayor Elected in a First-Class City (1974)

Mrs. Joyce Ferguson took office January 1, 1975, as the first woman mayor of West Memphis.

First Governor Elected to Second Non-Consecutive Term

Democrat Bill Clinton served as governor from 1979-1981. He lost to Republican Frank White in 1980. Clinton ran against White a second time in 1982 and won his second term in office.

First Arkansan Elected President of the United States

William Jefferson "Bill" Clinton was elected President of the United States in November 1992. Tennesseean Al Gore was his running mate and subsequent vice-president.

First Scenic Byway (1993)

Arkansas Highway 7 from Arkadelphia to Harrison was designated by the state Highway Commission as a scenic byway on November 18, 1993. The stretch runs from the northern city limits of Harrison near U.S. 65 to the Ouachita River in Arkadelphia which is about 194 miles.

First State to Designate All Shopping Malls Smoke-Free (1994)

First Black Woman on the Arkansas Supreme Court (1995)

Andrée Layton Roaf was appointed by Governor Jim Guy Tucker to replace retiring Justice Steele Hays on January 17.

TAKING THE CLOTHES
OFF THEIR BACKS

Two rare hand-painted animal skins, given to French colonists in the 18th century by the Quapaw, returned to Arkansas in January 1995 after 200 years in French museums. The unique buffalo and deer skins were loaned to the Territorial Restoration through May 1995, from the Musee de l'Homme in Paris (France, not Arkansas). The exhibit was entitled "Robes of Splendor: symbols of Quapaw Culture and the Grand Alliance with Colonial France." The robes were made between 1730 and 1760 and given to the French colonists before 1789.

The "Three Villages Robe" is the only colonial-era representation of Arkansas Post anywhere. Arkansas Post was the first French settlement in Arkansas and the territory's first capital. The sketches on the hide appear to be replicas of homes at Arkansas Post and the words "ACKANSAS," "OUZOVTOVOVI," "TOVARIMON" and "OVOAPPA." The first word is a reference to the Arkansas or Quapaw tribe. The other words are names of Quapaw villages. The second robe in the exhibit is the "Buffalo Dancers Robe" depicting a traditional plains Indian ceremony in which the dancers wear buffalo heads to honor the great beast. A third robe was stolen while on display in France, May 1982. The robes represent the only document we have from the colonial era that was produced by the Indians. All other information we have about their culture is filtered through the writings of Europeans. Like most Indians, the Quapaw left no written history. Their history was passed on by storytelling. The skins' Arkansas roots have only been known for about ten years. The Quapaw hides were mistakenly identified as originating with the Illinois Indians.

Squirrels in the family tree?

If you'd like to trace your ancestry, here are some places to start. If your forefathers and foremothers were rooted in Arkansas, the state History Commission houses old census rolls and other records from all over the state. If your relatives came from elsewhere, the Family History Center at the Little Rock headquarters of the Church of Jesus Christ of Latter-Day Saints may be able to help with their microfilmed records. The Mormon Church has incredible archives in Utah and if they don't have what you need locally, they can order it from Salt Lake. (You need not be Mormon to use the facilities.) You can trace your ancestors all the way back to the old country. There is also a local genealogy society that meets once a month at the Laman Library in North Little Rock. It's called The Heritage Seekers (501) 666-9211.

NATIONAL HISTORIC LANDMARKS

Arkansas has nearly 2,000 properties on the National Register of Historic Places, and due to the desire to preserve and protect the physical remnants of our state's past, that list continues to grow. But only 12 of those notable properties have landmark status. The National Historic Landmark status is reserved for properties important in American history, as well as Arkansas history. Nominations go to the U.S. Secretary of the Interior who makes the final decision. The following is a list of Arkansas' National Historic Landmarks, their location and date of admission:

- **Arkansas Post** Desha County, October 9, 1960.
- **Bathhouse Row** Hot Springs, Garland County. May 28, 1987.
- **Central High School** Little Rock, Pulaski County. May 20, 1982.
- **Fort Smith National Historic Site** Fort Smith, Sebastian County. December 19, 1960.
- **Louisiana Purchase Marker Initial Survey Point** Junction of Lee, Phillips & Monroe counties. April 19, 1993.
- **Menard-Hodges Mounds** Nady vicinity, Arkansas County. April 11, 1989.
- **Nodena Site** Wilson vicinity, Mississippi County. July 19, 1964.
- **Parkin Indian Mound** Parkin, Cross County. July 19, 1964.
- **Rohwer Relocation Center Memorial Cemetery** Rohwer vicinity, Desha County. July 6,1992.
- **Toltec Mounds** Scott vicinity, Lonoke County. June 2, 1978.
- **Camden Expedition Sites** Camden, Ouachita County. April 1994
- **Joe T. Robinson House** Little Rock, Pulaski County. 1995

SOURCE: Arkansas Historic Preservation Program

Hernando de Soto: Guest From Hell

Hernando de Soto landed on Florida's Gulf Coast in 1539. His fleet of nine ships carried supplies, pigs, horses and 600 conquistadors accompanied by tailors, trumpeters, shoemakers, servants, slaves, notaries, friars, a couple of women and war dogs trained to disembowel human beings. King Charles V of Spain who dispatched this crew, made it very clear that he wanted De Soto to pacify La Florida, the southeastern United States, without bloodshed, without "death and robbery of the Indians." De Soto and his men had other ideas. They wanted the sort of treasure the Spanish conquerors had found in Central and South America and they were determined to get it by any means necessary. So began a trail of destruction from the Gulf to the mouth of the Mississippi by one of America's most celebrated explorers.

De Soto employed a variety of techniques to subdue the Indians he encountered along his route. Enslavement was frequently used. The Spaniards carried iron collars and chains for shackling Indians who were used as burden bearers. The war dogs – mastiffs, wolfhounds and greyhounds – were great for intimidation purposes. Guides who misled the expedition were thrown to the dogs to be gutted as an example to the others. While many Indians met their deaths by the Spanish weapons, many others appear to have perished in epidemics of new diseases introduced into North America by the invaders – small pox, whooping cough, influenza. By the end of the sixteenth century, the native cultures were in serious decline, many of them having disappeared altogether.

After a lifetime of searching for gold, De Soto died at the age of 42, June 1542. It is said that upon his death, his belongings were sold at auction. They consisted of two slaves, three horses, and 700 swine (probable razorback ancestors). These were to be paid for in gold – when gold should be discovered.

SOURCES: *Arkansas: Yesterday and Today*, Knoop and Grant; *Archeology*, May/June 1989

WWII: NO DAY AT THE BEACH

A shoreline on Hog Island, one of Alaska's Aleutian Islands, has been designated as "Arkansas Beach" to honor the Arkansas National Guard's 206th Artillery who defended the island's harbor against a Japanese attack in World War II. Three Arkansans lost their lives in the attack: Sgt. James Arthur Allen of West Helena, Cpl. John Falls Bowen of Altheimer, and Sgt. Cecil Kenneth Dix of Little Rock. Forty other Americans also died.

INDIANS OF ARKANSAS

Information is pretty sketchy about the earliest inhabitants of what is now Arkansas. The prehistoric period (before Europeans arrived and took notes) begins around 10,000 B.C. During those thousands of years a variety of cultures existed. Like the later Indians, they had no written language, so what we know or assume about these cultures we learned by going through their trash and exhuming bodies (also known as archeology). The following is brief survey of what the experts believe to be true about these native Arkansans.

➨ PREHISTORIC PERIOD (9500 B.C. - 1650 A.D.)

Paleo-Indian Period (9500-8500 B.C.)

These folks enter the picture following the most recent Ice Age. Small hunter-gatherer bands with plenty to eat so they don't travel much.

Dalton Period (8500-7500 B.C.)

Small band of hunters, totaling only about 300 people at one time, form base settlements from which hunters go forth and hunt. They have centers for slaughtering with distinctive Dalton points used as knives and saws.

Corner-notched Period (7500-7000 B.C.)

Little known of this period except they experimented with notching their hunting points.

Hypsithermal Archaic Period (7000-3000 B.C.)

Drought conditions in lowlands cause forests and vegetation to die out. Hunter-gatherers move to more fertile mountain areas around Ozark Mountains. Around 4500 B. C. moisture starts to return to climate. By the end of this period there may be 3,000 inhabitants in the region.

Poverty Point Period (3,000-500 B.C)

Multi-family tribes with chief replace extended-family bands. Farming probably begins. Cooking methods include earthen ovens. Large earthen ceremonial mounds.

Tchula Period (500 B.C. - 0)

Not much known about his period. Pottery appears, farming continues, trading with other peoples.

Marksville Period (0-400 A.D.)

Big burial mounds appear. Tribal chiefs become more important in the village culture. Farming important. Rituals become increasingly important and the natives trade with people from the Great Lakes to the Gulf Coast for seashells and precious metals so their ceremonies won't be tacky.

Baytown Period (400-700 A.D.)

Not much going on here. Pottery boring. Lacks creative sparkle.

Early Mississippian Period (700-1000 A.D.)

Things start clicking during this period. Stable, prosperous time perhaps connected to the introduction of corn to the culture. Tribes give way to multi-village chiefdoms centered around fortified villages built near lakes. Single-family farms lie outside the forts where they return for rituals, and social functions. Bow and arrow appears changing hunting and warfare. Shell-tempering creates stronger, lighter pots and better more varied cooking methods. The Toltec mounds southeast of Arkansas are from this period. There were originally 19 temple mounds at this site.

Middle Mississippian Period (1000-1350 A.D.)

Villages are increasingly important as centers for ceremonies, social and civic activities. Plenty of food allows leisure time and artisans create beautiful pottery. Population hard to guess because the sites were continuously inhabited for long periods. Individual chiefdoms may have consisted of thousands of people. For some unknown reason, at the end of this period larger villages are burned and abandoned.

Late Mississippian Period (1350-1650 A.D.)

Population up to 50,000. Population shift continues with people from far-flung villages moving into walled cities. This society was destroyed by De Soto and his merry men who brought European diseases over in 1541. The Quapaw may be a remnant of this culture.

➤➤ THE HISTORIC PERIOD (1700-1835)

While the De Soto expedition provided a brief glimpse of Indian life in Arkansas, the historic records concerning Arkansas Indians cannot really be said to begin until after the expedition of French explorers Joliet and Marquette who in 1673 traveled down the Mississippi River to the mouth of the Arkansas River before turning north. During the nearly 150 years between De Soto and Marquette, there evidently had been some drastic changes among the Indians. The De Soto chronicles specifically state that in northeast Arkansas from one village the smoke could be seen rising from many others, and throughout the Spaniards' journey in Arkansas there was seemingly almost constant contact with Indian villages and groups. The three tribes they would have met with were the Quapaw, Caddoes and Osage. Yet in 1673 Joliet and Marquette found only one or two villages along the Mississippi River in eastern Arkansas. The first large villages they encountered were of Indians we have come to know as the Quapaw (the downstream people for whom Arkansas is named) located near the mouth of the Arkansas River.

The Quapaw

In the 1500s, the Quapaw dominated an area which included most of the lowlands of northeastern Arkansas, but by the late 1600s they seem to have been along the Arkansas River from the mouth possibly upstream as far as Russellville. By 1800 the Quapaw were living in four villages located on both the north and south banks of the river, all in the immediate vicinity of Arkansas Post. Perhaps the reduction in territory resulted from raids by the Chickasaw who lived across the Mississippi River just to the east and/or the Osage to the north. It's all speculative. The Quapaw are described as being well-mannered, liberal and "of a gay humor." Another early source describes them as "the tallest and best shaped of all the savages on the continent." We don't know much about their clothes. Apparently they wore tanned skins as well as grass and woven fabrics. Often they painted their bodies with designs sometimes covering the entire body. They grew corn, beans and squash and also hunted and fished. Although much of the pottery of the Quapaw closely resembled that made in northeastern Arkansas earlier, including similar incised decorations and human and animal effigies, new shapes did appear and there was greater use of red and white paint on vessels, a decorative technique not found among the Caddo. The Quapaw apparently liked Caddo pottery, however, for many Caddo vessels are found on Quapaw sites.

They lived in long bark-covered rectangular houses with domed roofs. Several families lived together, each family having its own area and fireplace within the house. The Quapaw spoke a Siouan language closely related to that of the Omaha, Kansa, Ponca and Osage tribes

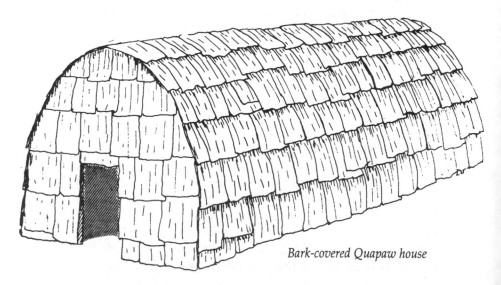

Bark-covered Quapaw house

who lived up the Missouri River to the north and west. The Quapaw population continued to decline, primarily due to the introduction of small pox and other diseases since they had no immunity to them. By the 1750s there were probably only about 1,500 Quapaw. In 1805 a U.S. government factory, as the official government Indian trading posts were called, was established at Arkansas Post specifically to trade with the Quapaw. The post closed in 1810. In 1818, the Quapaw sold all their land to the U.S. except for a small reservation located south of the Arkansas River in the area of Pine Bluff. In 1824 because of continued government pressure they sold the reservation and were moved to the Red River to join the Caddo. The move was miserable and they had to take whatever land the Caddo would give them, which, of course, was the land the Caddo least wanted. The Quapaw ended up with swampy land that flooded constantly. Consequently, the Quapaw gradually wandered back to their old homeplace, living in squalor along the riverbanks, hoping not to be discovered and sent back. Finally in 1833, they were assigned a new reservation by the U.S. government in what is now northeast Oklahoma and southeast Kansas. By the time they were forced out of Arkansas they numbered around 500.

An Osage warrior

The Osage

The Osage lived in large villages in southern Missouri and used northern Arkansas primarily as a hunting territory. No Osage villages or campsites have been identified in Arkansas. The Osage were active and aggressive, constantly raiding groups adjacent to them, including both the Quapaw and the Caddo. On several occasions the Caddo threatened the European settlement at Arkansas Post although they never actually attacked it. They did attack the Quapaw settlement nearby and in return were raided by the Quapaw. The Osage men wore breechclouts, leggings and moccasins of tanned skins. They later adopted skin shirts. The women wore skirts and dresses of skin. The clothing of both were decorated with fringe and shell. They were farmers, growing corn, beans and squash, but hunting and warfare were also favorite pastimes. Their villages consisted of houses grouped by family. The houses themselves were rectangular and constructed of saplings covered with brush, mats or hides. Several families occupied one house. In 1808, shortly after the United States obtained Arkansas through the Louisiana Purchase, the Osage sold all their land in Arkansas to the government and moved to Indian Territory in Oklahoma.

The Caddo

By the arrival of the Europeans, there were three separate but closely related Caddo Confederations, each made up of several tribes. Around 1700, there were about 8,000 Caddo in all three confederations. By 1800, their population had been reduced to 1,500. The first Europeans were horrified by their custom of tattooing and painting much of their bodies. They were expert tanners and their clothing was mostly of tanned deerskin, often fringed with small white seeds. The men wore breechclouts in the summer, adding mocca-

sins, leggings and skin shirts in the winter. The women wore skirts of woven grass or sometimes soft cloth woven from nettles or made from mulberry bark. They were excellent farmers often raising two crops of corn a year. They held over a supply of seeds for two years to guard against crop failures. They also raised five or six varieties of beans.

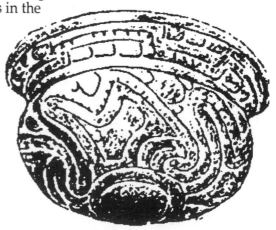

Both men and women worked the gardens. The men hunted deer, buffalo and small game. House-building like farming was a community activity. Long posts were set in the ground in a circle and tied together at the top. To this frame was applied a thick grass cover. Their houses varied considerably in size, depending upon the number of occupants and their social position.

There seems to have been little permanent contact between the early Europeans and the Caddo in Arkansas, although in the middle of the 1700s there was a small French settlement among them, and in 1818 the U.S. government established

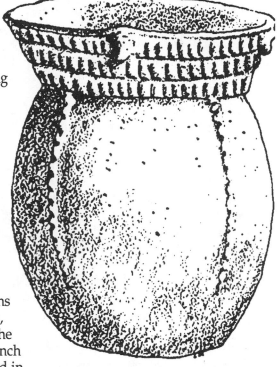

Typical late Caddo vessel

a trading post on the Sulphur River which operated until 1822. In 1835 the Caddo sold all their land in Arkansas to the government and moved to Texas. They were the last group of Indians to leave the state. After a few years in Texas, they were moved again to the reservation in Oklahoma.

The Cherokee and Others

A small number of Indians from various other tribes lived in Arkansas during the late 1700s and very early 1800s. These were members of tribes whose homeland was east of the Mississippi River, but who had been displaced and pushed west by the continued pressure of European and American settlers. These groups lived mostly in northeastern Arkansas and along the Arkansas River. They were never numerous nor did any of them stay very long, aside from the Cherokee. For a brief time they were numerous here. Because of pressure from American settlers in their homeland in Tennessee, Alabama and Georgia, a considerable number of Cherokee moved west in the early 1800s, living first along the St. Francis River in northeast Arkansas. Later they moved to the area of the Arkansas River around Russellville and up the White

River to around Harrison. The Cherokee adapted quickly to European customs and tools. Between 1817 and 1828, a Cherokee reservation was established in northwest Arkansas directly across from the Osage in Oklahoma. They didn't get along and the first Fort Smith was established to prevent open warfare between the two groups. Dwight Mission was established by Cephas Washburn among the Cherokee near Russellville and was active between 1820 and 1828. The Mission was then bought by the government and the Cherokee removed to Oklahoma.

In the late 1820s and 1830s several other groups of southeastern Indians passed through Arkansas on their way to Indian Territory. The largest and best-known of these "migrations" was that made by another group of Cherokee. By 1835, the Cherokee who had remained in Tennessee, Alabama and Georgia had adopted Christian religion and education, European style clothes and houses and a form of government patterned after that of the whites. In 1836 a few of these Cherokee signed a treaty with the U.S. government giving up all Cherokee land east of the Mississippi River. Most Cherokee protested the treaty as illegal contending that the signers had no legal authority to represent the entire Cherokee Nation. They protested to no avail and in the harsh winter of 1838-39 with little help from the government, 18,000 Cherokee were forced from a settled community life to a harsh frontier one. It is estimated that more than 4,000 died on their way to the reservation and this horrific journey became known as the "Trail of Tears."

SOURCES: *Archeology of the Central Mississippi Valley* by Dan & Phyllis Morse; *Indians of Arkansas* by Charles R. McGimsey III, Arkansas Archeological Survey; *"The Quapaws: Native Arkansans"* by Bob Lancaster, *Arkansas Times*, June 1984.

DID YOU KNOW?

Telltale Tails

All Quapaw women had long hair which was worn to distinguish married from unmarried women. Unmarried women parted their hair down the middle and fastened it up in a knot behind each ear. The married women parted their hair in the middle and braided it into two pigtails which hung loose behind each ear.

ARKANSAS GOVERNMENT

As predictable as a hog on ice!

During *the first-ever meeting of the Arkansas Legislature in 1837, the speaker of the house plunged a bowie knife into the chest of a colleague to settle a debate over a piece of legislation. In the trial that followed, the killer hired a mob to agitate on his behalf outside the courtroom and even took the judge to dinner a few times. He was found guilty of "excusable homicide" and went free. It would be thickheaded, of course, to consider this incident typical of Arkansas politics; but it may have set the tone. Traditionally, our state's politics have been a wild and woolly business.*

VOTE
FOR
"BUBBA"

For years our office-holders generally fell into two camps: flamboyant fire-breathers or tight-faced, no-nonsense pols. Today that's mostly all changed, with the cornpone giving way to the blow dryer. A successful candidate now sports an entourage of media consultants, image advisors and spin doctors. Certainly since the election of Bill Clinton to the presidency in 1992, our state's government has been under the microscope like no other. (Consequently, it's a lot harder to stab a politician and get away with it than it was in the good ol' days.)

Predicting Arkansas elections is like predicting the direction a hog on ice will take. The only thing for certain is that Arkansas goes its own way. Perhaps the best illustration of the paradoxical nature of Arkansas politics can be found in the general election of 1968. The voters cast their ballots for (1) a moderate Republican, Winthrop Rockefeller, for governor, (2) a liberal Democrat, J. William Fulbright, for senator, and (3) a reactionary American Party candidate, George Wallace, for president. What's a pollster supposed to make of that?

TO VOTE:

- You must be at least 18 years of age and a U.S. citizen.
- You must register in person at the county clerk's office or other specified registration locations like libraries, etc. (Call the clerk's office and ask for details). You must be registered 20 days prior to casting a vote.
- You must re-register if you fail to vote in four successive years, change your name or change your legal residence outside of the county.
- You may vote by absentee ballot by requesting a ballot (in person or in writing) from the county clerk's office one to 60 days before election day.

STATEHOOD

Arkansas was admitted to the Union as the 25th state on June 15, 1836.

CONSTITUTION

Adopted 1874; amendments may be passed by majority vote in each house or by initiative of the people; ratified by majority voting on it in an election.

CAPITALS

Arkansas has had several capitals. In 1819, the territorial capital was located at Arkansas Post. In 1821, the capital was moved to Little Rock, but there was no adequate Capitol building. The Legislature met in cabins, rented rooms and churches. In 1833 construction began on what is now the Old State House. It was here the first state Legislature met in 1836, though the building was still incomplete. It served as the state Capitol until 1911. Today it houses the Arkansas Museum of History and Archives. It was in front of this landmark that Bill Clinton held a press conference to announce his candidacy for president and where he spoke to the nation the night he claimed victory. From 1863 to 1865, Washington was the Confederate capital of the state. After the war, the seat of government resumed in Little Rock. The current Capitol has been in use since 1915 and is a scaled down replica of the U.S. Capitol.

REPRESENTATION IN U. S. CONGRESS

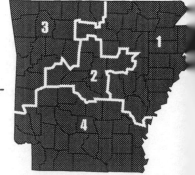

Senate: two members (six-year terms)

House of Representatives: four members (two-year terms). The state is divided into four congressional districts with one representative elected from each district. The districts are redrawn every ten years following the census. Arkansas has six electoral votes.

STATE GENERAL ASSEMBLY

Meets on odd-numbered years in Little Rock from January to March, and sometimes longer. The Assembly is comprised of 135 elected members: **Senate:** 35 members (four-year terms), **House** 100 members (two-year terms).

EXECUTIVE OFFICERS

These seven elected officers, also known as constitutional officers, serve four-year terms:

Governor   State Treasurer

Lieutenant Governor   State Auditor

Secretary of State   Commissioner of State Lands

Attorney General

JUDICIARY

All judges and justices are elected. Supreme court: seven justices (eight-year term). Court of civil appeals: six judges (eight-year term). Chancery judges (six-year term); chancery and circuit chancery judges (four-year terms).

June 1, 1982, the Arkansas Supreme Court struck down the archaic blue laws thereby allowing the retail sale of everything but alcoholic beverages on Sunday.

DRIVER'S ED, ANYONE?

During 1993-94, there were 632 accidents involving state-owned vehicles totally $915,340 in damages. A total of 6,747 vehicles are owned by the state. Four agencies: the Arkansas Highway and Transportation Department, Arkansas State Police, U of A System and Game and Fish Commission account for almost 60% of these vehicles and 74% of the accidents.

SOURCE: *Department of Finance and Administration*

Arkansas is the only state in the Union in which the theory of evolution was outlawed by a vote of the people. It happened in 1927 when Representative A. L. Rottenberry, distressed that the Senate had killed his anti-evolution bill, took the issue to the public. The vote: 108,991 for the anti-evolution bill; 63,406 against. In 1968 the U.S. Supreme Court ruled the law unconstitutional. But Arkansas politicians never let a bad idea die. In 1981 the state Legislature passed the so-called "creation science" act which was signed into law by Republican governor Frank White. The law mandated that biblical precepts on creation should be taught in public classrooms along with Darwin's theory of evolution. The law was later ruled unconstitutional by a federal judge, but not before this controversial law focused unwelcome national and international attention to the state and gave credence to those who saw this action as proof that Arkansas was terminally backward.

ARKANSAS GOVERNORS

The early politics of Arkansas was pretty murky since land in the New World was still being swapped back and forth among the French and Spanish. Then the United States played around with dividing up land and trying to decide which chunk of land went in which jurisdiction. They pretty much had to figure it all out as they went along. There were no guidelines for this sort of thing. We were a brand new country. Here's a run-down on what was going on before Arkansas became a state. The explorer La Salle claimed what is now Arkansas for France in 1682. Then in 1762, Louisiana (which included us) was ceded to Spain by the Treaty of Fontainebleau. Then in 1800, Spain ceded Louisiana back to France in a secret treaty. In 1803 the United States purchased the Province of Louisiana (which included us) and Arkansas became part of the territory of the United States. In 1806, the Territorial Legislature of Louisiana set off the southern part of the New Madrid District as the "District of Arkansas." In 1812, the Missouri Territory (which included Arkansas) was created by Congress. In 1819 Congress created the Territory of Arkansas and in 1821 we set up our own territorial capital. In 1836 Arkansas became a state and started electing our own officials.

Under French Rule

Marquis de Sanvolle 1699-1701
Bienville 1701-1712
Lamothe Cadillac 1712-1716
De L'Epinay 1717-1718
Bienville 1718-1724
Boisbrant (ad interim) 1724-1726
Perier 1726-1734
Bienville 1734-1743
Marquis de Vaureuil 1743-1753
Baron de Kelerec 1753-1763
D'Abbadie 1763-1765

M. Aubry 1765-1766

Under Spanish Rule

Antonia de Ulloa 1767-1768
Alexander O'Reilly 1769-1770
Luis de Unzaga 1770-1777
Bernardo de Galvez 1777-1784
Estevan Miro 1784-1791
Francisco de Luis Horto,
  Baron of Carondelet 1791-1797
Gayoso de Lemos 1797-1799
Sebastian de Caso
  Calvoy O'Farrell 1799-1801
Juan Manual de Salsedo 1801-1803

Louisiana Territory

C.C. Claiborne 1803

District of Upper Louisiana

General William Henry Harrison 1804

Territory of Louisiana

General James Wilkerson 1805-1806
Merriweather Lewis 1807-1808
Benjamin A. Howard 1809-1812

Territory of Missouri

Benjamin A. Howard 1812-1813
Captain William Clark 1813-1819

Governors appointed by the President of the United States during Arkansas' territorial days.

James Miller 1819-1825
George Izard 1825-1829
John Pope 1829-1835
William Fulton 1835-1836

Governors elected after Arkansas became a state in 1836 (We include only those governors who have been elected to this office, although throughout history there have been many interim governors or lieutenant governors who have served.)

James S. Conway 1836-1840	Carl E. Bailey 1937-1941
Archibald Yell 1840-1844	Homer M Adkins 1941-1945
Thomas S. Drew 1844-1849	Ben T. Laney 1945-1949
John S. Roane 1849-1852	Sid McMath 1949-1953
Elias N. Conway 1852-1860	Francis Cherry 1953-1955
Henry M. Rector 1860-1862	Orval E. Faubus 1955-1967
Harris Flanagin 1862-1864	Winthrop Rockefeller 1967-1971
Isaac Murphy 1864-1868	Dale Leon Bumpers 1971-1975
Powell Clayton 1868-1871	David H. Pryor 1975-1979
Elisha Baxter 1873-1874	Bill Clinton 1979-1981
Augustus H. Garland 1874-1877	Frank White 1981-1983
William R. Miller 1877-1881	Bill Clinton 1983-1992
Thomas J. Churchill 1881-1883	Jim Guy Tucker 1992-

SOURCE: *Historical Report of the Secretary of State*

James H. Berry 1883-1885

Simon P. Hughes 1885-1889

James P. Eagle 1889-1893

William M. Fishback 1893-1895

James P. Clarke 1895-1897

Dan W. Jones 1897-1901

Jeff Davis 1901-1907

John S. Little 1907-1909

George W. Donaghey 1909-1913

Joseph T. Robinson 1913

(Jan - Mar., then joined Senate)

George W. Hays 1913-1917

Charles H. Brough 1917-1921

Thomas C. McRae 1921-1925

Tom J. Terral 1925-1927

John E. Martineau 1927-1928

Harvey Parnell 1928-1933

J.M. Futrell 1933-1937

"I'm a hard-shell Baptist in religion. I believe in foot-washing, saving your seed potatoes and paying your honest debts."

Governor Jeff Davis (1901-1907)

• • • • • • • • • • • • • • • • • • • •

GOVERNOR'S MANSION

Arkansas' first official Governor's Mansion was completed in January 1950 after a two-year construction period. The Mansion is Georgian Colonial in style and is constructed of age-mellowed oversized brick from old state properties. Located at Center and West 18th Streets in Little Rock, the two-story home occupies six and a half acres. The main building is 140 feet by 60 feet and the overall width of all buildings, including guest houses flanking the Mansion on each side, is 254 feet. The Mansion was formerly occupied by the Arkansas School for the Blind.

THE OLD STATE HOUSE

Located at 300 West Markham Avenue in Little Rock, this was Arkansas' first state Capitol. The building now houses the Arkansas Museum of History and Archives. It is recognized architecturally as one of the most beautiful antebellum structures in the South. Construction was begun in 1833 and completed about ten years later at a cost of $125,000. In 1836, while still incomplete, the building was used as the meeting place of the first state Legislature and for the inauguration of Arkansas' first gover-

nor, James S. Conway. The building and property are owned and maintained by the state. By 1951 legislative action, the former designation of War Memorial building was officially changed to The Old State House.

STATE CAPITOL

Construction of the Capitol building in Little Rock was started on November 27, 1900, and was finished in 1915. The greater part of the stone used in the construction is commonly known as Batesville marble, being quarried in Batesville, Arkansas. The Legislature of 1911 was the first to sit in the new building, then only partially completed. The Arkansas state Capitol is a scaled down replica of the U.S. Capitol in Washington, D.C.

COUNTIES

Arkansas is divided into 75 counties each with a county seat to administer county business. Each county is governed by a county judge and quorum court composed of justices of the peace. All are elected and serve two-year terms. Of the 75 counties, 60 are named for individuals. The names for the other 15 counties come from topography, geography, nature or Indian tribes. Arkansas County is the oldest, established in 1813. Cleburne is the youngest, created in 1883. Union County is the largest in area with 1,052 square miles; White is second largest with 1,042. Sebastian County is the smallest in area with only 536 square miles. Pulaski County has the largest population; Calhoun has the fewest residents. The following is a list of counties and their seats.

County	Seat
Arkansas	Dewitt and Stuttgart
Ashley	Hamburg
Baxter	Mountain Home
Benton	Bentonville
Boone	Harrison
Bradley	Warren
Calhoun	Hampton
Carroll	Eureka Springs
Chicot	Lake Village
Clark	Arkadelphia
Clay	Corning and Piggott
Cleburne	Heber Springs
Cleveland	Rison
Columbia	Magnolia
Conway	Morrilton
Craighead	Jonesboro
Crawford	Van Buren
Crittenden	Marion
Cross	Wynne

Dallas	Fordyce	Jackson	Newport
Desha	Arkansas City	Jefferson	Pine Bluff
Drew	Monticello	Johnson	Clarksville
Faulkner	Conway	Lafayette	Lewisville
Franklin	Ozark	Lawrence	Walnut Ridge
Fulton	Salem	Lee	Marianna
Garland	Hot Springs	Lincoln	Star City
Grant	Sheridan	Little River	Ashdown
Greene	Paragould	Logan	Booneville
Hempstead	Hope	Lonoke	Lonoke
Hot Spring	Malvern	Madison	Huntsville
Howard	Nashville	Marion	Yellville
Independence	Batesville	Miller	Texarkana
Izard	Melbourne	Mississippi	Blytheville and Osceola

Sevier	De Queen	Van Buren	Clinton
Sharp	Ash Flat	Washington	Fayetteville
St. Francis	Forest City	White	Searcy
Stone	Mountain View	Woodruff	Augusta
Union	El Dorado	Yell	Danville and Dardanelle

A Woman's Place

Arkansas has sent a total of four women to serve in Congress – all Democrats, and all in this century. They are:

• **Effiegene Locke Wingo** Wingo was appointed in 1930 to fill out the term of her late husband, Rep. Otis Wingo. She served from 1930 to 1931. She died in 1962 and is buried in Washington.

• **Pearl Peden Oldfield** Oldfield also succeeded her dead husband, Rep. William Oldfield, who died in 1928. She served until 1931, attending every session.

• **Hattie Caraway** In 1932 Caraway became the first woman ever elected to the U. S. Senate. She was first appointed to serve out the term of her late husband, Thaddeus H. Caraway upon his death in 1931, but was elected in her own right the following year, and re-elected in 1938. She served until 1945.

• **Blanche Lincoln** A native of Helena, she won election in 1992 as the unmarried Blanche Lambert, the first woman elected to Congress from Arkansas without first being appointed to serve out a husband's term. Married in July 1993, she continued to serve under her maiden name until after her November re-election. When her colleagues in the House seemed to be in a tizzy over how she should be addressed, she instructed them to call her "Mrs. Lincoln," to which several committee colleagues, all male, responded with a round of applause. Pregnant with twins, Mrs. Lincoln chose not to seek re-election in 1996.

ARKANSAS BUSINESS

Whole log of movin' and shakin' goin' on!

Some of the business world's best-known movers and shakers first started moving and shaking right here in Arkansas. Among the business empires our state has spawned are Sam Walton's Wal-Mart, William Dillard's Dillard Department Stores, Frank Hickingbotham's TCBY, Patti Upton's Aromatique and J. B. Hunt's J. B.Hunt Transport. Agriculture, however, is still number one in Arkansas, with almost half of the state's 33,245,000 acres in farmland. We produce practically every crop grown in the temperate zone, with the exception of citrus fruit, and we lead the nation in the production of rice and broilers. But over the past few decades, Arkansas has successfully forged a more favorable balance of agriculture and industry. Today, we produce everything from greeting cards to refrigerators. Tourism is another major growth industry, bringing in close to $3 billion in 1994 (a native son in the White House hasn't hurt). Here's the bottom line on Arkansas bidness.

ARKANSAS' FORTUNE 500 FIRMS

Rank	Company	Headquarters	1994 Sales (in billions)
#4	**Wal-Mart**	Bentonville	$83.412
#206	**Dillard's**	Little Rock	$5.729
#225	**Tyson Foods**	Springdale	$5.110
#377	**Beverly Enterprises**	Fort Smith	$2.984
#384	**Alltel**	Little Rock	$2.962

MANUFACTURING FIRMS HEADQUARTERED IN ARKANSAS

Allen Canning Company
American Transportation Corporation
Baldor Electric Company
Crain Industries
George's Inc.
Hudson Foods
Munro and Company

OK Industries
Peterson Farms, Inc.
Petit Jean Poultry, Inc.
Riceland Foods
Riverside Furniture Corporation
Simmons Foods, Inc.
Tyson Foods

NON-MANUFACTURING FIRMS WITH CORPORATE HEADQUARTERS IN ARKANSAS

Acxiom Corporation
Affiliated Food Stores Southwest
Alltel Information Systems
Arkansas Best Corporation
Arkansas Blue Cross & Blue Shield
Arkansas Department of Human Services
Arkansas Freightways Corporation
Arkansas Highway & Transportation Dept.
Beverly Enterprises, Inc.
Cannon Express
Dillard Department Stores, Inc.
Donrey Media Group
Fairfield Communities
First Commercial Corporation
Harp's Food Stores
J. B. Hunt Transport, Inc.
Murphy Oil Corporation
Southland Racing Corporation
Southwestern Energy Company, Inc.
Stephens Group, Inc.
TCBY Enterprises
Wal-Mart Stores, Inc.

The 40-story TCBY Tower in downtown Little Rock is the tallest building in the state.

TOP 10 MANUFACTURING EMPLOYERS

Here are the top 10 manufacturing employers in Arkansas, what they manufacture and the number of jobs they provide.

1. TYSON FOODS, INC. 18,562
   Poultry processing, feeds and related products, tortillas, corn chips, taco shells, pre-plated frozen entrees and prepared foods.

2. CONAGRA, INC. 5,318
   Poultry processing and feeds, frozen dinners and specialties.

3. EMERSON ELECTRIC COMPANY 4,967
   Fractional horsepower motors, power tools, electronic air cleaners, transformers, circular saws, eddy current clutch drives, pilot and main burners, thermostats, solenoid valves.

4. GEORGIA-PACIFIC CORPORATION 4,791
   Paper, pulp, bleached food board, multiwall paper sacks, plywood, hardboard, fiberboard, lumber, resin, plastics for wood industry and urea for fertilizer use.

5. WHIRLPOOL CORPORATION 3,400
   Products: Refrigerators

6. INTERNATIONAL PAPER COMPANY 3,167
   Paper and paper products, bleached paperboard, corrugated shipping containers, polyethylene film, lumber and lumber products.

7. WHITE CONSOLIDATED INDUSTRIES 3,067
   Refrigeration equipment, shelving, check-out counters, trimmers, edgers, chain saws, blowers.

8. AMERICAN GREETINGS CORPORATION 2,664
   Greeting cards, gift wrap and accessories, picture frames.

9. OK INDUSTRIES 2,492
   Poultry products, poultry feeds, frozen entrees and side dishes.

10. MUNRO & COMPANY 2,289
   Military oxfords, men's women's and children's shoes, shoe components.

SOURCE: Arkansas Industrial Development Commission, 1994

BIG BUCKS!

Eleven of the 400 richest Americans live in Arkansas. Five of those eleven derive their wealth from Wal-Mart, which, as you can see, has been very, very good to them. Here are the home folks by rank on the list, net worth in millions, source of wealth, hometown.

#8. Alice L. Walton, $4.34 billion, inheritance (Wal-Mart), Rogers.

#9. Helen Walton, $4.34 billion, inheritance (Wal-Mart), Bentonville.

#10. Jim C. Walton, $4.34 billion, inheritance (Wal-Mart) Bentonville.

#12. S. Robson Walton, $4.34 billion, inheritance (Wal-Mart) Bentonville.

#82. Winthrop Paul Rockefeller, $1 billion, inheritance (oil) Morrilton.

#83. James Lawrence Walton, $1 billion, Wal-Mart, Bentonville.

#85. Donald John Tyson, $925 million, Tyson Foods, Springdale.

#117. Barbara Tyson, $745 million, Tyson Foods, Springdale.

#164. Jackson Thomas Stephens, $600 million, investment banking, Little Rock.

#310. Charles H. Murphy, Jr., $385 million, Murphy Oil, El Dorado.

#358. Johnnie Bryan Hunt, $335 million, J. B. Hunt Trucking, Goshen.

* Another of Sam Walton's sons, John T. Walton, of San Diego, is listed at #11 with $4.34 billion.

SOURCE: Forbes , October 1994

RAZORBACKS TO GREENBACKS

There are 166 businesses in Arkansas with the word "razorback" in the name. (This does not include businesses with the words "hog" or "pig.")

SOURCE: American Business Directory 1994

DID YOU KNOW?

WHOOPS!

Whoops!, the latex puddle of pretend barf that delights eleven-year-old boys, was invented by Ray Suggett of West Fork. While working for a plastic surgeon in Chicago, Suggett developed a number of novelty devices including "The Horrible Finger," an extremely popular swollen disfigured finger, and "The Schnoz," a large, Durante-like nose. Suggett's success helped start the Rubbercraft Corp. Over the years, Suggett thrilled the public with such novelties as "The Black Eye," "The Giant Olive," and "The Melted Ice Cream Bar," a favorite of fastidious moms everywhere. Around 1950, fake vomit was born. In 1964, Suggett left the fast track and retired in the Ozarks where he continued to freelance gag gifts.

TOP TEN FUNKY BIDNESS NAMES

1.**Hogg's Meat Market,** North Little Rock
2.**Sharp-Payne Grocery,** Damascus
3.**Arsenic & Old Lace** (bed & breakfast), Eureka Springs
4.**De Queen Bee,** De Queen's newspaper
5.**Mary's Curl Up and Dye** (hair salon), Russellville
6.**Wag-A-Bag** (convenience store), El Dorado
7.**Itch-Ta-Fish** (bait and tackle), Jacksonville
8.**Toot 'N' Moo** (convenience stores), North Little Rock
9.**Hog Wash** (laundry), Fayetteville
10.**Bone A Petit,** (canine bakery), North Little Rock

ARKANSAS' RANK AMONG STATES

Commodity	Rank	Value of Production (thousand dollars)
CROPS		
Corn for grain	32	23,760
Cotton	4	571,576
Cottonseed	4	66,928
Hay	25	133,110

Oats	24	3,003
Rice	1	477,546
Sorghum for grain	5	37,669
Soybeans	8	664,700
Wheat	16	129,536
Apples, commercial	32	1,230
Grapes	12	2,619
Peaches	14	1,960
Pecans	12	1,300
TRUCK CROPS		
Strawberries	12	325
Tomatoes	13	9,889
LIVESTOCK & POULTRY		
Cattle	16	378,408
Milk	34	104,667
Hogs	16	142,387
Broilers, commercial	1	1,820,138
Eggs	8	329,593
Farm chickens (sold)	2	16,575
Turkeys (raised)	3	224,400
Catfish	3	34,812

TOP 20 IN VALUE OF PRODUCTION

1. Broilers	$1,684,366,000
2. Soybeans	$590,813,000
3. Rice	$558,846,000
4. Cattle	$403,350,000
5. Cotton	$299,844,000
6. Eggs	$285,280,000
7. Turkeys	$205,000,000
8. Hogs	$146,951,000
9. Hay	$130,990,000
10. Wheat	114,000,000
11. Milk	$104,584,000
12. Cottonseed	$44,590,000
13. Catfish	$29,540,000
14. Corn for grain	$20,066,000
15. Chickens	$13,965,000
16. Tomatoes	$5,451,000
17. Peaches	$3,069,000
18. Grapes	$2,745,000
19. Oats	$2,380,000
20. Apples	$1,881,000

SOURCE: Arkansas Agricultural Statistics 1994 (most recent available)

BIG BIRD COMES TO ARKANSAS – AGAIN.

There are more than 300 ostrich farms in Arkansas, 31 being members of the Arkansas Ostrich Association. Ostriches are said to be easy to raise on a small amount of land and one bird can yield six pair of ostrich leather cowboy boots. The meat is comparable to lean red beef, only slightly gamy. The feathers are anti-static and can be used to clean computer parts and dust cars before paint is applied. But this isn't the first time the big birds have reared their lofty heads in our state.

In the late 1800s, ostrich feathers were valued for their beauty, not their practicality. Feathered hats and boas were all the rage, and American farmers decided to profit from their popularity. At the turn-of-the century there were over 6,000 ostriches in the United States. Since the incubation periods was only 42 days and the birds could live 80 years, a lot of plumes could be had for the plucking. However, fashion being fickle, the styles changed and by 1920 the ostrich population dropped to a little over 200. The U.S. farmers made income from the few remaining ostriches by charging tourists to ride on the 300-pound birds. In 1900, Thomas Cockburn brought 300 ostriches to Hot Springs and opened the 27-acre Ostrich Farm on Whittington Avenue. Here the ostriches raced and gave rides to Spa City tourists. Cockburn was also noted for harnessing his big birds to carts and driving them along Central Avenue as a publicity stunt.

TOURISM

The scenic beauty of The Natural State appeals to travelers from all over, which makes tourism a major factor in the state's economy. Travel and tourism expenditures in Arkansas in 1994 totaled $2,914,296,000. Tourism in Arkansas was up 6% while nationally tourism was up only 5%. The travel industry in Arkansas generates 46,0365 jobs and $131,143 in state taxes. In 1994 the typical Arkansas tourist was a 47-old-year-old Texan traveling with the family visiting relatives or friends in Arkansas and spending two to three nights in the state. The average family income of a typical visitor was $36,745. Forty-five percent of visitors had been here before and would come back again.

SOURCE: Arkansas Department of Parks and Tourism

BITS O' BIDNESS

■ **No More Five and Dime** Arkansas' last F.W. Woolworth store closed in 1993. The 21-year-old store at the Northwest Arkansas Mall was one of 400 Woolworth stores that closed in 1993 – half of the 800 stores in the U.S.

■ **Cleaning Up** Alda Ellis of Little Rock's Alda's Forever Soap sold over $2.5 million in soap in 1994. What is unique about her product is that the designs on the bar soap(from kitty cats to monograms) stay in tact as long as the bar lasts. She has sold soap to Michael Jackson with his Neverland Ranch logo. Her soap bearing the presidential seal can also be found cleaning up at the White House.

■ **Crappy Critters** Fort Smith chicken-farmer-turned-entrepreneur Jerry Sherrill recycles composted chicken litter into animal shapes. The cutesy four-inch bunnies and bears known as Crappy Critters are made to be stuck in flower pots as fertilizer.

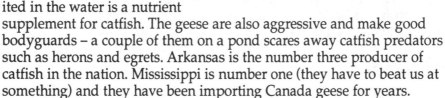

■ **Goosing the Catfish** Some catfish farmers in eastern and central Arkansas have been busy importing giant Canada geese in hopes of developing residential flocks of these non-migratory birds. It seems that the geese's fecal material that is deposited in the water is a nutrient supplement for catfish. The geese are also aggressive and make good bodyguards – a couple of them on a pond scares away catfish predators such as herons and egrets. Arkansas is the number three producer of catfish in the nation. Mississippi is number one (they have to beat us at something) and they have been importing Canada geese for years.

■ **Chicken Feed** As a response to fat and cholesterol concerns, Americans consume more than 90 pounds of chicken per person each year (which comes as no surprise to Don Tyson). In 1910, they ate only 15 pounds per person annually and wolfed down 77 pounds of beef per person.

■ **Mortgage Lifter** In the mid-1800s, hogs became known to financially strapped Arkansas farmers as the "mortgage lifter" because they are cheap to raise and there is little waste – everything but the "oink" being edible and/or saleable. Farmers learned they could buy a sow, fatten her up with corn, raise a few litters and make a good return on their investment.

ARKANSAS SPORTS

Whooooo, Pig! Sooie! – and more

Arkansas' love of sports is deeply entrenched. And for a small, sparsely-populated state, we've produced a disproportionately large number of splendid athletes over the years.

From Dizzy Dean to Bear Bryant to Sidney Moncrief, Arkansas athletes have excelled nationally and achieved great public acclaim.

In team sports, the U of A football and basketball Razorbacks dominate the field. The unique cry of "Whooooo, Pig! Sooie!" has incited pandemonium from the Orange Bowl to the Final Four.

However, the Hogs aren't the only game in town, as alumni of ASU or UALR are quick to tell you. In addition, there's the Arkansas Travelers, a St. Louis Cardinal farm club that has provided many thrilling seasons at Ray Winder Field in Little Rock.

Still, it's the porkers that hog most of the headlines, the crowds and the hearts of Arkansans everywhere. And it's likely that the state will continue to rally 'round the Razorbacks for years to come.

For more information about individual Arkansas sports figures, see listings in Famous Arkansans *section.*

THE ARKANSAS SPORTS HALL OF FAME

The Arkansas Hall of Fame was founded in 1959 to honor the state's outstanding athletes and sports figures. Here's a list of those who've made the cut:

1959
Bill Dickey, *baseball*
Hazel Walker, *basketball*
Jim Lee Howell, *football*
Wear Schoonover, *football*
Ivan Grove, *college athletics*

1960
Jim Benton, *football*
Don Hutson, *football*
John Barnhill, *football,
  college athletics*
Travis Jackson, *baseball*
Steve Creekmore, *football, golf*
Jimmy Haygood, *football*

1961
Lon Warneke, *baseball*
Paul Runyan, *golf*
Earl Quigley, *high school athletics*
Morley Jennings, *football*
Hugo Bezdek, *football, baseball*

1962
Schoolboy Rowe, *baseball*
Carey Selph, *baseball, football*
Rube Robinson, *baseball*
John Tucker, *football*
Ray Winder, *baseball*

1963
Clyde Scott, *football, track*
Dutch Harrison, *golf*
George Cole, *football,
  college athletics*
Russell May, *football*

1964
Julius Petty, *trapshooting*
Bill Carr, *track*
George Kell, *baseball*
Glen Rose, *basketball, football*
Dan Estes, *football*

1965
Paul "Bear" Bryant, *football*
Gordon Carpenter, *basketball*
Tom Murphy, *basketball, football*
Nick Carter, *football*

Clyde Scott, with ball

1966
Johnny Sain, *baseball*
Ken Kavanaugh, *football*
Francis Schmidt, *football*
Quinnie Hamm, *basketball*

1967
Preacher Roe, *baseball*
Frank Broyles, *football,
  college athletics*
Tommy Freeman, *boxing*

1968
Elmer Smith, *football*
Red Hickey, *football*
Bo Rowland, *football*
Gene Davidson, *football*

1969
Wally Moon, *baseball*
Allen Dunaway, *football*
Glenn Rice, *track*

1970
Mel McGaha, *baseball, basketball, football*
Duke Wells, *football*
Fred Thomsen, *football*
George Harper, *baseball*

1971
Wilson Matthews, *football*
Pat Summerall, *football*
Eddie Hamm, *track*
Swede McCormack, *college athletics*
Foy Hammons, *football*
1972
Maurice "Footsie" Britt, *football*
Dave Hanner, *football*
Charles McClendon, *football*
Boyd Cypert, *college athletics*
1973
Ray Hamilton, *football*
Sherman Lollar, *baseball*
Sam Coleman, *high school athletics*
Bill Walton, *football*
1974
Raymond Burnett, *football*
Reece "Goose" Tatum, *basketball*
Jack Robbins, *football*
John Thompson, *high school athletics*
1975
Miller Barber, *golf*
Lamar McHan, *football*
Bobby Winkles, *baseball*
Allan Berry, *football*
Charles Clements, *football*
1976
Billy Ray Smith, Sr., *football*
John Hoffman, *football*
George Terry, *football*
Billy Mitchell, *amateur athletics*
Walter Dowell, *golf*
1977
Leon Campbell, *football*
Bobby Mitchell, *football, track*
Willis Hudlin, *baseball*
Johnie Burnett, *high school athletics*
Tom Pickkell, *basketball*
1978
Eddie Meador, *football*
Brooks Robinson, *baseball*
Fred Williams, *football*
Joan Crawford, *basketball*
Alvin Bell, *officiating*
1979
Lance Alworth, *football*
Johnny Adams, *basketball*
Jim Abraham, *high school athletics*

Warren Woodson, *football*
Ike Tomlinson, *baseball*
1980
Marilyn McRae Houston, *tennis*
Elijah Pitts, *football*
Barry Switzer, *football*
Curtis King, *high school athletics*
Ellis Kinder, *baseball*
Arky Vaughan, *baseball*
Buster Brannon, *basketball*
1981
Don Kessinger, *baseball, basketball*
Clifford Shaw, *officiating*
Sam Hindsman, *basketball*
Jim Mooty, *football*
Wayne Harris, *football*
1982
Hugh Taylor, *football*
Bro Erwin, *high school athletics*
Jim Pace, *football, track*
Aubrey Fowler, *football, track*
Deward Dopson, *basketball*
Milan Creighton, *football, basketball*
1983
Lou Holtz, *football*
Eddie Sutton, *basketball*
Dizzy Dean, *baseball*
Paul Dean, *baseball*
Lee Rogers, *baseball*
Willie Davis, *football*
1984
Fred Akers, *football*
Thomas Hill, *track*
Sonny Gordon, *high school athletics*
Gayle Kaundart, *juco basketball*
Kay Eakin, *football*
1985
Eugen Lambert, *basketball*
Floyd Sagely, *football*
Cliff Harris, *football*
Eugene Sherman, *football*
Ragon Kinney, *boxing*
1986
Bill Bergey, *football*
Loyd Phillips, *football*
Howard Pearce, *football, stadium management*
Bill Vining, *basketball*
Bill Irving, *football*

1987
John McDonnell, *track*
Jim Lindsey, *football*
Larry Snyder, *horse racing*
Clair Bates, *basketball*
Alton Baldwin, *football*

1988
George Kok, *basketball*
Dwight Sloan, *football*
Gene Bearden, *baseball*
Lewis Carpenter, *football*
Jimmy "Red" Parker, *football*

1989
Ken Hatfield, *football*
Harold Horton, *football*
Eddie Miles, *basketball*
Sam Cooke, *football*
Brad Scott, *football*
R. H. Sikes, *golf*

1990
Hubert Ausbie, *basketball*
Henry Moore, *football*
Bobby Tiner, *football*
Bennie Ellender, *football*
Leoth Barham, *women's basketball*
Lowell Manning, *football*

1991
Norm DeBriyn, *baseball*
Pat Foster, *basketball*
George Dunklin, *tennis*
Francis Garroutte, *basketball*
Gerald Nesbitt, *football*

1992
Don Dyer, *basketball*
Preston Carpenter, *football*
Dan Hampton, *football*
Lorietta Blann, *basketball*
Tom Gulley, *baseball*

1993
Sidney Moncrief, *basketball*
Earl Bell, *track*
Buddy Bob Benson, *football*
Leo Nonnecamp, *baseball*
Jerry Dalrymple, *football*
Orville Henry, *sports writer*

1994
Joe Ferguson, *football*
Ron Brewer, *basketball*
Ike Poole, *football, basketball*
Buddy Coleman, *football, officiating*

1995
Lou Brock, *baseball*
Clell Burnet, *football*
Chuck Dicus, *football*
Bob Courtway, *swimming*
Bill Dunaway, *basketball*
Billy Ray Smith, Jr. *football*

1996
Billy Bock, *baseball*
Bill Burnett, *football*
Larry Lacewell, *football*
Kevin McReynolds, *baseball*
Houston Nutt, *baseball*
Raymond Peters, *football*

THE ARKANSAS RAZORBACKS

HOW 'BOUT THEM HOGS!

In 1896 the University of Arkansas held a student contest to select the school's official colors. The winners: white and cardinal (which edged out heliotrope). And so for the next 15 years, Arkansas athletic teams competed as the Cardinals. Then, according to legend, at a pep rally celebrating the unbeaten 1909 football season, coach Hugo Bezdek likened his players to "a wild band of razorbacks." The rest, as they say, is history.

In the 1920s, fans first started calling the hogs with the unique "Whooooo, Pig! Sooie!" yell. It wasn't until the mid-1960s that the U of A adopted a live mascot. Some ardent Razorback rooters donated a duroc hog – Big Red, who promptly died of a heart attack.

Today the distinctive symbol of the Arkansas Razorbacks – a snorting, rooting, bristling downright mean-looking hog – is recognized throughout the nation. Inside the state it's hard to walk a block without spotting the familiar red porker on store signs or T-shirts.

WHAT IS A RAZORBACK, ANYWAY?

The *razorback* is not a species of hog, rather a general term for feral (wild) domestic pigs, which at one time were quite plentiful in the southeastern United States. No one is quite certain of their origin. On his second voyage in 1493, Columbus first bought swine to the West Indies. Later, in 1539, hogs were transported to the mainland by Hernando de Soto. Here they thrived and multiplied.

Pigs became a very important resident on early farms. Since many farm animals were left to roam the range, or were fenced in rather crudely, it was not uncommon for some to escape and return to the wild.

It is generally believed that it is the descendants of these escapees that we lovingly refer to as razorbacks – so called because of their sharp, narrow backs.

These wild hogs were quite different from your basic porker wallowing about the barn lot. They had long, strong legs that enabled them to move with speed and power. The wild hogs lived on acorns, nuts, grass and tender roots of trees, beetles, bugs and grubs. In the constant pursuit of these foods, the razorback developed two large teeth, or tusks, for rooting. They also sported a scruffy, bristly coat unlike their domestic relatives.

Although there is evidence of wild hogs still roaming the Ozark hills and south Arkansas timberlands, it is generally believed that these creatures are few and far between. It is also conceded that if you do happen to run across one, you should take great care not to anger him. Because as any Arkie knows, Razorbacks can be very ferocious.

SOURCE: Little Rock Zoo, *Collier's Encyclopedia*.

THE LEGEND OF THE RAZORBACK

One of the principle pleasures of Arkansas life in the old days was the telling of tall tales. Some of the biggest were told by farmers waiting around the grist mills for their corn to be ground into meal. Mainly, they liked to swap stories about their hogs, who often had to forage in the open range to avoid starvation.

In *Living in Arkansas*, O.E. McKnight tells of one fellow who swore his hogs were so thin that "two of them would have to stand together to make a shadow." Another claimed his razor was so dull he hadn't been able to shave for weeks. Then he noticed that one of his hogs coming off the range had a backbone sharper than his razor had ever been. So he "picked up the hog and with his razor-sharp back got one of the closest and smoothest shaves he had ever had in his life." It was from whoppers like these that the legend of the Arkansas razorback evolved.

RAZORBACK FOOTBALL

The Razorbacks have now competed in football for over a century, with all the thrills and heartbreak a fan could ask for. During that time, they've even managed to win a national championship.

It all began back in 1893 when the university formed an athletic association to "foster and encourage the growing interest which the student body is manifesting in the development of the physical man." The following year a team was put together under the tutelage of a young Latin professor, John C. Futrall. A pair of tuneup games were arranged with Fort Smith High School (actually with an athletic club representing the school) and soon the "Cardinals" had rolled up 80 points without having been scored upon. Then came the University of Texas, and a 54-0 pasting in Austin – and the school's first football season was over.

Fortunately, things improved over the years that followed. Here's a brief look at the colorful history of the Hogs.

MOST MEMORABLE MOMENTS

Here are a few standouts among the many memorable games in Razorback football history:

1978

Arkansas 31, Oklahoma 6
In the most famous upset in Razorback history, the Hogs ripped the #2-ranked, 18-point-favorite Sooners before 65 million TV viewers. What made this Orange Bowl victory so startling was that coach Lou Holtz had suspended all but one player of his starting backfield for rules infractions, causing oddsmakers to temporarily drop the game from the boards.

1965

Arkansas 27, Texas 24
For years, nothing thrilled Hog fans like a Texas defeat – and no game ever provided more thrills than this one. After jumping to a 20-zip lead against the #1 Horns, the Razorbacks fell behind, 24-20. Then, late in the fourth quarter, Arkansas rallied for a classic 80-yard drive behind the throwing of Jon Brittenum and the catching of Bobby Crockett.

1969

Texas 15, Arkansas 14
The Hogs' most heartbreaking loss occurred on a cold December day in Fayetteville with millions watching on TV and President Richard Nixon

in the stands. The game was hyped to the max, with Texas ranked #1 and Arkansas #2, and both teams at 9-0. After three quarters of play the Razorbacks were ahead 14-0, thoroughly dominating the Horns. Then Texas pulled it out of the fire with two quick touchdowns and a two-point conversion – and took home the national title.

1965

Arkansas 10, Nebraska 7

A fourth-quarter 80-yard-drive capped by a Bobby Burnett touchdown allowed Arkansas to finish its perfect 11-0 season in style at the Cotton Bowl. Although the AP and UPI handed out their championship prizes *before* the bowls to 10-0 Alabama, the Tide later lost to Texas. Arkansas picked up the Football Writers of America award. The confusion led to changes in the voting. Under today's rules, the Razorbacks would be hands-down winners.

1936

Arkansas 6, Texas 0

The famous tandem of quarterback Jack Robbins (still the sixth leading passer in U of A history) and Jim Benton (number six in career receiving) brought Arkansas its first SWC title after defeating Texas in this rainy final game at Little Rock.

1951

Arkansas 16, Texas 14

A lousy 5-5 season was partially redeemed when Pat Summerall kicked a field goal just before halftime. It proved decisive as Arkansas upset number four Texas for the first time ever at Fayetteville, and the first time anywhere since 1938.

1954

Arkansas 6, Mississippi 0

What the U of A Sports Media Guide calls "one of the most, if not the most famous single play in school history" took place when Arkansas scored the only touchdown of the day – a 66-yard pass from Buddy Bob Benson to Preston Carpenter. The famed "Powder River Play" allowed Bowden Wyatt's Razorbacks to knock off previously undefeated, #1-ranked Ole Miss.

1964

Arkansas 14, Texas 13

An 81-yard TD punt return by future U of A coach Ken Hatfield set the stage for this classic victory over defending national champ Texas at Austin. It was victory number five in Frank Broyles' 11-0 national championship season.

Lou Holtz

1966

LSU 14, Arkansas 7
One of the Razorbacks most bitter defeats came in this Cotton Bowl tragedy. The 10-0 Razorbacks, ranked number two, had a clear shot at the undisputed national title when number-one-ranked Michigan State fell to UCLA. But the Hogs couldn't seize the moment, as a pumped-up LSU squad snapped Arkansas' 22-game winning streak.

1975

Arkansas 31, Texas A&M 6
In the final game of the regular season, with a Cotton Bowl berth on the line, Arkansas pulled a stunning upset by mauling the #2 Aggies at Little Rock. The Hogs, who rolled up most of their points in the second half after a nearly scoreless first half, went on to whip Georgia on New Year's Day.

1995

Arkansas 20, Alabama 19
With six seconds left, flanker J.J. Meadors dove to catch a fourth-down Barry Lunney pass and tie the game. Moments later, after the successful point-after kick, the Hogs celebrated their first-ever victory over #13 Alabama. It was only the Tide's tenth loss at Tuscaloosa since the start of the Bear Bryant era.

RAZORBACK FOOTBALL: SEASON BY SEASON

1894
Coach: John C. Futrall
Overall record: 3 years, 5-2
42	Fort Smith High	0
38	Fort Smith High	0
0	Texas	54
Won 2, Lost 1, Tied 0

1895
Coach: John C. Futrall
30	Fort Smith High	0
Won 1, Lost 0, Tied 0

1896
Coach: John C. Futrall
10	Fort Smith High	0
6	Fort Smith High	2
0	Drury College	34
Won 2, Lost 1, Tied 0

1897
Coach: B. N. Wilson
Overall record: 2 years, 4-1-1
12	Fort Smith High	0
6	Drury College	6
24	Ouachita College	0
Won 2, Lost 0, Tied 1

1898
Coach: B. N. Wilson
17	Drury College	0
12	Drury College	6
8	Fort Scott High	36
Won 2, Lost 1, Tied 0

1899
Coach: Colbert Searles
Overall record: 2 years, 5-2-2
10	Drury College	0
11	Tulsa	0
0	Tulsa	0
5	Oklahoma	11
11	Joplin High	10
Won 3, Lost 1, Tied 1

1900
Coach: Colbert Searles
15	Webb City High	0
6	Joplin High	6
10	Pierce City College	0
5	Drury College	17
Won 2, Lost 1, Tied 1

1901
Coach: Charles Thomas
Overall record: 2 years, 9-8
0	Pierce City College	5
22	Drury College	0
6	Fort Scott High	17
0	Little Rock High	5
48	Tulsa	0
6	Kansas City Medics	10
0	Louisiana State	15
16	Louisiana Tech	0
Won 3, Lost 5, Tied 0

1902
Coach: Charles Thomas
6	Neosho High	0
15	Kingfisher College	6
0	Oklahoma	28
33	Tulsa	0
50	Tahlequah Seminary	0
5	SW Missouri State	15
2	Pierce City College	24
16	Fort Scott High	0
11	Missouri-Rolla	0
Won 6, Lost 3, Tied 0

1903
Coach: D. A. McDaniel
Overall record: 1 year, 3-4
5	SW Missouri State	10
6	Missouri Mines	17
10	Drury College	6
0	Texas	15
0	Texas A&M	6
17	Fort Smith High	9
12	Oklahoma	0
Won 3, Lost 4, Tied 0

1904
Coach: A. D. Brown
Overall record: 2 year, 6-9
0	Drury College	12
22	Fort Scott High	0
0	Dallas Medics	5
6	Baylor	17
12	Fairmount College	6
11	Fort Smith High	5
11	Missouri-Rolla	10
Won 4, Lost 3, Tied 0

1905

Coach: A. D. Brown
0	Kansas	6
0	Washington-St. Louis	6
0	Drury College	12
6	Chiloco College	0
0	Texas	4
0	Kentucky	6
0	Missouri-Rolla	16
26	Kansas City Medics	0

Won 2, Lost 6, Tied 0

1906

Coach: F. C. Longman
Overall record: 2 years, 5-8-3
0	Chiloco College	6
0	Drury College	0
5	Kansas	37
0	Texas	11
12	SE Missouri State	0
0	Missouri	11
22	Tulane	0
6	Louisiana State	6

Won 2, Lost 4, Tied 2

1907

Coach: F. C. Longman
0	Haskell College	0
23	Drury College	0
17	Drury College	6
6	St. Louis University	42
6	Texas	26
12	Louisiana State	17
2	Tennessee	14
7	Missouri-Rolla	5

Won 3, Lost 4, Tied 1

1908

Coach: Hugo Bezdek
Overall record: 5 years, 29-13-1
6	Haskell College	0
33	Ole Miss	0
0	St. Louis University	24
51	Henderson State	0
5	Oklahoma	27
0	Texas	21
42	Pittsburg State	12
4	Ouachita College	0
4	Louisiana State	36

Won 5, Lost 4, Tied 0

1909

Coach: Hugo Bezdek
24	Henderson State	0
12	Drury College	6
23	Fairmount College	6
21	Oklahoma	6
16	Louisiana State	0
56	Ouachita College	0
34	Washington-St. Louis	0

Won 7, Loss 0, Tied 0

1910

Coach: Hugo Bezdek
33	Drury College	0
63	Henderson State	0
0	Kansas State	5
13	Texas Southwestern	12
5	Texas A&M	0
50	Washington-St. Louis	0
6	Missouri-Rolla	2
51	Louisiana State	0

Won 7, Lost 1, Tied 0

1911

Coach: Hugo Bezdek
100	SW Missouri State	0
65	Drury College	5
45	Hendrix College	0
0	Texas	12
0	Texas Southwestern	0
44	Missouri-Rolla	3
0	Kansas State	3
3	Washington-St. Louis	0
11	Louisiana State	0

Won 6, Lost 2, Tied 1

1912

Coach: Hugo Bezdek
39	Henderson State	6
52	Hendrix College	0
7	Oklahoma State	13
0	Texas A&M	27
0	Baylor	7
25	Texas Southwestern	0
7	Wisconsin	64
6	Louisiana State	7
13	Washington-St. Louis	7
0	Texas	48

Won 4, Lost 6, Tied 0

1913

Coach: E. T. Pickering
Overall record: 2 years, 11-7
3	Henderson State	0
26	Hendrix College	0
3	Oklahoma State	0
34	Baylor	0

26 Austin College 7
7 Louisiana State 12
10 Ole Miss 21
14 Ouachita College 3
14 Tulane 0
Won 7, Lost 2, Tied 0

1914

Coach: E. T. Pickering
13 Hendrix College 7
9 Ouachita College 15
26 St. Louis University 0
0 Missouri-Rolla 44
0 Oklahoma State 46
20 Louisiana State 12
1 Ole Miss (forfeit) 0
7 Oklahoma 35
7 Drury College 28
Won 4, Lost 5, Tied 0

1915

Coach: T. T. McConnell
Overall record: 2 years, 8-6-1
41 Hendrix College 0
13 Ouachita College 9
14 Oklahoma State 9
0 St. Louis University 0
7 Louisiana State 13
0 Oklahoma 24
46 Missouri-Rolla 0
Won 4, Lost 2, Tied 1

1916

Coach: T. T. McConnell
34 Pittsburg State 20
58 Hendrix College 0
82 Oklahoma Mines 0
60 Missouri-Rolla 0
7 Louisiana State 17
0 Texas 52
13 Oklahoma 14
7 Mississippi State 20
Won 4, Lost 4, Tied 0

1917

Coach: Norman Paine
Overall record: 2 years, 8-3-1
34 Central Missouri State 0
19 Hendrix College 0
32 Missouri-Rolla 0
19 Tulsa 7
14 Louisiana State 0
0 Oklahoma 0
0 Texas 20
Won 5, Lost 1, Tied 1

1918

Coach: Norman Paine
0 Camp Pike 6
6 Missouri-Rolla 0
0 Oklahoma 103
23 Tulsa 6
12 SW Missouri State 6
Won 3, Lost 2, Tied 0

1919

Coach: J. B. Craig
Overall record: 1 year, 3-4
7 Hendrix College 0
20 Missouri-Rolla 0
0 Louisiana State 20
7 Tulsa 63
7 Texas 35
7 Oklahoma 6
7 Rice 40
Won 3, Lost 4, Tied 0

1920

Coach: G. W. McLaren
Overall record: 2 years, 8-5-3
0 Hendrix College 0
2 Texas Christian 19
6 Southern Methodist 0
14 Missouri-Rolla 0
0 Louisiana State 3
20 Phillips College 0
0 Rice 0
Won 3, Lost 2, Tied 2

1921

Coach: G. W. McLaren
28 Hendrix College 0
40 Drury College 0
28 Ouachita College 0
0 Oklahoma State 7
14 Southern Methodist 0
7 Louisiana State 10
0 Phillips College 0
13 Baylor 12
14 Texas Christian 19
Won 5, Lost 3, Tied 1

1922

Coach: Francis Schmidt
Overall record: 7 years, 42-20-3
39 Hendrix College 0
22 Drury College 0
7 Ouachita College 13
13 Baylor 60
40 Louisiana State 6

1	Tulsa (forfeit)	0
7	Rice	31
9	Southern Methodist	0
0	Oklahoma State	13

Won 5, Lost 4, Tied 0

1923

Coach: Francis Schmidt

32	Arkansas State Teachers	0
26	Drury College	0
23	Rice	0
0	Baylor	14
26	Louisiana State	13
0	Ouachita College	0
6	Southern Methodist	13
32	Phillips College	0
13	Oklahoma State	0

Won 6, Lost 2, Tied 1

1924

Coach: Francis Schmidt

54	Northeast Oklahoma	6
47	SW Missouri State	0
34	Hendrix College	3
0	Baylor	13
20	Ole Miss	0
10	Louisiana State	7
14	Southern Methodist	14
28	Phillips College	6
0	Oklahoma State	20
20	Texas Christian	0

Won 7, Lost 2, Tied 1

1925

Coach: Francis Schmidt

0	Iowa	26
0	Oklahoma Baptist	6
9	Rice	13
45	Phillips College	0
12	Louisiana State	0
0	Southern Methodist	0
0	Texas Christian	3
9	Oklahoma State	7
20	Tulsa	7

Won 4, Lost 4, Tied 1

1926

Coach: Francis Schmidt

60	Arkansas State Teachers	0
21	Ole Miss	6
6	Oklahoma	13
14	Hendrix College	7
33	Centenary	6
7	Kansas State	16

0	Louisiana State	14
7	Texas Christian	10
24	Oklahoma State	2
7	Tulsa	14

Won 5, Lost 5, Tied 0

1927

Coach: Francis Schmidt

32	College of Ozarks	0
13	Baylor	6
6	Texas A&M	40
34	Missouri-Rolla	0
28	Louisiana State	0
10	Texas Christian	3
33	Oklahoma State	20
42	Austin College	0
20	Hendrix College	7

Won 8, Lost 1, Tied 0

1928

Coach: Francis Schmidt

0	Ole Miss	25
21	College of the Ozarks	0
14	Baylor	0
7	Texas	20
27	Texas A&M	12
7	Louisiana State	0
45	Missouri-Rolla	6
57	Oklahoma Baptist	0
73	Texas Southwestern	0

Won 7, Lost 2, Tied 0

1929

Coach: Fred Thomsen
Overall record: 13 years, 56-61-10

37	College of the Ozarks	0
30	Henderson State	7
0	Texas	27
20	Baylor	31
14	Texas A&M	13
32	Louisiana State	0
52	East Central Oklahoma	7
13	Centenary	2
32	Oklahoma State	6

Won 7, Lost 2, Tied 0

1930

Coach: Fred Thomsen

27	College of Ozarks	0
6	Tulsa	26
0	Texas Christian	40
7	Rice	6
13	Texas A&M	0
12	Louisiana State	27

0   Oklahoma State 26
7   Baylor 22
6   Centenary 2
Won 3, Lost 6, Tied 0

1931
Coach: Fred Thomsen
13   College of Ozarks 6
19   Hendrix College 0
6   Southern Methodist 42
7   Baylor 19
6   Louisiana State 13
0   Texas Christian 7
13   Chicago 13
12   Rice 26
6   Centenary 7
Won 3, Lost 5, Tied 1

1932
Coach: Fred Thomsen
0   Hendrix College 0
19   Missouri-Rolla 20
12   Texas Christian 34
20   Baylor 6
0   Louisiana State 14
7   Rice 12
7   Southern Methodist 13
0   Texas 34
0   Centenary 0
Won 1, Lost 6, Tied 2

1933
Coach: Fred Thomsen
40   College of Ozarks 0
42   Oklahoma Baptist 7
13   Texas Christian 0
19   Baylor 7
0   Louisiana State 20
3   Southern Methodist 0
6   Rice 7
63   Hendrix College 0
20   Texas 6
0   Tulsa 7
*7   Centenary 7
Won 7, Lost 3, Tied 1
* *Dixie Classic*

1934
Coach: Fred Thomsen
13   College of Ozarks 0
24   Texas Christian 10
6   Baylor 0
0   Louisiana State 16
20   Missouri-Rolla 0

7   Texas A&M 7
0   Rice 7
6   Southern Methodist 10
12   Texas 19
7   Tulsa 7
Won 4, Lost 4, Tied 2

1935
Coach: Fred Thomsen
12   Pittsburg State 0
7   Texas Christian 13
6   Baylor 13
7   Louisiana State 13
51   College of Ozarks 6
14   Texas A&M 7
7   Rice 20
6   Southern Methodist 17
28   Texas 13
14   Tulsa 7
Won 5, Lost 5, Tied 0

1936
Coach: Fred Thomsen
53   Pittsburg State 0
14   Texas Christian 18
14   Baylor 10
6   George Washington 13
7   Louisiana State 19
18   Texas A&M 0
20   Rice 14
17   Southern Methodist 0
23   Tulsa 13
6   Texas 0
Won 7, Lost 3, Tied 0

1937
Coach: Fred Thomsen
25   Central State (OK) 0
7   Texas Christian 7
14   Baylor 20
21   Texas 10
13   Southern Methodist 0
26   Texas A&M 13
20   Rice 26
32   Ole Miss 6
0   George Washington 0
28   Tulsa 7
Won 6, Lost 2, Tied 2

1938
Coach: Fred Thomsen
27   Oklahoma State 7
14   Texas Christian 21
6   Baylor 9

42	Texas	6
6	Santa Clara	21
7	Texas A&M	13
0	Rice	3
6	Southern Methodist	19
14	Ole Miss	20
6	Tulsa	6

Won 2, Lost 7, Tied 1

1939

Coach: Fred Thomsen

32	East Central Oklahoma	6
0	Mississippi State	19
14	Texas Christian	13
7	Baylor	19
13	Texas	14
0	Villanova	7
0	Texas A&M	27
12	Rice	12
14	Southern Methodist	0
23	Tulsa	0

Won 4, Lost 5, Tied 1

1940

Coach: Fred Thomsen

38	East Central Oklahoma	0
0	Texas Christian	20
12	Baylor	6
0	Texas	21
21	Ole Miss	20
0	Texas A&M	17
7	Rice	14
0	Southern Methodist	28
7	Fordham	27
27	Tulsa	21

Won 4, Lost 6, Tied 0

1941

Coach: Fred Thomsen

56	East Central Oklahoma	0
0	Texas Christian	9
7	Baylor	20
14	Texas	48
9	Detroit	6
0	Texas A&M	7
12	Rice	21
7	Southern Methodist	14
0	Ole Miss	18
13	Tulsa	6

Won 3, Lost 7, Tied 0

1942

Coach: George Cole
Overall record: 1 year, 3-7

| 27 | Wichita State | 0 |

6	Texas Christian	13
7	Baylor	20
6	Texas	47
7	Ole Miss	6
0	Texas A&M	41
9	Rice	40
6	Southern Methodist	14
14	Detroit	7
7	Tulsa	40

Won 3, Lost 7, Tied 0

1943

Coach: John Tomlin
Overall record: 1 year, 2-7

59	Missouri-Rolla	0
0	Texas Christian	13
12	Monticello Navy	20
0	Texas	34
0	Texas A&M	13
7	Rice	20
14	Southern Methodist	12
13	Oklahoma State	19
0	Tulsa	61

Won 2, Lost 7, Tied 0

1944

Coach: Glen Rose
Overall record: 2 years, 8-12-1

7	Missouri	6
0	Oklahoma State	19
6	Texas Christian	6
7	Norman Navy	27
0	Texas	19
26	Ole Miss	18
7	Texas A&M	6
12	Rice	7
12	Southern Methodist	20
2	Tulsa	33
41	Arkansas A&M	0

Won 5, Lost 5, Tied 1

1945

Coach: Glen Rose

12	Barksdale Field	6
14	Oklahoma State	19
27	Texas Christian	14
13	Baylor	23
7	Texas	34
19	Ole Miss	0
0	Texas A&M	34
7	Rice	26
0	Southern Methodist	21
13	Tulsa	45

Won 3, Lost 7, Tied 0

John Barnhill

1946
Coach: John Barnhill
Overall record: 4 years, 22-17-3
21	NW Louisiana State	14
21	Oklahoma State	21
34	Texas Christian	14
13	Baylor	0
0	Texas	20
7	Ole Miss	9
7	Texas A&M	0
7	Rice	0
13	Southern Methodist	0
13	Tulsa	14
0	Louisiana State	0

Won 6, Lost 3, Tied 2

1947
Coach: John Barnhill
64	NW Louisiana State	0
12	North Texas State	0
6	Texas Christian	0
9	Baylor	17
6	Texas	21
19	Ole Miss	14
21	Texas A&M	21
0	Rice	26
6	Southern Methodist	14
27	Tulsa	13
*21	William & Mary	19

Won 6, Lost 4, Tied 1
* *Dixie Bowl*

1948
Coach: John Barnhill
40	Abilene Christian	6
46	East Texas State	7
27	Texas Christian	14
7	Baylor	23
6	Texas	14
28	Texas A&M	6
6	Rice	25
12	Southern Methodist	14
55	Tulsa	18
0	William & Mary	9

Won 5, Lost 5, Tied 0

1949
Coach: John Barnhill
33	North Texas State	19
27	Texas Christian	7
13	Baylor	35
14	Texas	27
7	Vanderbilt	6
27	Texas A&M	6
0	Rice	14
6	Southern Methodist	34
0	William & Mary	20
40	Tulsa	7

Won 5, Lost 5, Tied 0

1950
Coach: Otis Douglas
Overall record: 3 years, 9-21
7	Oklahoma State	12
50	North Texas State	6
6	Texas Christian	13
27	Baylor	6
14	Texas	19
13	Vanderbilt	14
13	Texas A&M	42
6	Rice	9
7	Southern Methodist	14
13	Tulsa	28

Won 2, Lost 8, Tied 0

1951
Coach: Otis Douglas
42	Oklahoma State	7
30	Arizona State	13
7	Texas Christian	17
7	Baylor	9
16	Texas	14
12	Santa Clara	21
33	Texas A&M	21
0	Rice	6

7   Southern Methodist 47
24   Tulsa 7
Won 5, Lost 5, Tied 0
1952
Coach: Otis Douglas
22   Oklahoma State 20
7   Houston 17
7   Texas Christian 13
20   Baylor 17
7   Texas 44
7   Ole Miss 34
12   Texas A&M 31
33   Rice 35
17   Southern Methodist 27
34   Tulsa 44
Won 2, Lost 8, Tied 0
1953
Coach: Bowden Wyatt
Overall Record: 2 years, 11-10
6   Oklahoma State 7
13   Texas Christian 6
7   Baylor 14
7   Texas 16
0   Ole Miss 28
41   Texas A&M 14
0   Rice 47
7   Southern Methodist 13
27   Tulsa 7
Won 3, Lost 7, Tied 0
1954
Coach: Bowden Wyatt
41   Tulsa 0
20   Texas Christian 13
21   Baylor 20
20   Texas 7
6   Ole Miss 0
14   Texas A&M 7
28   Rice 15
14   Southern Methodist 21
6   Louisiana State 7
19   Houston 0
*6   Georgia Tech 14
Won 8, Lost 3, Tied 0
* *Cotton Bowl*
1955
Coach: Jack Mitchell
Overall record: 3 years, 17-12-1
21   Tulsa 6
21   Oklahoma State 0
0   Texas Christian 26

20   Baylor 25
27   Texas 20
7   Ole Miss 17
7   Texas A&M 7
10   Rice 0
6   Southern Methodist 0
7   Louisiana State 13
Won 5, Lot 4, Tied 1
1956
Coach: Jack Mitchell
21   Hardin-Simmons 6
19   Oklahoma State 7
6   Texas Christian 41
7   Baylor 14
32   Texas 14
14   Ole Miss 0
0   Texas A&M 27
27   Rice 12
27   Southern Methodist 13
7   Louisiana State 21
Won 6, Lost 4, Tied 0
1957
Coach: Jack Mitchell
12   Oklahoma State 0
41   Tulsa 14
20   Texas Christian 7
20   Baylor 17
0   Texas 17
12   Ole Miss 6
6   Texas A&M 7
7   Rice 13
22   Southern Methodist 27
47   Texas Tech 26
Won 6, Lost 4, Tied 0
1958
Coach: Frank Broyles
Overall record: 19 years, 144-58-5
0   Baylor 12
14   Tulsa 27
7   Texas Christian 12
0   Rice 24
6   Texas 24
12   Ole Miss 14
21   Texas A&M 8
60   Hardin-Simmons 15
13   Southern Methodist 6
14   Texas Tech 8
Won 4, Lost 6, Tied 0

Frank Broyles

1959

Coach: Frank Broyles

28	Tulsa	0
13	Oklahoma State	7
3	Texas Christian	0
23	Baylor	7
12	Texas	13
0	Ole Miss	28
12	Texas A&M	7
14	Rice	10
17	Southern Methodist	14
27	Texas Tech	8
*14	Georgia Tech	7

Won 9, Lost 2, Tied 0
* *Gator Bowl*

1960

Coach: Frank Broyles

9	Oklahoma State	0
48	Tulsa	7
7	Texas Christian	0
14	Baylor	28
24	Texas	23
7	Ole Miss	10
7	Texas A&M	3
3	Rice	0
26	Southern Methodist	3
34	Texas Tech	6
*6	Duke	7

Won 8, Lost 3, Tied 0
* *Cotton Bowl*

1961

Coach: Frank Broyles

0	Ole Miss	16
6	Tulsa	0
28	Texas Christian	3
23	Baylor	13
7	Texas	33
42	NW Louisiana State	7
15	Texas A&M	8
10	Rice	0
21	Southern Methodist	7
28	Texas Tech	0
*3	Alabama	10

Won 8, Lost 3, Tied 0
* *Sugar Bowl*

1962

Coach: Frank Broyles

34	Oklahoma State	7
42	Tulsa	14
42	Texas Christian	14
28	Baylor	21
3	Texas	7
49	Hardin-Simmons	7
17	Texas A&M	7
28	Rice	14
9	Southern Methodist	7
34	Texas Tech	0
*13	Ole Miss	17

Won 9, Lost 2, Tied 0
* *Sugar Bowl*

1963

Coach: Frank Broyles

21	Oklahoma State	0
6	Missouri	7
18	Texas Christian	3
10	Baylor	14
13	Texas	17
56	Tulsa	7
21	Texas A&M	7
0	Rice	7
7	Southern Methodist	14
27	Texas Tech	20

Won 5, Lost 5, Tied 0

1964

Coach: Frank Broyles

14	Oklahoma State	0
31	Tulsa	22
29	Texas Christian	6
17	Baylor	6
14	Texas	13

The 1964 national champion Razorbacks

17	Wichita State	0
17	Texas A&M	0
21	Rice	0
44	Southern Methodist	0
17	Texas Tech	0
*10	Nebraska	7

Won 11, Lost 0, Tied 0
* Cotton Bowl, National Championship

1965

Coach: Frank Broyles

28	Oklahoma State	14
20	Tulsa	12
28	Texas Christian	0
38	Baylor	7
27	Texas	24
55	North Texas State	20
31	Texas A&M	0
31	Rice	0
24	Southern Methodist	3
42	Texas Tech	24
*7	Louisiana State	14

Won 10, Lost 1, Tied 0
* Cotton Bowl

1966

Coach: Frank Broyles

14	Oklahoma State	10
27	Tulsa	8
21	Texas Christian	0
0	Baylor	7

12	Texas	7
41	Wichita State	0
34	Texas A&M	0
31	Rice	20
22	Southern Methodist	0
16	Texas Tech	21

Won 8, Lost 2, Tied 0

1967

Coach: Frank Broyles

6	Oklahoma State	7
12	Tulsa	14
26	Texas Christian	0
10	Baylor	10
12	Texas	21
28	Kansas State	7
21	Texas A&M	33
23	Rice	9
35	Southern Methodist	17
27	Texas Tech	31

Won 4, Lost 5, Tied 1

1968

Coach: Frank Broyles

32	Oklahoma State	15
56	Tulsa	13
17	Texas Christian	7
35	Baylor	19
29	Texas	39
17	North Texas State	15
25	Texas A&M	22

46   Rice 21
35   Southern Methodist 29
42   Texas Tech 7
*16   Georgia 2
Won 10, Lost 1, Tied 0
* *Sugar Bowl*

1969
Coach: Frank Broyles
39   Oklahoma State 0
55   Tulsa 0
24   Texas Christian 6
21   Baylor 7
52   Wichita State 14
35   Texas A&M 13
30   Rice 6
28   Southern Methodist 15
33   Texas Tech 0
14   Texas 15
*22   Ole Miss 27
Won 9, Lost 2, Tied 0
* *Sugar Bowl*

1970
Coach: Frank Broyles
28   Stanford 34
23   Oklahoma State 7
49   Tulsa 7
49   Texas Christian 14
41   Baylor 7
62   Wichita State 0
45   Texas A&M 6
38   Rice 14
36   Southern Methodist 3
24   Texas Tech 10
7   Texas 42
Won 9, Lost 2, Tied 0

1971
Coach: Frank Broyles
51   California 20
31   Oklahoma State 10
20   Tulsa 21
49   Texas Christian 15
35   Baylor 7
31   Texas 7
60   North Texas State 21
9   Texas A&M 17
24   Rice 24
18   Southern Methodist 13
14   Texas Tech 0
*13   Tennessee 14
Won 8, Lost 3, Tied 1
* *Liberty Bowl*

1972
Coach: Frank Broyles
10   Southern California 31
24   Oklahoma State 23
21   Tulsa 20
27   Texas Christian 13
31   Baylor 20
15   Texas 35
42   North Texas State 16
7   Texas A&M 10
20   Rice 23
7   Southern Methodist 22
24   Texas Tech 14
Won 6, Lost 5, Tied 0

1973
Coach: Frank Broyles
0   Southern California 17
6   Oklahoma State 38
21   Iowa State 19
13   Texas Christian 5
13   Baylor 7
6   Texas 34
20   Tulsa 6
14   Texas A&M 10
7   Rice 17
7   Southern Methodist 7
17   Texas Tech 24
Won 5, Lost 5, Tied 1

1974
Coach: Frank Broyles
22   Southern California 7
7   Oklahoma State 26
60   Tulsa 0
49   Texas Christian 0
17   Baylor 21
7   Texas 38
43   Colorado State 9
10   Texas A&M 20
25   Rice 6
24   Southern Methodist 24
21   Texas Tech 13
Won 6, Lost 4, Tied 1

1975
Coach: Frank Broyles
35   Air Force 0
13   Oklahoma State 20
31   Tulsa 15
19   Texas Christian 8
41   Baylor 3
18   Texas 24
31   Utah State 0

20 Rice 16
35 Southern Methodist 7
31 Texas Tech 14
31 Texas A&M 6
*31 Georgia 10
Won 10, Lost 2, Tied 0
* *Cotton Bowl*

1976
Coach: Frank Broyles
33 Utah State 16
16 Oklahoma State 10
3 Tulsa 9
46 Texas Christian 14
14 Houston 7
41 Rice 16
7 Baylor 7
10 Texas A&M 31
31 Southern Methodist 35
7 Texas Tech 30
12 Texas 29
Won 5, Lost 5, Tied 1

1977
Coach: Lou Holtz
Overall record: 7 years, 60-21-2
53 New Mexico State 10
28 Oklahoma State 6
37 Tulsa 3
42 Texas Christian 6
9 Texas 13
34 Houston 0
30 Rice 7
35 Baylor 9
26 Texas A&M 20
47 Southern Methodist 7
17 Texas Tech 14
*31 Oklahoma 6
Won 11, Lost 1, Tied 0
* *Orange Bowl*

1978
Coach: Lou Holtz
48 Vanderbilt 17
19 Oklahoma State 7
21 Tulsa 13
42 Texas Christian 3
21 Texas 28
9 Houston 20
37 Rice 7
27 Baylor 14
26 Texas A&M 7
27 Southern Methodist 14
49 Texas Tech 7

*10 UCLA 10
Won 9, Lost 2, Tied 1
* *Fiesta Bowl*

1979
Coach: Lou Holtz
36 Colorado State 3
27 Oklahoma State 7
33 Tulsa 8
16 Texas Christian 13
20 Texas Tech 6
17 Texas 14
10 Houston 13
34 Rice 7
29 Baylor 20
22 Texas A&M 10
31 Southern Methodist 7
*9 Alabama 24
Won 10, Lost 2, Tied 0
* *Sugar Bowl*

1980
Coach: Lou Holtz
17 Texas 23
33 Oklahoma State 20
13 Tulsa 10
44 Texas Christian 7
27 Wichita State 7
17 Houston 24
16 Rice 17
15 Baylor 42
27 Texas A&M 24
7 Southern Methodist 31
22 Texas Tech 16
*34 Tulane 15
Won 7, Lost 5, Tied 0
* *Hall of Fame Bowl*

1981
Coach: Lou Holtz
14 Tulsa 10
38 Northwestern 7
27 Ole Miss 13
24 Texas Christian 28
26 Texas Tech 14
42 Texas 11
17 Houston 20
41 Rice 7
41 Baylor 29
10 Texas A&M 7
18 Southern Methodist 32
*27 North Carolina 31
Won 8, Lost 4, Tied 0
* *Gator Bowl*

1982
Coach: Lou Holtz

38	Tulsa	0
29	Navy	17
14	Ole Miss	12
35	Texas Christian	0
21	Texas Tech	3
38	Houston	3
24	Rice	6
17	Baylor	24
35	Texas A&M	0
17	Southern Methodist	17
7	Texas	33
*28	Florida	24

Won 9, Lost 2, Tied 1
* *Bluebonnet Bowl*

1983
Coach: Lou Holtz

17	Tulsa	14
17	New Mexico	0
10	Ole Miss	13
38	Texas Christian	21
3	Texas	31
24	Houston	3
35	Rice	0
21	Baylor	24
23	Texas A&M	36
0	Southern Methodist	17
16	Texas Tech	13

Won 6, Lost 5, Tied 0

1984
Coach: Ken Hatfield
Overall record: 6 years, 55-17-1

14	Ole Miss	14
18	Tulsa	9
33	Navy	10
31	Texas Christian	32
24	Texas Tech	0
18	Texas	24
17	Houston	3
28	Rice	6
14	Baylor	9
28	Texas A&M	0
28	Southern Methodist	31
*15	Auburn	21

Won 7, Lost 4, Tied 1
* *Liberty Bowl*

1985
Coach: Ken Hatfield

24	Ole Miss	19
24	Tulsa	0

45	New Mexico State	13
41	Texas Christian	0
30	Texas Tech	7
13	Texas	15
57	Houston	27
30	Rice	15
20	Baylor	14
6	Texas A&M	10
15	Southern Methodist	9
*18	Arizona State	17

Won 10, Lost 2, tied 0
* *Holiday Bowl*

1986
Coach: Ken Hatfield

21	Ole Miss	0
34	Tulsa	17
42	New Mexico State	11
34	Texas Christian	17
7	Texas Tech	17
21	Texas	14
30	Houston	13
45	Rice	14
14	Baylor	29
14	Texas A&M	10
41	Southern Methodist	0
*8	Oklahoma	42

Won 9, Lost 3, Tied 0
* *Orange Bowl*

1987
Coach: Ken Hatfield

31	Ole Miss	10
30	Tulsa	15
7	Miami (FL)	51
20	Texas Christian	10
31	Texas Tech	0
14	Texas	16
21	Houston	17
38	Rice	14
10	Baylor	7
0	Texas A&M	14
43	New Mexico	25
38	Hawaii	20
*17	Georgia	20

Won 9, Lost 4, Tied 0
* *Liberty Bowl*

1988
Coach: Ken Hatfield

63	Pacific	14
30	Tulsa	26
21	Ole Miss	13
53	Texas Christian	10

31	Texas Tech	10
27	Texas	24
26	Houston	21
21	Rice	14
33	Baylor	3
25	Texas A&M	20
16	Miami (FL)	18
*3	UCLA	17

Won 10, Lost 2, Tied 0
* *Cotton Bowl*

1989

Coach: Ken Hatfield

26	Tulsa	7
24	Ole Miss	17
39	Texas-El Paso	7
41	Texas Christian	19
45	Texas Tech	13
20	Texas	24
45	Houston	39
38	Rice	17
19	Baylor	10
23	Texas A&M	22
38	Southern Methodist	24
*27	Tennessee	31

Won 10, Lost 2, Tied 0
* *Cotton Bowl*

1990

Coach: Jack Crowe
Overall record: 2 years, 9-15-0

28	Tulsa	3
17	Ole Miss	21
31	Colorado State	20
26	Texas Christian	54
44	Texas Tech	49
17	Texas	49
28	Houston	62
11	Rice	19
3	Baylor	34
16	Texas A&M	20
42	Southern Methodist	29

Won 3, Lost 8, Tied 0

1991

Coach: Jack Crowe

3	Miami (FL)	31
17	Southern Methodist	6
9	SW Louisiana	7
17	Ole Miss	24
22	Texas Christian	21
29	Houston	17
14	Texas	13
5	Baylor	9

21	Texas Tech	38
3	Texas A&M	13
20	Rice	0
*15	Georgia	24

Won 6, Lost 6, Tied 0
* *Independence Bowl*

1992

*Coach: Jack Crowe/Joe Kines**
Kines' overall record: 1 year, 3-6-1

3	The Citadel	10
45	South Carolina	7
11	Alabama	38
6	Memphis State	22
3	Georgia	27
25	Tennessee	24
3	Ole Miss	17
24	Auburn	24
3	Mississippi State	10
19	Southern Methodist	24
30	Louisiana State	6

Won 3, Lost 7, Tied 1
* *Crowe was discharged following*
the Citadel loss

1993

Coach: Danny Ford

10	Southern Methodist	6
18	South Carolina	17
3	Alabama	43
0	Memphis State	6
20	Georgia	10
14	Tennessee	28
0	Ole Miss	19
21	Auburn	31
13	Mississippi State	13
24	Tulsa	11
42	Louisiana State	24

Won 5, Lost 5, Tied 1

1994

Coach: Danny Ford

34	SMU	14
0	South Carolina	14
6	Alabama	13
15	Memphis	16
42	Vanderbilt	6
21	Tennessee	38
31	Ole Miss	7
14	Auburn	31
7	Mississippi State	17
30	Northern Illinois	27
12	LSU	30

Won 4, Lost 7, Tied 0

1995

Coach: Danny Ford

14	SMU	17
51	South Carolina	21
20	Alabama	19
27	Memphis	20
35	Vanderbilt	7
31	Tennessee	49
13	Ole Miss	6
30	Auburn	28
26	Mississippi State	21
24	SW Louisiana	13
0	LSU	28
*3	Florida	34
** 10	North Carolina	20

*   *SEC championship game*
** *Carquest Bowl*
Won 8, Lost 5, Tied 0

RAZORBACK BOWL APPEARANCES

1934 DIXIE BOWL
Arkansas 7, Centenary 7

1947 COTTON BOWL
Arkansas 0, LSU 0

1948 DIXIE BOWL
Arkansas 21, William & Mary 19

1955 COTTON BOWL
Georgia Tech 14, Arkansas 6

1960 GATOR BOWL
Arkansas 14, Georgia Tech 7

1961 COTTON BOWL
Duke 7, Arkansas 6

1962 SUGAR BOWL
Alabama 10, Arkansas 3

1963 SUGAR BOWL
Mississippi 17, Arkansas 13

1965 COTTON BOWL
Arkansas 10, Nebraska 7

1966 COTTON BOWL
LSU 14, Arkansas 7

1969 SUGAR BOWL
Arkansas 16, Georgia 2

1970 SUGAR BOWL
Mississippi 27, Arkansas 22

1971 LIBERTY BOWL
Tennessee 14, Arkansas 13

1976 COTTON BOWL
Arkansas 31, Georgia 10

1978 ORANGE BOWL
Arkansas 31, Oklahoma 6

1978 FIESTA BOWL
Arkansas 10, UCLA 10

1980 SUGAR BOWL
Alabama 24, Arkansas 9

1981 HALL OF FAME BOWL
Arkansas 34, Tulane 15

1981 GATOR BOWL
North Carolina 31, Arkansas 27

1982 BLUEBONNET BOWL
Arkansas 28, Florida 24

1984 LIBERTY BOWL
Auburn 21, Arkansas 15

1985 HOLIDAY BOWL
Arkansas 18, Arizona State 17

1987 ORANGE BOWL
Oklahoma 42, Arkansas 8

1987 LIBERTY BOWL
Georgia 20, Arkansas 17

1989 COTTON BOWL
UCLA 17, Arkansas 3

1990 COTTON BOWL
Tennessee 31, Arkansas 27

1991 INDEPENDENCE BOWL
Georgia 24, Arkansas 15

1995 CARQUEST BOWL
North Carolina 20, Arkansas 10

ROUND-ONE RAZORBACKS

Hog players drafted by the pros in the first round include:

1938   Jack Robbins, *Chicago Cardinals*
1940   Kay Eakin, *Pittsburgh Steelers*
1948   Clyde Scott, *Philadelphia Eagles*
1954   Lamar McHan, *Chicago Cardinals*
1956   Preston Carpenter, *Cleveland Browns*
1962   Lance Alworth, *San Francisco '49ers*
1967   Loyd Phillips, *Chicago Bears*
          Harry Jones, *Philadelphia Eagles*
1978   Steve Little, *St. Louis Cardinals*
1979   Dan Hampton, *Chicago Bears*
1983   Billy Ray Smith, Jr., *San Diego Chargers*
          Gary Anderson, *San Diego Chargers*
1989   Steve Atwater, *Denver Broncos*
          Wayne Martin, *New Orleans Saints*
1994   Henry Ford, *Houston Oilers*

FOOTBALL ALL-AMERICANS

1929
Wear Schoonover, *end*
1937
Jim Benton, *end*
1948
Clyde Scott, *tailback*
1954
Bud Brooks, *guard*
1959
Jim Mooty, *halfback*
1960
Wayne Harris, *linebacker*
1961
Lance Alworth, *halfback*
1962
Billy Moore, *quarterback*
1964
Ronnie Caveness, *center*

1965
Glen Ray Hines, *offensive tackle*
Bobby Crockett, *end*
Loyd Phillips, *defensive tackle*
1966
Loyd Phillips, *defensive tackle*
Martine Bercher, *safety*
1968
Jim Barnes, *guard*
1969
Rodney Brand, *center*
Cliff Powell, *linebacker*
Chuck Dicus, *end*
1970
Chuck Dicus, *end*
Dick Bumpas, *defensive tackle*
Bruce James, *defensive end*
Bill McClard, *kicker*

1971
Bill McClard, *kicker*
1976
Steve Little, *kicker*
1977
Steve Little, *kicker*
Leotis Harris, *guard*
1978
Jimmy Walker, *defensive tackle*
Dan Hampton, *defensive tackle*
1979
Greg Kolenda, *offensive tackle*
1981
Bruce Lahay, *kicker*
Billy Ray Smith, *defensive end*

1982
Billy Ray Smith, *defensive end*
Steve Korte, *offensive guard*
1983
Ron Faurot, *defensive end*
1986
Greg Horne, *punter*
1987
Tony Cherico, *nose guard*
1988
Wayne Martin, *defensive tackle*
Kendall Trainor, *kicker*
1989
Jim Mabry, *offensive tackle*

THE ALL-CENTURY TEAM

In 1994, as part of the centennial celebration of University of Arkansas football, Razorback fans from across the state voted on the best players of the past hundred years. The team included:

Lance Alworth
Steve Atwater
Alton Baldwin
Jim Benton
Martine Bercher
Bud Brooks
Leon Campbell
Ronnie Caveness
Freddie Childress
Steve Cox
Bobby Crockett
Chuck Dicus
Joe Ferguson
Barry Foster
Quinn Grovey
Dan Hampton
Dave Hanner
Leotis Harris
Wayne Harris

Ken Hatfield
Glen Ray Hines
Steve Korte
Steve Little
Wayne Martin
Lamar McHan
Bill Montgomery
Billy Moore
Jim Mooty
Loyd Phillips
Cliff Powell
Wear Schoonover
Clyde Scott
Billy Ray Smith, Jr.
Billy Ray Smith, Sr.
Pat Summerall
R. C. Thielemann
Fred Williams
Dennis Winston

RAZORBACK BASKETBALL

MOST MEMORABLE MOMENTS

Here are the most memorable Razorback basketball games of all time, as selected by the U of A Sports Information Office [all editorial comments are those of *The Arkansas Handbook*]:

1994

Arkansas 76, Duke 72
In the game that decided the national championship, the Razorbacks beat the Blue Devils in their own backyard in Charlotte. With the game tied 70-70 and no time left on the shot clock, Scotty Thurman launched the most famous basket in Hog history, a desperate three-pointer that stunned the opposition. Although over a minute remained to play, Duke couldn't recover – and Nolan Richardson's Razorbacks won the school's first-ever NCAA basketball title.

1984

Arkansas 65, North Carolina 64
Freshman Charles Balentine hit an eight footer to put the Hogs over the top against the 19-0 #1-ranked Tar Heels in Pine Bluff. Other Hog stars: Joe Kleine, Alvin Robertson.

Corliss Williamson

1979

Indiana State 73, Arkansas 71
Larry Bird's unbeaten, #1 Sycamores kept Sidney Moncrief's Hogs out of a return trip to the Final Four with this heartbreaking NCAA Midwest Regional final matchup in Cincinnati. After U.S. Reed tripped and got called for walking, Bob Heaton banged the rim to break a 71-71 tie.

1978

Arkansas 74, UCLA 70
Underdog Arkansas' famed Triplets (Ron Brewer, Marvin Delph, Sidney Moncrief) stunned the second-ranked Bruins with a 40-29 halftime score in Albuquerque, but UCLA fought back hard, eventually seizing the lead. They couldn't hold it, however. In the end, it was all Hog.

1981

Arkansas 74, Louisville 73
With only a second remaining on the clock, and defending national champion Louisville leading by one point, U. S. Reed entered into legend. His 49-foot nothing-but-net desperation basket kept Hog hopes alive in the second round of the NCAA tournament at Austin. No one who saw it will ever forget it.

1992

Arkansas 106, LSU 92
It was Arkansas' first season in the SEC, and they were tied with LSU for the lead. Whoever won the game in Fayetteville, won the title. The Razorbacks came from behind to force the game into overtime, where Shaquille O'Neal and his teammates were ripped 19-5. Lee Mayberry hit nine three-pointers on his way to 35 points, while Todd Day finished with 27.

1990

Arkansas 103, Texas 96
The Hogs jumped to a three-game lead and an eventual SWC title as the result of this victory over the desperate Horns. Lee Mayberry's three-pointer with three seconds left send the game into overtime, where the Razorbacks led all the way.

1993

Arkansas 101, Kentucky 94
No. 14 Razorbacks raced to a 10-point lead in the first 10 minutes of play against second-ranked Kentucky in their first Fayetteville matchup. After the Hogs led 73-58 with nine minutes left, the Wildcats clawed their way back to within four points before Arkansas, led by Clint McDaniel and Corliss Williamson, put it away for good.

1994

Arkansas 108, LSU 105
This typical LSU-Arkansas dogfight was decided by two miraculous three-pointers. The first came from ace Al Dillard, who tied the score with seconds remaining to send the game into overtime. The second came later, when Scotty Thurman launched an NBA-range field goal to give the Hogs the extra-period lead they kept.

RAZORBACK BASKETBALL: SEASON BY SEASON

1923 - 24
Coach: Francis Schmidt

19	NE Oklahoma State	13
33	NE Oklahoma State	12
46	Boynton Boys School	18
25	Jonesboro YMCA	38
34	Gay Oil Company	19
35	North Little Rock High	28
69	Fort Smith High Faculty	8
61	Ozark Athletic Club	36
43	NE Oklahoma State	22
42	NE Oklahoma State	14
62	Arkansas Normal	27
34	Arkansas Normal	14
31	SW Missouri State	38
22	SW Missouri State	21
11	SMU*	17
21	SMU*	15
30	TCU*	31
21	TCU*	23
28	Hendrix College	18
39	Hendrix College	21
29	Baylor*	33
28	Baylor*	14
27	Texas A&M*	35
17	Texas A&M*	32
19	Rice*	22
29	Rice*	22
26	Texas*	30
21	Texas*	32

Won 17, Lost 11
* SWC (3-9), 7th

1924 - 25
Coach: Francis Schmidt

27	College of the Ozarks	18
31	Gay Oil Company (LR)	13
31	England National Bank (LR)	22
34	Stuttgart Athletic Club	18
28	Jonesboro YMCA	24
21	SE Missouri State	28
35	Cairo (IL) Aces	7
31	Bemis(TN) YMCA	24
31	Arkansas State	9
78	England Athletic Club	22
40	Hendrix College	16
34	Hendrix College	25
29	SMU*	25
39	SMU*	20

26	TCU*	28
21	TCU*	20
39	Baylor*	14
23	Baylor	14
37	Rice*	19
29	Rice*	9
54	Texas A&M*	18
38	Texas A&M*	17
18	Texas*	20
12	Texas*	21
21	Oklahoma State	17
23	Oklahoma State	25

Won 21, Lost 5
* SWC (10-4), 3rd

1925 - 26
Coach: Francis Schmidt

81	Ozark Athletic Club	7
64	Ft. Smith National Guard	6
35	Union Trust Company (LR)	22
64	England Athletic Club	18
29	Jonesboro YMCA	22
32	Arkansas State	14
29	Centralia (IL) Lions	13
29	New Coliseum Athletic Club	20
30	St. Louis	40
43	Hendrix College	25
39	Hendrix College	21
29	SMU*	27
28	SMU*	8
22	Baylor*	9
19	Baylor*	14
69	Centenary	21
43	Centenary	9
35	Texas*	12
27	Texas*	7
54	Rice *	15
25	Rice*	17
37	Texas A&M*	27
35	Texas A&M*	21
24	TCU*	23
15	TCU*	30

Won 23, Lost 2
* SWC (11-1), 1st

1926 - 27
Coach: Francis Schmidt

27	NE Oklahoma State	13
25	NE Oklahoma State	19
38	Graham & Broening (LR)	34

42	Southwestern Bell (LR)	26
49	Jonesboro YMCA	25
42	Arkansas State	12
36	Rice*	18
34	Rice*	18
24	TCU*	16
23	TCU*	22
37	Texas A&M*	34
25	Texas A&M*	16
29	Texas*	32
24	Texas*	28
32	SMU*	30
32	SMU*	31

Won 14, Lost 2
* SWC (8-12), 1st

1927 - 28

Coach: Francis Schmidt

59	NE Oklahoma State	29
61	NE Oklahoma State	24
39	Drury College	20
31	SW Missouri State	45
53	College of the Ozarks	27
59	College of the Ozarks	20
23	TCU*	18
28	TCU*	24
42	Texas*	26
59	Texas*	29
69	Hendrix College	30
50	Hendrix College	24
59	Baylor*	21
34	Baylor*	21
48	SMU*	26
34	SMU*	22
20	Rice *	11
28	Rice*	23
42	Texas A&M*	18
46	Texas A&M*	31

Won 19, Lost 1
* SWC (12-0), 1st

1928 - 29

Coach: Francis Schmidt

54	NE Oklahoma State	28
54	NE Oklahoma State	34
32	Little Rock All-Stars	21
45	Fort Smith Collegians	22
43	Jonesboro YMCA	30
47	Earle Cardinals	25
32	SMU*	26
39	SMU*	17
41	TCU*	24

66	TCU*	26
59	Baylor*	24
71	Baylor*	23
52	Drury College	25
42	Drury College	22
48	Texas*	32
25	Texas*	36
51	Rice*	18
44	Rice*	13
49	Texas A&M*	32
38	Texas A&M*	29

Won 19, Lost 1
* SWC (11-1), 1st

1929 - 30

Coach: Charles Bassett

57	NE Oklahoma State	26
37	NE Oklahoma State	17
32	SE Oklahoma State	29
24	SE Oklahoma State	22
25	Drury College	28
13	St. Louis	32
21	SW Missouri State	40
23	Pittsburg State (KS)	36
20	Pittsburg State (KS)	51
32	TCU*	21
22	TCU*	18
22	Texas*	19
27	Texas*	29
30	Baylor*	33
27	Baylor*	21
30	Oklahoma State	20
30	Oklahoma State	23
28	SMU*	27
44	SMU*	29
28	Texas A&M*	24
25	Texas A&M*	23
30	Rice*	26
16	Rice*	37

Won 16, Lost 7
* SWC (10-2), 1st

1930 - 31

Coach: Charles Bassett

36	NE Oklahoma State	29
39	NE Oklahoma State	21
31	Pittsburg State (KS)	40
26	Pittsburg State (KS)	28
30	Colonial Baking AAU	27
30	Colonial Baking AAU	27
21	Butler	37
18	St. Louis	24

29	Texas*	21
25	Texas*	27
36	Rice*	32
31	Rice*	25
30	Texas A&M*	19
34	Texas A&M*	37
26	TCU*	35
30	TCU*	29
33	St. Louis	30
27	Baylor*	29
29	Baylor*	25
37	Oklahoma State	22
29	Oklahoma State	22
32	SMU*	27
27	SMU*	40

Won 14, Lost 9
* SWC (7-5), T 3rd

1931 - 32

Coach: Charles Bassett

46	NE Oklahoma State	28
43	NE Oklahoma State	31
33	Tulsa	28
37	Tulsa	29
41	SW Missouri State	38
20	Pittsburg State (KS)	36
45	Drury College	26
23	St. Louis	25
24	Texas*	21
25	Texas*	27
35	Drury College	14
32	Pittsburg State (KS)	21
46	SMU*	20
29	SMU*	20
28	Baylor*	34
42	Baylor*	31
27	TCU*	31
37	TCU*	24
33	St. Louis	19
37	SW Missouri State	19
23	Texas A&M*	28
25	Rice*	23
34	Rice*	19
33	Texas A&M*	27

Won 18, Lost 6
* SWC (8-4), 3rd

1932 - 33

Coach: Charles Bassett

31	NE Oklahoma State	16
33	NE Oklahoma State	20
41	Nebraska	24
28	Creighton	29

33	South Dakota	27
35	Tulsa	25
34	North Texas State	20
36	North Texas State	26
28	Texas*	36
28	Texas*	31
36	Rice*	32
33	Rice*	23
19	TCU*	29
26	TCU*	30
40	SMU*	23
26	SMU*	25
28	Tulsa	19
21	Texas A&M*	25
23	Texas A&M*	25
34	Baylor*	19
39	Baylor*	30

Won 14, Lost 7
* SWC (6-6), 4th

1933 - 34

Coach: Glen Rose

30	NE Oklahoma State	19
27	NE Oklahoma State	23
13	SW Missouri State	16
39	Diamond Oilers Ft. Smith	31
54	Central Arkansas	30
54	Colonial Baking AAU	37
37	Colonial Baking AAU	28
22	SW Missouri State	15
18	Tulsa	13
31	TCU*	15
21	TCU*	28
46	Oklahoma State	22
28	Oklahoma State	23
24	Tulsa	25
31	Baylor*	29
20	Baylor*	21
26	Texas*	28
32	Texas*	29
31	Rice*	20
22	Rice*	25
23	Texas A&M*	22
23	Texas A&M*	35
39	SMU*	35
37	SMU*	44

Won 16, Lost 8
* SWC (6-6), T 3rd

1934 - 35

Coach: Glen Rose

38	NE Oklahoma State	21
53	NE Oklahoma State	14

21	Tulsa	25
26	Diamond Oilers (Tulsa)	28
50	E. Central State (OK)	21
33	Tulsa	14
31	Rice*	30
37	Rice*	19
41	TCU*	20
42	TCU*	24
60	Ft. Smith Vehicle Sports	32
37	Baylor*	27
48	Baylor*	30
47	Texas*	30
23	Texas	33
22	SMU*	30
27	SMU*	41
45	Texas A&M*	41
51	Texas A&M*	31

Won 14, Lost 5
* SWC (9-3), T 1st

1935 - 36

Coach: Glen Rose

47	NE Oklahoma State	19
50	NE Oklahoma State	19
21	Oklahoma State	33
24	Oklahoma State	15
47	Tulsa	30
52	Ft. Smith Vehicle Sports	24
42	Central Arkansas	38
66	Cenral Arkansas	27
42	Oklahoma Tire AAU	39
22	Texas A&M*	18
34	Texas A&M*	27
33	Rice*	26
29	Rice*	35
42	Tulsa	28
34	SMU*	23
40	SMU*	28
44	Baylor*	26
39	Baylor*	14
47	TCU*	15
40	TCU*	29
38	Texas*	37
43	Texas*	31
27	Texas	16
53	Stephen F. Austin	24
43	Western Kentucky	36
39	Western Kentucky	30
29	Hollywood Universal	40

Won 24, Lost 3
* SWC (11-1), 1st

1936 - 37

Coach: Glen Rose

31	Drake	22
33	SE Oklahoma State	19
39	SE Oklahoma State	28
42	Tennessee	34
29	Brown Paper Mill AAU	31
22	Baylor*	25
42	Baylor*	24
25	SMU*	29
37	SMU*	28
28	Texas*	39
31	Texas*	43
45	Texas A&M*	19
36	Texas A&M*	32
52	Rice*	29
52	Rice*	34
33	Phillips 66ers	39
38	TCU*	35
43	TCU*	21

Won 12, Lost 6
* SWC (8-4), 2nd

1937 - 38

Coach: Glen Rose

52	Staff-O-Life AAU	26
40	Murray State (KY)	43
47	Ole Miss	43
48	Ole Miss	46
45	NW Oklahoma State	44
43	Central State (MO)	36
33	SW Kansas State	36
32	North Texas State	21
45	Texas A&M*	32
33	Texas A&M*	22
28	Parks Clothiers AAU	25
38	Rice*	31
59	Rice*	37
57	Marianne (AR) AAU	25
53	TCU*	26
57	TCU*	38
74	Texas*	38
42	Texas*	37
47	Baylor*	54
54	Baylor*	45
32	SMU*	23
34	SMU*	26

Won 19, Lost 3
* SWC (11-1), 1st

1938 - 39
Coach: Glen Rose

51	SE Oklahoma State	33
36	SE Oklahoma State	21
32	Phillips 66ers	31
44	Drury College	21
27	Drury College	19
39	Oklahoma	31
36	Oklahoma	30
28	Parks Clothiers AAU	66
51	Purdue	57
61	Fort Smith Buick AAU	19
31	SMU*	47
19	SMU*	32
37	Texas*	41
65	Texas*	41
46	Baylor*	38
40	Baylor*	36
44	TCU*	32
51	TCU*	38
48	Parks Clothiers AAU	45
61	Texas A&M*	42
66	Texas A&M*	38
50	Rice*	45
40	Rice*	35

Won 18, Lost 5
* SWC (9-3), 2nd

1939 - 40
Coach Glen Rose

32	SE Oklahoma State	20
25	SE Oklahoma State	26
50	Pittsburg State (KS)	62
49	Pittsburg State (KS)	42
36	Oklahoma	49
40	Oklahoma	38
48	West Texas State	43
44	Pittsburg State (KS)	33
26	Oklahoma State	32
60	Central State (MO)	46
33	Texas*	52
54	Texas*	44
24	Baylor*	40
39	Baylor*	47
75	SMU*	40
36	SMU*	26
37	Texas A&M*	25
38	Texas A&M*	41
43	Rice*	60
28	Rice*	42
59	TCU*	45

52	TCU*	36

Won 12, Lost 10
* SWC (6-6), 4th

1940 - 41
Coach: Glen Rose

62	Drury	17
46	Drury	20
52	Murray State (KY)	30
58	Southwestern (TN)	35
38	Phillips 66ers	24
33	Phillips 66ers	35
48	Pittsburg State (KS)	45
50	Texas*	38
44	Texas*	34
68	Texas A&M*	33
58	Texas A&M*	36
71	Pittsburg State (KS)	45
62	Baylor*	48
36	Baylor*	31
66	Rice*	41
48	Rice*	43
26	Phillips 66ers	31
67	TCU*	42
66	TCU*	43
40	SMU*	23
40	SMU*	32

NCAA Western Regional

52	Wyoming	40
43	Washington State	64

Won 20, Lost 3
* SWC (12-0), 1st

1941 - 42
Coach: Glen Rose

30	SE Oklahoma State	19
38	SE Oklahoma State	36
43	Central State (OK)	23
42	Central State (OK)	25
44	Central State (MO)	36
41	West Texas State	54
52	SMU	22
54	East Central (OK)	28
33	Phillips 66ers	34
35	SMU*	33
36	SMU*	34
38	Rice*	51
59	Tulsa	30
53	Baylor*	43
50	Baylor*	45
47	Texas A&M*	45
40	Texas A&M*	31

42	Texas*	34
37	Texas*	58
69	Tulsa	27
41	TCU*	33
63	TCU*	37

Won 19, Lost 4
* SWC (10-2), T 1st

1942 - 43

Coach: Eugene Lambert

43	Camp Crowder (MO)	31
50	East Central (OK)	48
57	Pittsburgh St. (KS)	46
40	Camp Crowder (MO)	29
42	Drury College	29
47	SW Missouri St.	31
44	Ouachita College	29
43	Texas Tech*	38
52	Texas Wesleyan	46
66	Texas*	44
25	TCU*	37
27	Phillips 66ers	48
43	Pittsburgh St. (KS)	38
37	St. Louis	43
39	SMU*	35
36	SMU*	29
52	Rice*	35
37	Rice*	41
68	Baylor*	25
40	Baylor*	38
31	Texas*	45
35	Texas*	48
74	Texas A&M*	49
52	Texas A&M*	67
33	TCU*	23
54	TCU*	39

Won 19, Lost 7
* SWC (8-4), 3rd

1943 - 44

Coach: Eugene Lambert

60	Conway (AR) AAU	33
42	Pittsburg State (KS)	37
65	Springfield (MO) AAU	40
58	Camp Chaffee	52
39	City College New York	37
40	Albright College	47
30	DePaul (Buffalo, NY)	59
71	TCU*	50
60	TCU*	29
42	Rice*	41
41	Rice*	67
68	SMU*	58

74	SMU*	49
41	Oklahoma State	66
15	Oklahoma State	17
42	Phillips 66ers	57
45	Baylor*	28
36	Baylor*	34
59	Texas*	48
54	Texas*	46
42	Pittsburg State (KS)	50
70	Texas A&M*	35
60	Texas A&M*	38
42	Camp Chaffee	58

Won 16, Lost 8
* SWC (11-1), T 1st

1944 - 45

Coach: Eugene Lambert

45	Pittsburg State (KS)	37
76	Blytheville AAB	45
59	City College, NY	47
61	Westminster College (PA)	71
50	Denver	36
54	Oklahoma	51
34	Oklahoma State	43
94	Baylor*	28
90	Baylor*	30
40	Phillips 66ers	60
41	Oklahoma State	38
40	Oklahoma State	49
40	Texas*	49
74	Texas*	38
46	Rice*	57
56	Rice*	69
37	TCU*	33
60	TCU*	35
76	Pittsburg State (KS)	45
59	SMU*	52
65	SMU*	49
80	Texas A&M*	21
87	Texas A&M*	36
34	Phillips 66ers	62

NCAA Midwest Regional

79	Oregon	76
41	Oklahoma State	68

Won 17, Lost 9
* SWC (9-3), 2nd

1945 - 46

Coach: Eugene Lambert

76	Camp Chaffee	35
101	Sedalia AAB (MO)	37
66	Western Kentucky	46
67	Western Kentucky	38

52	Memphis NATTC	47
62	New York University	63
42	Kentucky	67
55	Texas*	47
90	Texas*	63
49	Baylor*	37
28	Baylor*	40
62	Camp Hood (TX)	53
81	SMU*	53
74	SMU*	46
62	Rice*	45
68	Rice*	25
50	TCU*	53
58	TCU*	36
29	Oklahoma State	53
31	Oklahoma State	46
31	Camp Robinson (AR)	53
55	Texas A&M*	56
53	Texas A&M*	43

Won 16, Lost 7
* *SWC (9-3), 2nd*

1946 - 47

Coach: Eugene Lambert

56	Tulsa	21
57	Nebraska	46
52	Kansas	53
41	Kansas State	56
46	New York University	67
46	St. Joseph's (PA)	36
52	Pittsburg State (KS)	53
52	Rice*	51
66	Rice*	53
54	TCU*	39
63	TCU*	53
55	University of Mexico	37
38	Oklahoma State	42
44	Oklahoma State	49
59	Central Arkansas	39
55	Baylor*	50
68	Baylor*	57
62	SMU*	64
44	SMU*	47
62	Texas A&M*	56
71	Texas A&M*	58
44	Texas*	49
46	Texas*	66

Won 14, Lost 10
* *SWC (8-4), T 2nd*

1947 - 48

Coach: Eugene Lambert

75	Pittsburg State (KS)	42

68	Culver-Stockton (MO)	36
62	New York Univversity	85
58	LaSalle (PA)	69
62	North Texas State	49
58	Brigham Young	68
60	Loyola (CA)	47
70	Pepperdine	44
74	San Francisco	58
53	Standard	60
58	Texas A&M*	51
57	Texas A&M*	46
47	SMU*	40
58	SMU*	57
42	Alabama	35
76	Arkansas State	59
38	Baylor*	42
47	Baylor*	55
37	TCU*	30
47	TCU*	38
54	Texas*	40
43	Texas*	54
49	Rice*	61
66	Rice*	63

Won 16, Lost 8
* *SWC (8-4), 3rd*

1948 - 49

Coach: Eugene Lambert

40	Phillips 66ers	58
31	Oklahoma City	29
28	Oklahoma State	53
42	Long Island University	56
51	Canisius	60
39	Kentucky	76
79	Pittsburg State (KS)	53
45	Oklahoma State	50
58	Tennessee	55
37	Baylor*	41
32	Phillips 66ers	58
54	SMU*	45
41	TCU*	36
48	Rice*	49
62	Texas A&M*	47
52	Baylor*	46
60	Texas*	54
54	Texas*	50
47	SMU*	39
67	TCU*	52
48	Rice*	54
61	Texas A&M*	46

NCAA Regional

50	Rice	34

65	Arizona	44
38	Oregon State	56
61	Wyoming	48

Won 15, Lost 11
* SWC (9-3), T 1st

1949 - 50

Coach: Presley Askew

59	Pittsburg State (KS)	41
41	Oklahoma State	43
46	LSU	62
42	Tulane	41
53	Illinois	65
50	Indiana	75
36	Oklahoma State	44
41	Alabama	33
26	Wyoming	40
33	Oklahoma State	57
53	Kentucky	57
60	Texas*	51
35	Texas A&M*	43
60	Rice*	56
63	SMU*	55
49	Baylor*	60
51	Texas*	37
42	Baylor*	52
41	Pittsburg	36
52	Texas A&M*	46
52	TCU*	43
61	Rice*	38
48	SMU*	57
45	TCU*	39

Won 12, Lost 12
* SWC (8-4), T 1st

1950 - 51

Coach: Presley Askew

50	Arkansas Tech	45
59	Tulsa	46
53	Oklahoma State	55
46	Tulsa	48
33	Oklahoma State	44
32	Missouri	54
45	Ole Miss	35
41	Ole Miss	45
53	Tulsa	44
46	Alabama	34
41	Oklahoma State	54
31	TCU*	42
45	SMU*	60
42	Texas*	50
69	Baylor*	55

33	Texas A&M*	34
50	Rice*	42
50	SMU*	48
45	Texas A&M*	38
64	LSU	50
55	Baylor*	44
40	Texas*	38
42	TCU*	52
57	Rice*	43

Won 13, Lost 11
* SWC (7-5), 4th

1951 - 52

Coach: Presley Askew

52	Central (MO) College	42
39	Philips 66ers	74
66	Ole Miss	58
68	Ole Miss	66
44	Tulsa	48
39	Mississippi State	79
49	Missouri	43
48	Tulsa	66
46	Texas A&M	49
40	SMU	54
58	Baylor	44
42	Texas A&M*	47
51	Texas*	62
54	Baylor*	38
46	Rice*	48
53	Pittsburg State (KS)	37
56	TCU*	54
50	SMU*	54
55	Rice*	59
49	Texas A&M*	40
39	Baylor*	44
48	SMU*	57
56	TCU*	68
45	Texas*	44

Won 10, Lost 14
* SWC (4-8), T 6th

1952 - 53

Coach: Glen Rose

50	Tulsa	69
102	Mississippi State	71
65	Missouri	64
104	Ole Miss	72
68	Arizona	51
62	SMU	65
59	Baylor	54
50	Tulsa	61
48	Texas A&M*	56

57	Texas*	62
87	Rice*	68
49	Baylor*	47
79	Pittsburg State (KS)	63
46	TCU*	49
71	SMU*	66
45	Rice*	70
65	Texas*	70
66	Texas A&M*	46
68	Baylor*	74
63	TCU*	65
74	SMU*	79

Won 10, Lost 11
* SWC (4-8), T 5th

1953 - 54

Coach: Glen Rose

50	Tulsa	51
71	NW Louisiana State	62
69	Washington (MO)	55
64	Missouri	63
68	Washington (MO)	50
60	TCU	50
65	Texas	66
66	SMU	70
55	Tulsa	49
89	Ole Miss	76
61	Texas*	64
59	Baylor*	63
61	SMU*	58
55	Rice*	80
80	Texas A&M*	55
66	TCU*	59
68	SMU*	92
70	TCU*	55
73	Baylor*	51
62	Rice*	76
67	Texas A&M*	54
57	Texas*	67

Won 13, Lost 9
* SWC (6-6), T 3rd

1954 - 55

Coach: Glen Rose

68	NW Louisiana State	74
81	Oklahoma City	76
47	Tulsa	63
58	Missouri	77
74	Ole Miss	64
73	Rice	66
67	Alabama	87
74	Texas A&M	70

68	Tulsa	60
62	TCU*	67
59	Texas A&M*	62
83	Rice*	61
73	Baylor*	63
55	Oklahoma City	52
85	SMU*	74
74	Texas*	75
75	Baylor*	72
86	Rice*	75
72	St. Louis	99
79	Texas*	74
69	SMU*	83
73	Texas A&M*	63
110	TCU*	89

Won 14, Lost 9
* SWC (8-4), T 2nd

1955 - 56

Coach: Glen Rose

64	SE Oklahoma State	65
45	Tulsa	53
66	Oklahoma State	70
59	Oklahoma	69
62	SMU	67
63	Baylor	67
80	Texas A&M	49
50	Missouri	51
85	Baylor*	64
70	Texas*	67
84	Rice*	70
98	Texas A&M*	66
85	Ole Miss	69
74	TCU*	72
53	SMU*	58
36	Baylor*	31
65	Rice*	86
61	Texas A&M*	52
79	Texas*	69
72	SMU*	80
90	TCU*	71
51	Tulsa	55
66	St. Louis	68

Won 11, Lost 12
* SWC (9-3), 2nd

1956 - 57

Coach: Glen Rose

59	Oklahoma	55
47	Wichita State	64
77	Tulsa	70
50	Oklahoma State	59

52	Missouri	72
80	Wichita State	67
89	Texas	76
81	Rice	70
60	SMU	64
73	Texas A&M*	65
68	Rice*	78
51	Baylor*	52
67	Texas*	66
56	Kansas State	70
62	TCU*	58
55	SMU*	69
63	Texas A&M*	46
52	Tulsa	43
57	TCU*	64
69	Rice*	82
61	Baylor*	67
70	Texas*	54
59	SMU*	87

Won 11, Lost 12
* SWC (5-7), 5th

1957 - 58
Coach: Glen Rose

52	Oklahoma	64
59	New Mexico State	50
79	Tulsa	61
61	Ole Miss	58
48	Kansas State	63
55	Missouri	45
83	Texas	67
49	Rice	50
71	Texas Tech	67
57	Texas*	55
68	Baylor*	53
65	TCU*	49
58	Texas Tech*	55
50	Tulsa	43
67	Texas A&M*	51
46	SMU*	49
56	TCU*	46
59	Rice*	63
65	SMU*	63
48	Texas Tech*	69
57	Texas A&M*	66
59	Rice*	61
79	Baylor*	55
74	Texas*	60
61	SMU	55

NCAA Midwest-Regional

40	Oklahoma State	65
62	Cincinnati	97

Won 17, Lost 10
* SWC (9-5), T 1st

1958 - 59
Coach: Glen Rose

71	Missouri	74
61	Oklahoma	52
58	LSU	67
83	Ole Miss	81
52	Tulsa	54
64	SMU	65
60	Baylor	57
62	Texas Tech	72
61	Texas Tech*	57
45	TCU*	52
72	Rice*	61
62	Texas A&M*	63
54	Tulsa	61
58	Baylor*	64
50	SMU*	59
77	Texas*	74
62	Rice*	68
71	TCU*	76
59	Baylor*	53
72	Texas A&M*	71
51	SMU*	56
63	Texas*	56
69	Texas Tech*	80

Won 9, Lost 14
* SWC (6-8), T 5th

1959 - 60
Coach: Glen Rose

71	Missouri	75
54	Oklahoma State	50
65	Tulsa	51
63	Ole Miss	78
75	Centenary	55
71	Baylor	66
56	SMU	67
68	Texas	58
74	TCU*	60
90	Baylor*	83
66	Texas*	72
74	Rice*	63
65	Tulsa	78
79	Texas Tech*	82
70	SMU*	72
68	Texas A&M*	77
66	TCU*	61
78	Texas Tech*	55

61	Texas A&M*	82
94	Rice*	74
57	Texas*	71
83	Baylor*	74
82	SMU*	93

Won 12, Lost 11
* SWC (7-7), T 4th

1960 - 61

Coach: Glen Rose

84	Missouri	75
50	Oklahoma State	59
94	North Texas State	80
77	Ole Miss	71
59	Tulsa	64
71	Centenary	61
83	Alabama	76
89	Tennessee	76
58	Texas*	68
76	SMU*	74
62	Texas A&M*	81
80	Rice*	55
66	Tulsa	58
74	Baylor*	58
88	TCU*	75
66	Texas Tech*	72
84	Rice	72
74	Texas*	59
81	Texas Tech*	87
96	TCU*	76
70	Baylor*	48
88	SMU*	82
68	Texas A&M*	70

Won 16, Lost 7
* SWC (9-5), 3rd

1961 - 62

Coach: Glen Rose

74	Kansas	85
72	Missouri	68
68	North Texas State	61
63	Oklahoma State	54
87	Tulsa	59
59	Ole Miss	54
84	LSU	81
62	Clemson	60
72	Georgia Tech	42
64	Texas A&M*	59
59	Texas*	73
70	SMU*	77
64	TCU*	61
99	Tulsa	77

104	Rice*	84
64	Texas Tech*	66
60	Baylor*	76
90	TCU*	80
55	Rice*	63
64	Texas Tech*	76
76	Baylor*	75
79	Texas A&M*	89
60	Texas*	61
81	SMU*	84

* SWC (5-9), 6th
Won 14, Lost 10

1962 - 63

Coach: Glen Rose

64	Kansas	62
70	Missouri	61
45	Oklahoma State	46
68	Tulsa	76
90	Ole Miss	60
70	LSU	72
62	Loyola (Chicago)	81
58	Toledo	55
73	Creighton	61
73	SMU*	71
63	Texas*	69
81	TCU*	59
70	Rice*	85
66	Tulsa	68
66	Texas A&M*	55
75	Texas Tech*	80
75	Baylor*	65
65	Rice*	69
78	Texas A&M*	80
83	Texas Tech*	78
67	Baylor*	61
82	SMU*	79
86	Texas*	99
104	TCU*	94

* SWC (8-6), 4th
Won 13, Lost 11

1963 - 64

Coach: Glen Rose

71	SW Louisiana	65
74	Missouri	76
60	Kansas	73
65	Oklahoma State	74
77	Vanderbilt	101
86	Lamar Tech	80
57	Tennessee	77
76	Ole Miss	68
84	Texas Tech*	93

58	Texas*	53
66	TCU*	60
86	Tulsa*	95
74	Baylor*	70
63	Rice*	76
64	Texas A&M*	72
83	SMU*	71
73	Baylor*	61
69	Rice*	77
57	Texas A&M*	60
71	SMU*	86
86	Texas Tech*	87
67	Texas*	80
108	TCU*	77

* SWC (6-8), 6th
Won 9, Lost 14

1964 - 65

Coach: Glen Rose

60	Kansas	65
71	Missouri	81
52	Oklahoma State	66
68	Hardin-Simmons	63
65	Tulsa	64
82	Ole Miss	48
70	VMI	72
88	TCU*	70
78	Texas Tech*	93
79	Rice*	61
75	Baylor*	84
84	Mississippi State	69
83	Georgia Tech	93
79	Texas A&M*	82
76	SMU*	84
65	Texas*	81
96	TCU*	72
78	Baylor*	73
77	Texas A&M*	91
72	Texas*	74
77	Rice*	64
80	Texas Tech*	87
75	SMU*	88

Won 9, Lost 14
* SWC (5-9), 5th

1965 - 66

Coach: Glen Rose

52	Kansas	81
75	Missouri	62
55	Oklahoma State	52
90	Centenary	61
78	Texas-Arlington	64
75	Iowa	77

67	Loyola (LA)	57
85	TCU*	88
74	Texas Tech*	65
72	Texas A&M*	75
93	Texas*	82
69	Mississippi State	61
75	Georgia Tech	88
74	SMU*	75
78	Baylor*	59
76	Rice*	71
71	Baylor*	82
73	Rice*	67
66	SMU*	67
91	TCU*	73
74	Texas Tech*	79
70	Texas*	74
94	Texas A&M*	71

Won 13, Lost 10
* SWC (7-7), T 4th

1966 - 67

Coach: Duddy Waller

57	Kansas	73
66	Missouri	73
51	Oklahoma State	46
80	Centenary	81
36	Memphis State	43
43	Oklahoma State	50
67	Southern Cal	70
65	Arizona	61
72	Michigan	82
62	Texas*	71
70	Texas Tech*	65
53	Baylor*	65
47	Texas A&M*	46
59	SMU*	69
61	TCU*	78
56	Rice*	60
61	Texas*	67
53	Texas A&M*	60
66	Rice*	63
66	SMU*	69
83	TCU*	78
59	Texas Tech*	73
55	Baylor*	68

Won 6, Lost 17
* SWC (4-10), T 7th

1967 - 68

Coach: Duddy Waller

52	Missouri	74
52	Oklahoma State	61
64	Ole Miss	62

85	Centenary	65
90	Centenary	82
65	Alabama	82
58	Auburn	65
73	Fordham	80
75	Idaho State	77
75	Texas A&M*	70
61	Rice*	73
69	Baylor*	80
85	Texas*	80
90	Oklahoma City	92
68	TCU*	67
70	SMU*	68
61	Texas Tech*	56
75	TCU*	77
72	Texas Tech*	74
87	SMU*	95
67	Texas A&M*	71
78	Rice*	65
64	Baylor*	71
74	Texas*	73

Won 10, Lost 14
* SWC (7-7), 5th

1968 - 69

Coach: Duddy Waller

59	Missouri	60
68	Oklahoma State	73
61	Ole Miss	65
64	Centenary	61
80	Texas-Arlington	69
79	Centenary	50
52	Alabama	48
87	Texas-Arlington	78
56	Centenary	48
67	Rice*	62
68	Texas A&M*	73
59	Texas*	67
73	Oklahoma City	84
72	Baylor*	74
79	TCU*	85
64	Texas Tech*	53
69	SMU	84
63	TCU*	47
68	SMU*	76
57	Texas Tech*	59
67	Rice*	74
66	Texas A&M*	79
54	Baylor*	66
69	Texas*	65

Won 10, Lost 14
* SWC (4-10), 8th

1969 - 70

Coach: Duddy Waller

51	Missouri	58
67	Oklahoma State	80
66	Tulsa	74
74	Mississippi State	76
85	Texas-Arlington	73
75	Kentucky Wesleyan	76
85	SW Louisiana	94
69	Oklahoma	85
81	NW Louisiana	74
59	Texas A&M*	64
69	Texas*	75
70	Oklahoma City	73
76	Baylor*	110
68	TCU*	82
48	Texas Tech*	50
69	Rice*	76
75	SMU*	76
76	Baylor	75
88	SMU*	72
78	Rice*	85
71	Texas Tech*	76
60	Texas A&M*	72
78	Texas*	61
95	TCU*	97

Won 5, Lost 19
* SWC (3-11), 8th

1970 - 71

Coach: Lanny Van Eman

78	Missouri	80
96	Hardin-Simmons	112
65	Oklahoma State	67
107	Pittsburg State (KS)	82
78	Southern Illinois	99
77	Iowa State	86
67	Mississippi State	69
71	Centenary	61
91	Missouri-St. Louis	84
100	Oklahoma	115
110	Hardin-Simmons	101
79	Texas*	88
68	Texas Tech*	98
82	Rice*	85
75	Washburn (KS)	80
88	SMU*	90
87	TCU*	89
83	Texas A&M*	87
99	SMU*	112
91	Baylor*	92
86	TCU*	92

88	Texas*	87
87	Texas Tech*	89
93	Rice*	97
110	Baylor*	111
89	Texas A&M*	92

Won 5, Lost 21
* SWC (1-13), 8th

1971 - 72
Coach: Lanny Van Eman

93	Georgia Southern	91
73	Missouri	74
79	Missouri-St. Louis	85
102	Rockhurst	72
92	Southern Illinois	93
90	Oklahoma State	76
81	San Francisco State	84
93	Iowa State	96
94	Utah State	95
73	Idaho State	88
77	Memphis State	92
75	Mississippi State	79
77	TCU*	95
100	Texas A&M*	89
71	SMU*	85
93	Texas*	117
73	Texas Tech*	76
103	Rice*	95
84	Baylor	93
90	TCU*	98
85	Texas A&M*	86
88	SMU*	74
86	Texas*	92
85	Texas Tech*	86
131	Baylor*	109
113	Rice*	108

Won 8, Lost 18
* SWC (5-9), 6th

1972 - 73
Coach: Lanny Van Eman

87	Rockhurst	76
85	Missouri Western	81
67	Illinois State	81
87	Tulane	83
80	Indiana State	75
70	Georgia State	39
86	Memphis State	87
77	Cornell	78
97	Southern Illinois	96
72	Centenary	80
104	Missouri-St. Louis	78
81	Tulsa	85

84	Texas A&M*	73
76	Texas*	72
70	Baylor*	76
90	TCU*	75
94	SMU*	110
90	Rice*	69
64	Texas Tech*	73
82	Texas A&M*	108
86	Texas*	74
76	Baylor*	74
96	TCU*	95
103	SMU*	96
63	Texas Tech*	64
105	Rice*	79

Won 16, Lost 10
* SWC (9-5), T 2nd

1973 - 74
Coach: Lanny Van Eman

79	UCLA	101
80	Cal-Santa Barbara	109
100	Western Kentucky	102
80	Tennessee-Martin	68
83	Wabash	77
66	Ole Miss	117
72	Tulsa	95
96	VMI	86
83	Pittsburgh	91
96	Centenary	98
82	Indiana State	92
89	Tulane	73
77	Texas Tech*	80
69	Rice*	77
89	SMU*	88
86	TCU*	74
68	Baylor*	94
81	Texas*	96
80	Texas A&M*	86
106	Rice*	81
83	Texas Tech*	89
87	SMU*	95
109	TCU*	99
92	Baylor*	62
82	Texas*	99
97	Texas A&M*	86

Won 10, Lost 16
* SWC (6-8), 5th

1974 - 75
Coach: Eddie Sutton

78	Rockhurst	61
75	Mississippi State	72

Eddie Sutton

63	Western Kentucky	74
73	Ole Miss	84
63	Hofstra	58
60	Tulsa	64
77	Oklahoma City	79
100	MacMurry (IL)	66
72	Centenary	74
84	Oklahoma City	75
88	Western Illinois	51
71	Kansas State	73
65	Texas Tech*	62
73	SMU*	69
74	Rice*	67
69	Baylor*	73
56	Texas*	52
95	Texas A&M*	89
70	TCU*	61
60	Texas A&M*	62
81	TCU*	57
55	Texas Tech*	63
86	Rice*	51
72	SMU*	50
68	Texas*	56
83	Baylor*	64

Won 17, Lost 9
* SWC (11-3), 2nd

1975-76
Coach: Eddie Sutton

83	SW Missouri State	57
67	Tulane	55
58	Air Force	59
72	Boise State	56
64	Oklahoma	56
84	Oklahoma City	63
102	Eastern New Mexico	55
91	Indiana State	71
92	Houston*	47
81	SMU*	82
71	Houston*	72
80	Rice*	62
100	TCU*	65
57	Texas*	59
93	Texas A&M*	91
81	Baylor*	84
92	Texas Tech*	86
76	SMU*	82
78	Texas Tech*	86
75	Western Illinois	72
111	Rice*	68
83	TCU*	66
75	Texas*	68
69	Texas A&M*	70
86	Baylor*	64
81	TCU	65
74	SMU	70
63	Texas Tech	70

Won 19, Lost 9
* SWC (9-7), 4th

1976 - 77
Coach: Eddie Sutton

72	Air Force	54
89	California-Hayward	59
72	SW Missouri State	71
91	Southern Colorado	43
71	Oklahoma City	60
67	Kansas	63
80	Kansas State	65
81	Tulsa	66
62	Memphis State	69
41	Texas Tech*	38
81	Houston*	70
60	Texas Tech*	53
72	Rice*	45
62	TCU*	45
86	Texas*	58
72	Texas A&M*	58
77	SMU*	59
68	Baylor*	59
82	Houston*	80
76	Tulane	73
77	Baylor*	57

78 Rice* 51
79 TCU* 64
73 Texas* 61
63 Texas A&M* 62
80 Houston 74
NCAA Midwest Regional
80 Wake Forest 86
Won 26, Lost 2
* SWC (16-0), 1st

1977 - 78
Coach: Eddie Sutton
65 SW Missouri State 47
94 Mississippi State 61
79 Hawaii 60
78 Hawaii 53
99 Rockhurst 63
64 Oklahoma 53
86 Hardin-Simmons 55
78 Kansas 72
67 LSU 62
95 Memphis State 70
95 Hofstra 70
84 Houston* 65
87 Missouri-St. Louis 65
69 Rice* 60
69 Texas* 75
84 Texas A&M* 68
43 TCU* 35
56 Baylor* 55
72 SMU* 65
54 Texas Tech* 49
75 Texas* 71
69 Rice* 48
80 Texas A&M 79
77 TCU* 57
82 Baylor* 56
86 SMU* 75
75 Houston* 84
58 Texas Tech* 49
84 TCU 42
94 SMU 73
69 Houston 70
NCAA Western Regional
73 Weber State 52
74 UCLA 70
61 California-Fullerton 58
NCAA Finals
59 Kentucky 64
71 Notre Dame (3rd Place) 69
Won 32, Lost 4
* SWC (14-2), T 1st

1978 - 79
Coach: Eddie Sutton
80 Oklahoma 74
84 West Texas State 54
90 SE Missouri State 51
77 Centenary 57
67 Ole Miss 66
93 Southern Mississippi 79
82 Memphis State 69
96 North Texas State 71
62 Houston* 61
79 Rice* 66
63 Texas* 66
57 North Carolina 63
69 Texas A&M* 74
90 TCU* 51
67 Baylor* 70
79 SMU* 67
63 Texas Tech* 57
68 Texas* 58
68 Rice* 50
60 Texas A&M* 56
108 TCU 65
71 Baylor* 62
71 SMU* 55
78 Houston* 58
66 Texas Tech* 65
93 Texas Tech 77
39 Texas 38
NCAA Midwest Regional
74 Weber State 63
73 Louisville 62
71 Indiana State 73
Won 25, Lost 5
* SWC (13-3), T 1st

1979 - 80
Coach: Eddie Sutton
76 Loyola (CA) 66
65 Centenary 53
79 Missouri-St. Louis 50
70 Centenary 62
67 Ole Miss 59
86 Oklahoma City 68
55 LSU 56
67 Memphis State 74
57 Kansas State 66
84 SMU* 69
74 Northeast Louisiana 51
70 TCU* 58
55 Texas* 50

71	Baylor*	57
60	Houston*	57
39	Texas A&M*	45
73	Rice*	64
71	Texas Tech*	69
60	Texas*	59
74	TCU*	47
70	Baylor*	51
84	Houston*	90
45	Texas A&M*	44
77	Rice*	73
58	SMU*	62
84	Texas Tech*	60
64	Texas	62
50	Texas A&M	52

NCAA Midwest Regional

53	Kansas State	71

Won 21, Lost 8
* SWC (13-3), 2nd

1980 - 81

Coach: Eddie Sutton

81	Missouri	73
86	LSU	76
58	North Carolina	64
98	SW Missouri State	65
65	Michigan	78
76	Oklahoma City	70
78	Centenary	64
80	Eastern Kentucky	74
76	Southern Mississippi	68
46	Kansas State	47
64	Nebraska	52
92	SMU*	50
92	Alaska	58
85	TCU*	51
60	Texas*	62
58	Baylor*	67
54	Houston*	57
52	Texas A&M*	47
57	Rice*	52
60	Texas Tech*	35
54	Texas*	48
63	TCU*	48
67	Baylor*	50
70	Houston*	55
65	Texas A&M*	61
75	Rice*	59
47	SMU*	33
64	Texas Tech*	61
73	Texas	76

NCAA Midwest Regional

73	Mercer	67
74	Louisville	73
56	LSU	72

Won 24, Lost 8
* SWC (13-3), 1st

1981 - 82

Coach: Eddie Sutton

83	Michigan	72
71	Texas-San Antonio	42
85	San Diego State	68
84	Wisconsin-Parkside	59
87	Centenary	60
91	Biscayne	61
63	Southern Mississippi	54
91	Kent State	49
74	Texas Tech*	79
68	SMU*	48
51	Nebraska	50
62	TCU*	59
73	Texas*	87
70	Baylor*	58
67	Houston*	66
64	Texas A&M*	63
60	Rice*	54
48	Wake Forest	49
62	Texas*	55
79	TCU*	69
55	Baylor*	56
53	Houston*	55
92	Texas A&M*	75
72	Rice*	65
54	SMU*	53
67	Texas Tech*	61
80	TCU	70
84	Houston	69

NCAA Midwest Regional

64	Kansas State	65

Won 23, Lost 6
* SWC (12-4), 1st

1982 - 83

Coach: Eddie Sutton

74	SE Missouri State	57
78	Texas-San Antonio	59
79	Centenary	51
87	SW Missouri State	66
108	Alabama State	65
89	NE Louisiana	76
64	Southern Mississippi	62
52	St. Peter's	48

64	Nebraska	58
83	Mercer	62
65	Baylor*	60
66	Texas A&M*	64
63	SMU*	56
69	TCU*	55
60	Houston*	75
83	Texas*	64
62	Texas Tech*	59
68	Wake Forest	65
70	Rice*	43
81	Baylor*	66
62	Texas A&M*	55
71	SMU*	61
64	TCU*	56
84	Texas*	67
77	Texas Tech*	63
66	Houston*	74
82	Rice*	55
59	TCU	61

NCAA Midwest Regional

| 78 | Purdue | 68 |
| 63 | Louisville | 65 |

Won 26, Lost 4
* SWC (14-2), 2nd

1983 - 84
Coach: Eddie Sutton

62	Fordham	61
84	Oklahoma	78
60	North Carolina State	65
98	SE Missouri State	69
79	East Tennessee State	50
56	SW Missouri State	41
54	Nebraska	67
93	North Texas State	64
86	Alabama State	80
82	St. Peter's	49
68	Austin Peay	63
57	Baylor*	50
77	Texas A&M*	54
70	SMU*	69
70	TCU*	62
70	Texas	66
67	Texas Tech*	57
62	Rice*	65
54	Villanova	58
63	Baylor*	44
59	Texas A&M*	58
80	SMU*	71
65	North Carolina	64
55	TCU*	48

59	Texas*	41
55	Texas Tech*	49
61	Houston*	64
79	Rice*	54
73	Houston*	68
49	Texas A&M	47
56	Houston	57

NCAA East Regional

| 51 | Virginia | 53 |

Won 25, Lost 7
* SWC (14-2), 2nd

1984 - 85
Coach: Eddie Sutton

65	Southeast Louisiana	62
59	Central Florida	45
84	Ohio State	85
70	SW Missouri State	56
74	Baptist College	55
70	Tulsa	66
74	Texas-San Antonio	67
56	Minnesota	46
64	Oral Roberts	57
52	Georgia Tech	72
84	Iowa State	79
52	Iowa	71
70	Texas A&M*	67
60	SMU*	63
67	TCU*	59
64	Texas*	58
48	Texas Tech*	64
73	Houston*	78
67	Rice*	56
52	Virginia	54
64	Baylor*	57
58	Texas A&M*	53
39	Georgetown	56
69	SMU*	66
66	TCU*	72
60	Texas*	51
50	Texas Tech*	52
73	Houston*	59
68	Rice*	71
106	Baylor*	71
66	Texas	46
68	SMU	55
64	Texas Tech	67

NCAA West Regional

| 63 | Iowa | 54 |
| 65 | St. John's | 68 |

Won 22, Lost 13
* SWC (10-6), 2nd

Nolan Richardson

1985 - 86
Coach: Nolan Richardson

86	Southern Illinois	72
76	Southern University	75
68	SW Missouri State	67
76	San Diego State	64
72	Samford	51
64	Minnesota	71
79	Ohio State	70
87	Alabama State	69
78	Kansas	89
54	Oral Roberts	51
66	SMU*	71
62	TCU*	71
55	Texas*	59
46	Texas Tech*	48
85	Houston*	87
58	Rice*	50
74	Southern California	88
81	Baylor*	76
67	Texas A&M*	81
80	SMU*	90
71	TCU*	73
57	Texas*	61
79	Texas Tech*	72
83	Houston*	93
60	Rice*	59
64	Baylor*	65
76	Texas A&M*	93
51	Texas A&M	67

Won 12, Lost 16
* SWC (4-12), 7th

1986 - 87
Coach: Nolan Richardson

84	Grambling	65
90	Louisiana Tech	64
70	Ole Miss	56
103	Kansas	86
76	Alabama	87
106	Morgan State	57
98	Mississippi Valley	79
66	Virginia	78
49	SW Missouri State	56
97	Ohio State	94
82	Pittsburgh	114
74	California	58
77	TCU*	80
99	North Texas State	96
79	Texas*	62
73	Texas Tech*	95
62	Rice*	54
55	Houston*	60
62	Baylor*	63
87	Texas A&M*	69
76	SMU*	63
66	TCU*	73
73	Texas*	78
93	Texas Tech*	75
54	Houston*	57
88	Rice*	68
95	Oral Roberts	75
71	Baylor*	67
100	Texas A&M*	97
76	SMU*	93
59	Texas Tech	73

National Invitational Tournament

67	Arkansas State	64
71	Nebraska	78

Won 19, Lost 14
* SWC (8-8), 5th

1987 - 88
Coach: Nolan Richardson

78	Chicago State	68
47	Tulsa	68
77	NW Louisiana	55
53	SW Missouri State	47
79	Ole Miss	40
66	Virginia	52
101	Alcom State	55
91	Mississippi Valley	71
80	Alabama	55
61	Maryland	88
81	Coastal Carolina	59

91	Texas*	62
96	TCU*	53
85	SMU*	83
67	Texas A&M*	74
70	Baylor*	62
80	Rice*	61
71	Houston*	62
69	Texas Tech*	48
72	Texas*	79
63	TCU*	61
63	SMU*	73
79	Texas A&M*	58
57	Baylor*	58
112	Rice*	87
77	Houston*	82
75	Texas Tech*	65
76	Texas A&M	64
73	Baylor	74

NCAA Southeast Regional

| 74 | Villanova | 82 |

Won 21, Lost 9
* SWC (11-5), T 2nd

1988 - 89

Coach: Nolan Richardson

98	Rider	69
65	Virginia	75
73	Maryland	68
74	Ole Miss	68
97	Texas Southern	79
97	Sam Houston	79
78	Missouri	83
103	S. Alabama	71
69	Texas Tech*	62
99	Texas*	92
45	TCU*	51
93	SMU*	73
75	Texas A&M*	60
105	Florida State	112
88	Baylor*	58
109	Southern Utah	76
81	Rice*	77
88	Houston*	87
73	Texas Tech*	84
105	Texas*	82
100	TCU*	60
81	SMU*	68
71	Texas A&M*	82
89	Baylor*	54
118	Tulsa	69
83	Rice*	70
107	Houston*	79
108	Rice	72

94	Texas A&M	84
100	Texas	76

NCAA Midwest Regional

| 120 | Loyola-Marymount | 101 |
| 84 | Louisville | 93 |

Won 25, Lost 7
* SWC (13-3), 1st

1989 - 90

Coach: Nolan Richardson

97	Samford	67
102	Oregon	75
105	South Alabama	90
90	Ole Miss	76
166	U.S. International	101
88	Missouri	89
91	Bethune-Cookman	61
92	Virginia Military	61
117	Delaware State	75
93	Nevada-Las Vegas	101
82	Houston*	78
92	Texas Tech*	75
99	Baylor*	84
93	TCU*	79
80	SMU*	61
100	Texas A&M*	84
100	Houston*	89
109	Texas*	100
109	Alabama-Birmingham	95
70	Rice*	66
103	Texas*	96
100	Texas Tech*	77
77	Baylor*	82
79	TCU*	81
77	SMU*	46
114	Texas A&M*	100
104	Rice*	80
84	SMU	51
115	Baylor	75
96	Houston	84

NCAA Midwest Regional

68	Princeton	64
86	Dayton	84
96	North Carolina	73
88	Texas	85

NCAA Finals

| 83 | Duke | 97 |

Won 30, Lost 5
* SWC (14-2), 1st

1990 - 91

Coach: Nolan Richardson

| 107 | Vanderbilt | 70 |

110	Oklahoma	88
98	Duke	88
77	Arizona	89
96	Mississippi College	57
112	Kansas State	88
114	Louisiana Tech	97
95	Missouri	82
101	South Alabama	91
71	Oregon	68
126	Jackson State	88
114	NE Louisiana	92
86	Rice*	62
95	Houston*	79
101	Texas*	89
113	Texas Tech*	86
93	TCU*	73
98	SMU*	70
109	Florida State	92
113	Texas A&M*	88
73	Baylor*	68
104	Alabama-Birmingham	72
100	Rice*	87
81	Houston*	74
105	UNLV	112
87	Texas Tech*	69
97	TCU*	61
79	SMU*	70
111	Texas A&M*	72
106	Baylor*	74
86	Texas*	99
108	Texas A&M	61
109	Rice	80
120	Texas	89

NCAA Southeast Regional

117	Georgia State	76
97	Arizona State	90
93	Alabama	70
81	Kansas	93

Won 34, Lost 4
* SWC (15-1), 1st

1991 - 92

Coach: Nolan Richardson

92	Minnesota	83
99	Chaminade	84
71	Michigan State	86
96	Alabama State	80
128	Bethune-Cookman	46
76	Missouri	87
70	Kansas State	59
91	Montevallo	70
65	Arizona	59

74	Tulsa	64
89	Jackson State	66
101	South Alabama	82
123	Quincy College	60
110	Auburn*	92
63	Alabama*	65
101	LSU*	90
99	Mississippi State	78
114	Ole Miss*	93
75	Florida*	62
105	Kentucky*	88
81	Tennessee*	83
88	Memphis State	92
91	Vanderbilt*	71
89	South Carolina	73
78	Georgia*	87
90	Alabama*	87
82	Auburn*	74
84	Mississippi State*	76
106	LSU*	92
100	Ole Miss	83
73	Georgia	60
89	Alabama	90

NCAA Midwest Regional

80	Murray State	69
80	Memphis State	82

Won 26, Lost 8
*SEC (13-3), 1st

1992 - 93

Coach: Nolan Richardson

81	Memphis State	76
90	Tennessee-Martin	69
86	Arizona	80
96	SE Missouri State	72
73	Missouri	68
123	Jackson State	76
101	Tulsa	87
93	Coastal Carolina	74
78	Northeast Louisiana	87
72	SMU	53
90	Ole Miss*	78
86	South Carolina*	76
74	Alabama*	66
89	Vanderbilt*	102
89	Auburn*	100
76	Mississippi State*	80
97	Georgia*	79
91	LSU*	79
74	Florida*	66
101	Kentucky*	94
82	Alabama*	93

91	Tennessee*	101
115	Mississippi State*	58
85	Ole Miss*	63
88	LSU*	75
80	Auburn*	81
65	Georgia	60
81	Kentucky	92

NCAA East Regional

94	Holy Cross	64
80	St. John's	74
74	North Carolina	80

Won 22, Lost 9
*SEC (10-6), 3rd

1993 - 94

Coach: Nolan Richardson

93	Murray State	67
120	Missouri	68
111	Northwestern State	76
96	Memphis State	78
123	Delaware State	66
96	Jackson State	80
93	Tulsa	91
129	Texas Southern	63
96	SMU	70
87	Ole Miss*	61
64	Alabama*	66
84	LSU*	83
117	Auburn*	105
71	Mississippi State*	72
79	South Carolina*	53
65	Tennessee*	64
89	Vanderbilt*	76
131	Montevallo	63
90	Kentucky*	82
99	Florida*	87
102	Alabama*	81
90	Ole Miss*	73
74	Georgia*	65
91	Auburn*	81
108	LSU*	105
80	Mississippi State*	62
95	Georgia	83
78	Kentucky	90

NCAA Midwest Regional

94	North Carolina A&T	79
85	Georgetown	73
103	Tulsa	84
76	Michigan	68

NCAA Finals

91	Arizona	82

76	Duke	72

Won 31, Lost 3
*SEC (14-2), 1st

1994 - 95

Coach: Nolan Richardson

80	Massachusetts	104
97	Georgetown	79
103	Jackson State	87
94	Missouri	71
121	Centenary	94
78	SMU	66
94	Murray State	69
97	Florida A&M	57
82	Tulsa	63
86	Oklahoma	84
84	Cincinnati	75
101	Iowa	92
71	Ole Miss	76
97	Tennessee	79
79	Mississippi State	74
90	Auburn	104
84	Georgia	82
88	South Carolina	73
70	Alabama	88
94	Kentucky	92
105	LSU	81
62	Mississippi State	83
88	Memphis	87
97	Vanderbilt	94
86	Alabama	80
85	Ole Miss	70
92	LSU	90
122	Montevallo	64
94	Florida	85
68	Auburn	66
73	Vanderbilt	72
69	Alabama	58
93	Kentucky	95

NCAA Midwest Regional

79	Texas Southern	78
96	Syracuse	94
96	Memphis	91
68	Virginia	61

NCAA Finals

75	North Carolina	68
78	UCLA	89

Won 32, Lost 7
SEC (12-4)

1995 - 96

Coach: Nolan Richardson

75	NE Louisiana	67
73	Arizona	83
62	Michigan State	75
103	North Carolina A&T	49
116	Alcorn State	75
104	Missouri	93
67	Cincinnati	82
73	SMU	46
86	Tennessee State	67
86	Jackson State	77
75	Florida	60
76	Auburn	100
63	Mississippi	62
73	Vanderbilt	80
72	Memphis	94
80	Mississippi State	68
71	Alabama	63
66	Oral Roberts	65
76	LSU	68
81	South Carolina	69
63	Mississippi State	78
73	Kentucky	88
79	Mississippi	73
87	Auburn	77
59	Tennessee	66
59	Georgia	71
89	Alabama	98
94	LSU	79
80	South Carolina	58
75	Kentucky	95

NCAA East Regional

86	Penn State	80
65	Marquette	56
63	UMass	79

Won 20, Lost 13
SEC (9-7)

HOGS IN THE FINAL FOUR

The Arkansas Razorbacks have made it to the NCAA Final Four on six separate occasions. Here's how they fared:

1941

Only eight teams comprised the field in 1941, when All-American John Adams took the Hogs past Wyoming and on to the Final Four (although that phrase hadn't yet entered the sports lexicon). In the semifinals, Arkansas lost to Washington State, which then fell to Wisconsin.

1945

The previous spring, a devastating car accident had killed one player and badly injured two others, forcing Gene Lambert's Razorbacks to withdraw from the 1944 NCAA West Regional. (Utah, the team that took the Hogs' place, won the championship.) In 1945 Arkansas received another bid. The team beat Oregon in the first round, then lost 68-41 to eventual winner Oklahoma State, coached by the great Henry Iba.

1978

After a long dry spell, the Razorbacks returned to the Final Four under the tutelage of Eddie Sutton. Arkansas' famous Triplets (Sidney Moncrief, Ron Brewer and Marvin Delph) upset UCLA in the semifinals, then whipped California State-Fullerton, only to be eliminated by eventual champion Kentucky. Later, the Hogs beat Notre Dame in the since-discontinued consolation game.

1990

Nolan Richardson's spunky squad of overachievers, led by standout players Todd Day and Oliver Miller, surprised everyone by going all the way to the Final Four, losing to Duke, which fell to champion UNLV.

1994

Ranked #1 longer than any other team during the regular season, Richardson's Razorbacks went into the tournament the odds-on favorite. One by one, they took out all comers – North Carolina A&T, Georgetown, Tulsa, Michigan, Arizona and, finally, Duke. On the evening of April 4, 1994, sparked by Corliss Williamson and Scotty Thurman, the Hogs finally won the national championship, 76-72.

1995

As defending champs, the Hogs were everybody's target. By the end of January, after suffering the worst home loss in 27 years, the Razorbacks stood 4-3 in the SEC. But Nolan Richardson wasn't throwing in the towel. "Where we are today has nothing to do with where we'll be tomorrow," he promised. Sure enough, the Hogs went on a tear. In the NCAA tournament they eked out victories over Texas Southern, Syracuse and Memphis, then knocked out Virginia and North Carolina before finally losing the title match to UCLA, 89-78.

Sidney Moncrief

BASKETBALL ALL-AMERICANS

1928
Glen Rose
1929
Tom Pickkell
Gene Lambert
1936
Ike Poole
1941
John Adams

1977
Ron Brewer
1978
Ron Brewer
Sidney Moncrief
1979
Sidney Moncrief
1983
Darrell Walker

1984
Alvin Robertson
1991
Todd Day
1992
Todd Day
1993
Corliss Williamson
1994
Corliss Williamson

THE ARKANSAS TRAVELERS

Arkansas' only professional sports team, the Travs are a Double-A farm club allied with the St. Louis Cardinals baseball organization.

Originally called the Little Rock Travelers, the club changed names in 1961 – the first professional sports team named after an entire state. The franchise began life in 1901, as a member of the old Southern Association, playing teams like the Atlanta Crackers and the Memphis Chicks. Today it belongs to the Texas Baseball League.

Until the end of the 1931 season, the Travelers played at Kavanaugh Field, now the site of Little Rock Central High School's Quigley Stadium. The next year they moved into their present home, what is now known as Ray Winder Field in War Memorial Park (formerly Travelers' Field in Fair Park).

During its long history, the club has weathered many a crisis. On a couple of occasions, the Travs have been forced to shut the gates or even leave town, but somehow always returned. In 1961, in an effort to resume play after a two-year hiatus, the organization became a community-owned corporation – the Arkansas Travelers Baseball Club, Inc. The fan-owned concept has proved the club's salvation. Today, with over 1,200 stockholders, it is one of the few pro teams anywhere that maintains its own field without assistance from local government.

As a farm team, the Travs provide a training ground for future major leaguers. Players are generally signed directly from high school or college, then sent by the parent club to one of a series of farm teams to have their skills developed. Farm teams are classed from AAA, the highest, to Rookie, the lowest. Players are passed up and down the system depending on their abilities. Most players spend from two to four years in the farm system before moving on to the majors – if at all.

Established in 1888, the Texas League is among the oldest in professional baseball. Currently it fields eight teams from five states – Arkansas, Kansas, Louisiana, Oklahoma and Texas. The league is divided into two divisions, Eastern and Western. The Travs belong to the Eastern Division.

ARKANSAS STATE UNIVERSITY

Since 1991 the ASU Indians have competed in the Sun Belt Conference in 13 sports programs, excluding football.

Located in Jonesboro, A-State's colors are scarlet and black. The school's first entry in athletic competition came in 1911.

WHATEVER HAPPENED TO INJUN JOE?

In 1911, ASU athletes were called the "Aggies," and sometimes the "Farmers." Then, in 1925, the school decided to switch to the "Gorillas," a nickname that failed to inspire the fans. Five years later, this was changed to the "Warriors," which evolved the following year into the "Indians."

Officially, the nickname was a tribute to the fierce Osage tribe that ranged northern Arkansas before the whites arrived.

In 1952 a big-nosed mascot called "Jumpin' Joe" was designed and popularized. Later, in the 1980s, this Indian caricature developed into "Runnin' Joe," a leaner, meaner savage who chased his enemies with a tomahawk.

ARKANSAS STATE UNIVERSITY

Bending to the winds of political correctness, ASU finally sent old runnin', jumpin' Joe to happier hunting grounds, replacing him with a more modern, more corporate – and certainly more sterile – logo in 1994.

THE HOGS VS. THE INDIANS

After 39 years, the Arkansas Razorbacks finally played the ASU Indians in basketball. It happened in Fayetteville on March 13, 1987, during the first round of the NIT. The Hogs, who are highly resistant to allowing any in-state rivalries to develop, eked out a 67-64 victory in overtime.

INDIANS IN THE SUPER BOWL

Four former ASU players have played in pro football's crowning event – the Super Bowl. They include:

- **Maurice Carthon** (1979-82), fullback, XXI and XXV, New York Giants

- **Bill Bergey** (1965-68), linebacker, XV, Philadelphia Eagles

- **Leroy Harris** (1975-76), running back, XV, Philadelphia Eagles

- **Oren Middlebrook** (1975-76), XII, Denver Broncos

Maurice Carthon

ASU FOOTBALL ALL-AMERICANS

1953
Richie Woit, *running back*
1955
Tommy Spiers, *quarterback*
1957
Frank Farella, *offensive guard*
1964
Dan Summers, *linebacker*
1965
Dan Summers, *linebacker*
1968
Bill Bergey, *linebacker*
1969
Clovis Swinney, *defensive tacle*
Dan Buckley, *center*

1970
Bill Phillips, *offensive guard*
Calvin Harrell, *running back*
1971
Calvin Harrell, *running back*
Dennis Meyer, *defensive back*
Wayne Dorton, *offensive guard*
1973
Doug Lowrey, *offensive guard*
1975
Ken Jones, *offensive guard*
1976
T. J. Humphreys, *offensive guard*
1984
Carter Ray Crawford, *nose guard*

1985
Carter Ray Crawford, *nose guard*
Ray Brown, *offensive tackle*
1986
Randy Barnhill, *offensive guard*
1987
Charlie Fredrick, *defensive tackle*
Jim Wiseman, *center*

UALR

Bill Bergey

The University of Arkansas at
Little Rock participates in 16
athletic programs in both men's
and women's sports. UALR is a
division I school in the Sun Belt
Conference, playing under the
nickname of the Trojans. In 1994 Wimp Sanderson, a former national
coach of the year at Alabama, was signed to lead the UALR basketball
program. The basketball Trojans play their home games at Barton
Coliseum on the Arkansas State Fairgrounds in Little Rock. UALR does
not field a football team.

Wimp Sanderson

ABOUT THE AUTHOR

A native Arkansan, Diann Sutherlin is the author of four non-fiction books, including *The Arkansas Handbook*. Her essay "Worldly Goods,"written about her grandmother in south Arkansas, was originally published in *House Beautiful*, and is included in the anthology *Thoughts of Home* (Hearst Books, 1995). A graduate of El Dorado High School, Ms. Sutherlin holds BA and MA degrees in English from the University of Arkansas at Fayetteville. She and her husband, writer Craig Smith, make their home in Little Rock with their children Quentin, Lindsey and Blair.

THANK YOU NOTE

With heartfelt gratitude...

I want to express my sincere appreciation to everyone who helped me get this book to press. Thank you for returning my phone calls, answering my questions and so generously sharing your time and expertise. Some of you I know personally. Many more of you I do not. I was just another voice on the phone to those who work at state and federal agencies, chambers of commerce, museums, souvenir shops, historic sites, cafes, hotels, libraries and caves around the state. But with few exceptions, my inquiries were handled professionally, with courtesy and good humor. If you didn't know the answers to my frequently off-the-wall requests, you tried to put me on the right track. And often you shared Arkansiana more enticing than the information I was seeking.

To the conscientious staff at the Central Arkansas Library Reference Department, you are an invaluable resource. All of you contributed enormously to the success of this book.

To those of you I can thank individually, I now do – Tim Schick, Dorene Harris, Tim Nutt, Linda Pine, John L. Ferguson, Lynn Ewbank, Lisa Loporto, Lynn Bulloch, John D. McFarland, Karen Yaich, Debbie Strobel, Keith Brenton, Pat LaGrone, Nancy Griebel, Bill Jennings and Rebecca Esterer.

I am also grateful to the talented, tireless Pat Tribell for her production assistance and hard work on this often overwhelming project. Thanks for hangin' in there with me when I was nit-picking, and not giving up until we got it right.

A belated thank you to Dr. Lyna Lee Montgomery whose 18th Century British Literature class at the U of A was pivotal for me. Your vivid descriptions of everyday life in the 1700s led me to appreciate that history is not exclusively the province of the spectacular, the heroic, the grandiose.

I am enormously indebted to my husband Craig Smith whose literary, artistic and editorial contributions to the *Handbook* were considerable – I *could* have done it without you, but the book is so much better with you, as am I.

SELECTED REFERENCES

No one attempting a book of this kind could do so without frequent reliance on back issues of state newspapers, magazines and historical journals. In addition to the works listed below, I am especially indebted to the *Arkansas Democrat-Gazette*, the old *Arkansas Gazette*, the *Arkansas Times* and the *Arkansas Historical Quarterly* for information gleaned from news and sports reports, historical articles, obituaries and feature stories too numerous to cite.

The American Spa: Hot Springs, Arkansas, by Dee Brown, Rose Publishing, 1982.

Archeology of the Central Mississippi Valley, by Dan and Phyllis Morse.

Arkansans of the Years, by Fay Williams, Democrat Printing and Litho, 1952.

Arkansas, by John Gould Fletcher, University of North Carolina Press, 1947.

The Arkansas Challenge, by Avantus Green, illustrated by Jon Kennedy, 1969.

Arkansas Gazette: The Early Years 1819-1866, by Margaret Ross, Arkansas Gazette Foundation, 1969.

Arkansas in the Gilded Age 1874-1900, by Waddy W. Moore, Rose Publishing, 1976.

Arkansas Lives, edited by Dr. John L. Ferguson, 1965.

Arkansas Roadsides, by Bill Earngey, East Mountain Press, 1987.

The Arkansas Travelers: 79 Years of Baseball, by Jim Bailey, Arkansas Travelers Baseball Club, Inc.

Arkansas, Off the Beaten Path, by Patti Delano, Globe Pequot Press, 1992.

Arkansas: A History, by Harry S. Ashmore, W.W. Norton & Company, 1978.

Authentic Voices: Arkansas Culture 1541-1860, edited by Sarah M. Fountain, University of Central Arkansas Press, 1986.

The Autobiography of Sir Henry Morton Stanley, edited by Dorothy Stanley, Houghton Mifflin, Boston, 1937.

The Ballplayers: Baseball's Ultimate Biographical Reference, edited by Mike Shatzkin, Arbor House, 1990.

The Baseball Encyclopedia, Fourth Edition, edited by Joseph L. Reichler, Macmillan Publishing Co., 1979.

Bear: The Hard Life and Good Times of Alabama's Coach Bryant, by Paul W. Bryant and John Underwood, Little Brown & Company, 1975.

Biographical Almanac, Second Edition, edited by Susan L. Stetler, Gale Publishing, 1983.

Biographical and Pictorial History of Arkansas, by John Hallum, Southern Historical Press, 1975.

Biographical Dictionary of Afro-American Musicians, edited by Eileen Southern, Greenwood Press, 1982.

Biographical Dictionary of American Sports: Football, edited by David L. Porter, Greenwood Press, 1987.

Blood Sport: The President and His Adversaries, by James B. Stewart, Simon & Schuster, 1996.

Bootlegger's Boy, by Barry Switzer with Bud Shrake, William Morrow & Company, 1990.

Centennial History of Arkansas, edited by Dallas T. Herndon, S. J. Clarke Publishing Company, 1922.

Challenging Skies, by C. R. Roseberry, Doubleday & Co., 1966.

College Football Almanac, edited by Robert Ours, Barnes & Noble, 1984.

Concise Dictionary of American Biography, Fourth Edition, American Council of Learned Societies, Scribners, 1990.

The Congressional Medial of Honor, Sharp & Dunnigan, 1984.

Contemporary Poets, Third Edition, St. Martin's Press, edited by James Vinson.

Dictionary of American Biography, by J. G. Fletcher, Scribners, 1950.

Discovering America's Past, Reader's Digest, 1993.

A Documentary History of Arkansas, by Williams, Bolton, Moneyhon and Williams, University of Arkansas Press, 1984.

Down-Home Talk: An Outrageous Dictionary of Colorful Country Expressions, by Diann Sutherlin Smith, Macmillan Publishing, 1988.

Early Louisiana and Arkansas Oil, by Kenny A. Franks and Paul F. Lambert, Texas A & M University Press, 1982.

Encyclopedia of American Architecture, edited by William Dudley Hunt, Jr., McGraw-Hill Book Co., 1980.

Encyclopedia of American Crime, by Carl Sifakis, Facts on File, 1982.

Encyclopedia of Black America, edited by W. A. Low and Virgil A. Clift, McGraw Hill.

The Encyclopedia of Folk, Country and Western Music, Second Edition, by Irwin Stambler and Grelun Landon, St. Martin's Press, 1983.

The Evolution of an Architect, by Edward Durell Stone, Horizon Press, 1962.

Famous First Facts, Fourth Edition, Joseph Nathan Kane, H. W. Wilson Co.

Fanne Foxe: The Stripper and the Congressman, by Fanne Foxe with Yvonne Dunleavy, Pinnacle Books, 1975.

Fayetteville, A Pictorial History, by Kent R. Brown, The Donning Company, 1982.

Fierce Solitude: A Life of John Gould Fletcher, by Ben F. Johnson III, University of Arkansas Press, 1994.

The Film Encyclopedia, by Ephraim Katz, Putnam Publishing Group, 1982.

Finding Her Voice: The Saga of Women in Country Music, by Mary A. Bufwack and Robert K. Oermann, Crown Publishing, 1993.

First In His Class: A Biography of Bill Clinton, by David Maraniss, Simon & Schuster, 1995.

Folk Songs of North America, by Alan Lomax.

Folklore of Romantic Arkansas, by Fred W. Allsopp, Grolier Society, 1931.

Garden Sass: A Catalog of Arkansas Folkways, by Nancy McDonough, Coward, McCann & Geoghegan, 1975.

The Glen Campbell Story, by Freda Kramer, Pyramid Books, 1970.

Greater Little Rock, by Jim Lester and Judy Lester, The Donning Company, 1986.

H.L. Hunt, by Stanley H. Brown, Playboy Press, 1976.

The Harmony Illustrated Encyclopedia of Rock, edited by Ray Bonds, Harmony Books, 1982.

Historic Arkansas, by John L. Ferguson and J.H. Atkinson, Arkansas History Commission, 1966.

Historical Report of the Secretary of State, 1958.

Hog Wild: The Autobiography of Frank Broyles, by Frank Broyles and Jim Bailey, Memphis State University Press, 1979.

How We Lived: Little Rock, An American City, by F. Hampton Roy and Charles Witsell, August House, 1984.

Huey Long, by T. Harry Williams, Alfred A. Knopf, 1970.

Hurrah for Arkansas: From Razorbacks to Diamonds, by Marguerite Lyon, The Bobbs-Merrill Company, 1947.

I Didn't Know That About Eureka Springs, by Susan Schaefer, Ozark Mountain Press, 1993.

I Know Why the Caged Bird Sings, by Maya Angelou, Bantam Books, 1970.

Indians of Arkansas, by Charles R. McGimsey, III, Arkansas Archeological Survey, 1969.

Ladd: The Life, The Legend, The Legacy of Alan Ladd, Beverly Linet, Arbor House, 1979.

Law West of Fort Smith: Frontier Justice in the Indian Territory, 1834-1896, by Glenn Shirley, Collier Books, 1961.

Let Us Build Us a City, by Donald Harington, Harcourt, Brace, Jovanovich, 1986.

Living in Arkansas, by O.E. McKnight, Harlow Publishing, 1952.

Martha: The Life of Martha Mitchell, by Winzola McClendon, Random House, 1979.

Maxine: "Call Me Madam" The Life and Times of a Hot Springs Madam, by Maxine Temple Jones, Pioneer Press, 1983.

Mug Shots, Jay Acton, et. al., World Publishing, 1972.

The New Edition of The Encyclopedia of Jazz, by Leonard Feather, Horizon Press, 1960.

The NFL's Official Encyclopedic History of Professional Football, MacMillan Publishing Co., 1977.

Obituaries on File, edited by Felice Levy, Facts on File, 1979.

The Official NBA Basketball Encyclopedia, edited by Zander Hollander and Alex Sachare, Villard Books, 1989.

The Official NFL Encyclopedia, edited by Beau Riffenburgh, New American Library, 1968.

Old Fort Smith: Cultural Center on the Southwestern Frontier, by Ruth B. Mapes, Pioneer Press, 1965.

On a Slow Train Through Arkansas, by Thomas W. Jackson, 1903.

101 Wacky Facts About Bugs & Spiders, by Jean Waricha, Scholastic, 1992.

1,000 Makers of the Twentieth Century, edited by Godfrey Smith, Times Newspapers Ltd., 1971.

The Penguin Encyclopedia of Popular Music, edited by Donald Clark, Viking, 1989.

Pissing In The Snow & Other Ozark Folktales, by Vance Randolph, Avon Books, 1976.

Profiles: Real Arkansas Characters, by Margaret Arnold, August House, 1980.

The Razorbacks, by Orville Henry and Jim Bailey, Strode Publishers, 1973.

Reptiles and Amphibians, by Herbert Zim and Hobart Smith, Golden Press, 1956.

Roads of Arkansas, Shearer Publishing, 1990.

Rock Movers and Shakers, edited by Barry Lazell, Billboard Publications, 1989.

Sears Roebuck Catalogue Replica (1908), edited by Joseph J. Schroeder, Jr., Digest Books, Inc., 1969.

The Sporting News Pro Football Register, edited by Mark Shimabukuro, The Sporting News, 1993.

The Story of Arkansas, by Hazel Presson and David Y. Thomas, Democrat Printing & Lithographing Company, 1942.

The Story of the Blues, by Paul Oliver, Chilton Books, 1982.

This Wheel's On Fire, by Levon Helm, William Morrow & Company, 1993.

The Top Ten: 1956 - Present, by Bob Gilbert and Gary Theroux, Simon & Schuster, 1982.

Trees of Arkansas, by Dwight M. Moore, Arkansas Forestry Commission, 1981.

True Grit, by Charles Portis, Simon & Schuster, 1968.

Vance Randolph: An Ozark Life, by Robert Cochran, University of Illinois Press, 1985.

Who's Who in America 1994, 48th Edition, Marquis Who's Who, 1994.

Who's Who in Professional Baseball, by Gene Karst and Martin J. Jones, Jr., Arlington House, 1973.

The WPA Guide to 1930s Arkansas, University Press of Kansas, 1987.

PHOTO AND ILLUSTRATION CREDITS

Arkansas Department of Parks & Tourism: photographs on pages 130, 206, 209, 216, 221, 227, 230, 231, 235, 249, 252, 255, 258, 286, 298, 301, 303, 306, 311, 334, 339, 342, 345, 347, 348, 349, 350, 351, 355, 411, 412.

Arkansas History Commission: photographs on pages 20, 41, 57, 70, 84, 101, 245, 274, 279, 328.

Arkansas State University Sports: photos on page 477, 478.

Craig Smith: illustrations on pages 9 (top), 133, 135 (bottom), 149, 191 (bottom).

Lindsey Smith: photos on page 253, 479.

Quentin Smith: photo on page 280.

Joe Thibideau: illustrations on pages 103, 104, 105, 106, 108, 109.

Pat Tribell: illustrations on pages 102, 110, 118, 185, 192, 361, 421 (bottom).

UALR Archives: photograph on page 95. Photos on pages 46, 53, 92 from the Heiskell Collection. Photo on page 89 from the Simon Collection.

UALR Sports: photo on page 478.

University of Arkansas Sports Information: photographs on pages 424, 431, 438, 440, 441, 449, 465, 469, 474.

Photos by the author: pages 208, 210, 212, 273, 304, 326, 343.

SUGGESTIONS?

They're as welcome as the flowers in spring!

Do you know some fascinating Arkansas trivia, a sure-fire cure for
warts, a famous Arkansan? Do you have a beloved down-home expression or a secret recipe guaranteed to remove the slime from boiled okra?
If you want to share your knowledge through future editions of
The Arkansas Handboook, we'd like to hear from you. Send all comments,
suggestions and materials (with your sources, please) to:

Fly-By-Night Press
200 North Bowman Road
Suite 482
Little Rock, AR 72211

or FAX them to 501-228-4825

We regret we cannot acknowledge or return material – so for Pete's sake
don't send your *only* copy of that okra recipe!

INDEX

You can look it up!

LOOKING FOR A UNIQUE GIFT?

Books! Books! more Books!

The Arkansas Handbook is guaranteed to make any friend, relative, business associate or transplanted Arkie happy as a coon in a roastin' ear patch! So share the fun for **ONLY $22.50!** (Order 5 or more and pay only $20 each!)

Down-Home Chic!™

You'll be happy as a dead hog in the sunshine with our unique T-shirt. Heavyweight 100% natural unbleached cotton. Image printed in black. Adult sizes: medium, large and extra-large. Wear it with pride or delight someone special with this one-of-kind gift. And chic is cheap – **ONLY $15!**

ORDER FORM ON BACK ☞

Mail orders: **Fly-By-Night Press**
                  200 North Bowman Road, Suite 482, Little Rock, AR 72211
Phone orders: 501-228-4825 Mon-Fri, 8:30 a.m. - 4:30 p.m.
FAX orders: 501-228-4825

○ _____ copies of The Arkansas Handbook
            (1 - 4 copies: $22.50 each; 5 or more: $20 each)   _____

○ _____ Down-Home Chic T-shirts
            $15.00 each (state adult sizes M, L, or XL)
            M [   ]   L [   ]   XL [   ]   _____

○ Arkansas residents add 7% sales tax   _____
○ Shipping & Handling *(see chart below)*   _____
                                        TOTAL DUE: $ _____

Check or money order [ ]   VISA [ ]   Mastercard [ ]

Credit Card Number [ ][ ][ ][ ][ ][ ][ ][ ][ ][ ][ ][ ][ ][ ][ ][ ]

Signature for credit ————————————————— Exp. Date ——/——/——

Name _____

Street Address _____
                    (UPS won't deliver to P.O. Box)

City_____ State _____ Zip _____

Daytime phone (_____)_____ *(in case we have a question about your order)*

Ship to: (if different from above address)

*Name*_____

Address _____

*City*_____ *State* _____ *Zip* _____

Shipping & Handling	Order Total	Charge
	$ 15.00 – $ 30	$ 4.95
	$ 30.01 – $ 50	$ 6.95
	$ 50.01 – $ 75	$ 8.95
	$ 75.01 – $100	$10.95
	$100.01 – $250	$12.95